The Joy of Humility

The Joy of Humility

The Beginning and End of the Virtues

Drew Collins
Ryan McAnnally-Linz
Evan C. Rosa
Editors

BAYLOR UNIVERSITY PRESS

© 2020 by Baylor University Press
Waco, Texas 76798

All Rights Reserved. No part of this publication may be reproduced, stored in a retrieval system, or transmitted, in any form or by any means, electronic, mechanical, photocopying, recording, or otherwise, without the prior permission in writing of Baylor University Press.

Cover and book design by Kasey McBeath
Cover art: *Finding the Thin Places* (2016), by Ty Nathan Clark, part of the "Cosmos in the Chaos: The Harmony of Spirit and Matter" series

Hardcover ISBN: 978-1-4813-1182-3
Library of Congress Control Number: 2020018005

Printed in the United States of America on acid-free paper with a minimum of thirty percent recycled content.

NATIONAL ENDOWMENT FOR THE HUMANITIES

The Joy of Humility has been made possible in part by a major grant from the National Endowment for the Humanities: Exploring the human endeavor. Any views, findings, conclusions, or recommendations expressed in this book do not necessarily represent those of the National Endowment for the Humanities.

Contents

Acknowledgments	ix
Contributors	xi
Introduction: Contesting Humility *Drew Collins and Ryan McAnnally-Linz*	1

I
Normativity

Introduction to Part 1		9
1	**OPPRESSIVE HUMILITY** A Womanist View of Humility, Flourishing, and the Secret of Joy *Stacey M. Floyd-Thomas*	**13**
	RESPONSE TO STACEY M. FLOYD-THOMAS *Robert C. Roberts*	28
	REPLY TO ROBERT C. ROBERTS *Stacey M. Floyd-Thomas*	32
2	**LIBERATING HUMILITY** A Variation on Luther's Theology of Humility *Miroslav Volf*	**43**
	RESPONSE TO MIROSLAV VOLF *Lisa Sowle Cahill*	59

	REPLY TO LISA SOWLE CAHILL *Miroslav Volf*	64
3	**MAGNANIMOUS HUMILITY** The Lofty Vocation of the Humble *Jennifer A. Herdt*	**79**
	RESPONSE TO JENNIFER A. HERDT *Lisa Sowle Cahill*	93
	REPLY TO LISA SOWLE CAHILL *Jennifer A. Herdt*	97
4	**CREATURELY HUMILITY** Placing Humility, Finding Joy *Norman Wirzba*	**107**
	RESPONSE TO NORMAN WIRZBA *Jane Foulcher*	122
	REPLY TO JANE FOULCHER *Norman Wirzba*	126

II
Methodology

Introduction to Part 2		137
5	**OBSERVING HUMILITY** Relational Humility and Human Flourishing *Don E. Davis and Sarah Gazaway*	**139**
	RESPONSE TO DON E. DAVIS AND SARAH GAZAWAY *Jane Foulcher*	155
	REPLY TO JANE FOULCHER *Don E. Davis and Sarah Gazaway*	160
6	**DEFINING HUMILITY** The Scope of Humility *Jason Baehr*	**173**
	RESPONSE TO JASON BAEHR *Robert C. Roberts*	185
	REPLY TO ROBERT C. ROBERTS *Jason Baehr*	189

7	**EMPLOYING HUMILITY**	199

The Role of Humility in Servant Leadership
Elizabeth J. Krumrei-Mancuso

    RESPONSE TO ELIZABETH J. KRUMREI-MANCUSO   215
        Everett L. Worthington Jr.
    REPLY TO EVERETT L. WORTHINGTON JR.   219
        Elizabeth J. Krumrei-Mancuso

8	**LIVING HUMILITY**	237

How to Be Humble
Kent Dunnington

    RESPONSE TO KENT DUNNINGTON   257
        Everett L. Worthington Jr.
    REPLY TO EVERETT L. WORTHINGTON JR.   262
        Kent Dunnington

Index of Subjects   271
Index of People and Groups   279
Index of Scripture   283

Acknowledgments

This volume emerged in 2017 as a collaboration between the Yale Center for Faith & Culture (YCFC) and Biola University's Center for Christian Thought (CCT) on mutual projects related to humility, human flourishing, and joy. YCFC's project, "The Theology of Joy & the Good Life," was supported by the John Templeton Foundation, with additional support from the McDonald Agape Foundation; and CCT's project, "Humility: Religious, Moral, Intellectual," was supported by the Templeton Religion Trust.

As we discovered the common ground between each of our projects, we imagined an interactive volume that would generate new conversations about humility across disciplines of theology, psychology, philosophy, and ethics. We, the editors, would like to thank the following individuals for their support and friendship throughout the process: Mike Murray, Chris Stewart, Thomas Crisp, Steve Porter, Gregg Ten Elshof, Barry Corey, Laura Pelser, Carey Newman, Peter McDonald, Phil Love, Leon Powell, Karin Fransen, Susan dos Santos, Ryan Darr, Ryan Ramsey, Spencer French, Marta Jiménez, and Caitlyn Mack. And, of course, we are deeply grateful to the contributors and to Baylor University Press, especially Cade Jarrell, for their insights and professionalism over the course of the publishing process.

Contributors

JASON BAEHR, Professor of Philosophy, Loyola Marymount University

LISA SOWLE CAHILL, J. Donald Monan Professor, Boston College

DREW COLLINS, Associate Research Scholar, Yale Center for Faith & Culture, Yale Divinity School

DON E. DAVIS, Assistant Professor of Psychology, Georgia State University

KENT DUNNINGTON, Associate Professor of Philosophy, Biola University

STACEY M. FLOYD-THOMAS, E. Rhodes and Leona B. Carpenter Chair in Ethics and Society, Vanderbilt Divinity School

JANE FOULCHER, Senior Lecturer, School of Theology, Charles Sturt University, Barton, Australia

SARAH GAZAWAY, Georgia State University

JENNIFER A. HERDT, Gilbert L. Stark Professor of Christian Ethics, Yale Divinity School

ELIZABETH J. KRUMREI-MANCUSO, Associate Professor of Psychology, Pepperdine University

RYAN MCANNALLY-LINZ, Associate Director, Yale Center for Faith & Culture, Yale Divinity School

ROBERT C. ROBERTS, Professor Emeritus, Baylor University

EVAN C. ROSA, Assistant Director for Public Engagement, Yale Center for Faith & Culture, Yale Divinity School

MIROSLAV VOLF, Henry B. Wright Professor of Systematic Theology, Yale Divinity School

NORMAN WIRZBA, Gilbert T. Rowe Distinguished Professor of Christian Theology, Duke Divinity School

EVERETT L. WORTHINGTON JR., Commonwealth Professor Emeritus, Virginia Commonwealth University

Introduction

Contesting Humility

Drew Collins and Ryan McAnnally-Linz

A young artist eagerly presents his mentor with a meticulously designed plan to build his personal brand through social media, a series of critical reviews of more established artists, and a new, edgier personal look. All this will position him as the painter uniquely equipped to express his generation's mix of rage, hope, and despondency over environmental degradation. The mentor nods, unimpressed, as she looks over the plan. "If you're going to stay in this business without losing your soul," she says, "one thing you'll need more than this is a good helping of humility." Fresh off a triumphant IPO and the company's first ever profitable quarter, the CEO of an up-and-coming tech company lays out a plan to acquire the firm's nearest competitor and expand into three international markets within a year. A skeptical board member pipes up: "I wonder if we shouldn't take a more humble stance toward all this recent success." A woman struggles with the nagging sense that her family does not respect her, that they devalue her and fail to acknowledge her steady service to them. She feels constrained, belittled, unrecognized. She looks to her pastor for advice. "The way of Jesus is the way of humility," the pastor observes, counseling patient endurance in faith.

If, inspired by these conversations, any of these characters resolved to learn more about humility in hopes perhaps of becoming more humble, they would be met with a problem. Humility, they would find, is a matter of persistent debate or, rather, debates. There are debates about whether humility is good or bad, about its effects, its precursors, and its relationships to various virtues, vices, and emotions, about how we might cultivate it (if we wanted to cultivate it at all), and about what previous thinkers thought about it and whether it is a peculiarity of Christianity. But, at an even more fundamental level, there are ongoing, thoroughly unresolved debates about what "it" is. Humility is not like hydrogen—an object of study with a widely agreed upon definition that picks it out from the crowd and provides coherence to a delimited field of inquiry. There is no widely agreed upon definition of humility. Just what it is we are disagreeing about when we disagree about humility is itself a matter of much disagreement.[1]

The situation evokes Plato's *Cratylus*, which begins with a petition for Socrates to adjudicate a disagreement between Hermogenes and Cratylus regarding "the correctness of names." Cratylus, Hermogenes says, holds "that there is a correctness of name for each thing, one that belongs to it by nature" (*Crat.* 383a).[2] Hermogenes is unpersuaded. He thinks "that any name you give a thing is its correct name." All that matters is "convention and agreement" (384c–d). Over the course of the dialogue, Socrates leads Hermogenes out of his conventionalism and somewhat toward Cratylus' position, but he proceeds to push Cratylus beyond his linguistic naturalism, urging him not to focus on the correctness of names but to pursue non-discursive understanding of the forms, the characters of which determine what would make a name correct in the first place.

It can seem as though scholars working on humility are persistently performing a bizarre variation on the Cratylan project: not, like Cratylus, seeking the names that correspond by nature to "the things that are," but rather, possessed of a name ("humility"), searching feverishly for the thing to which it corresponds by nature.[3] In P. D. Eastman's children's book *Are You My Mother?* a newborn bird knows that he has a mother (who, in fact, has left the nest immediately before his birth to find a first meal for her coming child), but he has no idea how to identify her. He proceeds from kitten to hen to dog to cow to boat to airplane to hydraulic excavator (a "Snort," as he dubs it), asking each in turn, "Are you my mother?" The excavator finally lifts him back into the nest whence he came, just in time for the return of his mother, whom he greets joyfully: "I know who *you* are. You are not a kitten. You are not a hen. You are not a dog. You are not a cow. You are not a boat or a plane or a Snort. You are a bird, and you're my mother." The burgeoning literatures on humility can feel rather like a whole brood of baby birds running around arguing among themselves: "*Here* is our mother!" "No, *this* is our mother!" "That is not our mother. That is a Snort!" Two problems arise. First, unlike in the case of the bird's mother, it is not at all clear that there is some *thing* out there waiting to be appropriately identified as humility, and what is more, even if there were, it is not at all clear that scholars would agree whether they had recognized it. Second, the search for *a* humility, and in particular the confidence of various scholars that they have found it, can lead to significant cross-cultural misunderstandings. Richard Brislin describes something like this when he notes a tendency in cross-cultural psychological research toward prioritization of the *etic* over the *emic*, where a theoretical formulation is employed as "a category or code for which ratings from various cultures are already available," obscuring the particular shape and content of norms or patterns of behavior that are culturally located and specific.[4]

For those of us who are dismayed by this situation but disinclined to take Socrates' route and try to forgo language in favor of nondiscursive investigation of unchanging rational truths,[5] two responses are tempting, each a variation on the preformed Hermogenes' conventionalism. On the one hand, we might give up on trying to define humility at all, submit to the flow of anchorless signifiers, and play with the language of humility however we see fit. "'Humility' means whatever I mean with it, and that's all that counts, after all," we might say. On the other hand, we might think it important not merely to mean but to be understood, to conform our use to a *shared* convention. And so we might, pace Socrates, take a vote, as it were, and let everyday usage among contemporary English speakers define humility for us. "'Humility' means whatever *we* mean with it," we might (rather more plausibly) say.

Yet neither of these responses will do. They both miss the special character that histories of normative usage can give to particular terms. Someone who extends the word "tell" to include what we mean by "ask" for no particular reason or includes drinks made from tea leaves under the category "coffee" because she feels no need to distinguish between bitter caffeinated beverages would be confused—and rather confusing—but not *depraved* or *morally blameworthy*. Even substituting one term for another ("tea" for "coffee" and "coffee" for "tea") would merely inhibit communication, not spark outrage. "Woe unto them that call coffee tea and tea coffee" could only ever be exaggeration. "Woe unto them that call evil good and good evil," however, is an earnest exclamation of dismay and judgment. As Charles Taylor has shown, the "correctness" of normative terms matters.[6] We cannot keep it from mattering, try as we might. To call evil good is to approve of, to commend, even to command that which ought not to be approved of, commended, or commanded.⁷ "Good" carries its normative weight with it wherever it goes.

"Humility" is a normative term of this sort. For certain communities, it carries a positive valence, so to misdefine it is to misconstrue the shape of flourishing human life. To talk of humility is thus necessarily to talk of broader visions of the good life. And, for some, to talk of the good life is necessarily to talk also of humility. Moreover, since visions of flourishing life bear upon the actual living of lives, debates about how to understand humility are matters of ethics and not merely of semantics. They have the potential to inform, perhaps even to transform, our lives.

What is more, normative terms like "humility" are not without histories. Indeed, their histories are how they come to carry their normative weight.⁸ Humility's history is driven by Christianity's adoption and extension of the Hebrew prophets' ethical valorization of a category (Heb. *ănâvâh*, translated with Lat. *humilitas*, Gk. *tapeinotēs*) that had applied primarily to certain lowly social classes.⁹ (Nietzsche was not entirely wrong about this.) This category, for early Christians, named something important about Jesus Christ and therefore also—because they took Christ to be decisive for the shape of human life as it ought to be—something important about true life for all of us. The Gospel of Matthew and the apostle Paul both ascribe humility to Christ (Matt 11:39; Phil 2:8), and various epistles urge their readers to lives of humility (e.g., Phil 2:3; Col 3:12; 1 Pet 5:5). In dialogue with scriptural texts such as these, Aphrahat the Persian Sage exhorts his readers, "So great a humility did our Saviour manifest to us in himself! Let us *therefore* make ourselves humble" (*Demonstrations* 6.10).¹⁰ In the Latin tradition, Augustine speaks of "the humble Christ" and Christ's "saving humility [*saluberrima humilitate*]" (*Serm.* 51.18, 142.2; *Trin.* 4.12.15; *Civ.* 10.28). And, as several authors in this volume note, with respect to the Christian life, he says, "If you ask and as often as you ask about the rules of the Christian religion, I would answer only, 'Humility'" (*Ep.* 118.3.22).¹¹

For Christian communities, then, the die is loaded in favor of humility. But what if the Christian presumption in favor of humility is pernicious? What if the ways Christians have understood humility, preached it, tried to live it, tried to enforce it in *others'* lives, have been at odds with other, perhaps more basic, normative commitments, to justice or love of neighbor, for example? What if humility is not a virtue, at least not for the oppressed? What if taking it to be a virtue leads not to flourishing but to languishing for many of God's creatures? Stacey Floyd-Thomas levels just such a critique in the first chapter of this volume. Her rather uncomfortable (implied) question for us: Should the rest of this book even exist? Although they were not written in direct response to Floyd-Thomas' chapter, the remaining chapters in part 1 are all attuned to the possibility that Christian humility might be subject to a critique along her line of argument. (See the introduction to part 1 for a more detailed discussion of the interplay between the four chapters of part 1.) The stakes of the implicit debate in these chapters are high: Can Christians go on preaching humility, as we have for two millennia, in good conscience? If so, under what conditions? What conceptions of humility are consonant with a broader Christian vision of flourishing life? Who can legitimately advocate for humility? And to whom?

Christian discourse on humility cannot, however, limit itself to theological responses to the questions of the nature and normative import of humility. As we define and attempt to operationalize humility both for research and for living our lives, we must continuously consider why, and how, Christians should engage with accounts of humility that are not explicitly, or primarily, Christian. This is not to argue that theology qua theology must be interdisciplinary to be legitimate. But if Christian theology has *anything* to do with actual human life, it behooves Christians to listen to and consider alternative accounts of humility derived in or through disciplines that are not explicitly Christian, for example, psychology and philosophy. At a minimum, it is hard to contest that accounts of humility offered in other-than-theological terms are shaping the lives of those outside the tradition. This is nothing new. But in our ever more connected world, such alternative accounts of human flourishing, and the lives shaped by such accounts, have ever more bearing on our own lives and therefore must be considered as alternative sources of our own existential formation. As Christians discerning the good life and the place of humility therein, we are enmeshed in a complex web of cultural forces, intellectual currents, and popular and scholarly discourses. It is increasingly difficult to duck the question of what bearing these have on our Christian discernment and practice of humility.

The chapters of part 2 enact a series of interdisciplinary debates about how best to study humility, not by posing methodological questions, but by tackling substantive questions about humility and exploring the way in which different approaches to it bear fruit, or do not. Indeed, these are the stakes raised explicitly in the opening exchange between collaborators Don E. Davis and Sarah Gazaway, on the one hand, and Jane Foulcher, on the other. For Foulcher, her encounter with Davis and Gazaway's chapter raises a crucial question: "Is Christian humility really comparable with the construct labeled 'humility' being explored in the field of positive psychology?" (159). Davis' response, significantly, demurs from answering Foulcher's question head on. Instead, he entreats us to approach such exchanges with patience, hoping that we might "do our work 'alongside each other' with confidence that something new could happen between us" (162). This can be messy, difficult, and frustrating for all involved, as might be observed at certain points in the exchanges in part 2. (See the introduction to part 2 for a more detailed discussion of the structure and stakes of the conversations it contains.)

"Truly flourishing life," Miroslav Volf and Matthew Croasmun write, "is the most important concern of our lives, the pearl for which it's worth selling everything else we might have."[12] The most fundamental task of our lives is to discern, articulate for ourselves and others, and pursue that life. If that is so, and if humility is either essential or antithetical to the true flourishing of particular lives, working out the place of humility in human flourishing is a matter of urgent practical, existential importance. This is no easy task. For those of us who live within the cultural current Taylor calls the "Nova Effect," the proliferation of conceivable and livable accounts of the good life in late modernity, discernment is always fraught, unstable, and provisional.[13] We are "cross-pressured" and aware, sometimes painfully, that even the best account of the good life we can muster is one option among many. Material conditions, too, can militate against discernment of humility's place in (or opposed to) flourishing life and pursuit of a humble (or appropriately unhumble) life in response to that discernment.

This book is meant to be a help in this difficult task. It does not, however, arrive at any conclusions or definitive statements about humility. Rather, even though it is a conversation almost entirely among Christians, it enacts something of the cross-pressure Taylor identifies. It is full of different, competing claims about life and humility's place in it—claims that are also discernible within our culture and might therefore be shaping, even if implicitly, our own accounts of humility and its place in human flourishing. In offering their different accounts of humility, the authors in this book are commending importantly different ways of life. In compiling these and putting them in dialogue with each other, this book seeks both to point toward (incompletely, of course) the plurality of voices that might be shaping our perspectives on humility and thereby to present you with a challenge: What are you going to do about it? How are you going to live?

• • •

NOTES TO THE INTRODUCTION
(DREW COLLINS AND RYAN MCANNALLY-LINZ)

1   In addition to the various, mostly philosophical, debates referenced in Kent Dunnington's and Jason Baehr's chapters, see Stephen T. Pardue, *The Mind of Christ: Humility and the Intellect in Early Christian Theology* (London: Bloomsbury T&T Clark, 2013), 1–29. For a review of some recent psychological

work on humility, see Don E. Davis, Joshua N. Hook, Ryan McAnnally-Linz, Elise Choe, and Vanessa Placeres, "Humility, Religion, and Spirituality: A Review of the Literature," *Psychology of Religion and Spirituality* 9 (2017): 242–53. At the risk of running afoul of at least some definitions of humility, one of the present authors might also point toward a portion of his dissertation: Ryan McAnnally-Linz, "An Unrecognizable Glory: Christian Humility in the Age of Authenticity" (Yale University, 2016), 186–207.

2 Plato, *Cratylus*, trans. C. D. C. Reeve, in *Plato: Complete Works*, edited by John M. Cooper (Indianapolis: Hackett, 1998).

3 "The things that are" (*ta onta*) is a favorite formulation of Plato's Socrates. It appears throughout his lines in *Cratylus* as well as in various other dialogues.

4 Richard W. Brislin, "Cross-Cultural Research Methods: Strategies, Problems, Applications," in *Human Behavior and Environment*, vol. 4, *Environment and Culture*, ed. Irwin Altman, Amos Rapoport, and Joachim F. Wohlwill (New York: Plenum, 1980), 73.

5 See *Crat.* 438–39b.

6 See Charles Taylor, "What Is Human Agency?" and "Self-Interpreting Animals," in *Human Agency and Language*, Philosophical Papers 1 (Cambridge: Cambridge University Press, 1985) for Taylor's clearest early statement of his argument about the place of what he calls "strong evaluation" (synonymous with our "normativity") in human life.

7 Isaiah 5:20 (KJV). An eager objector might contend that what distinguishes the coffee/tea from the evil/good inversion and makes the latter an object of strong condemnation is not the normative character of the latter but the fact that it is an inversion of opposites, while the former is not. It is striking, in fact, just how many sets of opposites carry a normative valence, sometimes faint but often quite strong: up/down, dark/light, left/right, full/empty. If we consider more arcane oppositional terms like precipitation/solvation in chemistry, it becomes clear that the *normativity* of these terms, their being matters of strong evaluation, is what leads us to object to inverting them.

8 See Charles Taylor's recurrent example of how *isonomia* and *isēgoria* became strongly evaluative terms among the ancient Greeks, in its most elaborated form in *The Language Animal: The Full Shape of Human Linguistic Capacity* (Cambridge, Mass.: Belknap Press of Harvard University Press, 2016), 280–83; but also in "Theories of Meaning," in *Human Agency and Language*, 272–73; and Hubert Dreyfus and Charles Taylor, *Retrieving Realism* (Cambridge, Mass.: Harvard University Press, 2015), 121–23.

9 See Klaus Wengst, *Humility: Solidarity of the Humiliated; The Transformation of an Attitude and Its Social Relevance in Graeco-Roman, Old Testament-Jewish and Early Christian Tradition*, trans. John Bowden (Philadelphia: Fortress, 1988), 4–57; Erich Auerbach, "*Sermo Humilis*," in *Literary Language and Its Public in Late Latin Antiquity and in the Middle Ages*, trans. Ralph Manheim, 25–66 (Princeton: Princeton University Press, 1965).

10 Aphrahat, *Demonstrations*, trans. Kuriakose Valavanolickal (Changanassery, India: HIRS, 1999) (emphasis added).

11 *The Works of Saint Augustine: A Translation for the 21st Century*, vol. 2/2, *Letters 100–155*, trans. Roland Teske, ed. Boniface Ramsey (Hyde Park, N.Y.: New City Press, 2003).
12 Miroslav Volf and Matthew Croasmun, *For the Life of the World: Theology That Makes a Difference* (Grand Rapids: Brazos, 2019), 19.
13 See Charles Taylor, *A Secular Age* (Cambridge, Mass.: Harvard University Press, 2007), 299, for the introduction of the term, and 539–776, for his wide-ranging discussion of the cultural condition of secular modernity.

Introduction Bibliography

Aphrahat. *Demonstrations*. Translated by Kuriakose Valavanolickal. Changanassery, India: HIRS, 1999.

Auerbach, Erich. "*Sermo Humilis*." In *Literary Language and Its Public in Late Latin Antiquity and in the Middle Ages*, translated by Ralph Manheim, 25–66. Princeton: Princeton University Press, 1965.

Augustine. *The Works of Saint Augustine: A Translation for the 21st Century*. Vol. 2/2, *Letters 100–155*. Translated by Roland Teske. Edited by Boniface Ramsey. Hyde Park, N.Y.: New City Press, 2003.

Brislin, Richard W. "Cross-Cultural Research Methods: Strategies, Problems, Applications." In *Human Behavior and Environment*, vol. 4, *Environment and Culture*, edited by Irwin Altman, Amos Rapoport, and Joachim F. Wohlwill, 47–82. New York: Plenum, 1980.

Davis, Don E., Joshua N. Hook, Ryan McAnnally-Linz, Elise Choe, and Vanessa Placeres. "Humility, Religion, and Spirituality: A Review of the Literature." *Psychology of Religion and Spirituality* 9 (2017): 242–53.

Dreyfus, Hubert, and Charles Taylor. *Retrieving Realism*. Cambridge, Mass.: Harvard University Press, 2015.

McAnnally-Linz, Ryan. "An Unrecognizable Glory: Christian Humility in the Age of Authenticity." Ph.D. diss., Yale University, 2016.

Pardue, Stephen T. *The Mind of Christ: Humility and the Intellect in Early Christian Theology*. London: Bloomsbury T&T Clark, 2013.

Plato. *Cratylus*. Translated by C. D. C. Reeve. In *Plato: Complete Works*, edited by John M. Cooper. Indianapolis: Hackett, 1998.

Taylor, Charles. *Human Agency and Language*. Philosophical Papers 1. Cambridge: Cambridge University Press, 1985.

———. *The Language Animal: The Full Shape of Human Linguistic Capacity*. Cambridge, Mass.: Belknap Press of Harvard University Press, 2016.

———. *A Secular Age*. Cambridge, Mass.: Harvard University Press, 2007.

Volf, Miroslav, and Matthew Croasmun. *For the Life of the World: Theology That Makes a Difference*. Grand Rapids: Brazos, 2019.

Wengst, Klaus. *Humility: Solidarity of the Humiliated; The Transformation of an Attitude and Its Social Relevance in Graeco-Roman, Old Testament-Jewish and Early Christian Tradition*. Translated by John Bowden. Philadelphia: Fortress, 1988.

I
Normativity

Introduction to Part I

Because humility is such a contested subject, to understand it well requires entering into and getting a grip on the debates that swirl around it. Hence the structure of this book: Nine scholars offer their takes on how to understand humility and its place in flourishing life. Four others respond, bringing their own (often opposing) perspectives into dialogue with two of the original chapters. Rather than leaving critiques and questions hanging in the air, the chapters' authors then each have a chance to reply and defend, or modify, their approach and conclusions.

Of course, in real life, not all of our debates about humility happen in explicit conversations. Even when they do, rarely do they unfold in a structured sequence like those arranged here. More common, and of no less importance, are the implicit debates that unfold between people pursuing their own interests and questions. Debates of *this* sort take place *between* the chapters of each of the book's two parts, and are no less significant than those explicit exchanges comprising each chapter.

While there is widespread agreement that humility is important, it is a live question whether humility belongs in an account of human flourishing at all. *Stacey Floyd-Thomas* presents an emancipatory critique of humility discourse as obstructing the flourishing of Black women and advocates for a recovery of the virtue of pride within a contextually attentive womanist social ethical framework. When imposed as a norm on Black women, humility functions as an ideological instrument of oppression. The problem, as she sees it, is twofold. On the one hand, there is the unacknowledged erasure of Black women's experiences in the surreptitious elevation of particular (White, male) persons' exercises of reason to the level of a supposedly universally binding norm. On the other hand, humility as it has been articulated in Christian ethics is especially well-suited to pernicious social use, since it has been taken to entail lowliness, submissiveness, and so on.

One response to this critique would be to reject Christianity for being intrinsically tied to an oppressive form of humility, housed in a supposedly universal normative ethic. We might plausibly read Mary Daly as taking roughly this stance, for instance.[1] Another response, antithetical to the first, would be to accept the validity of the critique (advocating humility regardless of context does reinforce hierarchical social relations organized on racial and sexual lines) but deny its significance (there is nothing wrong with such social relations). The authors here all reject such bald-faced anti-egalitarianism as contrary to Christian faith rightly understood. Two possible stances are left for our authors: either (1) develop a Christian vision shorn of affirmation of humility (at least for some groups and social contexts) or (2) offer an account of Christian humility that both avoids the imposition of oppressive norms and retains a place for humility within a vision of human flourishing that applies across various social contexts.

Floyd-Thomas takes the first approach: the vision of womanist virtue and joy that she presents does not depend on a virtue of humility. The remaining three chapters were not, we should emphasize, commissioned as responses to Floyd-Thomas or written in explicit dialogue with her text. Even so, each can be seen as sensitive to the kind of emancipatory critique of humility she offers and as taking the second of the two stances identified above. In these chapters, it is argued that a true account of humility will be one that all could adopt without reinforcing systems of social exclusion and oppression. *Miroslav Volf* contends that we can find a surprisingly emancipatory account of humility in the theology of Martin Luther, somewhat despite Luther's own social vision. Volf distinguishes between "humility of being" and "humility in acting." The former is the recognition that one does not stand on one's own but receives all that one is—including one's immense value—as a gift from God. Humility in acting, which follows from humility of being, is that by which we join in God's movement toward, on behalf of, and with the socially lowly. It thus ought to fund a struggle to realize in social relations what is true theologically: that all are equally nothing in themselves and equally exalted in Christ. *Jennifer Herdt* focuses on the theology of Thomas Aquinas, developing his account of humility and its relation to magnanimity in dialogue with Robert C. Roberts' philosophical account of humility.[2] The result is a view of humility as a posture of openness to grace and recognition that one's talents, accomplishments, and so forth are gifts and thus no cause for self-exaltation. Humility so understood, she claims, "is indeed a virtue and thus necessary to living well." *Norman Wirzba* roots humility in the soil (humus), that is to say, in our inescapable dependence on the whole "meshwork" of creaturely existence and the responsibilities toward others (including the soil) that this enmeshment places on us. He argues that to be a creature is to receive life from beyond oneself, that we receive life originally from God but also in and through the community of other creatures, and that humility is the proper stance of recognition of this reality.

While their interlocutors and arguments are at points quite different, the three latter chapters of part 1 share certain common convictions. Perhaps most basic is the claim that humility involves a recognition of what it is to be a creature. In systematic theological terms, the doctrine of creation takes center stage in their accounts of humility. It is not surprising, therefore, that they share an emphasis on humility's connection to dependence and gift, as well as a concern to downplay any comparative aspect of humility. Implied in this appeal to createdness is an affirmation of the universal appropriateness of humility. There is a form of humility that we all ought to have, they claim, whether explicitly or implicitly. And articulations of humility that would enforce the sorts of social injustices that Floyd-Thomas' critique identifies must, on Volf's, Herdt's, and Wirzba's views, be mistaken. So there is a question that hangs over this half of the volume: Do these shared convictions, or any of the particular accounts of humility the authors develop from them, adequately address emancipatory critiques of humility in general or Floyd-Thomas' challenge in particular? Can universal and normative accounts of humility cogently meet the charge that they impose an anti-flourishing form of normativity on oppressed and marginalized peoples?

Whether as an essential feature of living well or an oppressive pseudo-virtue, humility never stands on its own. Rather, humility always figures within accounts of human life that inescapably go beyond agency to address the emotional content or affective tonality of human flourishing. For Christians, joy bubbles to the surface of these broader Christian accounts of flourishing life, in no small part because of its centrality in the scriptural witness and the church's worship.[3] Hence, even if humility and joy might at first glance appear a rather odd pairing, from a Christian perspective it is fitting that considerations of humility also be reflections on joy.

For Floyd-Thomas, the kind of joy that can be built from the four tenets of womanism—radical subjectivity, traditional communalism, redemptive self-love, and critical engagement—is part of a lived struggle to get beyond oppressive, traditional virtue ethics. It is a generative "contemplative practice" that foments flourishing in unexpected places and rejects "the dominant objectification of others." Volf poses the question of how the joy of the humble Mary relates to the exultant joy in liberation of the dancing Miriam. He answers that they are one and the same. Humility opens the way for joy as the affective response to having received good gifts from God, gifts that include oneself, the ordinary things of the world, and also the achievement of justice. Herdt, too, sees humility as conducive to joy, a "joy-enhancer." Humility, she says, removes our tendencies to invest our joy in the fragile vessel of comparative self-importance and plants it instead "in something that is not subject to fluctuation," in friendship and God's work of drawing creation into communion. Moreover, as a virtue, humility disposes us to *good* joy, to rejoice in that which is genuinely good. Wirzba sees humility and joy as sharing a common root. Humility thus opens us up toward joy. Indeed, it is a prerequisite of true joy, for without humility, we cannot recognize that others in their own "integrity and sanctity" are a blessing to our lives. "There can be no joy . . . apart from the humble realization that life is always together and never alone."

• • •

Notes to the Introduction to Part I

1 Humility figures in Mary Daly's critique of patriarchal theology in *Beyond God the Father: Toward a Philosophy of Women's Liberation* (Boston: Beacon, 1973), 53, 77, 100–101; her subsequent works decisively break with Christianity.
2 Roberts is a respondent to other chapters in this volume.
3 On joy in the Scriptures, see Marianne Meye Thompson, "Reflections on Joy in the Bible," and N. T. Wright, "Joy: Some New Testament Perspectives and Questions," in *Joy and Human Flourishing: Essays on Theology, Culture, and the Good Life*, ed. Miroslav Volf and Justin E. Crisp (Minneapolis: Fortress, 2015), 17–38 and 39–62, respectively.

Introduction to Part I Bibliography

Daly, Mary. *Beyond God the Father: Toward a Philosophy of Women's Liberation*. Boston: Beacon, 1973.

Thompson, Marianne Meye. "Reflections on Joy in the Bible." In *Joy and Human Flourishing: Essays on Theology, Culture, and the Good Life*, edited by Miroslav Volf and Justin E. Crisp, 17–38. Minneapolis: Fortress, 2015.

Wright, N. T. "Joy: Some New Testament Perspectives and Questions." In *Joy and Human Flourishing: Essays on Theology, Culture, and the Good Life*, edited by Miroslav Volf and Justin E. Crisp, 39–62. Minneapolis: Fortress, 2015.

1

Oppressive Humility

A Womanist View of Humility, Flourishing, and the Secret of Joy

Stacey M. Floyd-Thomas

In her 1982 memoir entitled *African Saga*, Mirella Ricciardi, an Italian woman raised in Kenya, writes:

> I had always got on well with the Africans and enjoyed their company, but commanding the people on the farm, many of whom had watched [me] grow up, was different. With the added experience of my safaris behind me, I had begun to understand the mode of "birth, copulation and death" by which they lived. Black people are natural, they possess the secret of joy, which is why they can survive the suffering and humiliation inflicted upon them. They are alive physically and emotionally, which makes them easy to live with. What I had not yet learned to deal with was their cunning and their natural instinct for self-preservation.[1]

This excerpt serves as the impetus for why Alice Walker, renowned novelist and creator of the term "womanist," wrote the sequel to her widely celebrated novel, *The Color Purple*. As an epigraph to *Possessing the Secret of Joy*, Walker paraphrases the author by writing, "There are those who believe Black people possess the secret of joy and that it is this that will sustain them through any spiritual or moral or physical devastation."[2]

The racist implications of Ricciardi's anthropological reading of the supposed pejorative view of how the nature of Black people is characterized not only normalizes her "mastery" of African culture but maintains her colonizing role in being master over them. There is a fearsome asymmetry at the core of the author's false assumption. The words of Ricciardi—identified as a "white colonialist author" by Walker—speak to the moral sphere of Black life captured within the perspective of dominant descriptive ethics. As the lowest echelon of moral thinking, descriptive ethics works out theories of human nature based on generalizations of empirical theory rather than bearing on the more pressing ethical questions of one's "real-lived" experience of flourishing. To this end, Ricciardi, seeing through her ethnocentric myopia, makes moral judgments, based on her limited observations, concerning the indigenous Kenyans over whom she lorded herself. Her pejorative observation connects their humble circumstances to their joy and their pride in self-preservation to their moral failure. Ironically, in the paraphrasing of Ricciardi's words (which becomes her preface to a novel that inspires her activism against female genital mutilation), Walker's reframing of Ricciardi's descriptive moral thinking does the due diligence of metaethically analyzing joy—and by extension humility and pride—as a disclaimer effectively deconstructing the constitutive arrogance of the original statement.

Therefore, the query must be posed: What is the "secret of joy" that Black people possess? In this case, neither is joy an emotion nor does it have an object. To the contrary, I assert that joy is the intrinsic capacity of Black people to bear yet sidestep the dynamics of their oppression. Thus, joy is the ultimate virtue in Black life, which is marked by resilience. What allows Black women, men, and children to bear witness to life-giving joy in the midst of death-dealing circumstances is the sociohistorical and psychological connection of experiences that allow for pleasure, efficacy, and imagining a future so that one's place in the world is meaning-making for the individual yet meaningful for her community and her place within it. It is illogical for the marginalized to make sense of Aristotelian-Thomist virtues (like humility) when fundamentally the ordering of their lives is experiential. Ricciardi is looking at the effects of virtue; Walker is looking at the affects of virtue. Ricciardi does not see a phenomenological experience of the virtue of joy (or humility) but only its effects. Conversely, Walker sees its affectivity because (a) she has experienced its interiority by being a Black woman who inhabits the intersectional space wherein her identity is indivisible from the Black people Ricciardi merely observes and (b) her integrity (as the self that is ever thus) involves not an observation but rather a subjective experience in their joy.[3]

For too long, ethicists have had the tendency to erroneously privilege virtue along Aristotelian and Thomistic lines. However, I want us to think more carefully about the way we approach virtue and how it reifies racial injustice and racialized ideologies. Therefore, this chapter offers a womanist theological exploration of joy as a sustained state of "being-ness" and consciousness in which the so-called virtue of humility and vice of pride are debunked, demystified, and disentangled from the dominant ethical perspectives that keep them entrenched and in place. It proceeds by suspending the culturally relevant belief that humility is a virtue and pride is a vice and instead insists that inverting these normative understandings of humility/pride and virtue/vice is central to the moral trajectory of intersectional oppression (racism, sexism, and classism most especially) by revealing the ephemeral quality of happiness that masks itself as joy that is transcendent. Herein, I suggest that womanist ethics offers an alternative metaethical definition of joy. The constitutive elements of this particular schema of joy can be found in the four tenets of womanism: namely, radical subjectivity, traditional communalism, redemptive self-love, and critical engagement. These principles represent the moral practices that sustain a life of joy irrespective of one's social conditions or normative standards of virtue. It shows how joy is far more than an emotion. It is, rather, a state of being-ness forged by ethical actions that have taken on the dimensions of spiritual disciplines. Joy is a form of consciousness that evolves from a familiar form of self, communal, embodied, and worldly consciousness in which normative assumptions of humility and pride cannot coexist. This being-ness specifically is a womanist consciousness, an unapologetic and unashamedly critical consciousness of what does or does not get noticed when joy provides a horizon of human flourishing despite death-dealing conditions.

It is commonplace in the Black church tradition to hear a church mother strike up the familiar gospel song "This Joy I Have" and for the entire church to rejoice in singing along:

> This joy I have the world didn't give to me
> This joy I have the world didn't give to me
> Oh! This joy I have the world didn't give to me
> The world didn't give it and the world can't take it away.[4]

Inspired from the New Testament passage "Though now you see [God] not, yet believing, you rejoice with joy unspeakable and full of glory" (1 Pet 1:8b, AKJV), this song reveals that the secret of joy is actually a literal, albeit extraordinary, possession, appearing as what womanist ethicist Barbara Holmes calls "an exultation of body and soul that extends far beyond our ordinary pleasures."[5] One might argue that Holmes' adage is indicative of the Black church tradition as well as a reflection of Jonathan Edwards' "joy unspeakable." According to firebrand Congregationalist preacher and theologian Jonathan Edwards, there are only two virtues of the Christian life: "joy unspeakable" and "beneficence (love)."[6] Humility works more as spiritual disciplining, which is necessary for the increase of joy and love. Habits are necessary, but they are disciplined and enriched as they provide the possibility of enrichment and flourishing in joy and in love. Humility is essential for the possibility of establishing cooperative life. Humility is not lowering oneself but putting one's sense of self in relation to community with others. Humility can only take place in subjective contexts—where one already has an affirmed and confirmed sense of the beauty of life. The virtue of tradition counters the long-overblown Thomistic framework that sees virtue as merely the formation of habits. Ultimately the manifestation of joy occurs when personal yearnings are ensconced within the embrace of shared realities, needs, and aspirations. Practical theologian Mary Clark Moschella presents this sense of joy as a countercultural spiritual path, a fruit of the Spirit wherein spirit and reason are not ultimately opposed.[7]

When contemplating the secret of joy, what should we make of the fact that humility is juxtaposed with pride? As always, ethics is rooted in the moral confluence of causation and consequence in human life—individual and collective, spontaneous and systemic, hyperlocal and global. The challenge of distilling the power of red-lettered scripture into the principles and praxis governing the lives of Christians is to negotiate the purpose of both our peace and pain in this world separate from the oppression and persecution of the modern world. But, in the face of a perspective framed by the ironies of the living gospel compounded by living in a white supremacist patriarchal world, the experience and expression of joy for Black women is something both wholly and holistically different from the normative claims that tend to be advanced in the public square as well as sacred contexts. Moreover, caught somewhere between the inflection point of vice and virtue, this ethical analysis suggests an exploration of joy as a constant dialectical tension between the ephemeral notion promoted by Western normativity and the existential concern embraced by Black liberationist and womanist viewpoints.

There is, however, the chance that this glimpse of Black human flourishing's expression of the freed self overflowing the strictures of its formerly prescribed limits appears to be petty particularism or mere identity politics. However, I beg to differ. The swirling torrent of memories, emotions, dreams, proclamations, and questions that are constitutive to the vision of joy I am articulating finds common cause with what Black feminist bell hooks calls the form of moral agency that strips away the pressures and problems imposed by the precarious nature of the present moment in the hopes of finding the strength to survive in the complexity of oneself. Yet we need to understand that "opposition is not enough," as hooks insists about the quest for joy qua real-lived moral agency, because "in that vacant space after one has resisted there is still the necessity to become—to make oneself anew."[8] In a womanist sense, joy is an ongoing effort to navigate beyond the inherent contradictions of humility and pride for the suffering subaltern. In the pages that follow, I will illustrate how womanist theological ethics shows us how to accomplish such a feat.

Troubling Virtues and Triumphant Vices

As David Hume notes in the *Treatise*, philosophy "cannot go beyond experience; and any hypothesis, that pretends to discover the ultimate original qualities of human nature, ought at first to be rejected as presumptuous and chimerical." He goes on to say further that the method of sticking to the limits of experience is "very skeptical, and tends to give us a notion of the imperfections and narrow limits of the human understanding."[9] While virtue is normatively a disposition or habitual inclination to act in ways consistent with forging the good life, what is considered "the human good" is, in fact, not always something held in common. Consequently, to apprehend the good life necessitates giving particular attention to differing epistemologies, lest we fall into colonial perspectives like Ricciardi's that view human flourishing by people of color as vice. To the contrary, mujerista ethicist Ada María Isasi-Díaz states that such perspectival shifts are essential in virtue ethics. In *En La Lucha*, Isasi-Díaz highlights the revelatory value of perspectival discourse when she states that it is necessary to "believe that the voices of particular . . . women have validity in themselves and that without claiming to be representative they point to the reality of all . . . because they make our reality more understandable. Just as radical immanence is a different way of understanding what up to now has been called transcendence, so, too, the more specific and particular the voices we present . . . the more they encompass the reality of all."[10] That being said, this white troubling of Black "virtue" leads to Black people valuing what white people call "vice." One might ask what prompts such a reality inversion. What are we to make of moral systems that have been reversed, with vice replacing virtue as the guiding force for many who often find themselves trampled underfoot by the human flourishing of others? This reversal of moral codes is not meant so much as a valuing of vice per se but rather bears witness to the mocking or appropriation of virtue and those ideologies, institutions, and individuals who promote it but fail to practice it. But this demands that we pursue a line of inquiry. Why should the downtrodden be humble? Why should they not take pride in their self-preservation in the face of their dehumanization? When such moral practices are deemed vices, the individuals/communities who practice them become the raw material and the evidence for moral failure. Defiance in the face of death must fully reject the virtue of moral codes that suggest that one should take comfort in their demoralized circumstances that occur at the hand of the devious systems and the deviant practices that have dominant agency and authority within our society and that suggest that powerful and privileged positions also have taken principled stances. Thus, normative accounts of virtue and vice, with the vice of humiliation (read as humility) vanquishing the virtues of proud people (read as pride), do further harm by undermining the enterprise of moral reasoning or, even worse, serve as the proof that ethics/virtues have failed or no longer exist. But taking another turn, what would happen if we use this perspectival shift to neither demolish ethics nor question its viability but instead treat ethics as a new enterprise for a more thoroughgoing ethic of human flourishing?

This assumption does not reside in an ethical vacuum. Akin to sociologist of religion Peter Berger's sacred canopy, this is a subjective statement posing itself as an objective reality that everyone has internalized.[11] However, according to ethicist and public intellectual Michael Eric Dyson, ethics—like hubris—has hues. "If Aristotle's 'proper pride' is a virtue to blacks whose self-respect has been battered, then white pride is often the vice that makes black pride necessary."[12] Further, psychologists have often noted that perceptions of hubris versus aggression are regarded differently across race. Building on prior research, psychologists Livingston and Pearce make the case that pride, arrogance, and agency are esteemed and rewarded traits for high-achieving and profiled people but are disparaged traits for working-class and marginalized people. Functioning as "disarming mechanisms," character traits, social dispositions, and physical behaviors that signal humility (read: passivity and deference) are considered virtuous characteristics and beneficial to the success of people of color, and particularly Black males.[13] But these same characteristics are irrelevant or even detrimental to the success of white males. The gendered-racialized public responses to Barack Obama and Donald Trump bear witness to this as real-world referents that illustrate that the expression of humility and its consistent traits (e.g., deference, warmth) benefit Black male leaders like Obama but hurt white male leaders, whereas the opposite pattern of humility (e.g., dominance, aggression) benefits Trump.

Now, before it appears that I have simply added a modifier for manipulative effect, stop and think. Is Black humility in America lost? Do the aims of Black people in America—to be recognized as citizens worthy of civil rights as well as fair and equal treatment—threaten their sense of joy? Is the sense that Black people are entitled to have inalienable rights or demand human rights an inhibitor of their joy? No, of course not! Freedom, and the fight for it, represent the essence of joy for Black life and trouble everything that up to now has been considered virtue or vice in our pursuit of it. As a moral theologian best known as leader of the Civil Rights Movement for practically pinioning his civil disobedience to his Black Christian beliefs, Rev. Dr. Martin Luther King Jr. stated:

> Psychological freedom, a firm sense of self-esteem, is the most powerful weapon against the long night of slavery. No Lincolnian Emancipation Proclamation, no Johnsonian civil rights bill can totally bring this kind of freedom. [Blacks] will only be free when [the community] reaches down to the inner depths of [their] own being and signs with the pen and ink of assertive [humanity their] own emancipation proclamation. Psychological freedom, a firm sense of self-esteem, is the most powerful weapon against the long night of physical slavery. And, with a spirit straining toward true self-esteem, the [African American] must boldly throw off the manacles of self-abnegation and say [inwardly] and to the world, "I am somebody. I am a person. I am a [person] with dignity and honor. I have a rich and noble history. How painful and exploited that history has been." . . . Yes, we must stand up and say, "I'm black and I'm beautiful," and this self-affirmation is the black [community's] need, made compelling by the white [people's] crimes against [them].[14]

King's observation must be acknowledged by the Christian social ethicist. As he noted, and as the generalized fear and conventional wisdom of U.S. race relations reflect, Black human flourishing threatened the flourishing of white power. Thus, the only moral course for redeeming the ideals of America was to disobey both the laws and its moral practices by calling out its hypocrisy and the privileges it held out for whites alone. Moreover, despite our history as a democratic republic, the rights of the racial ethnic minorities of our nation have given way to the power of the majority. And even decades later, when the demographics change, the majority is measured not by numbers but by those who still hold the power.

Within recent memory, in an August 2016 essay deconstructing the now-infamous Trump campaign slogan as a racially coded catchphrase, *New York Times* op-ed columnist Charles Blow insightfully observed: "'Make America Great Again' is in fact an inverted admission of loss—lost primacy, lost privilege, lost prestige."[15] But these losses among many so-called Trump voters have become magnified and take on added force because they generate the perception of uncertainty regarding one's status and, correspondingly, the fear of falling to a level that would make white Americans merely equal to their nonwhite counterparts. This legitimation crisis, as Habermas might rightly diagnose it, is especially critical for white Americans because it is largely being defined by a growing sense of deprivation, ambiguity, and insecurity that runs contrary to what whiteness as a collective identity once afforded them less than a generation ago. Dyson suggests that "this mode of whiteness parallels Renato Rosaldo's description of imperialist nostalgia, where a colonial power destroys a culture only to lament its demise with colonialism's victims."[16]

In his 1927 work *The Public and Its Problems*, philosopher and educator John Dewey made clear that democracy involves treating the negotiation of citizens in public life as an open network of sorts, across which multiple and often competing problems and concerns get communicated by different groups. In this perpetual process, all seek aid in order to participate more fully and freely in the larger society. In turn, our coordinated effort to address such concerns leads us as a people and a nation to build a shared life together grounded in the principle of equality as mutual regard. By contrast, however, the virulent strain of white supremacy advanced by the alt Right involves a perversion of democratic empathy by treating the concerns of white Americans as the only legitimate concerns of the body politic, and therefore whiteness prompts the only concerns in need of remedy or redress. Consequently, the very nature of our democratic society becomes deformed, since the interests of people of color are deemed either less important or unworthy of any consideration when doing so involves even the slightest devaluation of whiteness.

Womanist Vision of Joy

Take for instance the status of African American women as the United States witnessed their movement from enslavement to emancipation and to enfranchisement back to enslavement again. Although significant progress has been made since key historical markers such as the 1865 Emancipation Proclamation and, much later, the 1954 *Brown v. Board of Education* U.S. Supreme Court decision, the 1964 Civil Rights Act, the 1965 Voting Rights Act, and the short-lived War on Poverty, Black women still remain:

- the women for whom having a baby can be deadly. The maternal mortality rate for Black women is three times that of white women and is on par with that in several developing nations. For the sake of comparison, women in Lebanon have a much greater likelihood of surviving childbirth than do African American women;

- the most likely group to remain single and/or unmarried;
- the most likely to die of breast cancer once diagnosed and the group with the highest cases of hypertension;
- more likely than any group in America to work for poverty-level wages, thereby making them the most likely of all Americans to be among the working poor, in spite of the great strides they have made in collegiate education;
- the group with the lowest household income of any demographic group in America (and they are especially at risk of poverty in their retirement years); and
- the most likely to be a victim of violence in America (and they are more likely to be beaten, either by a stranger or by someone they love and trust, and more likely than any other group of women in America today to go to prison for fighting for their lives and family).[17]

These key findings illustrate that Black women experience some of the most death-dealing circumstances of anyone in America and thus are in need of national attention and urgent action for social justice. Ironically, however, African American women are markedly more religious on a variety of measures than the U.S. population as a whole (while the United States is generally considered a highly religious nation), including any level of affiliation with a religion, attendance at religious services, frequency of prayer, and religion's importance in life. These women are overwhelmingly Christian.[18] And, as Christians whose pursuit of the good life should reflect the humanity of Jesus, who also was born into exigent circumstances and suffered, Black Christian women might point us to the more thoroughgoing ethic that we stand in need of in our current moment.

At this point, it might be fruitful to briefly revisit the definition of "womanist" in order to better understand how it offers an alternative reading of not only virtue (of pride) and vice (of humility) but the consciousness and agency necessary for realizing the virtue of joy itself. Womanist theologian Jacquelyn Grant contends: "A womanist . . . is a strong Black woman who has sometimes been mislabeled as a domineering castrating matriarch. A womanist is one who has developed survival strategies in spite of the oppression of her race and sex in order to save her family and her people."[19]

For some, that may involve going against the norms of what is considered a virtuous woman and refusing to have one's desires ordered in accordance with a Eurocentric and/or patriarchal ideal and instead cultivating coping mechanisms related to the conditions of their cultural circumstances to not merely survive but thrive in spite of the tyrannical systems of race, sex, and class oppression that is their true sphere of moral life and that resonates with the historical Jesus, who as the gospel song declares is "the center of [their] joy."

> Jesus, You're the center of my joy
> All that's good and perfect comes from You
> You're the heart of my contentment
> Hope for all I do. . . .
> When I've lost my direction
> You're the compass for my way
> You're the fire and light
> When nights are long and cold
> In sadness, You're my laughter
> That shatters all my fears
> When I'm all alone,
> Your hand is there to hold.[20]

According to womanist theologian Delores Williams, the didactic intent of womanist theological reflection fulfills much of this task.[21] Womanist theology points Christians to new insights about moral life that give authoritative status to Black folk wisdom and Black women's moral wisdom based on reasoning that annunciates celebration and good news in forging strategic options for survival, supports justice, and sustains a productive quality of life for an entire community of poor women, children, and men. This means that womanist theological ethics should be a departure point for the question, "How ought the Christian to live in the world?" Of course, as we have discovered, tensions will exist between the moral teachings derived from these sources and the moral teachings about humility and pride that have usually buttressed presuppositions about living the Christian life. Nevertheless, womanist theology, in its didactic intent, teaches and models for us the different ways God reveals a prophetic word about virtues and vices in real-lived action for Christian living that is deliberately reflective of the historical Jesus and not simply the risen Christ.

The social and religious locations of Black women are so distant and divergent from the aggregate social and religious experiences of most Americans, womanist ethicist Katie Cannon posits, that desirable ethical values and moral qualities that determine moral character and moral conduct must always take into account the circumstances, the paradoxes, and the dilemmas that constrict self-determination and virtually block human flourishing altogether. Consequently, Cannon claims that there is a need to separate normative virtue from womanist virtue. The life and testimony of the first published African American female poet and abolitionist, Phillis Wheatley, serve as an example of this. She details the process of her thoroughgoing evangelical conversion in her poem "On Virtue." From the outset, Wheatley describes virtue as being out of the realm of definition and comprehension of the mere human mind:

> O Thou bright jewel in my aim I strive
> To comprehend thee. Thine own words declare
> Wisdom is higher than a fool can reach.

A few months prior to this poem's publication, Jonathan Edwards' *True Virtue* (published posthumously in 1765) similarly argued the same point—that virtue is beyond most people's understanding because it is summed up in the being of God—that God's "being above our reach . . . [should not] hinder that he should be loved according to his dignity . . . we must allow that true virtue does primarily and most essentially consist in a supreme love to God." Because Wheatley's "On Virtue" is one of her earliest poems, written in her youth, it is often dismissed. But this poem, like Ricciardi's observation of the Kenyans' joy, demands reexamination, as it is where Wheatley experientializes for the reader a phenomenological engagement of Jonathan Edwards' theology. Though we have no evidence that Wheatley had been exposed to Edwards' writings, particularly the texts *The Freedom of the Will* (1754) and the posthumous *The Nature of True Virtue* (1765), which were published and sold a few blocks away from the Wheatleys' residence, one cannot help but be inspired to believe that Jonathan Edwards' theological account was a call to communion, and Phillis Wheatley's testament a response to its beauty. According to the "Proposals" for her volume of poetry, which was first printed in the *Boston Censor* on February 29, 1772, Wheatley wrote "On Virtue" in 1766. That Wheatley composed her poem within months after Edwards' text on the same topic posthumously appeared in print only further supports the possibility that "On Virtue" is Wheatley's poetic response to Edwards' conception of virtue.[22]

In agreement with Edwards, Wheatley argues that Virtue is a divine and "sacred" quality, "array'd in glory from the orbs above." Yet Wheatley additionally alludes to Edwards when she asks Virtue to "embrace" her soul and "guide [her] steps to endless life and bliss." For in *Freedom of the Will*, Edwards also claims that one's soul is capable of influencing the way one walks: "And God has so made and established the human nature . . . that the soul preferring or choosing such an immediate exertion or alteration of the body, such an alteration instantaneously follows. There is nothing else in the actings of my mind, that I am conscious of while I walk." The reason that Edwards is conscious of nothing while he walks is that his newly converted soul has suspended "the actings of [his] mind." By saying that his body only moves as a result of his soul's, and not his mind's, "preferring or choosing," Edwards argues that when one undergoes a conversion experience and gives one's self up to God, one no longer has complete control over one's own body. Wheatley's saying that her soul touched by Virtue can "guide [her] steps" is thus more than just a metaphor for God's ability to change a converted person's life: it is an acknowledgment of the immense power that God's virtuous character can have over a person's body and soul.

The space between knowing what is virtue and being virtuous is akin to knowing what is good and choosing to do it. Anyone who has ever faced a moral dilemma of any sort is fully aware that there is a vast distance between knowledge and agency. Yet it is one's choice (or more accurately, the power to choose) that makes said distance a concrete reality. Without agency, vice and virtue are not a choice, nor can they be ascribed. As John Harris reminds us, where freedom disappears, virtue is also swept away in its undertow, while only vice remains intact. One must have the agency to examine and choose virtue in light of the knowledge of good within one's moral condition. If joy is evident in the good life, then the good life at the very least must be an examined life. To be sure, as Walker posits in *Possessing the Secret of Joy*, "If you lie to yourself about your own pain, you will be killed by those who will claim you enjoyed it."[23] Thus, if Black women reflect upon their lot, the so-called virtue of humility is morally bankrupt for people who live in humiliating conditions. Likewise, pride as a vice is in no way an evil for people who would become complicit in their own oppression without it.

Womanist virtue is the moral wisdom that Black women live out in their existential context—one in which normative appraisals of right and wrong or good and bad assigned by the deontological rules of an oppressive society do not apply. Instead, Black women's rational prescriptivism is a critical shifting of moral principles from white heteropatriarchal tradition; exceptions to their imposed rules yield the right of way to new rules, life chances, and better consequences so that they never conflict or dispute the right of way for their own flourishing. These general conditions for moral reasoning evolve from a mediating ethic that is conscientious, aiming to do justice, evaluative of courses of actions, concerned for the common good and human well-being of all, and confident in the universalizing of its actions so that such actions can become universal maxims. So humility can be deemed as counterintuitive at best and counterproductive at worst for Black women who have been perennially undermined and despised in the United States. Instead, consider this definition of virtue from a womanist point of view:

> Fundamentally, [womanist] virtue is inseparable from three principles: "invisible dignity," "quiet grace," and "unshouted courage." *Invisible dignity* is the self-celebration of survival against great odds. Living with the tension of the irrational facticity of life, women of African ancestry learn how to deal with insults and humiliations of the larger society so that they do not make the wrong step or give the wrong response, which could jeopardize their lives. *Quiet grace* is the search for truth. It is defined as looking at the world with one's own eyes, forming judgments and demythologizing whole bodies of so-called social legitimacy. *Unshouted courage* is a virtue evolving from the forced responsibility of black women. In its basic sense, it means the quality of steadfastness, akin to fortitude, in the face of formidable oppression. The communal attitude is far more than "grin and bear it." Rather, it involves the ability to "hold on to life" against major opposition. Virtue is thus the practical attitudes and habits adopted in obedience to these three principles.[24]

Put another way, both womanism in general and womanist ethics in particular are indicative of a countercultural moral practice that yields a contemplative practice for human flourishing by articulating what religiously has been referred to as joy unspeakable but has been distilled into four tenets: *radical subjectivity, traditional communalism, redemptive self-love,* and *critical engagement*. These tenets best capture how joy unspeakable in an unspeakably joyless world can become a contemplative practice that nurtures the God-potential in unlikely people in unlikely circumstances, cultivates the courage to transgress false boundaries, and mines the motherlode of their own epistemological resources.

Radical Subjectivity

As the first tenet of womanism, radical subjectivity is the process that emerges as Black women in the nascent phase of their identity development come to understand moral agency as the ability to defy a forced humility or naïveté in an effort to influence the choices made in one's life and how conscientization incites resistance against marginality. This mediated knowledge is intergenerational yet still inchoate to the extent that it is always already accountable to the anecdotal evidence of the wisdom and discernment grounded in and born of the experiences of being Black and female. Whereas many might decry the notion of essentialism undergirding identity politics for marginalized people, it is the embodied reality that serves as a rite of passage for Black women that is navigated by empowering assertion and audacious acts of naming and claiming voice, space, and knowledge.

Traditional Communalism

The second tenet of womanism, traditional communalism, is the affirmation and pride illustrated in the loving connections and relational bonds formed by Black women—including familial, maternal, platonic, religious, sexual, and spiritual ties. By claiming space among enemies and making culture out of contradiction, this virtue is displayed in Black women's ability to create, re-member, nurture, protect, sustain, and liberate communities that are marked and measured not by those outside of one's own community but by the acts of inclusivity, mutuality, reciprocity, and self-care practiced within it (opposite of the biological deterministic assumption that a woman's role is to serve as nurturer and protector). The moral principles and practices of Black women are marked by a commitment to live in solidarity with and in support of those with whom they share a common heritage and contextual language. This entails womanists having a preferential option for Black women's culture, especially their constructive criticism, "tragicomic hope," "in/visible dignity," and "un/shouted courage," which furthers the survival and liberation of all Black women and their communities. In turn, these deep-seated goals necessitate the inherited and shared legacy of Black women who have had to "make a way out of no way" from one generation to the next.

Redemptive Self-Love

Serving as the third tenet of womanism, redemptive self-love is the literal embodiment of pride in that it is an assertion of the humanity, customs, and aesthetic value of Black women in vast contradistinction to the commonly held stereotypes characteristic of white solipsism. The admiration and celebration of the distinctive and identifiable beauty of Black women (e.g., "I am black and beautiful O ye daughters of Jerusalem," Song 1:5, NRSV) unapologetically and unashamedly prides one's life in the midst of suffering and walking in love in the midst of hate. Pride, in this sense, functions neither as a displacement of God nor as a denial of human limitation but instead as reaffirmation of the God-ordained power of wisdom, love, and creativity found in Black women being made in God's image. Moreover, this capacity for redemptive self-love is marked by their unconditional and relentless resolve to enjoy the range of their cultural, physical, and spiritual expression, even at the risk of doing it alone.

Critical Engagement

Lastly, the fourth tenet of womanism characterizes Black women's intellectual positioning. Critical engagement is the epistemological privilege of Black women, born of their totalistic experience with the forces of interlocking systems of oppression and strategic options they devised to undermine them. In this mode of moral thinking, Black women maintain an unequivocal belief that they hold the standard and normative measure for true liberation and the ability to view things in their true relations or at least assign relative importance that privileges them as those who should be chief arbiters of accountability, advocacy, and authenticity, while being faithful to the task of expanding their discourse, knowledge, and skills. Critical engagement, then, is considered a healthy hermeneutical suspicion, cognitive counterbalance, intellectual indictment, and perspectival corrective to those people, ideologies, movements, and institutions that hold a one-dimensional analysis of oppression. When all is said and done, this tenet depends on an unshakable belief that Black women's survival strategies must reject what others have provided as the gold standard.

Must I Be a Womanist to Be Virtuous?

In his legendary work *God of the Oppressed*, liberation theologian James Cone claimed that in order to be a Christian one must become ontologically Black by claiming that Jesus' blackness is an ontological symbol, "a visible reality which best describes what oppression means in America."[25] While I assert that Black Christian women's moral witness provides real lived evidence that models Jesus' life and ministry and that womanist theological ethics articulates it, I do not assert that one must be womanist to be virtuous or to know joy (as evidenced with the Stoics or Edwards). No, that is not my assertion. But rather, I do see it necessary that for one to know true joy, one must view the dominant objectification of others (i.e., whiteness) as a vice. This intentional and concomitant effort of others entails participating in solidarity with and on behalf of Black women who have made available, shared, and translated their wisdom, strategies, and methods for the universal task of liberating the oppressed and speaking truth to power. In the final analysis, this work is not merely the appropriation of joy (as Ricciardi exacted from the Kenyans she exploited) but the reciprocity of joy as articulated and acted out by those womanist allies who take pride in their allegiance and realize as Alice Walker did, as Edwards did, that the lives they save may be their own.

• • •

Response to Stacey M. Floyd-Thomas
Robert C. Roberts

Stacey Floyd-Thomas' rich and wide-ranging essay on joy and humility in womanist theological ethics merits a correspondingly rich discussion, one that is impossible in the brief compass of this comment. But one of her essay's central topics is the oppressive misuse of the language of humility and pride. Since I am better equipped to address that topic than I am most of the others she touches on, I will focus this short response on it.

The uses of "pride" and "humility" in English can be confusing. We will understand better the moral misuse of the language of humility and pride if we first put before us a clear taxonomy of the meanings that may attach to these words.

"Pride" can be used as a synonym for "conceit," "arrogance," "being overbearing" or "domineering," "self-righteousness," "vanity," "snobbery," "invidious triumph," and "grandiosity." It seems obvious that, when used in any of these senses, "pride" is the name not of a virtue but of a family of vices and modes of human dysfunction. If you look up the criteria for narcissistic personality disorder in the *Diagnostic and Statistical Manual*, fifth edition, you'll see several of these vice words. We could call these traits *the vices of pride*. On the other hand, pride in one's work, or children, or community can denote a happy sense of their excellence combined with a sense that they are one's own. Similarly, "pride" can function as a synonym for "integrity," "self-confidence," "self-respect," "secure sense of one's ability to do good things," "sense of one's own dignity," or "high aspiration." These attributes all seem to be important aspects of being a mature and excellent person. In any of these senses, then, "pride" designates a virtue. So is pride a virtue, or a vice? The answer seems to be that the word can go either way, depending on context.

"Humility" has a similar ambiguity. Some people use the word as a catch-all substitute for such other terms as "low self-esteem," "defeatist lethargy," "servility," "obsequiousness," "shame" (especially, the deeply dispositional shame that often results from living in squalor and not being respected by "respectable" people), "timidity," "slovenliness," "low ambition," and "pusillanimity" (small-mindedness). It seems clear that when "humility" is used in any of these ways, it designates a vice or, if that is too harsh a term, at least a trait that is unfortunate for its possessor and for the friends and family of its possessor. But "humility" can also name a virtue or family of virtues (and I think that in our contemporary world it usually does). It may be used as a stand-in for "unpretentious," "not being arrogant," "unvain," "not being domineering," "being down to earth," "nonjudgmental," "unconceited," "not puffed up," and perhaps others. It is interesting that when we look for specifications of "humble," used for virtue, we are drawn to privative, "negative," terms like the prefixes "un-," "non-," and "not being . . ." attached to terms for the vices of pride. Humility seems to be the absence of the vices of pride. Whether that is *all* it is is a contentious question at the moment, in the philosophy of humility.[1] But if that is all it is, it would be like the attribute of purity in pure water. For many purposes, purity is a very good quality for water to have, yet it is nothing but the absence of pollutants. Humility would be a certain "purity of heart"—the absence of pollutants like arrogance, vanity, conceit, and domination.

Despite the awkwardness of the term "humility" designating both virtue and vice, and the same for "pride," this all may seem rather harmless. After all, thousands of words in English may mean more than one thing, and we seem to be pretty good at catching, from the context, whatever meaning a speaker or writer currently intends. When someone says, "Compared with Donald Trump, Barack Obama was a humble leader," we know immediately that the speaker does not mean to say that Obama was obsequious, servile, and lethargic because of crushingly low self-esteem. We know that the speaker uses the term honorifically, as denoting a virtue. And when someone says that Satan's fall was due to his pride, we know that the speaker is not praising Satan for his self-confidence, sense of dignity, and noble aspirations.

But the ambiguity of "humility" and "pride" is problematic when exploited as a device of social oppression. How does this work? By crisscrossing the meanings, making vice virtue and virtue vice, the oppressor casts a spell on his victim (and maybe himself) and binds the spirit as surely as chains bind the body. The oppressor says to the oppressed, as it were, "In you, humility [read: servility, obsequiousness, low personal ambition] is a virtue and pride [read: self-confidence, a sense of dignity, and high personal aspirations] is a vice; in me, pride [read: self-confidence, a sense of dignity, and high personal aspirations, but also covertly mixed with more or less disguised and thus licensed arrogance, domination, and conceit] is a virtue, because I am [for example] white and male." That seems to be the bare logic of oppression by confusion of "humility" and "pride." But how does it work psychologically?

Of course, the oppressor does not literally *say* these things to the oppressed, at least not in the mainstream of our politically correct culture. But he does manage to *communicate* them—for example, by making sure that the oppressed are excluded, in certain ways, from positions of affluence, knowledge, and power, and kept, as much as possible, in humiliating conditions, in social conditions that reinforce the impression of inferiority, worthlessness, and inability. In this way, stereotypes of ignorance, ineptitude, and dangerousness are frequently reinforced in the minds of both oppressors and oppressed. Much of this is not consciously intentional on the part of oppressors but engineered with robotic automaticity by institutional inertia and dimly conscious assumptions. This is why explicit movements of resistance like Black Power and womanism and devices like affirmative action are useful to break the inertia and cast light on the assumptions.

We can go a little deeper in our understanding of the misuse of the language of humility and pride by exploring what the two kinds of humility and the two kinds of pride are, psychologically. If we start with the vices of pride, we will also be able to see how joy enters into the dynamism. The vices of pride are all dispositional concerns for a certain kind of personal importance, with an integrated understanding of what that importance is and means, and how it is acquired. Let us call the kind of importance in question *narcissistic importance*, to distinguish it from the kind of importance that a person who has proper self-respect and a sense of her own worth and her effectiveness as an agent attributes to herself. Narcissistic importance is the kind that the vain person feels he gets from being celebrated in the limelight, and the arrogant person feels he gets from claiming extraordinary entitlements, and the invidiously triumphant person feels he gets from besting a rival for all to see, and the racist person feels he gets from belonging to the supreme race—and so on through the vices of pride. We might call the second kind of importance *dignity* or *worthiness of respect and love*. We all have a need for this kind of importance, and when we implicitly feel that we have it, we have the healthy kind of pride.

When a person's desire for narcissistic importance is gratified, he feels joy (a vicious joy, of course), and when circumstances dramatically frustrate this desire, especially in a public way, he feels distress ("wounded pride"). For example, a white supremacist may feel a special invidious joy in working with Black subordinates (a joy he would not feel working with white subordinates), inasmuch as it gives him a concrete and exhilarating experience of his dominance as a member of the "superior" race. He revels in their inferiority to himself and his white "brothers." But if one of his supposed inferiors then demonstrates, for all the world to see, an intellectual ability incontrovertibly superior to his own, he will experience racist dudgeon and may become dangerous.

Speaking of joy, not in its evil edition as an expression of satisfied vicious concern but as virtuous, Floyd-Thomas comments that "joy is far more than an emotion [but] rather, a state of being-ness" (15). Here she echoes the apostle Paul, who includes joy in a list of the fruit of the Holy Spirit that also includes gentleness, self-control, patience, and love (see Gal 5:22-23). These qualities are something like character traits of a person who lives in fellowship with the Spirit of God. What does it mean to say that joy is a virtue? One thing it means, as Floyd-Thomas' word "being-ness" suggests, is that it has a certain permanence in a person; it is a characteristic of a mature Christian—not just an episodic feeling, but a way of *being*. The Christian is joyful, not just now and then, but characteristically.

It also means that the episodes of emotion that express the character trait of spiritual joy are virtuous and not of the vicious variety. Paul tells the church at Rome, "Rejoice with those who rejoice, and weep with those who weep" (Rom 12:15, NASB). Here, joy is an expression of love, of one's concerns being aligned with others' concerns. It is an expression of social harmony, of "unity" of mind and heart with your sisters and brothers. A person has the virtue of joy if her episodes of joy are consistently loving and are never (or almost never) invidious.

And this is where humility comes in as a necessary condition for spiritual joy. Spiritual joy is ruined and excluded by the vices of pride (among the works of the flesh that Paul contrasts with the fruit of the Spirit are envy, bitter competition, and conceit [Gal 5:20-21]). Humility, as the absence of the vices of pride, is a joy-purifier. If our joy is not purified by humility, it cannot be spiritual. Or, to put the point a bit more generously (and realistically, given the depths of our sin), we must be able to dissociate from our prideful joys.

Floyd-Thomas points out that to know true joy, we must recognize others' domineering reduction of us to be the vice that it is. This recognition buffers us against the bad kind of humility (the dispositional shame that is a natural response to being habitually put down by others) and liberates us for the joys of virtuous pride, as well as the joys of loving fellowship. Having a good sense of our own worth and confidence in our ability to accomplish good things positions us well for successes and for relatively undistorted enjoyment of them. We can go further: not only *others'* domineering reduction of us, but also *our own* domineering reduction of others is vice, and our joys are purified by humbly taking this fact to heart. Only if we are able to perceive with courage and contrition the viciousness of our own domineering reduction of others will our joy be a fruit of the Holy Spirit.[2]

• • •

Reply to Robert C. Roberts

Stacey M. Floyd-Thomas

This invitation places me in a most precarious predicament. On the one hand, my task as a Christian social ethicist is to transcend my blackness and femaleness and draft a blueprint of liberation ethics that somehow speaks to, or responds to, the universality of the human condition. On the other hand, my assignment as a womanist liberation ethicist is to debunk, unmask, and disentangle the historically conditioned value judgments and power relations that undergird the particularities of race, sex, and class oppression. Zora Neale Hurston described this dilemma as trying to hit a straight lick with a crooked stick. In essence, I have been invited to speak as "one of the canonical boys" and as "the noncanonical other" at one and the same time. These two tasks stand in opposition to each other. Thus, the question which has evolved from wrestling with this dilemma is the following: *What importance do race and gender have as meaningful categories in the development of a Black liberation ethic?*[1]

I preface my response to Robert C. Roberts with the epigraph that my mentor and the progenitor of womanist ethics, Katie Cannon, enunciated before the Society of Christian Ethics over three decades ago. I am both comforted and anguished by her words as I write this response. To be sure, Roberts offered a clear and well-expressed approach, demonstrating great skill approaching the concepts of vice and virtue for pride and humility. His perspective concerning the interactions between oppressors and oppressed demonstrates a critical inquiry that acknowledges the oppressive ideologies at play. Nevertheless, Roberts' philosophical approach responds to the taxonomy and semantics of the definitions and is based on normative understandings resting in the Western understanding of a subjective/objective experience of joy. *Therein lies the problem. There is nothing normative about joy for the oppressed.* In contrast to, and in critique of, normative assumptions that marginalize real-lived experiences, my approach and discussion of joy is phenomenological and metaethical. As a form of consciousness that is negotiated and resurrected from those of us who live left of center, joy evolves from a familiar form of self that is inextricably communal, embodied, and possessed by a worldly consciousness within which normative assumptions of humility and pride cannot really exist.

It is true that vices and virtues are interchangeable in their meanings depending on the subject and the context. One cannot claim an essentialist notion of what these terms mean within different contexts and without having a responsible knowledge of how oppressive ideologies are being manifested in those contexts, especially within the intersections of class, gender, sexuality, ethnicity, and citizenship. Only those who are inserted within these contexts and their construction of meanings will know what meaning will be assigned. Roberts defines a joy the world gives by providing virtuous humility to enhance virtuous pride in oppressed people, which actually misses my point. Womanists debunk the so-called vice of pride and virtue of humility by showing how there are actually virtues of pride and vices of humility because how virtue and vice are experienced arises from subjective contexts, not objective definitions.

According to philosopher Jacques Derrida in "Structure, Sign, and Play," the structurality of structures in the forms of language is always at play. Sometimes an author, by trying to govern the structure—in this case, to seek a "clear taxonomy" to explain the ambiguity of the form in language—could escape the intentional structurality at play.[2] Derrida further states that "it has always been thought that the center, which is by definition unique, constituted that very thing within a structure which while governing the structure, escapes structurality."[3] In other words, there cannot be a clear taxonomy of the meanings if the respondent is not addressing the systemic creation of ambiguity within the creation of the form of language itself. The different centers of power from which that center has been formed and re-formed suggest that there is always the sensible agent who ascertains what is or is not intelligible in that this is "a system in which the central signified, is never absolutely present outside a system of difference."[4]

Thus, the way in which one forms language or taxonomies must always be discussed in dialectic conversation with the historical formation of the form of discourse itself. Because "language bears itself the necessity of its own critique,"[5] that must constitute the first approach toward a discussion of the sensible and intelligible, morality or immorality, and categories of vices and virtues. Furthering Derrida's semiotic analysis, in the power play of language, the sensible signifier (moral agent / power broker) always has an intelligible sign (moral content / game piece) that is reduced to whatever the powerful wants to signify.[6] The one who wins the game is the one who makes the rules, and if you refuse to play by his rules, you lose. So, to engage Roberts' following observations proves his engagement of my contribution basically represents a kind of "power play of language": (1) "The ambiguity of 'humility' and 'pride' is problematic when exploited as a device of social oppression"; (2) "Stereotypes of ignorance, ineptitude, and dangerousness are frequently reinforced in the minds of both oppressors and oppressed"; and (3) the oppressor will "[make] sure that the oppressed are excluded, in certain ways, from positions of affluence, knowledge, and power . . . in social conditions that reinforce the impression of inferiority . . . This is why explicit movements of resistance like Black Power and womanism [*it is interesting that Roberts links these two*] and devices like affirmative action are useful to break the inertia and cast light on the assumptions" (29–30).

What arises in Roberts' articulation and discourse can also assume that the oppressed is not exerting her/his/their agency during or in the midst of oppression. Also, while stereotypes of arrogance and ineptitude could be reinforced in both the oppressor and the oppressed, they will not be manifested, treated, and healed in the same manner or level. Additionally, the oppressor might have more resources, privilege, and power to work on those, while the oppressed works on surviving. Sangeeta Ray's formulation of literary theorist Gayatri Spivak's methodology suggests that in order to deconstruct the manner in which language is formed, the oppressor needs to "[acknowledge] complicity, [learn] from below, [unlearn] one's privilege, . . . persistently [critique] the structures that one inhabits . . . and [give] attention to subject formation such that it 'produc[es] the reflective basis for self-conscious social agency.'"[7] In this statement, Ray asks the privileged readers to shift their perceptions from the anthropological or the psychological toward the historic-political, in which text lies as what Spivak calls a "cultural fabric."[8]

During her 1993 Nobel Prize lecture after winning the prize for literature, Toni Morrison provides poignant clarity about what makes up this cultural fabric:

> The systematic looting of language can be recognized by the tendency of its users to forgo its nuanced, complex, mid-wifery properties for menace and subjugation. Oppressive language does more than represent violence; it is violence; does more than represent the limits of knowledge; it limits knowledge. Whether it is obscuring state language or the faux-language of mindless media; whether it is the proud but calcified language of the academy or the commodity driven language of science; whether it is the malign language of law-without-ethics, or language designed for the estrangement of minorities, hiding its racist plunder in its literary cheek—it must be rejected, altered and exposed. It is the language that drinks blood, laps vulnerabilities, tucks its fascist boots under crinolines of respectability and patriotism as it moves relentlessly toward the bottom line and the bottomed-out mind. Sexist language, racist language, theistic language—all are typical of the policing languages of mastery, and cannot, do not permit new knowledge or encourage the mutual exchange of ideas.

The new knowledge I hoped to offer as part of this book was that Black women's countercultural moral practice of joy unspeakable (via their epistemological resources of *radical subjectivity, traditional communalism, redemptive self-love,* and *critical engagement*) yields a contemplative practice for human flourishing in an otherwise unspeakably joyless world. And that when truly seeking mutuality rather than power, joy-filled contemplative practice nurtures the God-potential in unlikely people in unlikely circumstances. This unspeakable joy of Black women also cultivates the courage to transgress false boundaries and capture how this joy creates a difference that is neither alienating nor deficient but might in fact signify what flourishing looks like when power is not the endgame. This calling into community (not to be mistaken as a calling out) represents the clarion call of my essay, to which Professor Roberts provides a normative response. Alas, "call and response" is, after all, a Black liturgical norm. Perhaps I confused this context with one that might be similar: communally akin and mutually affirmative. Only through that lens (one of accountability and atonement) is the oppressor able to recognize the difficulty of what Roberts claimed as necessary—to recognize humility as a virtue for spiritual joy conditioned by an action of purification from pollution (31).

As Roberts mentions with his water example, the humility of the oppressed cannot be spiritual if the oppressed is not able to disassociate from "prideful joy." Here Roberts is not addressing the systemic oppression that often rules over and regulates the context of the oppressed. The oppressed encounter themselves within a dialectic dynamic between addressing the systemic while simultaneously working for their individual and communal sense of joy.

When Roberts states that "the uses of 'pride' and 'humility' in English can be confusing," perhaps he is attempting to be deliberately didactic and nothing more. Yet in his attempt to instruct us all in ethical vocabulary, he misses the opportunity to learn, by reiterating the ambiguity of the concepts themselves and by referencing the deceptive forces of normativity always attached to them. This needs further discussion. Postcolonial theorist Homi Bhabha argues that "English" as a language has been used to create discourses, and this needs to be scrutinized by acknowledging its colonial roots of power.[9] Scholars, especially those at the intersections of sacred rhetoric and moral philosophy, know this and unfortunately wield their imperialist swords by pen and paper. Thus, the colonial presence has its forts in both church and academy as well. Consequently, there will always be a trace and a trademark of ambivalence and normativity that is either subconsciously or subversively placed in the politics, preaching, and publications of any who play the roles of privileged purveyors of the normative truth. In other words, though surely unintended by him, I read Roberts' lesson in ambivalence and normativity as yet another example of colonial power. Bhabha further complicates Roberts' statement about "resistance movements that are there to awake people from inertia" by arguing: "Resistance is not necessarily an oppositional act of political intention, nor is it the simple negation or exclusion of the 'content' of another culture. It is the effect of an ambivalence produced within the rules of recognition of dominating discourses as they articulate the signs of cultural difference and replicate them within the deferential relations of colonial power—hierarchy, normalization, marginalization and so forth."[10]

In the final analysis, it is unfortunate that the miseducation of the oppressor often results in the missed education that they could have gained if they had inclined their minds and hearts to the epistemological lessons afforded by the oppressed. A lesson in joy from a womanist perspective elicits the hope of a mutual liberative response, while acknowledging this as it explains how the form of language and discourse needs to be scrutinized a priori, where *all* are affirmed as agents capable of defining and defending that which can only be experienced before it can be explained.

I will end this response as I started, allowing the words of the late Katie Cannon, the first womanist ethicist, to have the last word on this present iteration of a perennial and pernicious act of colonial pride: "Even though there is no clearly written statement among Christian social ethicists regarding the nature of scholarship, enough areas of agreement do exist within the guild to make reasonable generalizations regarding the ethicist as scholar. Most of these have nothing to do with the realities of Black women. For instance, membership in this highly complex fraternity means investigation of abstract metatheory, traditional philosophical thought, and the established canon of ethical inquiry with supposedly calm and detached objectivity."[11] To prove that she is sufficiently intelligent, the Black woman as Christian ethicist must discount the particularities of her lived experiences and instead focus on the validity of generalizable external analytical data. The dilemma she faces in joining the canonical boys is that of succumbing to the temptation of only mastering the historically specified perspective of the Euro-American masculine preserve. In order to be a respected scholar in the discipline, the Black woman is placed under a double injunction. She has to face a critical jury, primarily white and male, that makes claims for gender-neutral and value-free inquiry as a model for knowledge.[12]

Notes to Chapter 1
(Stacey M. Floyd-Thomas)

1 Mirella Ricciardi, *African Saga* (New York: HarperCollins, 1981), 147.
2 Alice Walker, *Possessing the Secret of Joy* (New York: Harcourt Brace Jovanovich, 1992).
3 Ricciardi's observation resonates with dominant discourses in ethics that often attend to the Aristotelian accounts of the virtues (e.g., humility, temperance, etc.). The Aristotelian account of virtues is not the only account of virtues. Walker's estimation makes this point clear. In fact, I would venture to argue that Aristotelian forms of virtue are the least effective way of talking about African and African American experiences of virtue. We can consider the British tradition, from the Cambridge Platonists, who were not informed by Aristotelian virtue ethics but by Stoicism, onward. Within the Stoic tradition, virtues are not so much habits as they are a particular orientation or ordering of the heart, and as such they are far more experiential. In one instance, the virtues are experienced as beauty. There is an entire aesthetics for how we think about the virtues that leaves itself more aligned to poetry, beauty, experience, and singing and aesthetic virtues of beauty than it does to the Aristotelian-Thomist virtues of humility that we are supposed to practice. In the Renaissance, the Stoic tradition (as they read the classics by Cicero and Seneca) offered a new account of the virtues that was humanistic, as it took into serious consideration the passions, emotions, and interiority. So they began to define virtue as beauty. For them, beauty was the highest evaluation that one could give to life. When Augustine takes it up, virtue is not many things; virtue is love. For a womanist, this is a better paradigm for understanding virtue as the affect by which those moral tenets that make up our interiority travels and is appreciated through a multiplicity of artistic, experiential forms and affective forms. Joy is affectivity.
4 Shirley Caesar, "This Joy I Have," video, Pannell CTP Traditional Gospel Music, 4:11, November 21, 2010, https://www.youtube.com/watch?v=Tlgl54RaMmY.
5 Barbara A. Holmes, "Joy Unspeakable in an Unspeakably Joyless World," *Theology Today*, https://theologytoday.ptsem.edu/uploadedFiles/School_of_Christian_Vocation_and_Mission/Institute_for_Youth_Ministry/Princeton_Lectures/Holmes-Joy.pdf.
6 Jonathan Edwards, *The Works of Jonathan Edwards*, ed. Perry Miller, vol. 2, *Religious Affections*, ed. John E. Smith (New Haven: Yale University Press, 1959).
7 Mary Clark Moschella, *Caring for Joy: Narrative, Theology, and Practice* (Boston: Brill, 2016).
8 bell hooks, *Yearning: Race, Gender, and Cultural Politics* (Boston: South End, 1999), 15.

9 David Hume, *A Treatise of Human Nature*, vol. 1 (New York: Oxford University Press, 2007), 5.
10 Ada María Isasi-Díaz. *En La Lucha / In the Struggle: Elaborating a Mujerista Theology* (Minneapolis: Fortress, 2004), 63.
11 See Peter Berger, *Sacred Canopy: Elements of a Sociological Theory of Religion* (New York: Anchor Books, 1990).
12 Michel Eric Dyson, *Pride* (New York: Oxford University Press, 2006), 46.
13 See R. W. Livingston and N. A. Pearce, "The Teddy-Bear Effect: Does Having a Baby Face Benefit Black Chief Executive Officers?" *Psychological Science* 20, no. 10 (2009): 1229–36. This article unpacks the theoretical and practical implications for research on race, gender, and leadership among racial perceptions of success. Livingston and Pearce's research suggests that expressions and embodiment that are negatively correlated with success among white males in high positions of leadership have an inverse impact on the success of Black men. Taken together, these findings suggest that appearing naïve, young, and innocent (what they call "babyfacedness") are disarming mechanisms that facilitate the success of Black leaders by attenuating stereotypical perceptions that Blacks are threatening.
14 Martin Luther King Jr., "The President's Address to the Tenth Anniversary Convention of the SCLC, Atlanta, Ga., August 16, 1967," in *The Rhetoric of Black Power*, ed. Robert L. Scott and Wayne Brockriede (New York: Harper and Row, 1969), 155–56.
15 Charles M. Blow, "Trump Reflects White Male Fragility," *New York Times*, August 4, 2016, https://www.nytimes.com/2016/08/04/opinion/trump-reflects-white-male-fragility.html?_r=0>.
16 Dyson, *Pride*, 49.
17 "Black Women in the United States, 2014: Progress and Challenges," National Coalition on Black Civic Participation Black Women's Roundtable, https://www.washingtonpost.com/r/2010- 2019/WashingtonPost/2014/03/27/National-Politics/Stories/2FinalBlackWomenintheUS2014.pdf. This groundbreaking report assesses the overall conditions of Black women in the United States, examining virtually the full spectrum of their contemporary experience in America. The ones highlighted here are broad strokes but key findings from this report.
18 "A Religious Portrait of African-Americans," Pew Research Center Religion and Public Life, January 30, 2009, http://www.pewforum.org/2009/01/30/a-religious-portrait-of-african-americans/. For womanist historical/sociological context, see also works including Cheryl Townsend Gilkes, *If It Wasn't for Women: Black Women's Experience and Womanist Culture in Church and Community* (Maryknoll, N.Y.: Orbis Books, 2001); Daphne Wiggins, *Righteous Content: Black Women's Perspectives of Church and Faith* (New York: NYU Press, 2004); Judith Weisenfeld, *African-American Women and Christian Activism: New York's Black YWCA, 1905–1945* (Cambridge, Mass.: Harvard University Press, 1997); Evelyn Brooks Higginbotham, *Righteous Discontent: The Women's Movement in the Black Baptist Church, 1880–1920*

(Cambridge, Mass.: Harvard University Press, 1993); and Marla F. Frederick, *Between Sundays: Black Women and Everyday Struggles of Faith* (Berkeley: University of California Press, 2003).

19 Jacquelyn Grant, *White Women's Christ and Black Women's Jesus: Feminist Christology and Womanist Response* (Atlanta: Scholars Press, 1989), 205.

20 Gloria Gaither and Richard Smallwood, "Jesus, You're the Center of My Joy," http://www.azlyrics.com/lyrics/richardsmallwood/centerofmyjoy.html.

21 Delores Williams, "Womanist Theology: Black Women's Voice," *Christianity and Crisis* 47 (March 2, 1987).

22 Michael Monescalchi, "On Virtue: Phillis Wheatley with Jonathan Edwards," *Commonplace* 17, no. 3 (2017), http://commonplace.online/article/vol-17-no-3-monescalchi/. According to Monescalchi:

> The most authoritative edition of Wheatley's writings is *Complete Writings*, ed. Vincent Carretta (New York, 2001). Haynes's writings can be found in *Black Preacher to White America: The Collected Writings of Lemuel Haynes, 1774–1833*, ed. Richard Newman (Brooklyn, 1990). The most authoritative editions of Edwards's writings are from Yale University Press; *Freedom of the Will* is found in the collection's first volume and *True Virtue* is located in the eighth volume. Cedrick May is one of the only other scholars to discuss the affinity between Edwards's and Wheatley's theology; see his *Evangelism and Resistance in the Black Atlantic, 1760–1835* (Athens, 2008). For more information on Samuel Kneeland, see Jonathan Yeager, "Samuel Kneeland of Boston: Colonial Bookseller, Printer, and Publisher of Religion," *Printing History* 11 (2012): 35–61.

23 Walker, *Possessing the Secret of Joy*, 106.

24 Katie G. Cannon, "Womanist Virtue," in *Dictionary of Feminist Theologies*, ed. Letty M. Russell and J. Shannon Clarkson (Louisville: Westminster John Knox, 1996), 313.

25 James Cone, *A Black Liberation Theology* (Maryknoll, N.Y.: Orbis Books, 1996), 8.

NOTES TO CHAPTER 1 RESPONSE
(ROBERT C. ROBERTS)

1 See, for example, Dennis Whitcomb, Heather Battaly, Jason Baehr, and Daniel Howard-Snyder, "Intellectual Humility: Owning Our Limitations," *Philosophy and Phenomenological Research* 94, no. 3 (2015): 509–39; Robert C. Roberts and Ryan West, "Jesus and the Virtues of Pride," in *The Moral Psychology of Pride*, ed. Adam Carter and Emma Gordon (Totowa: Rowman and Littlefield, 2017), 99–121; Robert C. Roberts and Scott Cleveland, "Humility from a Philosophical Point of View," in *Handbook of Humility*, ed. Everett Worthington, Joshua Hook, and Donnie Davis (New York: Routledge, 2016), 33–46.

2 This essay was written with the support of the Templeton Religion Trust, by way of the Self, Motivation, and Virtue Project at the Institute for the Study of Human Flourishing at the University of Oklahoma. The opinions expressed in it are those of the author, and not necessarily of the Templeton Religion Trust.

Notes to Chapter 1 Reply
(Stacey M. Floyd-Thomas)

1 Katie G. Cannon, "Hitting a Straight Lick with a Crooked Stick: The Womanist Dilemma in the Development of a Black Liberation Ethic," *Annual of the Society of Christian Ethics* 7 (1987): 165 (emphasis modified).
2 Jacques Derrida, *Writing and Difference* (Chicago: University of Chicago Press, 1978), 278–79.
3 Derrida, *Writing and Difference*, 279.
4 Derrida, *Writing and Difference*, 280.
5 Derrida, *Writing and Difference*, 284.
6 Jacques Derrida, "*Différance*," in *Margins of Philosophy*, trans. Alan Bass (Chicago: University of Chicago Press, 1982), 5.
7 Sangeeta Ray, "An Ethics on the Run," *PMLA* 123, no. 1 (2008): 238; quoted in *Planetary Love: Spivak, Postcoloniality, and Theology*, ed. Stephen Moore and Mayra Rivera (New York: Fordham University Press, 2011), 17. The quotation in Ray's text is from Spivak in an interview with Tani E. Barlow, "Not Really a Properly Intellectual Response: An Interview with Gayatri Spivak," *Positions* 12 (2004): 153.
8 Quoted in Moore and Rivera, *Planetary Love*, 20.
9 Homi Bhabha, "Signs Taken for Wonders: Questions of Ambivalence and Authority Under a Tree outside Delhi, May 1817," *Critical Inquiry* 12, no. 1 (1985): 149.
10 Bhabha, "Signs Taken for Wonders," 153.
11 Cannon, "Hitting a Straight Lick," 165–66.
12 Cannon, "Hitting a Straight Lick," 165–66.

Chapter Bibliography

Barlow, Tani E. "Not Really a Properly Intellectual Response: An Interview with Gayatri Spivak." *Positions* 12 (2004): 139–63.

Berger, Peter. *Sacred Canopy: Elements of a Sociological Theory of Religion*. New York: Anchor Books, 1990.

Bhabha, Homi. "Signs Taken for Wonders: Questions of Ambivalence and Authority under a Tree outside Delhi, May 1817." *Critical Inquiry* 12, no. 1 (1985): 144–65.

Cannon, Katie G. "Hitting a Straight Lick with a Crooked Stick: The Womanist Dilemma in the Development of a Black Liberation Ethic." *Annual of the Society of Christian Ethics* 7 (1987): 165–77.

———. "Womanist Virtue." In *Dictionary of Feminist Theologies*, edited by Letty M. Russell and J. Shannon Clarkson. Louisville: Westminster John Knox, 1996.

Cone, James. *A Black Liberation Theology*. Maryknoll, N.Y.: Orbis, 1996.

Derrida, Jacques. "*Différance.*" In *Margins of Philosophy*, translated by Alan Bass, 3–27. Chicago: University of Chicago Press, 1982.

———. *Writing and Difference*. Chicago: University of Chicago Press, 1978.

Dyson, Michel Eric. *Pride*. New York: Oxford University Press, 2006.

Edwards, Jonathan. *The Works of Jonathan Edwards*. Edited by Perry Miller. Vol. 2, *Religious Affections*. Edited by John E. Smith. New Haven: Yale University Press, 1959.

Frederick, Marla F. *Between Sundays: Black Women and Everyday Struggles of Faith*. Berkeley: University of California Press, 2003.

Gilkes, Cheryl Townsend. *If It Wasn't for Women: Black Women's Experience and Womanist Culture in Church and Community*. Maryknoll, N.Y.: Orbis, 2001.

Grant, Jacquelyn. *White Women's Christ and Black Women's Jesus: Feminist Christology and Womanist Response*. Atlanta: Scholars Press, 1989.

Haynes, Lemuel. *Black Preacher to White America: The Collected Writings of Lemuel Haynes, 1774–1833*. Edited by Richard Newman. Brooklyn: Carlson, 1990.

Higginbotham, Evelyn Brooks. *Righteous Discontent: The Women's Movement in the Black Baptist Church, 1880–1920*. Cambridge, Mass.: Harvard University Press, 1993.

hooks, bell. *Yearning: Race, Gender, and Cultural Politics*. Boston: South End, 1999.

Hume, David. *A Treatise of Human Nature*. Vol. 1. New York: Oxford University Press, 2007.

Isasi-Díaz, Ada María. *En La Lucha / In the Struggle: Elaborating a Mujerista Theology*. Minneapolis: Fortress, 2004.

King, Martin Luther, Jr., "The President's Address to the Tenth Anniversary Convention of the SCLC, Atlanta, Ga., August 16, 1967." In *The Rhetoric of Black Power*, ed. Robert L. Scott and Wayne Brockriede. New York: Harper and Row, 1969.

Livingston, R. W., and N. A. Pearce, "The Teddy-Bear Effect: Does Having a Baby Face Benefit Black Chief Executive Officers?" *Psychological Science* 20, no. 10 (2009): 1229–36.

May, Cedric. *Evangelism and Resistance in the Black Atlantic, 1760–1835*. Athens: University of Georgia Press, 2008.

Monescalchi, Michael. "On Virtue: Phillis Wheatley with Jonathan Edwards," *Commonplace* 17, no. 3 (2017), http://commonplace.online/article/vol-17-no-3-monescalchi/.

Moore, Stephen, and Mayra Rivera, eds. *Planetary Love: Spivak, Postcoloniality, and Theology*. New York: Fordham University Press, 2011.

Moschella, Mary Clark. *Caring for Joy: Narrative, Theology, and Practice*. Boston: Brill, 2016.
Ray, Sangeeta. "An Ethics on the Run." *PMLA* 123, no. 1 (2008): 238.
Ricciardi, Mirella. *African Saga*. New York: HarperCollins, 1981.
Roberts, Robert C., and Scott Cleveland. "Humility from a Philosophical Point of View." In *Handbook of Humility*, edited by Everett Worthington, Joshua Hook, and Donnie Davis, 33–46. New York: Routledge, 2016.
Roberts, Robert C., and Ryan West. "Jesus and the Virtues of Pride." In *The Moral Psychology of Pride*, edited by Adam Carter and Emma Gordon, 99–121. Totowa: Rowman and Littlefield, 2017.
Walker, Alice. *Possessing the Secret of Joy*. New York: Harcourt Brace Jovanovich, 1992.
Weisenfeld, Judith. *African-American Women and Christian Activism: New York's Black YWCA, 1905–1945*. Cambridge, Mass.: Harvard University Press, 1997.
Wengst, Klaus. *Humility: Solidarity of the Humiliated; The Transformation of an Attitude and Its Social Relevance in Graeco-Roman, Old Testament-Jewish and Early Christian Tradition*. Translated by John Bowden. Philadelphia: Fortress, 1988.
Wheatley, Phillis. *Complete Writings*. Edited by Vincent Carretta. New York, 2001.
Whitcomb, Dennis, Heather Battaly, Jason Baehr, and Daniel Howard-Snyder. "Intellectual Humility: Owning Our Limitations." *Philosophy and Phenomenological Research* 94 (2017): 509–39.
Wiggins, Daphne. *Righteous Content: Black Women's Perspectives of Church and Faith*. New York: NYU Press, 2004.
Williams, Delores. "Womanist Theology: Black Women's Voice." *Christianity and Crisis* 47 (March 2, 1987).
Yeager, Jonathan. "Samuel Kneeland of Boston: Colonial Bookseller, Printer, and Publisher of Religion." *Printing History* 11 (2012): 35–61.

2

Liberating Humility

A Variation on Luther's Theology of Humility

Miroslav Volf

Humility is a signature virtue of the Christian faith. Joy is its signature emotion. Today, in the West at least, we love joy but are ambivalent about humility, partly because we suspect that humility cravenly elevates acquiescence to our own inadequacy and inferiority to the status of a virtue.

A certain iconographic depiction of Mary, the mother of God, is for many the image of humility: hands folded submissively over the chest, head neatly covered and a bit askew, eyes rolled slightly heavenward, and a face mildly pained by, so it seems, the very fact of her own worldly existence—in a phrase, a posture of lowly malleability and insignificance. Joy, on the other hand, is Miriam, the sister of the great liberator Moses: rhythmic movements of tambourine over her head, heavy necklaces—the spoils of the Egyptians—bouncing over her breasts, hair and clothes flying as she leads the dance of celebration for the destruction of the oppressor's armies. Miriam and Mary, joy and humility, are two irreconcilable souls of the Christian faith, or so many are prone to think.

But we have gotten humility wrong. The goal of this essay is to nudge us toward getting it right, thus opening up a new way to joy, to Miriam's kind of joy, exuberant over improbable fortunes and, perhaps more importantly, to a quieter kind of joy, both deeper and more pervasive, a delight in the wonder of life's abiding and recurring goods, both our own and those of our neighbors.

1

It is common to think that humility is about self-abasement, about considering oneself, in the famously self-deprecating phrases from the *Rule of St. Benedict*, as a "worthless workman" and of "less account than anyone else"[1]—or, worse, humility is about wanting to *appear* to do so. But the shadow of hypocrisy is not the worst of it. The rot of untruthfulness, both factual and existential, eats at the core of such humility. Factual untruthfulness: only one person can have the distinction of being lower than anyone else, and none but God can know who that is. Existential untruthfulness: many of those who seem to consider themselves worthless and the lowest are secretly hoping that others, including God, will see and publicly acknowledge them as worthy and, in their own way, great—and bejeweled with humility on top of it. As the great critic of Christian humility, Friedrich Nietzsche, puts it in a parody of Luke 18:14: "He that humbleth himself wants to be exalted."[2]

Humility's current troubles—including its modern homelessness—are not mainly the consequence of unresolved inner tensions in the way people tend to understand and practice it. Any plausible account of humility, and not just humility as self-abasement, seems at odds with the very shape of the modern self. Many of us moderns imagine ourselves as owners of ourselves and of our action, each engaged in the great endeavor of self-achievement. We walk through life as pop-cultural caricatures of Nietzsche's "sovereign individual"—sovereign individuals lite—though with an important disquieting modification.[3] For the sovereign man, writes Nietzsche, the consciousness of "freedom, of this power over himself and fate has settled in him to his uttermost depths and has become instinct, the dominating instinct."[4] These three lines from *On the Genealogy of Morality* describe well how those who were actually the owners of themselves and their action, *who had in fact achieved themselves*, would be. Only the most hardcore of narcissists would dare to describe themselves this way, and yet, from the depths below ordinary self-awareness, this vision guides much of what we hope for and do.[5]

Now the troubling qualification of our sovereignty: instead of knowing ourselves as masters so powerful and secure as to dispense even with pride, most of us tend to experience ourselves as inadequate and demeaned, as fragile and insecure. In the business of self-achievement, the self we crave to be eludes us. What troubles most of us is not a gnawing guilt in the face of an unfulfillable moral law (as was the case only six or seven decades ago), even less is it a crushing fear of an overbearing and angry omnipotent lawgiver (as was the case a few centuries ago, and certainly at the time of the Reformation). Our problem is a self-undoing sense of inadequacy in the face of an impossible task. For the oppressed and marginalized, upon whom the dominant culture has projected its disrespect, the sense of inadequacy is often heightened by an internalized inferiority.

Let us take first the general sense of inadequacy. Self-achievement is, arguably, impossible in any setting. But in contemporary modern societies we do the hard labor of self-achievement in a cultural environment in which (almost) everything is possible but (almost) nothing is forbidden[6] and in a social environment of competitive struggle for recognition. The "achieved self" is a moving target, and we are unequal in power. Competitors threaten at every turn to prove that we do not measure up.

A sovereign individual, as Nietzsche imagined him (for Nietzsche surely imagined a him), has an instinctive pride about his "power over himself and over fate." He is also a being full of zest for life, his very act of living being identical with joy unclouded by either inadequacy or guilt.[7] In contrast, contemporary individuals, who can never measure up, must incessantly work to "achieve" their pride. And when our efforts are crowned with success, the pride turns out fleeting, no more secure than the passing grandeur of the self of which it boasts. And joy? We do experience it in the celebrations of the victories of self-achievement and pride. But the dance of jubilation is too short-lived, as are the things it exalts; the Egyptian army, undefeated, stands ready for battle at the edge of the dance floor.

As Alain Ehrenberg has argued in *The Weariness of the Self*, depression, that "tragedy of inadequacy," is a more likely fate of contemporary self-achievers than is joy. And then there is depression's sibling, dependency, the very opposite of proud sovereignty. We reach for legal and illegal drugs to help us manufacture the kind of self that can sustain the impossible struggle or, more modestly, to keep the floods of inadequacy-fed depression at bay. Modern individuals look less like Nietzsche's "sovereign men" than like his "*last* men"—people who have given up on all striving and, half-drugged, blink, satisfied that they have invented happiness[8]—but mostly like some ill-fated mixture of the two.

Marginal groups in modern societies, people whose self-respect has been battered on account of the color of their skin, history of oppression, or a particular cultural or religious heritage, are saddled with a particular kind of feeling of inadequacy. Deemed inferior and treated as worthless, they often experience themselves as deficient.[9] As they push against humiliation, they seek to shore up their self-respect and enter boldly into the struggle for recognition.[10] During the Civil Rights Movement in the United States, Martin Luther King Jr. gave voice to the need of the downtrodden African Americans to reclaim pride and joy: "And, with a spirit straining toward true self-esteem, the Negro must boldly throw off the manacles of self-abnegation and say to himself and to the world, 'I am somebody. I am a person. I am a man with dignity and honor. I have a rich and noble history, however painful and exploited that history has been.' . . . [W]e must stand up and say, 'I'm black, but I'm black and beautiful,' . . . [T]his self-affirmation is the black man's need, made compelling by the white man's crimes against them."[11]

The struggle of the downtrodden and demeaned for self-respect and equal treatment and against a socially constructed sense of inferiority continues. Significantly, it is fought in the environment of general struggle for self-achievement and pride shadowed by depression and dependency.

An adequate proposal about humility has to address a general pattern of failure in the struggle for self-achievement as well as be compatible with "striving toward true self-esteem" on the part of the marginalized.

The pervasive sense of personal inadequacy and social inferiority nudges us to look for alternatives to the modern self, the joyless owner of itself and its action and a troubled slave of its own impossible achievement. An alternative, which draws a good deal of its inspiration from the apostle Paul, takes us back to humility and opens up the possibility of its unity with joy. In the following, I will explore Martin Luther's version of this alternative.[12] Luther's Reformation discovery centers on the self freed from the compulsion to achieve itself, a self both humble and joyous at the same time. The alternative is compelling, I believe, but in societies of self-achieving, sovereign individuals its acceptance is likely to face resistance at least as serious as was the resistance to humility in the honor societies in which it was first introduced.[13] But perhaps the conviction is gaining in currency that the personal, social, and ecological costs of our false anthropological imaginary are steeper than its purported benefit.

Before I come to the great reformer and propose a variant of his theology of humility, however, I need to pay a brief visit to Max Scheler, an early twentieth-century philosopher. He can serve as a bridge from the sixteenth-century self, plagued by its inability to love God and neighbor adequately, to the contemporary self, plagued by its nagging inadequacy. Building on Scheler and Luther, I will propose an account of humility that seeks both to liberate persons from the impossible task of self-achievement and to support them in striving for dignity and self-respect.

2

It is "the most ridiculous" misjudgment of Christian humility, writes Scheler, to represent it "as a type of 'servility' raised to the position of virtue and dedicated to God, as the 'virtue' of the poor, the weak, the little ones."[14] For such a misreading to seem compelling, Scheler believes, a person must place "singular emphasis on the value of everything 'self-earned' and of 'becoming someone by one's own initiative.'"[15] In the early twentieth century when he wrote his essay on humility, this was the posture of the bourgeoisie, struggling to assert itself against the hereditary privilege of "masters and kings."

In contrast to humility as the self-abnegation of the weak, Scheler proposes humility as a voluntary service of "born masters."[16] The phrase is reminiscent of Nietzsche, but its inspiration is Christ as portrayed in one of the earliest pieces of Christian literature, an ancient hymn to Christ that the apostle Paul quotes to motivate the church in Philippi to practice humility. Though Christ was originally "in the form of God," he "did not regard equality with God as something to be exploited, but emptied himself, taking the form of a slave" (Phil 2:6).[17] Humility, Scheler contends, is the "inner replica" in the soul of "the *one* great gesture of Christian divinity freely to abandon its grandeur and majesty, to come to man in order to become every man's and all creation's free and blessed servant."[18] The humble human is the image of the self-humbling God.

The proud cling to their insecure "grandeur" and "majesty" and always stretch out for more, as they would be undone without ascending. But there is something paradoxical in their climbing into their own superior greatness. Always elevating themselves above others, the proud ultimately reduce all values to the "naked center of the I." Scheler explains: pride "causes the subject, proud of himself, to leap again and again above all things and values until, with complete 'supremacy,' he can look down on all except on the total emptiness and nothingness which he has now achieved."[19] Two consequences follow. First, doomed to futile and joyless ascent to the position of absolute greatness, the proud show themselves as ineliminably poverty-stricken; "*all* pride is 'beggar's pride,'" notes Scheler tersely.[20] Second, in referring all values to themselves, the proud are caught in the gesture of contempt and are incapable of joy. Each value apart from himself that the proud person "beholds appears to him as a theft and robbery from his own worth," so he must always act as "a devil and negator."[21]

"Humility is the virtue of the rich, as pride belongs to the poor."[22] But what comes first, humility or "wealth"? "Be humble, and you will immediately be rich and powerful," counsels Scheler. The advice is too simple, of course. Its point is to underscore that, no matter how great we are, without humility we will experience ourselves as lacking and therefore continue to thirst. But the main thrust of Scheler's argument goes in the opposite direction: not that only the humble are great, but that only those who are great—those who are "born masters"—can be humble. But how does one become a humble master? How does one acquire what he calls "humility of being" so that one can act humbly in voluntary service? The path to humility leads through self-surrender, not self-exertion.

For a humble person, Scheler writes, "there is ever present the picture of his own individual self, which he constantly perceives as traced anew, as well as borne before him by the movement of God's love aimed at him."[23] This kind of picture of the self involves a twofold movement of self-perceiving: as a person penetrates into the divine sketch of himself, he is "sinking down as far as his conscious experience of himself is concerned," and simultaneously "this beautiful picture actually draws him up to God and, in the substance of his being, he rises gently into heaven."[24] *Humility of being is the effacement of the self-standing self through its arrival to itself as always already constituted by God.* It may seem that an "effaced" self has lost everything, both herself and her world. The exact opposite is the case, argues Scheler: the only self who "can win *all*" is a self who, not owning herself, "assumes that *nothing* is deserved, and *everything* is gift and wonder," including her "own strength" and "the smallest worthiness."[25] The humble receive themselves and the world with gratitude and "joyfully discover" ever anew those things—a foot, a hand, or an eye, for instance—whose value we otherwise seem able to grasp "only when they are rare and others do not possess them."[26]

A tension runs through Scheler's account of humility. It shows up most clearly in the ambiguity of the "love of God" through which the humble self is constituted. On the one hand, humility is rooted in "the movement of God's love aimed at" the person. On the other hand, in its purest form, humility "is only the delicate silhouette which the movement of holy, God-oriented love casts over the soul."[27] The first love is God's creative love for the self, and the self receives it, or, rather, *is* in receiving it; the second love is the self's love for God, and the self practices it. Humility, then, ends up being both a gift and an achievement.[28]

Perhaps the gift and the achievement can be united. A candidate for doing the job of unifying could be "absolute trust in being and in the root from which all things sprout,"[29] which, according to Scheler, lies at the heart of humility. For Martin Luther, too, trust was central to the generation of humility. As a monk, whose entire life was to be one of humility, he knew, however, that one can glory not just in the "worthiness" of one's achievement but in the "unworthiness" of one's nonachievement (LW 21:314).[30] To counter the attempts to make something out of the nothingness of one's utter self-renunciation, he came to believe that one should see humility-constituting trust as itself a gift of the very God in whom it is placed. In his mind, that insight followed from the more fundamental conviction that those doing the trusting—as well as those who refuse to trust—owe the existence of their entire selves and of their world to the God in whom they do or do not trust.

3

In his last work, *A Pluralistic Universe* (1908), William James identified Martin Luther as the first to break "with any effectiveness through the crust" of the self-sufficiency of pagan, naturalistic, and legalistic morality.[31] Scheler quoted the relevant passage from James at length and composed his essay on humility as a philosophical variation on Luther's theology of humility, especially Luther's Philippians 2–inspired account of the relation between master and slave in *The Freedom of a Christian* (November 1520). Luther himself discussed humility most extensively in his commentary on the Magnificat. He preached multiple sermons on it before committing it to writing shortly after composing the *Freedom* tractate (March 1521). In that text, on which I rely mainly here, the virgin mother of Jesus appears as the embodiment of the free, humble, and joyous self.[32] Singing joyously her song, Luther's Mary looks nothing like a life-weary Madonna. But she is not a dancing Miriam either, and that is where Luther's theology of humility will need a touchup or two.

Following Scheler's terminology, it may be useful to distinguish in Luther between *humility of being* and *humility in acting*, though the two are intimately related.

Seen from Luther's vantage point, all significant decisions for one's account of humility concern humility of being. It has two moments. The first is the realization that what we ordinarily understand as the self is "nothing"—or, rather, that it exists in powerful and perniciously active ways, but only in sinful personal and collective imagination. We project ourselves as something self-standing—as owners of ourselves and our actions, for instance—forgetting that God holds us, with all our powers and possessions, in existence.[33] We claim these powers and possessions as our own, and, in life's struggle for power and honor, we boast of them in thought, deed, and demeanor before neighbors and God.

To realize that we are nothing on our own, we often need the jolt of personal and social humbling—a pinch of sickness, poverty, or lowliness, a bout of despondency, or, at times, an avalanche of evil thundering down on us and taking us on a deadly ride (LW 21:346–47). But suffering and lowliness, though often necessary to make a person humble, are not indispensable aspects of humility proper, neither of the humility of being nor of the humility in acting.[34] When Luther insists that the self must "consider himself to be nothing" (LW 10:351), the self's nothingness is *not social*. It does not mean: I am nobody compared to others (not "I am of less account than anyone else," in the *Rule of St. Benedict*). This nothingness is also *not existential*. It does not mean: I am nothing compared to what I should or could be (not: "I am a bad and worthless workman," in the *Rule of St. Benedict*). The nothingness of the self is ontological: along with all other human beings and the rest of creation, *my own self is not the kind of thing that could be something on its own.*

The first moment of humility of being is a truthful recognition of the nothingness of the false self—what Luther calls in *The Freedom of a Christian* "the old man" (LW 31:334)—whether it is parading self-importantly in false glory or hiding self-dejectedly in false shame. Call the first moment "humiliation," though that would be to name it from the perspective of the *false* self, for it is that imagined usurper-self that is reduced to nothing, not the true self. The second moment of the humility of being—again from the perspective of the false self—is *exaltation*. Exaltation appears as exaltation from the perspective of the false self because, from the perspective of the true self, elevation is the placement of the self into the original and proper position of which the falsehood had robbed it. To call exaltation the second moment of the humility of being is a bit of a misnomer, though. It suggests that one *first* comes to see oneself as nothing and is *then* elevated into being something by participating in Christ's lordship. That is how Luther thought of it early on: self-abnegation as a condition of justification. But once he saw faith itself as a gift, the insight into the nothingness of the self shifted from being the condition to being the consequence of elevation.[35]

The second paragraph of Luther's commentary on the Magnificat, which identifies the pillar both of his account of humility and of his theology as a whole, begins as follows: "Just as God in the beginning of creation made the world out of nothing, whence He is called the Creator and the Almighty, so His manner of working continues unchanged. Even now and to the end of the world, all His works are such that out of that which is nothing, worthless, despised, wretched, and dead, He makes that which is something, precious, honorable, blessed, and living" (LW 21:299).[36] Exaltation as the second moment in the humility of being is the awareness of oneself as being something by virtue of God's generous creativity, and therefore also a sense of oneself as precious, honorable, and blessed.

In *The Freedom of a Christian*, Luther uses the term "lord" or "master" to describe such a self. That is because the exaltation of the self that needed to be humiliated on account of its enacted false image of itself takes place through the indwelling of the Lord Jesus Christ in the self. He is echoing the hymn to Christ that the apostle Paul quotes in Philippians 2: Christ is the Lord who did not graspingly cling to his divinity as if it were something that could be lost and had always to be regained; in union with Christ, every self is the lord and "Christ," always already achieved as the self and never in fear of losing itself as long as Christ indwells it. This is the exaltation of the self, which is identical with the self's return to itself—the second and central moment of the humility of being.[37]

This, then, is the configuration of proper relation between God and the self that constitutes humility of being. First, the God of Jesus Christ is a generous creator rather than a glory-hungry and law-imposing overlord; a humble and giving deity on account of God's utter exaltation rather than a proud and grasping deity always in need "to take what is ours" and "to have us as His benefactors" (LW 11:410).[38] Second, God's love for the self is not an achievement-conditioned attachment but an unconditional and unalterable commitment as creator and savior to make the self into something precious and honorable. Third, the creature's very self is constituted by divine presence and activity—"a cheerful guest chamber and willing hostess to a great Guest," as Luther says of Mary (LW 21:308)—not as a self-standing individual, owner of itself and its action. Fourth, such a God-created and God-indwelled self is not a passive object of God's action, as if the self were already there when God came onto the scene to pick it up and use it as some lifeless tool; the entirety of the self, including the self's proper action, owes its reality to God. Finally, the self who *is* and *has* and *does* all things on account of God's creative generosity—the self who is the lord over all things—is truthful only if it "ascribes everything to God alone" from whom it received them (LW 21:308).

According to Philippians 2, Christ is the Lord who, just because he is free both from the eager striving to become the Lord and from fearful clinging to being the Lord, can, in obedience to the law of love, reach down to those in need and humble himself to the point of self-sacrificial love. The gesture of giving rather than of grasping is characteristic of God. Luther's God is not a proud divinity, vacuuming up all glory into the divine Majesty. God has superior glory, of course, and possesses it inalienably; it is intertwined with God's unconditional love. To honor God is not to extol God as the greatest of all proud potentates but to recognize God as the omnipotent, indiscriminate lover. *Humility of being* is the fruit of trust in the humble God whose nature is to create something out of nothing and who "looks into the depths and helps only the poor" (LW 21:300), a mode of relating to God as the giver of all that is good and to oneself as "achieved" and exalted in God. *Humility in acting*—which is nothing but the other-oriented side of the humility of being—is participation in the movement of the humble God toward the lowly, in passing God's gifts to others who need them. In union with Christ, a Christian is "Christ" to others: a lord who considers proud grasping for lordship as the loss of lordship and humble service to others in love as its enactment.

Defining humility in acting, Luther writes: "Humility we call . . . a love and leaning to lowly and despised things," of having one's "heart set on things of low degree" (LW 21:314, 315). The truly humble will "cultivate" rather than merely "affect" humble "conduct, humble words, places, faces, and clothing, and shun as far as possible great and lofty things" (LW 21:315). They will "gladly associate" with "things of low degree" (LW 21:315). The goal is not self-diminishment, as if lowliness were inherently valuable. The goal is service to those who live in "the depths" and therefore identification with them. The proud strive after what is great for themselves and therefore flee the depths. God's humble servants, like the humble God, go near to those in the depths, assume their clothing and language—dispense with outward marks of their own higher standing—so that, without the insult of condescension, they can help people in "poverty, disgrace, squalor, misery, and anguish" (LW 21:300). Humility in acting is fearlessness in self-identification and association with the lowly for the purpose of lifting them up, and that not as a false self-sacrifice for which one expects a reward of glory, but as the expression of one's being.

4

Luther himself does not state explicitly that the main purpose of a person's self-identification and association with the lowly is to lift them up. He is more interested in the positive effects social lowliness has in generating and sustaining human recognition of their "nothingness." But he does insist that "lifting up" is the purpose of God's humility. God "looks" not up but down so as to "make something out of" the lowly; correspondingly, Christ comes down to serve the lowly to the point of self-sacrifice on the cross that he may raise us up. Luther is also clear that Christians, too, should "look" not on what is above them but on what is "beneath them" (LW 21:320) and that, indwelled by Christ, they are to be "Christs" to their neighbors (see

LW 31:367–68). The inference seems legitimate that the purpose of Christian self-identification and association with the lowly is, as Luther states of God, "helping them or . . . making something out of them" (LW 21:300). And yet he does not explicitly draw the inference. That is likely because, for soteriological reasons, he is invested in people staying lowly and thinking of themselves as lowly: humility of station feeds humility of being, a sense of nothingness of the self as a self-standing entity and its exaltation in God. He draws up a portrait of Mary to motivate his investment in humility of station. But this warps his broader account of humility.

As Luther sees it, the Virgin Mary is not just humble for having come "of poor, despised, and lowly parents" (LW 21:301) and therefore for being herself one of "the despised"; she is humble in that "she despises herself" (LW 21:321). Moreover, Luther believed that, because she was humble, she compared herself unfavorably with others: she "regarded herself *alone* as unworthy of such honor [being the bearer of God] and all others as worthy of it" (LW 21:308, emphasis added). We seem to have returned to the key elements of the problematic account of humility in the *Rule of St. Benedict*: Mary sees herself as worthless in herself and of less account than anyone else.

Do the humble need to despise themselves, to consider themselves worthless? Not if we are talking about the true self, the new self. For the *new self* to consider itself worthless is in tension with Luther's humility of being. "Created out of nothing" (LW 21:327), Mary is nothing in herself but exalted in God; that is how Luther encourages Christians to relate to Mary: not "to regard her alone and by herself" but in God so that in coming to her they are able to come "through her to God" (322–23). As it is with Mary, so it is, though to a lesser degree, with everybody else, or at least with every Christian: all Christians know themselves as nothing in themselves and as lords-freely-become-servants in Christ. But that is not compatible with the demand that the humble despise themselves. Humility should, then, include recognition that a self indwelled by Christ—in a sense, every self created by God—"is precious, honorable, and blessed" (LW 21:299) and that when it appears to the world and to itself as anything else but precious, honorable, and blessed it is so because of the self's and the world's refusal to recognize and live out the most basic truth of the self's character.

The "satisfaction with self . . . is the death of humility" (LW 21:317), Luther believes. But satisfaction with the self can be wrong, and despising of the self can be right, only in regard to the false self, the old self; indeed, the argument Luther uses to support his claim that Mary despises herself is her claim about herself *prior* to becoming the Mother of God: "She says that her low estate was regarded by God" (LW 21:321). It is right to despise and wrong to be satisfied with the *false self* that claims to be something great but is in fact nothing in its own right and everything in dependence on God. But what is the proper affective relation to the *true self*, the new self, that Mary as the Mother of God also is (and that, according to Luther, she *fully* is, given that at that point in his career he considers her sinless)? The proper affective relation to the new self as Luther saw it constituted should be gratitude and joy. But Luther resists saying so. That is perhaps because he cannot disassociate satisfaction with the self from glorying in the self and therefore from pride. But why could one not consider oneself to be nothing while at the same time being pride-lessly satisfied with oneself as God's creature indwelled by Christ? Might not despising oneself as the new self come close to inverted pride, a secret longing to be something in one's own right? Would it not bespeak of lack of faith, of clinging to the reality of one's false self in the act of despising oneself?

Luther's affirmation of humility as self-abnegation pushes against attempts to improve one's station. He believes that the positive affective relation to oneself as the bearer of particular gifts is contentment with one's lowly station (LW 21:315). The new self is content with whatever capacities it has and with whatever social position it occupies. For one, capacities and social position are God's gifts and as such good. Moreover, the self cannot serve others well while, out of discontentment, it works on "achieving" itself. So far so good. But if one effect of humility is a willingness to serve the despised and afflicted so as to, among other things, improve their lot, why would wishing and working for improvement of one's own lot be wrong? For no principled reason, it would seem, except one's own limited time and resources. Moreover, to serve others well, would one not need to cultivate many of one's capacities? If so, should we not, in contrast to Luther, insist that to the humble, contentment with their lowly station and diminished capacities is not essential but instrumental? It helps them in the task of lifting others into equality of honor and position.

Though all human beings are equal as creatures indwelled by Christ, all human beings differ in capacities, powers, possessions, and influence. Does humility require each to consider herself or himself as *less worthy than all others*, as Luther claims Mary did? If she did, she was clearly untruthful. In all cases, except one, the claim that one is of less account than everyone else could not possibly be true, and in no case would it be true in all regards. But Luther's position here does not only repeat the inadequacy of the classical account of humility; it is in tension with Luther's own account of humility of being, which undercuts competitive comparisons among people. The humble, Luther insists, glory neither in their worthiness nor in their unworthiness (see LW 21:314). And, according to his famous principle of "happy exchange," *everything* that is Christ's belongs to each person united with Christ (LW 31:349, 351–52). *All* are equally nothing in themselves; *all* are equally exalted in Christ. To consider all others worthier than oneself is to remain in the sphere of competitive comparisons and to engage in the futile attempt to conquer pride by inverting it. Luther is most consistent when he counsels about what to do when we are praised and honored: "We ought neither to reject this praise and honor as though they were wrong, nor despise them as though they were nothing, but refuse to accept them as too precious or noble, and ascribe them to Him in heaven, to whom they belong" (LW 21:330).

A genuinely humble person is free from compulsion to win in the game of competitive comparisons. She can make truthful assessments about the relative strengths and weaknesses of herself in relation to others and of others in all their relations. How else would she properly honor people, which we must do, at least "while we live on earth" (LW 21:330)? The apostle Paul, the great authority whose theology and account of humility Luther claims to channel, stressed the importance of truthful judgments both about our own qualities and those of others. He urged Christians in Rome "not to think of yourself more highly than you ought to think, but to think with sober judgment, each according to the measure of faith that God has assigned" (Rom 12:3). The characteristic feature of the proud is to think of themselves more highly than they ought; for instance, they "claim to be wiser than they are" (Rom 12:16). The characteristic feature of the humble, however, is *not* to think of themselves *as lower* than they ought to think; they *do not* claim, for instance, that they are *less wise* than they in fact are. Truthfulness is essential to humility. Like the God on account of whose humility they are humble and whose humility they mirror, the humble are humble not because they think of themselves as lowly but because they are happy to "associate with the lowly" (Rom 12:16) and to "weep with those who weep" (Rom 12:15).

Perhaps the most striking trait of the humble is that they "rejoice with those who rejoice" (Rom 12:15). Unlike the proud, who experience the good things over which others rejoice as their own diminishment, the humble experience these good things as their own good simply because they are good. The humble are in fact able to rejoice indiscriminately over any good they encounter, including their own capacities and achievements, because they see each good fundamentally as an undeserved divine gift.

"My soul magnifies the Lord, and my spirit rejoices in God my Savior," begins Mary's song. "These words," explains Luther, "express the strong ardor and exuberant joy with which all her mind and life are inwardly exalted in the Spirit" (LW 21:302). Mary's song is joyous because her entire life, the life of a lowly and humble servant, is joy.

Luther is careful to specify what kind of joy Mary's is: not joy over who she is or over any of the goods she has received from God. A person rejoices properly when she finds joy "not in the good things of God that she felt, but *only* in God" (LW 21:311, emphasis added). Alone the "bare goodness of God" (LW 21:312) is the proper object of joy, without any reference to the advantage that goodness is to the self (LW 21:309). Luther did grant that a Christian ought to rejoice over the goods God gives to *others*. That is consistent with his stress that Christians live not in themselves and for themselves; by faith they are "caught up beyond" themselves into God, and by love they "descend beneath" themselves into their neighbors in need (LW 31:371). But joy in ordinary things of one's own appears to him as a mode of self-centeredness. Correspondingly, the humble "despise" themselves.

Luther liked the adverb "alone"—God alone, grace alone, faith alone, Scripture alone. But perhaps his proclivity to exclusive polarities led him to misconstrue an aspect of joy and of humility. What if we rejoiced in God's bare goodness *and* rejoiced in good things that we have and that we are—which is to say rejoiced in one and the same act in God as the giver of all good things and in good things as God's gifts (rather than either in God apart from things or in things apart from God, this last stance being a form of falsehood as nothing good ever exists in itself without being God's gift)? To be truthful about our lives and counter pride, we do not need to rob ourselves of joy over the good things we are, have, and can do. If we were indifferent toward these goods and focused only on God, would we not prove ourselves unable or unwilling to recognize these goods as goods given out of love for us? Would we not fail to honor the basic fact that God's works are such "that out of that which is nothing, worthless, despised, wretched, and dead, He makes that which is something, precious, honorable, blessed, and living" (LW 21:299). What else would receiving oneself in faith result in at the emotional level if not in joy over the gift of one's true self? How can we then not rejoice in God's joy over us and in others' rejoicing in us? How could we then not participate in what Jennifer Herdt has called "reverberations of joy"[39]—my rejoicing over your rejoicing in my joy, your rejoicing in my rejoicing over your joy, and our both rejoicing in this shared joy? This seems to me to describe well the world of joy into which the Master bids his faithful servants to enter (Matt 25:21, 23).

Humility is the virtue that opens up space for just such non-self-inflating and non-self-serving joy.

5

As Scheler and Luther conceive of it, the joy to which humility opens the door is joy over having always already been "achieved" by love, joy over the goodness, the beauty, and the wonder of the world and of the self, all their deficiencies notwithstanding! Humility here leads to joy over what is.

But what about Miriam's kind of joy, joy not simply over what we and the world are constituted to be, but joy over tasks accomplished, misfortunes averted, evils conquered? What about joy over the fall of the mighty—hallelujahs over the destruction of the Egyptian army (Exod 15) or over the ruin of Babylon with its blood-drenched hands (Rev 17)? Can the humble rejoice with Miriam? The answer is yes, and the reason is simple: properly understood, a great and good task accomplished is a gift received, and while the glory belongs above all to the Giver, the joy belongs both to us and to the Giver. That is what Miriam's and Mary's songs celebrate.

But is humility of the kind Luther and Scheler advocated—humility of the "lords" who do not strive to achieve themselves by ascending—compatible with the *struggle* that arises in the longing for the joy of the world to become God's home among mortals? Might it even motivate such struggle?

Scheler treats pride as a personal tragedy: the proud see themselves as ascending but are in fact falling into nothingness; the humble are the exalted masters. His aim, however, is to undermine the cultural prevalence of a bourgeois morality of self-creation along with its "pride before kings' thrones."[40] But underneath this personal and cultural concern lies an anti-egalitarian political vision. He has completely detached pride and humility from actual differentials of power, wealth, and social honor. A humble ruler, for instance, will manifest "a deeply secret readiness to serve him whom" he rules.[41] But he will sit comfortably on the throne as an unself-conscious king, born a master; it will not occur to him to share power with those he rules or to seek legitimacy from and accept oversight by them. Humility here in no way unsettles his power and privilege.

In the biblical traditions, by contrast, whatever else pride may be, it is a decidedly political and economic malady. The proud must be taken down from their thrones, as the Virgin pregnant with God's Son sings, especially those among the proud whose realms and riches are vast. In their ultimately futile climbing, the proud do not just undermine themselves (as Scheler rightly insists); they also demean, oppress, and at times destroy those around them. Struggling to ascend, the proud do not just look down with contempt on what is beneath them; they pull down everything above them and push under everything around them. It might seem that, to solve the problem, it would suffice for the powerful to give up pride and assume the posture of humility. So why do biblical traditions assail their power and not just their pride?

Luther, who saw himself above all as an interpreter of Scripture, treats pride and humility primarily as modes of being human before God. Yet he is keenly aware that economic wealth, political might, and cultural influence—and, at least in his own day, especially religious authority (see LW 21:332–43)—feed the pride of those who possess them as well as enable the proud who are powerful to swagger their way through the world while covering the tracks of their ruinous iniquity. He wrote the commentary on the Magnificat for Prince John Frederick of Saxony. Addressing him directly in the epilogue, Luther writes: "For great possessions, glory, and favor, as well as the flatterers no lord may be without, surround and lay siege to the heart of a prince, moving it to pride" (LW 21:357).[42] As pride is insatiable, it demands even more possessions, greater glory, bigger favor, which, in turn, inflate pride even more. The feedback loop between pride and power suggests that the actual experience of lowliness—in Luther's phrase, lack "of all temporal goods" (LW 21:349)—is almost indispensable if a person is to become and remain humble (see LW 21:347–48).[43]

Luther knows, of course, that you do not have to be mighty to be proud and, inversely, that you do not need to be weak to be humble.[44] He also knows that the mighty are not the only ones who oppress and destroy; the weak and the impoverished who are proud oppress and destroy, too. The difference is that the pride of the lowly is more fragile and their injustice less consequential. That is why Mary sings of God, who, in Christ, "has brought down the powerful from their thrones, and lifted up the lowly," and who "has filled the hungry with good things, and sent the rich away empty" (Luke 1:52–53, NRSV).

But can the humble take part in bringing down the powerful? Luther does not entertain the thought; at least he does not mention it to the prince. But the answer must be positive: if Christ, the Lord-become-servant, can take down the mighty—for instance, overturn the tables of money changers—so can his followers whose humility is an echo of his. Moreover, once we acknowledge that might generates, confirms, and increases pride—at least "while we live on earth" (LW 21:330)—the interest in the good of humility adds motivation to the struggle against unchecked power. The virtue of humility will also preclude the lowly from striving merely to *replace* the dethroned mighty. When God "lifts the lowly," Luther writes, God does not put the lowly "in the seat of those He has cast out" (LW 21:345). Envy and pride drive the struggle for reversal of positions of privilege. But the humble will embrace the struggle for *equality* in political, economic, and cultural power. And, like Mary in the Gospel of Luke and Miriam in Exodus, they will rejoice.

6

Mary is Miriam and Miriam is Mary. Their humility and their joy are one humility and one joy, or rather, they are the two sides of one and the same humility and joy. Their kind of joy is carried on the wings of humility, on the sense that all the self's goods and its very existence—all the world's goods and the world's very existence—that everything good, both sought after and unbidden, deserved and undeserved, done by myself or by somebody else, is a gift, and therefore an occasion for joy.

• • •

Response to Miroslav Volf

Lisa Sowle Cahill

From the standpoint of an ethicist, there is a lot to like about this essay. It also reminds me why I am inspired by Luther, and it takes me back to some beloved texts: We are saved "by the Word of God, that is, by the promise of his grace, and by faith, that the glory may remain God's, who saved us not by works of righteousness which we have done, but by virtue of his mercy by the word of his grace when we believed." "Here faith is truly active through love, that is, it finds expression in works of the freest service, cheerfully and lovingly done, with which a man willingly serves another, without hope of reward, and for himself he is satisfied with the fullness and wealth of his faith."[1]

Yet despite ample appreciation, I will offer an alternative perspective on a few points. First is the invocation of Philippians as a model for humanity. Second are two aspects of Volf's interpretation of Luther's humility-related theology—namely, Luther's view of Mary's humility and Luther's reluctance to applaud the "new self" bestowed in Christ. Third and finally, I will raise a question about the intended audience or scope of this theology of humility. Is it limited to Christians, and if so, how useful is that for Christian social ethics today? I propose that interreligious efforts to heal inequality and violence can embody humble and joyful service to the vulnerable, as well as reconciliation of sinners, by grace.

Let me start with appreciation. Volf elucidates the meaning of humility as the self's awareness that its being is constituted by God's generous creativity. What Volf calls "the *true* self, the new self" appreciates that it "is precious, honorable, blessed" because it is indwelt by Christ (54, 56; citing LW 21:299). "*Humility of being is the effacement of the self-standing self through its arrival to itself as always already constituted by God*" (48). To have humility is thus to recognize ourselves in our true relation to God in Christ. But humility calls for gratitude and celebration, not self-abasement or fear. False shame and false glory are the antitheses of true humility. True humility arises at the intersection of God's love for us and our love for God. It consists in "trust as itself a gift of the very God in whom it is placed" (49). Humility is not only compatible with the joy of the Christian life; it is a necessary premise and concomitant, a counterpart of faith as acceptance of the gifts we are promised in Christ.

Humility of being bears fruit in humility of acting, as in Luther's "works of the freest service, cheerfully and lovingly done." Volf reappropriates Luther's insight that humility is "a love and leaning to lowly and despised things" (52; citing LW 21:314). In Volf's words, "*Humility in acting*—which is nothing but the other-oriented side of the humility of being—is participation in the movement of the humble God toward the lowly, in passing God's gifts to others who need them" (52). An especially important nuance contributed by Volf is that actively humble association with the lowly is "for the purpose of lifting them up"; empowerment of "the lowly" is the very "expression of one's being" as a Christian (52). As feminist ethics, liberation ethics, postcolonial ethics, and other Christian politics "from below" attest, true charity as practical love of neighbor goes beyond generous service, in its aspiration that the "poor" become not only the recipients of largesse but the authors of their destinies. Volf interprets the virtue of humility in such a way as to move from Luther's uplifting portrait of the Christian vocation as "faith active in love" to a very contemporary Christian social ethics in which personal and structural transformation guarantee broader and deeper social change than Luther himself envisioned.

As Gustavo Gutiérrez sees this process, Christian faith is not a matter of paternalism or reformism. Authentic faith brings awareness of one's own alienation and need for conversion.[2] This is the humility that becomes joyful when it recognizes the possibilities we are given in Christ. In the light of faith, charity, and hope, "one can identify radically and militantly with those—the people and the social class—who bear the brunt of oppression."[3] Volf adeptly brings Luther up to date, with an ethical "spin" that traces to Luther's sixteenth-century vision, yet travels creatively far beyond it into the twenty-first.

Now, some questions and possible modifications. First, I am ambivalent about the usefulness of Philippians as a model for human imitation or an analogue to Christian humility. On the one hand, it assumes a parallel to Christ's "greatness" that either undermines or is undermined by an interpretation of Philippians 2 as a christological hymn (bracketing the question whether Paul himself saw Jesus as "divine" in the sense proclaimed at Chalcedon). On the other hand, Volf compellingly shows how this text calls Christians to identify unreservedly with those who are unnoticed, brushed aside, exploited, or condemned.

Speaking of Christ, Philippians' point of departure is Christ's status as one who was "in the form of God" and even "shared equality with God" (2:6). Philippians assumes Godlike greatness that is willingly given up. Of course, this is precisely the opposite of what Volf himself is arguing in his delineation of humility as clear-eyed recognition of humanity's total dependence on God, and need for exaltation by God, in order to have and know the divinely bestowed worth that enables "humility in action." Volf takes from Luther's commentary on the Magnificat that it is God who makes the self "into something precious and honorable" (51; citing LW 21:308). Yet in discussing Philippians, Volf seems to say that human humility involves giving up "greatness" to side with those who are "beneath them" (52; citing LW 21:320). If we have authentic faith (according to both Luther and Volf), we will recognize that we do not have any such greatness in the first place.[4]

Despite this dissimilarity between Christ and Christians, however, Volf shows the importance of emulation. Jesus Christ becomes one of the lowly in an "anonymous" and risky way. This is evident in Jesus' association with outcasts and sinners; in his practice of "open table fellowship"; and in his sharing the lot of those condemned to death as a danger to the religious and political establishments. It is confirmed theologically and doctrinally in the formulae of Chalcedon and Nicaea, which assert that Christ is both of "one substance" with God and yet fully human, including subjection to suffering and death. Jesus neither publicizes nor protects his own status. He is willing to be taken for "one of them" even when this is mortally dangerous. Recognizing Christ in "the least of these" is what brings his followers into the same position and makes them subject to the same consequences as the crucified Christ (Matt 25). Volf makes the valid point that to be humble is to emulate Jesus in sharing the fate of the despised and subjugated without reserving the option to "back out" or to "exploit" one's own status when the situation turns desperate. One caveat here is that the privileged are also called to empower the poor, which requires using one's more abundant resources to that end. The ultimate point, though, still applies: empowering alignment with the poor is always risky, as we see in Christian martyrs to justice, such as Martin Luther King, Oscar Romero, and Dorothy Stang.

At this point, let us return to Luther. Luther is rarely consistent, which is one of the things that makes him interesting, as well as an ever-rich source of new ideas. In his reading of Luther's commentary on the Magnificat (49ff.), Volf applauds Luther's suggestion that humility requires recognition of the "nothingness" of the "false self." Mary is an exemplar of the joyful humility of one who rests her confidence in God. But Volf takes issue with Luther's further idea that even the person of grateful faith must continue to regard herself as wretched and despised, rather than as empowered by God's love to take Christlike action. Volf is quite right that such a provision would take away much of the basis for a transformative Christian ethics and politics; he is also right to find it in Luther and to reject it. A ray of hope for an energetic Lutheran social ethic, however, emerges from Luther's sometimes useful tendency to go off in different directions. As Volf does note (54–55), Luther promisingly slips in of Mary that, when endowed with God's "abundant grace," "she does not glory in her worthiness nor yet in her unworthiness, but solely in the divine regard."[5] As exemplified by Mary, true humility "is never aware that it is humble," for "all things are done gladly."[6] I believe the contemporary interpreter of Luther is justified in a selective appropriation of Luther's characterizations of this virtue that best suits a Luther-derived theology of humility as an appreciation of our own true standing in relation to God.

Elaborating on Luther's interpretation of the Magnificat's celebration of the mighty being cast down from their thrones, Volf asks a further question: Can the lowly participate in, even instigate, such a casting down, and can they even rejoice in it? Volf answers (and I again agree) that while the lowly should not usurp the roles of the powerful and claim them for themselves, they must surely "embrace the struggle for *equality* in political, economic, and cultural power" (58–59; presumably not strict equality but an equitable sharing of power and allocation of roles). I would only add here (as an ethicist) that what the lowly and their allies may properly rejoice in is not the disgrace and suffering of the powerful as such but the greater *justice* occasioned by the disruption and realignment of roles.

A most interesting question to me is, why does Martin Luther not affirm the "new self" that Volf believes Luther to show has been created by grace? "The proper affective relation to the new self as Luther saw it constituted should be gratitude and joy. But Luther resists saying so" (54). Perhaps the reason is that, as an Augustinian political theologian, Luther was highly skeptical that justification by grace through faith could bring any significant transformation of life, especially political life.

A deeper and related reason is that Luther would not have characterized the action of grace as creating an inherent change in the agent or self, for that would be too close to the repudiated doctrine of the "schoolmen" that the theological virtue of charity creates a new nature in sinful humanity, allowing humans to "merit" salvation by works.[7] Luther does speak of the justified sinner's relation to God as a type of participation, but the emphasis for Luther is that participation in Christ or God is always dependent on union with Christ in the Holy Spirit, or the indwelling of Christ in the believer (as Volf recognizes on p. 51). This is the basic idea conveyed by the marriage metaphor of *On Christian Liberty*.[8] In the new Finnish school of Lutheran interpretation,[9] for example, the works of the believer are transformed, but not on the basis of any changed nature of the self or "new self." Rather, Christ is present to the believer in faith, so that he or she participates in Christ's righteousness and works of love. Christ acts through the person of faith, so that Christ's works become his or her works. This is always by virtue of the believer's ongoing relation to Christ in the Holy Spirit, not by virtue of any change in his or her nature. But the outcome is the same in terms of the reliability and consistency of transformed action, which is the point of the new school of thought. In a salutary outcome for ethics, it turns out that Luther does have a strong theology of what might be termed regeneration or sanctification. Yet all is ever reliant on Christ.

The main concern of Volf's chapter is to show how a rightly construed Lutheran theology of humility leads to love and service of the neighbor and takes the form of empowering the neighbor via structural as well as personal change. This mission has been accomplished. I will thus conclude with some questions for further consideration, questions on which I hope Miroslav Volf can shed light. Structural change for justice in today's world necessarily requires interreligious commitment and cooperation, because exclusions, violence, memories of atrocities, and ongoing unjust structures have transcultural and transnational roots, manifestations, and effects.[10] How can an *interreligious* process of healing be explained and supported by Christian faith, theology, and ecclesial presence? Does Luther bring anything to the table? How has his theology been reinterpreted for a global Christian social ethics, or how might it be so in the future?

* * *

Reply to Lisa Sowle Cahill

Miroslav Volf

Lisa Cahill is a wonderful responder, erudite and incisive, generous and constructive. As she rightly sees, the chapter is an attempt not only to illuminate how humility, properly understood, is important for joy but also to show how humility can be not merely a private virtue but a social one, in fact, one that supports commitment to social relations marked by radical equality. This essay is a "Martin Luther-meets-Gustavo Gutiérrez" kind of a project, in which, without necessarily turning into a liberation theologian, Martin says to Gustavo, "Yes, I could have done both humility and social ethics better!" In the encounter between the two as the chapter tacitly imagines it, Martin also asks Gustavo, "But could you agree with the way I understand the self and its relation to Christ?" Cahill correctly writes, "The main concern of Volf's chapter is to show how a rightly construed Lutheran theology of humility leads to love and service of the neighbor and takes the form of empowering the neighbor via structural as well as personal change."

If I understand her rightly, Cahill has three main pushbacks against claims I make in the chapter and one question. The pushbacks concern (1) the appropriateness of Philippians 2 as the basis of a theology of humility, (2) the suggestion that it is possible to reinterpret Luther such that the redeemed self rejoices over itself, and (3) the description of our contemporaries' self-conception as "sovereign individuals, owners of themselves and their action, engaged in the great endeavor of self-achievement." These are the pushbacks. The question concerns the audience for this theology of humility, specifically the appropriateness of this strongly Christianly inflected humility, given the need for joint social engagement with adherents of other faiths.

In the following, I take up these four issues, starting with the last.

I take it that Christian theology is primarily about the true life and that it is therefore, like the Christian faith itself, addressed to every human being. At the same time, I believe that I am the primary addressee of the theological texts that I write. They address me not just as a Yale professor living currently in Guilford, Connecticut, but also as a boy growing up in an apartment at the far end of a large courtyard, with a kitchen, two rooms, and an outdoor latrine; a student of theology and philosophy sharing a 2.5 × 2.5 m room with a friend; and a teacher of theology in Osijek, Croatia. My primary audience, partly experienced and partly imagined, is me throughout my entire life. The true life that has a claim on everyone has (for me) first of all a claim on me.[1] Hopefully, such personal investment gives existential urgency to texts that have all human beings as potential audience members in view. But the consequence is that all my texts, including this one on humility, are always inflected by my experiences and concerns. They may therefore not be appropriate to all situations. At the same time, I have found that the more concrete, even situation-specific, writing about the human condition is, the wider reach it tends to have.

In asking about the scope of my Luther-inspired account of humility, Cahill has a specific audience in mind: adherents of other religions. As I see it, I am issuing an invitation to them to reflect about their own lives in the light of a Christian vision of humility. It may well turn out that some adherents of other religions reject this account of humility, say, because they find the anthropology underpinning it implausible. But this rejection need not hinder the collaborative interreligious social engagement required in a globalized world. For such engagement—say, for combating world hunger, pushing against ecological devastation, rescuing child soldiers from captivity—it is not necessary for all parties involved to agree about the nature of true humanity. Agreement on the proximate goals of their joint action and the means of achieving them suffices. If this is correct, the kind of humility I advocate here can in fact be helpful in an interreligious setting.

As a humble Christian, I will not need to achieve myself over against others in the process of cooperation or to prove that I and my faith are superior to them and their faith. In fact, I will not need to thematize myself and my convictions at all, but I will be able simply to act out of my convictions in collaboration with others on shared goals. As to my responsibility as a Christian to bear witness to Christ with more than just my deeds, my words would point not to something that I "possess" but my non-Christian collaborators do not, but to Someone who has constituted me and possesses me. If it were otherwise, Christian humility would morph into unchristian pride and the witness itself would become self-contradictory, pointing away from what it claims to be pointing toward, away from Christ and toward the self.

How appropriate is Philippians 2 as the foundation of a Christian account of humility? In sketching Christ's humility, Paul in Philippians assumes the "Godlike greatness" of the Pre-incarnate. In claiming to model human humility on Christ's humility, Luther's account of humility presupposes the utter dependence of human beings on God. Does not the incongruity between the nature of Christ ("Godlike greatness") and of humans (dependence on God) make Christ implausible as the model of humility? That is Cahill's question.

As did many theologians before him, Luther used Christ of Philippians 2 as the model of humility because St. Paul did so. In fact, in *The Freedom of a Christian*, Philippians 2 structures the entirety of the Christian life (LW 31:365–66). Now, to describe Christ as the *model* of humility would not be quite the right way to put what he was after, especially if we assume that the idea of the "model" pushes toward strict identity between the model and the modeled, rather than sitting comfortably with the similarity between the two. As Luther understood Philippians 2—and, arguably, he was a good interpreter of Paul, at least in this regard—for "the same mind [to] be in you that was in Christ Jesus" (Phil 2:5) is not a matter of merely aligning your thought and behavior with an external model ("observe and emulate"). It is above all the outworking of Christ's presence. Christ is not just a model to be emulated; Christ is not even just a model with an external power to enable emulation. By indwelling the self, Christ (re)constitutes the self and its agency. That is where the greatness of the human self comes from; it is a conferred greatness, as is appropriate for the creature, but it is a Christlike greatness nonetheless. As Luther saw it, the self's greatness is Christ's greatness.

The same is true of humility. The relation between Christ's and a believer's humility is as follows: As Christ, who was divine, did not hold to his glory but took the form of a servant to attend to the lowly, so also Christians ought to do the same and are empowered to do the same. In union with Christ, believers are already constituted as glorious, and therefore they can let Christ act through them in the world and they can be humble in a Christlike way. Only those who do not need to achieve and keep achieving their own greatness can be humble. Those who are not great but must make themselves great are likely to be proud.

"Christ was exalted in his own right," the objection of the kind Cahill is raising could continue, "whereas believers are great on account of the presence of Christ." But if we take Christ to be divine, as Luther did, and follow the inner logic of the two framing claims in the text, namely the one about his original equality with God (Phil 2:6) and the one about conference of Lordship upon him (Phil 2:9), he cannot be said to have had equality with God in his own right. For the second person of the Trinity is not a self-standing divine self. If this were the case, we would have in this text not an incipient form of monotheistic trinitarianism, but tritheism, a complete impossibility for a Jew like Paul.

As theologians in subsequent centuries realized, the second person of the Trinity is relationally constituted and has therefore its glory as something that is always being "given." If it were otherwise, the second person would either be a self-achieved glorious self (a divine bourgeois) or an axiomatically glorious self (a divine aristocrat). Either of these two options would make the idea of the One God being triune love problematic.

If the divine greatness is given in mutual glorification of the persons of the Trinity and then "given up" by one of the persons in incarnation and crucifixion, the space opens up for an analogous understanding of human greatness, both *given to* humans and *not held graspingly* by them but *given up* in service to the lowly. Such humility is the obverse of the constitution of the self in receptivity of faith as well as of the non-self-seeking practice of love, Luther's two main concerns.

Cahill pushes against my suggestion that Luther was not at his best when he refused to let the redeemed self rejoice about its own redeemed state. She argues that there was an insurmountable obstacle, essential to the character of his theology, to him affirming that kind of joy. The reason is, Cahill writes, that according to Luther, grace cannot create "an inherent change in the agent or the self." Before I respond, let me note how extraordinary it is to find a Catholic moral theologian so knowledgeable about the intricacies of Luther interpretation, even about debates within a still relatively marginal school of Luther interpretation, the so-called Finnish school, which, like Cahill, I find for the most part compelling.

As Cahill rightly notes, the crux of the matter in the debate between Martin Luther and the best of the Catholic tradition represented by someone like Thomas Aquinas was for many centuries the question of "an inherent change in the agent or the self" as a result of grace. Aquinas insisted on the reality of such change; Luther contested it. Finnish Luther interpretation, Cahill notes, has largely bridged the gap by arguing that Luther imagined the justified sinner's relation to God "as a type of participation." As a consequence, Cahill continues, "the works of the believer are transformed, but not on the basis of any changed nature of the self." So far so good. But I would argue along with at least some of his Finnish interpreters that Luther goes a step further.

In *The Freedom of a Christian*, Luther employs multiple metaphors to express what happens to the self in relation to Christ. Cahill mentions the marriage metaphor: the union of Christ and the believer makes all Christ's goods his bride's goods. But she fails to mention the "hot iron" metaphor (LW 31:349),[2] which pushes against thinking of the goods the bride has received as merely external to her. As the fire heats iron, the iron itself becomes hot even though the heat of the iron comes entirely from the fire, and it does so throughout the course of its being hot. As this metaphor suggests, actual transformation of the self occurs in union with Christ; the new quality of the self—in fact, the new self—is not external but internal to the self, and yet it remains in a crucial sense extrinsic, not the self's own. In union with Christ, the believer becomes "Christ," as Luther puts it famously in *The Freedom of a Christian* (LW 31:351), but the believer is Christ only as united with Christ. Transformation of the self is the effect of uncreated grace that lasts as long as union with uncreated grace is present.

Two important anthropological convictions help clarify what may seem the paradoxical idea of the transformation of the self that remains extrinsic to the self. First, Luther rejects the idea that in union with Christ humans are mere objects upon which God acts. They cannot be, for then as recipients of saving grace they would be like a stone or a tree and lose their very humanity. In *On the Bondage of the Will*, Luther articulates a fundamental principle of the relation between God and humans: God "does not work in us without us" (*LW* 33:243), which is to say, without involving our will and knowledge. Humans are in a crucial sense utterly passive in relation to God, but the passivity is at a level even deeper than their will and knowledge.

Second, being human, according to Luther, means living always as created out of nothing, as having one's entire existence given to oneself by God. It is not that we as iron are our own independent thing, to which then God's fire is added, as the metaphor Luther used suggests. The metaphor is not fully adequate to express our existential situation. For the belief in God the creator means for Luther that we in our entirety, at all moments of our existence, are the result of God's creatively relating to us.[3] When God acts in us, when Christ indwells us, we come into our own as created beings; that is what it means to be properly human. At the deepest level, our sin consists in thinking that we are our own work, that we can achieve ourselves, that we can ever possess goods that we have not received and are not always receiving from God. The problem of human beings, according to this interpretation of Luther, is not so much that they think that they are something but are in fact nothing. It is rather that they mistakenly take themselves to be and act as if they were the kind of entities that can be originators of their own goodness, as if they had anything good that they "did not receive" (1 Cor 4:7). The "I" that claims to be something in its own right is the false "I," telling itself and others a falsehood about itself and enacting that falsehood in its relation to itself, other humans, and God. The falsehood does not consist in the claim that the self is something—something good and even something great; that is actually the truth about the self. The falsehood consists in the claim that the self can be and in fact is good and great apart from God, on its own.

The result of this falsehood is the unending and futile effort of the self to achieve itself and to cling to and exploit in relation to itself and others any achievement it has made, always busy defending it, shoring it up, increasing it. The self then becomes self-absorbed, and never more than when it pursues self-achievement through holy and good causes. Such a self is incapable of genuine love. Such a self is incapable of true joy as well.

Against Luther's explicit claims but with the spirit of Luther's position, I claim that the new self who knows and enacts the truth about itself can and ought to rejoice over its own character as such a self. I speak of "rejoicing" and "joy" deliberately, rather than "being proud" and "pride." As Luther understands it, pride is a competitive emotion, always directed as much against the other as it is oriented toward itself; joy is not. True joy is at once more self-confident and more compliant, less other-dependent and more other-embracing, more stable and yet also more malleable, multifaceted and at one with itself.

Why not rejoice over the reality of the new self that has become properly itself as indwelled by Christ? If we should not, is it because we must assume that the self can rejoice only over what it has itself achieved by existing and acting as a fully independent entity? But would that not be the joy of the "old" proud self and therefore a twisted joy? Why could the self, constituted and active on account of being indwelled by Christ, not rejoice over the kind of creature that it has been made without making comparative judgments either of a positive or negative kind? Presumably that is what will happen in the world to come. One will recognize that everything one has is a gift, one will long for what one has (as Dante said of the souls in the lower regions of Paradise, *Paradiso* 3.3.71)—and rejoice in both having and in longing. It may be psychologically difficult to rejoice in such a way in the here and now, but at least something of that joy can be part of our ordinary experience, the reality of our being curved in on ourselves (*homo in se incurvatus*) notwithstanding.

In footnote 4, Cahill questions the degree to which the idea of the self as the owner of itself and its action engaged in a process of self-achievement in a competitive setting adequately describes the self-understanding of people today. An elite self is in view here, she believes. I largely agree. But it is important to keep in mind what "self-understanding" here means. At one level the image of the owner of the self is not even appropriate to those most elite and privileged among us; except for the narcissists, most of us do not experience ourselves as such. And yet, at least in the countries within a strong Western sphere of influence, *we imagine ourselves normatively as being such*. But this image of ourselves is not only false but also pernicious.

Cahill claims that "global insecurity, fear, and lack of control have led to increases in violence and the global resurgence of the political Right."

I agree, though the main cause has to do more with unconscionable and unjust disparities in wealth distribution and with an attenuated sense of cultural and personal identities. Still, it is also true that "insecurity, fear, and lack of control," though rooted in objective realities, are subjective states, not mere reactions to objective circumstances. In the United States and Europe, these subjective states have been in part manufactured and exploited for economic and political purposes, *so that* power and wealth would not be more equitably distributed. There is no getting out of the present global crisis by insisting on all humans becoming in fact self-achieving sovereign individuals; such individuals are at the heart of the crisis (though likely not the main motor of it).

The humility of being and of acting is a necessary condition not just of personal flourishing but also of global thriving. This conviction is central to my variation on Luther's theology of humility.

• • •

NOTES TO CHAPTER 2
(MIROSLAV VOLF)

1 Timothy Fry, ed., *Rule of St. Benedict* (Collegeville, Minn.: Liturgical, 1981), 7:49–50.
2 Friedrich Nietzsche, *Human, All Too Human*, trans. R. J. Hollingdale (Cambridge: Cambridge University Press, 1986), I.87.
3 See Alain Ehrenberg, *The Weariness of the Self: Diagnosing the History of Depression in the Contemporary Age* (Montreal: McGill–Queen's University Press, 2015).
4 Friedrich Nietzsche, "On the Genealogy of Morality," in *The Complete Works of Friedrich Nietzsche*, vol. 8, ed. Alan D. Schrift and Duncan Large (Stanford: Stanford University Press, 2014), 249.
5 When our agency does not suffice for us to achieve ourselves, we will happily claim gifts of fortune—qualities, material belongings, or social positions we have inherited, for instance—as not just our own, but as possessions others should consider we deserve. The life need of the modern self for either accomplishment or possession explains the indispensability of pride, pride being, in the opinion of David Hume, who deems it a virtue, "a certain satisfaction in ourselves, on account of some accomplishment or possession, which we enjoy" (*A Dissertation on the Passions*, section 2.1, http://www.davidhume.org/texts/fd.html).
6 See Ehrenberg, *Weariness of the Self*. In Nietzsche's language, we are on the open sea with land nowhere in sight (*Gay Science* §124).
7 For a meditation on unsatisfiable desire and undischargeable responsibility as inhibitors of joy, see Miroslav Volf, "What Is Good? Joy and the Well-Lived Life," *Christian Century*, July 1, 2016.

8 Friedrich Nietzsche, *Thus Spoke Zarathustra*, trans. Adrian Del Caro (Cambridge: Cambridge University Press, 2006), "Zarathustra's Prologue," §3.
9 See Frantz Fanon, *Black Skin, White Masks*, trans. Richard Philcox (New York: Grove, 2008). For a historical discussion of the issue in Western democratic traditions, see Charles Taylor, *Multiculturalism and "The Politics of Recognition"* (Princeton: Princeton University Press, 1992), 25–73.
10 For a womanist account of such a position, see Stacey M. Floyd-Thomas, "The Virtues and Vices of Possessing the Secret Joy: A Womanist Ethical Assessment," a paper presented at the consultation on "Humility, Pride, and Joy," April 28–29, 2017, at the Yale Center for Faith and Culture. Her paper, which appears in revised form as chapter 1 of this volume, and participation in the discussion inform much of the present paragraph.
11 Martin Luther King Jr., "Where Do We Go from Here?" address delivered at the Eleventh Annual Convention of the Southern Christian Leadership Conference, Atlanta, Georgia, August 16, 1967, in *A Call to Conscience*, ed. Clayborne Carson and Kris Shepard (New York: Grand Central, 2001), 184–85. See also Michael Eric Dyson, *Pride* (New York: Oxford University Press, 2006), 46: "White pride is often the vice that makes black pride necessary."
12 Another compelling Christian alternative is that of Thomas Aquinas. (See Jennifer A. Herdt's essay in this volume.)
13 For the history of a shift from the context of thinking about humility and practicing it in ancient "honor" societies to doing so in the context of modern "recognition" societies, see Ryan McAnnally-Linz, "An Unrecognizable Glory: Christian Humility in the Age of Authenticity" (Ph.D. diss., Yale University, 2016).
14 Max Scheler, "Humility," *Aletheia* 2 (1981): 217.
15 Scheler, "Humility," 217.
16 Scheler, "Humility," 218.
17 This translation of *harpagmos* in Phil 2:6 ("exploited," in the translation I use) is contested because much of the interpretation of the whole passage depends on it. Perhaps it is best to translate it as "something to be used for one's own advantage" as Gerald F. Hawthorne does ("In the Form of God and Equal with God," in *Where Christology Began: Essays on Philippians 2*, ed. Ralph P. Martin and Brian J. Dodd. [Louisville, Ky.: Westminster John Knox, 1998], 102).
18 Scheler, "Humility," 210.
19 Scheler, "Humility," 211–12. Scheler distinguishes sharply—perhaps too sharply—between pride and vanity. Vanity is ridiculous. A vain person "subjects himself to the judgment of those whom he, at the same time, seeks to surpass by showing off his superiority. This situation deserves a cheerful laugh, since he does not notice that he serves where he wishes to rule; that he succumbs to the ordinary where he claims to be extraordinary" (212). Pride, in contrast, dispenses with validation from others and, being dependent on no outside measure of greatness, is in its solitariness diabolical.
20 Scheler, "Humility," 214.

21 Scheler, "Humility," 214.
22 Scheler, "Humility," 214.
23 Scheler, "Humility," 213.
24 Scheler, "Humility," 213–14.
25 Scheler, "Humility," 214, 210.
26 Scheler, "Humility," 214.
27 Scheler, "Humility," 214.
28 The same tension appears in another form. Humility is a virtue of "born masters," Scheler states. Having been born is not one's achievement but the presupposition of any achievements. Like birth itself, humility, it would seem, cannot be achieved; if it were achieved, it would likely be a source of pride and therefore cancel itself. Confirming this line of thinking, Scheler writes that a person is humble through "the inner miracle of ever new re-birth" (216). At the same time, he insists that both the humility of being—"radical renunciation of one's own power and one's own worth"—and humbly acting in intercourse with others are possible through "utter daring" (216). To be humble, a person must cultivate one's soul into such daring, into the ability to walk "the way of abandonment" (215).
29 Scheler, "Humility," 215.
30 Martin Luther, *Luther's Works*, 55 vols. (St. Louis: Concordia, 1955–1986), hereafter cited as LW.
31 William James, *A Pluralistic Universe*, in *William James: Writings, 1902–1910* (New York: Library of America, 1988), 625–820. Luther, of course, thought that it was the great apostle Paul to whom the breakthrough should be ascribed. Commenting on this, William James notes, "And possibly he was right" (768).
32 We can trace Luther's road to the reformation breakthrough (or breakthroughs), which was behind him in 1520–1521 when the texts I engage here were composed, by narrating the story of the transformations of his account of humility—from humility preceding faith, through humility being part of faith, to humility proceeding from faith (though such a linear way of putting things does not do justice to the messy character of his public process of discovery as evident in his various lectures). On the relation between faith and humility in Luther, see Ronald K. Rittgers, *The Reformation of Suffering: Pastoral Theology and Lay Piety in Late Medieval and Early Modern Germany* (Oxford: Oxford University Press, 2012), 87–119.
33 It is important to be clear that the first moment in the humility of being does not consist in *making oneself* into nothing. Whatever one makes oneself into, that is still something, and it is something that one has a rightful claim to have made. In this case, humility would rest on an inner contradiction; one could legitimately be proud of one's humility. Neither does the first moment in humility of being consist in *considering oneself as nothing while in fact being something*. In this case humility would rest both on an inner contradiction and on untruthfulness. For Luther, humility of being rests on a truthful seeing of who one in fact is.

34 The relation between humility as "lowly estate" and humility as a "stance of the self" (understood both as a "mode of self-relating" [specifically being "nothing in oneself," which is humility of being] and as a "mode of relating to others" ["a love and leaning to lowly and despised things" (LW 21:314), which is humility in acting]) is complicated in Luther. Luther consistently insists on the connection between the two. A lowly state, especially suffering, can lead to humility becoming the stance of the self and is often a necessary condition of humility (LW 21:313; see Rittgers, *Reformation of Suffering*, 87–105); indeed, Luther often writes as if humility just is "nothing else than a disregarded, despised, and lowly estate, such as that of men who are poor, sick, hungry, thirsty, in prison, suffering, and dying. Such was Job in his afflictions" (LW 21:313). Correspondingly, an exalted state—possession of power, riches, honor, knowledge, in a phrase, large amounts of capital of whatever sort—tends to feed pride as a stance and keep a person captive to pride. The rich and the powerful then end up as the proud ones. But Luther is quite aware that it is possible to be in a lowly state and proud by "striving for that which is above" one, after "honor, power, wealth, knowledge, a life of ease, and whatever is lofty and great" (LW 21:300). Inversely, he knows that it is possible to be exalted and still humble by being both aware of being nothing on one's own and willing to "look into the depths with their poverty, disgrace, squalor, misery, and anguish" and associate with those who are in such a state, "helping them" or "making something out of them" (300).

35 This is not to say that Luther did not continue to believe that lowly estate, including suffering, is not needed to prepare the self for the insight into its nothingness as a self-standing entity and to keep that insight alive. This is the purgative function of suffering for Luther (see Rittgers, *Reformation of Suffering*).

36 In the same context, Luther puts what I have called the first moment in humility of being or "humiliation" in the following way: "On the other hand, whatever is something, precious, honorable, blessed, and living, He [God] makes to be nothing, worthless, despised, wretched, and dying" (LW 21:299). Luther's God may appear puzzlingly capricious here: God creates something out of nothing and then, as soon as it has become something, turns it back into nothing. But that is if one disregards Luther's peculiar ontology. Most of the discussion of Luther's ontology centers on his anthropology, especially after Wilfred Joest's *Ontologie der Person bei Luther* (Göttingen: Vandenhoeck & Ruprecht, 1967). Joest stressed the relational character of Luther's ontology. The best of subsequent scholarly work argues that Luther does not equate "being" with "being-for-consciousness," as does philosophy in the wake of Kant's transcendental turn, but superimposes relational ontology onto substantialist ontology. We can see this complex, not fully developed but intuitively plausible, ontology at work in the quote above. In the phrase "whatever is something," "is" must refer to more than just the "out-thereness" of something. Without in any way denying their "objective" being and characteristics, for Luther things are also always "there-for-us." Here are some other examples of

claims that illustrate just such complex, substantialist-cum-relational ontology. Without at all denying the reality of the one true God independent of the world, Luther claims in the *The Large Catechism* that "the truth and faith of the heart alone make both God and an idol" (*The Book of Concord: The Confessions of the Evangelical Lutheran Church*, ed. and trans. Theodore G. Tappert [Philadelphia: Fortress, 1959], 365); you can relate to the true God without the true God being a god to you, and you can relate to an idol in a way that the idol is a god to you. (In *The Essence of Christianity* [1841], trans. George Eliot [Amherst, N.Y.: Prometheus, 1989], Ludwig Feuerbach generalized the claim that trust creates God into a projectionist theory of religion; from trust co-constituting God for us to trust constituting God pure and simple.) Similarly, without denying the "objective" reality of pain and pleasure in their varied severities, or, more generally, of evil and good in their gradations, he claims, perhaps exaggerating, that "a man's evils are only as great as his knowledge and opinion of them; so it is with his blessings" (LW 42:146; see 42, 124). More to the point under discussion, without denying something like a personal "substratum" that endures over time (or "soul" as he sometimes puts it), Luther notes that "love "transforms the lover into the beloved" and "hope changes the one who hopes into what is hoped for" (LW 25:364). To return to the quote from the *Commentary on the Magnificat*, the self being something—precious, honorable, blessed, and living, or worthless, despised, wretched, and dying—is the mode of its existence *for* the self; its appearance *as* something is part of it being a particular something for the self. The destruction of the self as a presupposition of new creation is the destruction not of the enduring "soul" but of the certain kind of agency and self-perception of the soul. The "soul" comes to be "without the power of understanding and willing," abiding in "darkness," and in the self-experience of the soul this is "like going into destruction and annihilation" (LW 25:368). (In this footnote I draw on Sammeli Juntunen, "Luther and Metaphysics: What Is the Structure of Being according to Luther?" in *Union with Christ: New Finnish Interpretation of Luther*, ed. Robert E. Jenson and Carl E. Braaten [Grand Rapids: Eerdmans, 1998], 129–60.)

37 Luther writes of Mary that she "left all of God's gifts freely in His hands," rather than claiming them as her own, and "therefore she also kept all these things forever" (LW 21:308). Nothing of what the self acknowledges as having come from God—as being God's—is ever lost to the self.

38 God's humility is at the center of Luther's account of human humility. Christ's coming to become servant is an expression of the character of God. "The eyes of the world and of men . . . look only above them and are lifted up with pride. . . . Everyone strives after what is above him, after honor, power, wealth, knowledge, a life of ease, and whatever is lofty and great. And where such people are, there are many hangers-on" (LW 21:300). It is different with God. "For since He is the Most High, and there is nothing above Him, He cannot look above him; nor yet to either side, for there is none like him. He must needs, therefore, look within Him and beneath him; and the farther on is beneath Him, the better does He see

him" (299–300). Later on, Luther insists: "For he knows God aright who knows that He regards the lowly" (317).
39 See Herdt's essay in this volume.
40 Scheler, "Humility," 217.
41 Scheler, "Humility," 218. Perhaps this is because he sees pride in disjunctive relation to vanity and argues that the haughtiness of vanity is compatible with humility.
42 In the introduction, again addressing the prince directly, Luther writes: "Since the heart of man by nature is flesh and blood, it is of itself prone to presumption. And when, in addition, power, riches, and honor come to him, these form so strong an incentive to presumption and smugness that he forgets God and does not care about his subjects. Being able to do wrong with impunity, he lets himself go and becomes a beast, does whatever he pleases, and is a ruler in name, but monster in deed" (LW 21:298).
43 Luther thinks that this tight (though not unavoidable) connection between pride and power explains God's predilection for the weak.
44 Luther notes, as examples of godly power, "the holy fathers, Abraham, Isaac, and Jacob" (LW 21:346), perhaps giving them too much credit.

Notes to Chapter 2 Response
(Lisa Sowle Cahill)

1 Martin Luther, *On Christian Liberty*, ed. Harold J. Grimm, rev. ed. (Philadelphia: Fortress, 1957), 25–26 and 28, respectively. There is no need to add "[sic]" to the exclusive pronouns of a sixteenth-century writer, but contemporary readers will assume the inclusion of all genders.
2 Gustavo Gutiérrez, *A Theology of Liberation*, trans. and ed. Sister Caridad Inda and John Eagleson (Maryknoll, N.Y.: Orbis, 1973; originally published in Spanish, 1971), 146.
3 Gutiérrez, *Theology of Liberation*, 146.
4 A related issue is the degree to which people today (2020) really believe they are great creators of the "authentic selves" they choose to become, as Volf suggests in the modernity-bashing critique of "self-achievement" that opens his essay (44ff.; see also 69–70). He grants that ultimately no one ever measures up to their own aspirations. Yet in the post-2008 years of the gig economy, unaffordable higher education, out-of-control climate change, pervasive civil conflict in much of the world, and the displacement of huge waves of refugees, it is hard to think that all but a few elites "imagine themselves as owners of themselves and their action, engaged in the great endeavor of self-achievement" (64, paraphrased). I think it is rather global *insecurity, fear, and lack of control* that have led to increases in violence and the global resurgence of the political Right.
5 Martin Luther, "The Magnificat," in *The Annotated Luther*, vol. 4, *Pastoral Writings*, ed. Mary Jane Haemig (Minneapolis: Fortress, 2016), 333.
6 Luther, "Magnificat," 336.

7   See Luther, *On Christian Liberty*, 25; and *Lectures on Galatians 1535, Chapters 1–4*, LW 26:127–37. For Aquinas on charity as a participation in the divine nature, whereby humans are given a new nature appropriate to their supernatural end of friendship to God, see Thomas Aquinas, *ST* II–II.23.2.
8   Luther, *On Christian Liberty*, 14.
9   This school of interpretation arose in the 1980s largely through the work of Tuomo Mannerma and his students. It was occasioned by an Orthodox-Lutheran dialogue that debated the implications of the Lutheran doctrine of "forensic justification" for social ethics, and it asked whether the patristic, Eastern theology of *theosis* has any parallel in Luther's theology. Turning to Luther's *Lectures on Galatians*, the Lutherans realized that Luther does speak of faith as bringing a union of Christ and believer, or an indwelling of Christ in the believer, that allows transformed identity, dispositions, and action. Yet, unlike Aquinas (and the dissenting Lutheran Osiander), this theology-ethics of transformation does not presuppose an inherent change in the nature of the human being but bases it on the continual presence of Christ to faith. The Finnish school has by now several different proponents, whose theologies diverge in significant ways; it has undergone internal development; and its meaning, significance, and fidelity to Luther are debated. Yet, in my view, it productively challenges stereotypes of Luther and offers the possibility of strengthening a Lutheran social ethics in a way consistent with Luther's demand that Christians recognize their total dependence on Christ. See Toumo Mannerma, *Christ Present in Faith: Luther's View of Justification*, ed. Kirsi Stjerna (Minneapolis: Fortress, 1989); Carl E. Braaten and Robert W. Jensen, eds., *Union with Christ: The New Finnish Interpretation of Luther* (Grand Rapids: Eerdmans, 1998); Mark Totten (who thanks readers, including Miroslav Volf), "Luther on *Unio cum Christo*: Toward a Model for Integrating Faith and Ethics," *Journal of Religious Ethics* 31, no. 3 (2003): 443–62; and Gordon L. Isaac, "The Finnish School of Luther Interpretation: Responses and Trajectories," *Concordia Theological Quarterly* 76, nos. 3–4 (2012): 251–68.
10 Among Volf's many relevant works, see *Exclusion and Embrace: A Theological Exploration of Identity, Otherness, and Reconciliation* (Nashville: Abingdon, 1996).

Notes to Chapter 2 Reply
(Miroslav Volf)

1   On theology being primarily about the true life and on the importance of the lived life of a theologian, see Miroslav Volf and Matthew Croasmun, *For the Life of the World: Theology That Makes a Difference* (Grand Rapids: Brazos, 2019).
2   See Risto Saarinen, *God and the Gift: An Ecumenical Theology of Giving* (Collegeville, Minn.: Liturgical, 2004), 45–58.
3   This, too, is Luther's point in *On the Bondage of the Will*. In personal correspondence, Ronald Rittgers, a fine Luther scholar, drew my attention to

the passage where Luther objects against Erasmus that he "has separated God from the sailor in the piloting of a ship. God is all in all, both in the temporal kingdom and the spiritual kingdom, and human beings only 'cooperate' with God in both realms" (May 14, 2018; LW 33:241).

CHAPTER BIBLIOGRAPHY

Braaten, Carl E., and Robert W. Jensen, eds. *Union with Christ: The New Finnish Interpretation of Luther*. Grand Rapids: Eerdmans, 1998.

Dyson, Michael Eric. *Pride*. New York: Oxford University Press, 2006.

Ehrenberg, Alain. *The Weariness of the Self: Diagnosing the History of Depression in the Contemporary Age*. Montreal: McGill–Queen's University Press, 2015.

Fanon, Frantz. *Black Skin, White Masks*. Translated by Richard Philcox. New York: Grove, 2008.

Feuerbach, Ludwig. *The Essence of Christianity*. Translated by George Eliot. Amherst, N.Y.: Prometheus, 1989. First published 1841.

Fry, Timothy, ed. *RB 1980: The Rule of St. Benedict in English*. Collegeville, Minn.: Liturgical, 1981.

Gutiérrez, Gustavo. *A Theology of Liberation*. Translated and edited by Sister Caridad Inda and John Eagleson. Maryknoll, N.Y.: Orbis, 1973. First published 1971.

Hawthorne, Gerald F. "In the Form of God and Equal with God." In *Where Christology Began: Essays on Philippians 2*, edited by Ralph P. Martin and Brian J. Dodd, 96–110. Louisville, Ky.: Westminster John Knox, 1998.

Hume, David. *A Dissertation on the Passions*. http://www.davidhume.org/texts/fd.html.

Isaac, Gordon L. "The Finnish School of Luther Interpretation: Responses and Trajectories." *Concordia Theological Quarterly* 76, nos. 3–4 (2012): 251–68.

James, William. *A Pluralistic Universe*. In *William James: Writings, 1902–1910*, 625–820. New York: Library of America, 1988.

Joest, Wilfred. *Ontologie der Person bei Luther*. Göttingen: Vandenhoeck & Ruprecht, 1967.

Juntunen, Sammeli. "Luther and Metaphysics: What Is the Structure of Being according to Luther?" In *Union with Christ: New Finnish Interpretation of Luther*, edited by Robert E. Jenson and Carl E. Braaten, 129–60. Grand Rapids: Eerdmans, 1998.

King, Martin Luther, Jr. "Where Do We Go from Here?" Address delivered at the Eleventh Annual Convention of the Southern Christian Leadership Conference, Atlanta, August 16, 1967. In *A Call to Conscience*, edited by Clayborne Carson and Kris Shepard. New York: Grand Central, 2001.

Luther, Martin. *Luther's Works*. 55 vols. St. Louis: Concordia, 1955–1986.

―――. "The Magnificat." In *The Annotated Luther*, vol. 4, *Pastoral Writings*, edited by Mary Jane Haemig. Minneapolis: Fortress, 2016.

———. *On Christian Liberty*. Edited by Harold J. Grimm. Rev. ed. Philadelphia: Fortress, 1957.

Mannerma, Toumo. *Christ Present in Faith: Luther's View of Justification*. Edited by Kirsi Stjerna. Minneapolis: Fortress, 1989.

McAnnally-Linz, Ryan. "An Unrecognizable Glory: Christian Humility in the Age of Authenticity." Ph.D. diss., Yale University, 2016.

Nietzsche, Friedrich. *Human, All Too Human*. Translated by R. J. Hollingdale. Cambridge: Cambridge University Press, 1986.

———. "On the Genealogy of Morality." In *The Complete Works of Friedrich Nietzsche*, vol. 8, edited by Alan D. Schrift and Duncan Large. Stanford: Stanford University Press, 2014.

———. *Thus Spoke Zarathustra*. Translated by Adrian Del Caro. Cambridge: Cambridge University Press, 2006.

Rittgers, Ronald K. *The Reformation of Suffering: Pastoral Theology and Lay Piety in Late Medieval and Early Modern Germany*. Oxford: Oxford University Press, 2012.

Saarinen, Risto. *God and the Gift: An Ecumenical Theology of Giving*. Collegeville, Minn.: Liturgical, 2004.

Scheler, Max. "Humility." *Aletheia* 2 (1981): 2–209.

Tappert, Theodore G., ed. and trans. *The Book of Concord: The Confessions of the Evangelical Lutheran Church*. Philadelphia: Fortress, 1959.

Taylor, Charles. *Multiculturalism and "The Politics of Recognition."* Princeton: Princeton University Press, 1992.

Totten, Mark. "Luther on *Unio cum Christo*: Toward a Model for Integrating Faith and Ethics." *Journal of Religious Ethics* 31, no. 3 (2003): 443–62.

Volf, Miroslav. *Exclusion and Embrace: A Theological Exploration of Identity, Otherness, and Reconciliation*. Nashville: Abingdon, 1996.

———. "What Is Good? Joy and the Well-Lived Life." *Christian Century*, July 1, 2016.

Volf, Miroslav, and Matthew Croasmun. *For the Life of the World: Theology That Makes a Difference*. Grand Rapids: Brazos, 2019.

3

Magnanimous Humility

The Lofty Vocation of the Humble

Jennifer A. Herdt

We might not think immediately of humility in connection with joy.[1] After all, joy uplifts, expands our spirits; humility bends low, deflates, with its etymological connections to *humus*, the earth, to all that is humble, and to humiliation, being brought low. I want to argue, though, for an intimate connection between joy and humility. Humility is joyful, and lack of humility interferes with joy. In order fully to grasp why and how humility is joyful, we need to understand humility in connection with what Thomas Aquinas treats as its twin virtue, magnanimity. Magnanimity, literally, is greatness of soul. The point here is not that the meek and poor in spirit shall be exalted, that the humble shall be lifted up; it is not the notion that self-denigration induces glorification by some higher power. Unfortunately, Christian praise of humility has often been understood in this way, eliciting appropriate critique. True humility is not what Nietzsche branded *ressentiment*, and its joy does not wait upon any reversal of fortunes but can be always already present as an anticipation of eschatological delight. Or so I shall argue.

I understand joy, following Robert Roberts, as a "delight in the way the world is," a satisfaction or spiritual pleasure in something's being as it is.² It is as though one says Amen to something: this is as it ought to be, as I wish it to be. While joy is always pleasurable, joy is not always good, since one can delight in bad things as well as in good; I might delight in radiant fall splendor or in seeing a despised colleague taken down a peg.³ Our joys reveal what we care about, and we tend to care in distorted ways—for the wrong things, or too much, or too little. Assessing joy is thus not a neutral enterprise; we know whether someone else's joy is worth approving and rejoicing in only if we know whether it is indeed delight in the good.⁴ Furthermore, to assess someone's joys is also to assess his or her character, since our character is partially constituted by what we care about.

Humility seems an unlikely candidate for the role of "joy-enhancer." In part for that reason, it has often been the target of abuse and demotion from virtue to vice. Nietzsche associates it with *ressentiment*, with the slave morality that valorizes weakness. Hume identifies humility with the "disagreeable" passion of shame. It has seemed to many a kind of perverse self-abasement antithetical to healthy self-esteem and even to accurate self-knowledge, as it seems to require thinking better of others than oneself even where this disadvantageous comparison is unfounded. So understood, it has rightly been a target for feminist critique: women in particular have been measured by an ideal of humility to which men have been content to pay only lip service.⁵

Many Christian champions of humility have not helped matters; Benedict in his rule, for instance, includes among the degrees of humility "to believe and profess oneself lower than others" and "to believe and acknowledge oneself useless for anything."⁶ Anselm, for his part, enumerates among the degrees of humility "to acknowledge oneself contemptible"; "to convince others of this, that is to wish them to believe it"; and "to love" being treated "with contempt."⁷ Given such an understanding of humility, it is no wonder that it has been subjected to harsh critique. Is this not the Aristotelian vice of pusillanimity, that thinks oneself capable and worthy of less than one truly is (*NE* 1123b10)? Does this not suggest that modernity recovered a healthy self-esteem that had been pounded and driven underground by Christianity's displacement of classical pagan virtue? If a virtue is a stable disposition that makes a person good and capable of reliably acting well and thus of living a good human life, how is humility a virtue, let alone a disposition that enhances joy? Small wonder that Hume classed it with "monkish virtues" that "cross all . . . desirable ends; stupify the understanding and harden the heart, obscure the fancy and sour the temper."⁸ Moreover, given that Augustine tells us that "almost the whole of Christian teaching is humility," demoting humility would seem likely to strike at the root of Christian understandings of human goodness and flourishing.⁹

Defending humility seems, then, to be an uphill battle. Nevertheless, it is one worth undertaking. For rightly understood, humility is indeed a virtue and thus necessary to living well. It is, moreover, a source of lasting joy. To see this, we would do well to begin with Thomas Aquinas, who develops his account of humility with reference to both pagan and Christian inheritances, working to honor and render coherent all received wisdom as pointing to God's truth. Aquinas pairs humility with magnanimity as twin virtues—just as humility is not to be identified with pusillanimity, magnanimity is not to be identified with pride.[10] This proves immensely helpful for understanding both humility and humility's relationship with joy. This is wisdom worth recovering in a culture obsessed with greatness and self-promotion, but lacking in joy. And it is wisdom worth recovering, too, in light of the Christian tradition's tendency to slide into a one-sided valorization of humility uncomfortable with any aspiration to greatness. Humility, rightly understood, is bound together with God-enabled greatness. And God-enabled greatness is joyful.

Humility, in Aquinas' account, appears at moments to be just as objectionable as it is in the versions of some of his Christian predecessors. It is a "praiseworthy self-abasement to the lowest place" (*ST* II–II.161.1 ad2). It involves "suppressing hope or confidence in oneself" (II–II.161.2 ad3). Humility suppresses the passion of hope, "which is the movement of a spirit aiming at great things" (II–II.161.4). It "makes a man a good subject to ordinances of all kinds and in all matters" (II–II.161.5). Reading carefully, though, we begin to see the inner logic of humility. It tempers and restrains the impulse to "tend to high things *immoderately*" (II–II.161.1, emphasis added), not absolutely. It is not self-abasement as such, but only insofar as this is praiseworthy. But how are we to determine what is immoderate and what is praiseworthy in these regards? Most crucially, humility does not rule out aiming at great things, but only aiming "at greater things through confiding in one's own powers." In contrast, "to aim at greater things through confidence in God's help, is not contrary to humility" (II–II.161.2 ad2). This offers us an invaluable gloss on another comment, that humility "would seem to denote in the first place man's subjection to God," since "man ought not to ascribe to himself more than is competent to him according to the position in which God has placed him" (II–II.161.2 ad3). What, though, is the position in which humankind has been placed by God? A most exalted one, reference to which is woven into the very structure of the *Summa*: humankind is made to the image of God, as creatures capable of moral agency, of being the principles of their own actions. The turning point from the *exitus* of creation from God to its *reditus* in the *Summa* comes with the prologue to the *Prima Secundae*; having "treated of the exemplar, i.e., God, and of those things which came forth from the power of God in accordance with His will," attention now turns to the image of God, in whom creation no longer simply passively reflects God's glory but is capable of actively recognizing the divine goodness and accepting the invitation to enter into friendship with God.

With such a lofty vocation in view, what is it to ascribe to oneself more than that to which one is competent? The answer comes in Thomas' discussion of pride, humility's opposite vice, and more particularly in Thomas' discussion of humankind's first sin, a sin of pride. Pride, generally speaking, is "the appetite for excellence in excess of right reason" (II–II.162.1). Our first parents sinned by coveting God's likeness inordinately, above their measure. Humankind was made to God's image, so aspiring to this was not in itself inordinate but proper to human nature, Aquinas hastens to say. Nor did our first parents aspire to absolute equality with God, not even conceiving of such a thing. Rather, they desired to have through their own power what they ought to have received from God. They wanted to determine for themselves what was good and what was evil. And they wanted to obtain happiness by their own natural power. But happiness, constituted by living in the knowledge and love of God and of all in relation to God, is reached not by independent human action but by reliance on God's grace. We are to be tutored not toward self-sufficiency but toward friendship, toward a willingness to rely on our friend. Humility, by expelling pride, "makes man submissive and ever open to receive the influx of divine grace" (II–II.161.5 ad2). So humility is not essentially a matter of thinking less of oneself than of others. Nor is it a matter of groveling or of self-abasement before God. Rather, submission to God is essentially a matter of openness to grace, of being willing to be lifted above servanthood to friendship with God, a sharing in the self-giving Trinitarian life that comes only in acceptance of gift, not as independent achievement.

It is at this point that magnanimity can most helpfully be brought onto the stage. Humility and magnanimity are for Aquinas parts of distinct cardinal virtues, humility of temperance, by way of modesty, and magnanimity of courage. Nevertheless, Aquinas considers the two to be specially related to one another. Whereas the core definition of magnanimity is as a virtue that strengthens persons in hoping for or obtaining the greatest goods (II–II.129.5), magnanimity's special relation to humility emerges in a fuller definition of each: "Magnanimity makes a man deem himself worthy of great things in consideration of the gifts he holds from God," while "humility makes a man think little of himself in consideration of his own deficiency, and . . . makes us honor others and esteem them better than ourselves, so far as we see some of God's gifts in them" (II–II.129.3 ad 4).

Magnanimity and humility are thus complementary to one another. Humility cannot be groveling or self-abasement, because then it would be *contrary* to magnanimity, rather than being its complement.

Introducing magnanimity into the picture might be thought only to make matters worse. For magnanimity is just as contested a virtue as is humility. If humility embodies the suspect character of Christian virtue, magnanimity occupies that role for pagan virtue. Aristotelian magnanimity has come under particularly intense fire. For the magnanimous man, on Aristotle's account, is concerned especially with honor (*NE* 1124a 12). He wishes to be superior to others and to forget what he has received from others (1124b 10–15). He despises other people (1124b 5) and is so preoccupied with doing great things that he is "inactive and lethargic" with regard to everything else (1124b 24). Why ever would one think of the magnanimous person as the "best person," possessing all of the other virtues, and magnanimity as "a sort of adornment" (1123b 27, 1124a 1)? While scholarly opinion is far from united, there is much to be said in favor of a reading on which Aristotle begins with a report on common opinions regarding great-souled heroes and moves dialectically to quite a different, more Socratic moral heroism: the truly magnanimous have a *proper* concern for honor, which is to say that what they seek is not honor but virtue, even as they regard honor as an appropriate recognition of virtue.[11]

Aquinas, of course, did not have the benefit of modern scholarship on Aristotelian magnanimity. He did, though, inherit other traditions of reflection on magnanimity that offered lenses through which creatively redemptive readings of Aristotle were possible. Most significant was that stemming from Cicero, who enumerated four parts of fortitude: magnificence, confidence, patience, and perseverance (*Off.* 1.18.64–1.20.67). Aquinas makes room for the Aristotelian crown virtue by identifying it with Ciceronian confidence, as a virtue through which "the mind is much assured and firmly hopeful in great and honorable undertakings" (*ST* I–II.128).

Aquinas makes other similar moves, notably allowing Cicero's inclusion of endurance within the virtue of courage to modify Aristotelian battlefield courage in a direction favorable to martyrdom. The identification of magnanimity with confidence did not simply secure a place for magnanimity, of course. It also transformed it. Magnanimity strengthens the mind in great undertakings. It is peculiarly concerned with honor not for its own sake but only insofar as honor is indeed right recognition of great goodness. First and foremost, then, honor is to be given to God, and when accorded to human virtue, to be referred to God. Magnanimity, in strengthening persons in hoping for the greatest goods, strengthens them not in hope for honor but rather in hope for being able to fulfill the task to which human persons are called, that of participating actively, as creatures made to the image of God, in the *reditus* of creation to God. This greatest good toward which the soul can be stretched is that of entering into friendship with God, a friendship that turns outward in ever-widening invitation. And what is critical to achieving this heroic task, this great good, is precisely seeking to do so not as one's own independent achievement but rather in constant recognition of the gifts one has received from God. Hence one cannot be magnanimous without also being humble—that is, without recognizing that one's achievements are not independent accomplishments. Similarly, one cannot perfect the virtue of humility without also possessing the virtue of magnanimity: it would be the vice of pusillanimity to refuse to aim at the fulfillment of one's God-given calling.

All of this is seen most clearly in the virtues of Jesus Christ. Aquinas' portrait of the virtuous person is always indirectly a portrait of Christ's perfect virtue.[12] To be sure, Christ's virtues are perfect because Christ is perfectly united to God, always in possession of the beatific vision. Yet what this underscores is not that Christ's virtue is unattainable for the rest of us but rather that it was attainable for Christ *precisely as reliant on divine grace*, not as independent achievement. Hence, virtue is also attainable for Christ's followers precisely as grace-given. Christ displays perfect human virtue as receptive and self-giving friendship, not as independence or invulnerability. Jesus Christ thus corrects our likely misunderstandings of both magnanimity and humility. We are all to aim at the greatest goods—to rise to our lofty calling as part agents of the *reditus* of creation to God—but we are to do so by virtue of the abundant gifts we receive from God. This is not to ascribe to ourselves more than is competent to us according to the position in which God has placed us but rather precisely to hope and aspire well, attended by both magnanimity and humility (II–II.161.2 ad3).

Now, we may still be inclined to think that Aquinas nods a bit too approvingly in the direction of Christian understandings of humility as self-denigration. Need openness to divine grace be construed as submission and self-abasement? Need honoring God as the source of all grace involve honoring human others as better than ourselves? Doesn't common dependency on God's grace swamp the significance of all such human comparisons? Robert Roberts argues that while humility is often understood as a disposition to compare oneself disadvantageously to others, such a disposition is problematic insofar as it is built—just like the vice of pride—on comparison with others.[13] Instead, he suggests that it is better to conceive of humility as "a matter of viewing everybody as ultimately or basically equal."[14] It is not that comparisons with others must be precluded: we often need to know who can think with a clearer head under pressure, who can more effectively rally the troops, who can more sensitively broach the uncomfortable topic. But, argues Roberts, "humility is the ability, without prejudice to one's self-comfort, to admit one's inferiority, in this or that respect, to another. And it is the ability, without increment to one's self-comfort or prejudice to the quality of one's relationship with another, to remark one's superiority, in this or that respect, to another."[15] In order to be humble, we need grounds for conceiving of ourselves and others as essentially equals. And we need grounds for conceiving of ourselves as valuable apart from success in competition with others. Conceiving of all persons as equally beloved of God offers both.[16]

Roberts' account, while fully compatible with that of Aquinas, clarifies one point at which Aquinas might be read as suggesting that humility is based on comparative judgments. In fact, for Aquinas, too, humility radically relativizes comparative judgments. As we have seen, "humility," according to Aquinas, "makes a man think little of himself in consideration of his own deficiency, and . . . makes us honor others and esteem them better than ourselves, so far as we see some of God's gifts in them" (II–II.129.3 ad 4). Of course, Aquinas is guided here not just by predecessors in the theological tradition but by Scripture itself. "Do nothing from selfish conceit," says Paul, "but in humility count others better than yourselves" (Phil 2:3). Yet the truly humble do not *belittle* themselves with reference to the achievements of others; rather, they *think little* of themselves—that is, quietly confident of their self-worth, they need not be troubled by comparisons with others, whether favorable or unfavorable. As Roberts argues elsewhere, humility "is a striking or unusual *un*concern to be well regarded by others, and thus a kind of emotional *in*sensitivity to the issues of status."[17] This is not because all of the things for which one might be well regarded are unimportant (for example, moral character) but because "the concern for status is swamped or displaced or put on hold by some overriding virtuous concern."[18] Paul's verse above leads directly into the ancient hymn praising Christ's self-emptying humility. Christ's "love for humankind and for accomplishing his Father's will overrides the concern for his status and moves him to make himself vulnerable to some very unlordly humiliation."[19] For both Aquinas and Roberts, then, the virtue of humility involves a disposition to one's God-given task and to recognition of the God-given gifts that empower one to accomplish it, where humility's special contribution is by way of acknowledging the dependent character of one's being and accomplishments.[20]

Fleshing out just what sort of lack of concern for the regard of others is involved here turns out to be a fine-grained task. For starters, public honor and recognition of moral goodness is itself a good thing. Aquinas calls honor the greatest of external goods, rightly "offered to God and to the best" (II–II.129.1). We praise and honor God in public worship, and regard this as the anticipation of the great celebration of heaven: "worthy is the Lamb that was slain, to receive power, and riches, and honor, and glory!" Further, if our communities failed publicly to recognize and honor moral goodness, how would we as individuals come to recognize that goodness? It is essential that we aspire to become good, and that requires that we grasp certain ways of acting as good, as worthy of choice. Public recognition of them as good points us in the right way. Even if at some point we come to critique what those around us judge to be good, such critique is always internal criticism, intelligible only insofar as it rejects some alleged good in the name of others that are not currently being contested. Whatever humility is, then, it cannot require or be predicated on a lack of recognition or a failure to discriminate moral goodness.

Nor can humility be constituted by a peculiar blind spot where one's own self is concerned—that is, by a local inability to discriminate what in oneself might be worthy of honor or, indeed, of admiration more generally. For such blindness would hinder one's ability to act well. We must know both our capacities and our incapacities, our virtues and our vices. Am I able to galvanize a roomful of people to fight injustice? Able instead to build the sort of trust that makes room for a difficult intimate conversation? Keep a clear head in times of stress? Persist in an exacting task that requires endless repetition? Self-knowledge is indispensable. This requires, further, that we compare ourselves with others. Perhaps I can galvanize the roomful of people, but not as well as Bob can. Or that I can lead the difficult conversation even better than Jackie. The humble person is not lacking in such knowledge or the willingness to engage in the comparative judgments that are required. Moreover, this cannot be a sort of unconcerned, observational knowledge. We must also *care* about the quality of our own agency in a special way, since it is only by way of that agency that we can be for what is good, advance it, defend it. Only if I care about my agency can I hope to build my competencies. Further, we must concede that caring about what respected others think of us plays a significant role in the development of the virtues, even if we become less dependent on others' perceptions of us insofar as we develop our own stable sense of what is honorable. Short of a state of perfect virtue, we cannot afford to exclude the possibility that others' assessments of us give us much-needed information. Indeed, some degree of sensitivity to others' assessments, a willingness to take them into consideration, would seem to be ingredient in the virtue of humility itself.

What we might say, then, is that the humble person is fully aware of her strengths and weaknesses in relation to others, and of others' perceptions of her, but is neither inflated nor deflated by these. That is, her sense of self-worth is not dependent on these comparisons. They simply provide important information concerning what she should and should not aspire to in particular contexts. So what humility seems to involve is a relative independence of others' good regard, such that one is not dependent on that regard for one's sense of identity or self-confidence, even as one remains sensitive to others' regard or lack of regard insofar as that might make one aware of some previously unrecognized flaw or weakness. And the humble person's concern for comparison is not directed toward being better than others for the sake of being better than others. Comparison is rather directed toward becoming better than one presently is and toward acting as well as possible given one's present strengths and weaknesses. Attention is focused not on the self as such, but only insofar as various aspects of one's agency are significant for fulfilling one's task, one's vocation.

Humility, then, disposes us to regard our competencies as gifts rather than as achievements. For regarding something as an achievement focuses attention on oneself as achiever. To see our virtues and competencies instead as gifts, as unmerited, decisively reframes them, focusing attention on the giver and on oneself as fortunate recipient, as gift-ed. Instead of being puffed up with pride, we are suffused with gratitude at having been gifted in this way. Magnanimity likewise frees its possessor from preoccupation with herself as the achiever of great deeds, enabling her to focus on doing that to which she is called, on the goodness and importance of the task rather than of herself.[21] We are all equal in that we are all recipients of gifts, all counted worthy to receive such unmerited gifts, equally beloved. Yet we are recipients of varied and unequal gifts, as Thomas rightly notes. Given the importance for moral development of self-knowledge, sensitivity to others' regard, and comparison with others, the likelihood that we will fall into insecure self-preoccupation is great. We need the virtues of humility and magnanimity to assist us in turning outward rather than inward.

We are all summoned to the same high calling, and magnanimity, no less than humility, is a virtue that we all require. Reflecting further on what this high calling is reveals even more fully why it—unlike the civic euergetism of Aristotle's magnanimous man—can be achieved only with the assistance of humility. For our part in the *reditus* of creation to God is realized as we accept that God befriended us as sinners and that we are called to extend the community of God's friends by loving our enemies, the overlooked, and the outcast. It is a high, heroic calling that is realized in ways that look anything but heroic, a kind of magnanimity whose public works are not marble monuments but gestures of welcoming, reconciliation, and love. The God to whose image we are made is a God whose goodness is turned outward, not inward, a God of wholly self-giving love. It is also a calling whose way might well lead through the cross, as it did for the One who shows us the way and is the Way. So we need magnanimity to "strengthen us in hoping for the greatest goods" (*ST* II–II.129.5), but only by way of God's great gifts to us, freed through humility from preoccupation either with our own strength or our own weakness, our own ability or our own insufficiency.

It is not, then, simply that a preoccupation with some great good swamps concern for the self and its status.[22] We might think for a moment of Plato, who likens seeing the Good with falling in love; both have an ecstatic quality about them, as something is discovered that is worth giving oneself up for and over to. It might seem, then, that concern for the self and its status are here swamped by attention to the Good. And yet a dogged line of critique alleges that Platonic love is not genuinely ecstatic but rather pursues the Good as that which enhances the lover's own creativity.[23] Diotima tells Socrates in the *Symposium* that the "life above others which man should lead" is that spent contemplating absolute beauty. For it is in seeing "true beauty simple and divine" that we become able ourselves to bring forth true beauties—that is, in "bringing forth and nourishing true virtue to become the friend of God and be immortal, if mortal man may."[24] Essentially, the concern here is that Platonic magnanimity is not balanced by Platonic humility. It is not sufficient to have one's attention focused for the moment on some great good, some heroic task, rather than on oneself, if this concern is instrumental to or contingent on the enhancement of one's own glory. It would take us too far afield to attempt to adjudicate the complex question of whether or not Plato can be fairly charged with "spiritualized egocentrism."[25] My suggestion is simply that humility adds to magnanimity's ecstatic aspiration to the greatest goods not just an acceptance of fundamental human equality, but also the awareness that one's capacities are gifts rather than achievements, and therefore that the glory that accrues to one's accomplishments is to be referred elsewhere.

I have placed at least a question mark alongside the possibility of Platonic humility. Do I mean, then, to be asserting that only Christians, or those who acknowledge God-given tasks and gifts, can be truly humble (or magnanimous)? No. For there is a naturalistic attitude that can nurture humility: the awareness of the contingent and unearned character of all that comes together to constitute one's capacities—genetic endowment, upbringing, chance occurrences. Here, too, one can cultivate gratitude. Jeffrey Stout calls this piety and looks to Emerson for an apt expression of it: "When I receive a new gift, I do not macerate my body to make the account square, for, if I should die, I could not make the account square. The benefit overran the merit the first day, and has overrun the merit ever since. The merit itself, so called, I reckon part of the receiving."[26]

Emerson grasps that pusillanimity and self-abasement are no substitute for grateful acknowledgment. Similarly, I see no reason to deny a secular magnanimity that strengthens hope in seeking the common good rather than focusing on one's own glory—indeed, as rooted in this same acknowledgment that one's own merits and achievements, like those of others, are gift-enabled. If this magnanimity remains imperfect given its failure to acknowledge God as giver, Christian magnanimity, too, remains in manifold other respects short of its eschatological consummation.

Gratitude fosters humility, then, by disposing a person to regard her capacities as gifts, and thus by shifting her attention from herself and her merit to the great goods to which magnanimity hopefully aspires. Humility also stands in a special relationship with friendship. Where pride isolates, humility paves the way for friendship. For the prideful engage in just the kind of comparisons with others for which the humble have no need. The prideful are focused on themselves and their status and hence cannot but regard their friends through the lens of perceived inferiority or superiority, as those who enhance our standing by way of association, or whose subordinate status feeds our sense of self-esteem.[27] But we might also just as appropriately say that friendship fosters humility. We see this when we recall Aquinas' account of humility and magnanimity against the backdrop of the *exitus* and *reditus* of creation. There is a teleological character to these virtues that it is important to recognize. For we are called to grasp not simply that we are equally beloved children of God but also that we are summoned to participate in creation's return to God by realizing our call as creatures made to the divine image. God is revealed as the befriender, gifting Godself to us in Jesus Christ, who is preoccupied not with his own status in relation to God but with the task of befriending strangers and enemies. Grasping that we have been befriended by God in this way is what frees us for both humility and magnanimity, for awareness of our capacities as gifts and for the hopeful employment of those gifts in befriending others. We become *imago dei* as we more and more fully receive the gifts given to us and more and more fully pour ourselves out in self-gift. Where we grasp ourselves as beloved and befriended so absolutely, the gnawing insecurity that keeps us preoccupied with our own status and feeds competition with would-be friends is stilled. Friendship, then, prepares the ground for humility, which in turn opens the way for friendship.

Indeed, for Aquinas, charity—the infused theological virtue that becomes the form guiding and directing all Christian virtues—just *is* friendship with God. It is God communicating God's own goodness to human beings in such a way that they themselves become capable of *amicitia*, of self-giving friendship, with God and one another. Thomas is guided here by Scripture, notably by Jesus' farewell discourse in the Gospel of John: "I will not now call you servants . . . but My friends" (John 15:15); and 1 Corinthians 1:9: "God is faithful: by Whom you are called unto the fellowship of His Son" (II-II.23.1). Human beings, he tells us, are invited into a fellowship and communication (*conversatio*) with God that can be imperfectly experienced now but that will be eschatologically perfected (II–II.23.1 ad 1; 23.3).[28] Befriended by God, we begin to love all that is loved by our friend. Hence, out of charity our friendship extends to all, even enemies and sinners. God's be-friending of us, then frees us for a humility that fosters and invites friendship with others. That this is so helps us understand why human friendship, too, is not simply fostered by humility but also the gift that can make friendship possible.

It is time to circle back around to joy. For we are now in a position to see how humility, despite its association with deflation and bending low to the earth, actually fosters joy. For humility dismantles tendencies that interfere with our ability to take delight in the way things are. It also renders joy more durable, by rooting it in something that is not subject to fluctuation. Joy can, as we noted at the outset, be taken in pretty much anything that someone is capable of surveying with satisfaction or delight. Humility, together with its twin virtue of magnanimity, fosters durable joy in a particular domain, having to do with one's self and one's agency.

We might think that someone with an inflated sense of self-importance, while lacking in humility, finds in feelings of self-importance a source of significant joy. And this might indeed be the case. Think of Professor Top-of-the-Heap, who takes great delight and satisfaction in surveying his Amazon rankings and monitoring his citation reports. At the same time, Professor Top-of-the-Heap feels threatened when his rankings fall and envious of his colleague Professor Trendy, whose research seems to be garnering ever-increasing attention. Professor Top-of-the-Heap's joy is fragile, vulnerable to threats to his status. Moreover, the fact that his sense of self-esteem rests on rankings in this way blocks the possibility of friendship with Professor Trendy and others. And friendship is a source of joy—one rejoices in the very being of one's friend, and enjoys the company of one's friend, indeed, enjoys the friendship itself. One's friend's achievements enhance rather than threatening one's joy. The vices of pride and vanity deprive one of the joys of friendship. Professor Top-of-the-Heap also lacks the virtue of magnanimity and its attendant joys. He is preoccupied with his own importance, not the significance of his research undertakings. When his rankings fall, he is consumed with doubt over whether he has pursued the best line of research or ought rather to have anticipated Professor Trendy's topics. He cannot take joy in having contributed to something of genuine and lasting significance.

Contrast Professor-Top-of-the-Heap with Professor Perseverant, who has been working for twenty years to analyze the envelope glycoproteins of the HIV virus. Possessing the virtue of humility, Professor Perseverant is filled with gratitude for all that led her into this lifework—the undergraduate professor whose virology course captured her imagination, the postdoctoral fellowship that landed her a spot in a leading proteomic lab, the colleague whose effervescent imagination sparked Professor Perseverant's current line of investigation, the friends whose companionship makes time in the lab enjoyable. Professor Perseverant is grateful for her own character, and the way it enables her research—grateful that she has been gifted with the patience to persist through years of repetitive experiments and disappointing results, and with a skill at analyzing inconclusive masses of data. When a coauthored paper is published in the journal *Science*, she rejoices, knowing that this will boost the chances of further NIH funding, funding that could lead to a breakthrough with clinical implications. When she retires, no breakthrough in sight, she is nevertheless filled with joy, satisfied that her energies have been dedicated to something worthwhile.

Professor Perseverant's humility disposes her toward the joys of friendship. She is aware that both her own achievements and those of others are not pure achievement but rest on gifts received. Hence, both can be a source of joy, as she surveys with delight what these gifts make possible. Clearly, she also possesses the virtue of magnanimity, and this, too, gives rise to joy, for it strengthens her hope in contributing to the achievement of a great good. Given her humility, she does not regard this contribution as significant because it proves her own greatness; her attention is focused primarily on the great undertaking itself. Should she not succeed, or should success not be evident, she can nevertheless take satisfaction (and therefore find joy) simply in having been *for* this great good, and in having been *for* it together with others.

I have noted both that it is possible to take joy in anything one can survey with delight and satisfaction and that humility and magnanimity dispose us to more durable and stable joys. Of course, we ought to seek not simply maximally great and lasting joy, but good joy, joy that is taken in things and states of affairs that are good. To be virtuous is to take joy only in what is good. If Professor Perseverant discovers that her closest colleague and friend has been fabricating the data on which a decade's worth of publications have been based, her joy in having contributed to those publications evaporates. She is incapable of delighting in them now. Since humility and magnanimity are virtues, they dispose their possessors not just to stable and lasting joy but to good joy. They do so imperfectly, however, unless they are complemented by all of the other virtues. Had Professor Perseverant possessed greater prudence, for instance, she would have examined her colleague's data more closely. Had she been more courageous, she would have confronted her colleague earlier.

Magnanimity is a source of joy insofar as one surveys with delight the fact that one is devoted to the pursuit of a great good. It matters, of course, that this truly be a great good. But while one's joys are always revealing of what one cares about, not all joy is delight in something great. Some of the most easily accessible joys are simple joys: delight in a clear blue sky, in a child's smiling face, in the feel of a smooth, cool pebble. Of course, one can take joy in something that one would unhesitatingly lay aside were something of greater significance at stake—leave a savored hour of solitary reading without a backward glance, say, should a phone call come from a student in distress. I can take joy in visiting an invalid friend, but not if I am preoccupied the whole time with the thought that I should be getting a head start on the weekend's household chores. The perfectly magnanimous (i.e., those in whom magnanimity is attended by the full complement of virtues) are not less capable of simple joys because of their devotion to the pursuit of a great good; they are simply clear about when one undertaking ought properly be given up for the sake of another. Lack of clarity concerning how various concerns ought to be ordered, on the other hand, interferes with even the simplest joys, as one waffles and worries over whether one's energies are being aptly deployed. The perfectly humble, who regard both their own and others' achievements as gift-enabled, are disposed to view not just everything they do but everything they experience as gift-laden.

The humble-and-magnanimous, then, are capable of rejoicing in everything that they do. This is not to deny that their lives might be filled with loss and disappointment. Even if their joy is not destroyed by a sense of insecurity or threat from others, eroded by the vices of pride or pusillanimity, their virtues do not insulate them from all evils. Nevertheless, in fighting injustice, they rejoice to be aligning themselves with the just; in mourning a loved one, they rejoice that this loved one was present in their lives, and in the fittingness of mourning. They can, to be sure, imagine a fuller joy, in which there is no injustice to oppose, no loss to mourn. But they are nevertheless filled with joy. Not only do the good find occasion for joy everywhere and always, their joy echoes or reverberates: I can rejoice in your joy in something's being as it ought to be, and you can rejoice in my rejoicing over your joy. Humility and magnanimity facilitate the reverberation of joy. Humility does so by regarding this capacity to rejoice as gift, source of gratitude rather than of invidious pride. Magnanimity does so by recognizing this as a great good worthy of hopeful and energetic pursuit.

The perfectly humble-and-magnanimous grasp their hopeful pursuit of great goods as participating in the *reditus* of creation to God. They relate all that they do to this great pursuit, allow it to order all goods. And they regard the gifts that enable this participation, including their own great virtues, as gifts from God. They understand themselves as equally beloved children of God, called to *conversatio* with God, called into a circle of fellowship that invites in the stranger and the enemy, befriending others into endlessly reverberating joy. And they rejoice.

• • •

Response to Jennifer A. Herdt

Lisa Sowle Cahill

By showing its interdependence with joy and magnanimity, Jennifer Herdt illumines the importance of humility—an unfairly maligned virtue—and its essential role in human flourishing. The Christian recognizes that human flourishing is "a sharing in the self-giving Trinitarian life," a relationship Herdt characterizes, with Aquinas, as the "friendship" with God made possible by divine grace (82; see *ST* I–II.65.5 and II–II.23.2). In the same key, Herdt grounds humility, joy, and magnanimity in the conferral of worth on the subject by God, whose love is bestowed in Christ (85–87), a gift to which humility fosters increasing openness (82, citing *ST* II–II.161.5 ad2).

But there is an important difference between Jennifer Herdt's and Thomas Aquinas' portrayals of flourishing and virtue. Unlike Aquinas, Herdt does not differentiate forms of flourishing, friendship, and virtue that are *natural* to humans as humans from the graced counterparts that take human flourishing to an entirely new (supernatural) level, that of friendship with God. Instead Herdt only speaks of one, comprehensive sort of flourishing, one graced kind of friendship with God, that defines what humans are meant to be, and the happiness to which they are called.

This holistic approach to human nature, ends, and happiness seems to reflect Augustine better than Aquinas. Augustine insists that authentic human happiness (and any real virtue at all) necessarily rests in charity—love of God as the highest good (*summum bonum*), the anchoring good, in relation to whom all other goods are ordered and appropriately loved.[1] From a perspective in which humility rests in rightly ordered love, humility becomes an attractive virtue: the honest appreciation of one's own place in creation, the gift of true self-knowledge.

Such a rendering of the virtue includes an essential safeguard against the abusive view that humility is a special virtue of the lowly and the subjugated (for example, women). To the contrary, humility is the ability to see everyone and everything, including oneself, in its *proper* place, including the self's peculiar worthiness and limits. If we evaluate reality rightly, Herdt explains, we will "know both our capacities and our incapacities, our virtues and our vices," exaggerating or minimizing neither (86). Thus humility activates "God's great gifts to us, freed through humility from preoccupation either with our own strength or our own weakness, our own ability or our own insufficiency" (88). Far from being a deadweight of self-abasement, humility is a springboard for self-confidence. Humility attunes the self to convergences of actual capacities and opportunities.

Thus lived and understood, humility fosters joy—the ability to delight in reality as it is, as fit, acceptable, and good. Humility dismantles distorted perceptions that create anxiety, envy, scrupulosity, loss of self-respect, discouragement, and despair—as well as hubris, narcissism, self-promotion, and indifference to the plight of other people. Humility inspires us to embrace friends and friendships, knowing that we have already been befriended by God.

The humble person is freed to reach toward worthwhile goals and especially to serve and empower vulnerable neighbors. This outward goal-directed and service-oriented movement, explains Herdt, is the virtue of magnanimity in action. Herdt affirms Aquinas' insight that humility and magnanimity are counterparts. In a Christian vein, Herdt emphasizes that the premise of magnanimity is the recognition that all one's capacities are divinely bestowed gifts. Our gifts are then poured out in self-gift (89). The related emotion, joy, is the delight attendant on "the pursuit of a great good" (92), carried out within, and for the sake of, friendship with God. There has been a revival of theological interest in humility over the past few decades,[2] but the same has not been true of magnanimity. The common notion of magnanimity must also be corrected: magnanimity does not spring from greed for public honors or from assurance of one's superiority to others. Instead, aligned with humility, it radiates what Pope Francis calls "the joy of the gospel."[3]

This comprehensive and celebratory vision of the virtues as joyful propensities to love all things in relation to God; of all life as fulfilled in so loving; and of all human flourishing, virtue, and happiness as dependent on the grace of Christ, are strongly reminiscent of Augustine. And, like Herdt, Augustine believed humility to be key to the Christian life. "This way is first humility, second humility, third humility and no matter how often you keep asking me I will say the same over and over again."[4]

Aquinas certainly agreed with Augustine that perfect flourishing depends on grace, and on what he (Aquinas) termed the "theological" virtues (faith, hope, and charity; see *ST* I–II.62.1–3.). But Aquinas also specified that the natural or cardinal virtues (prudence, justice, fortitude, and temperance) "arise from certain natural principles pre-existing in us" (I–II.63.3) and are real (if imperfect) virtues. They are appropriate perfections of humanity's created nature, a participation in divine wisdom, and the embodiment of God's will for human creatures.

This comparison of Augustine and Aquinas on flourishing, virtue, and grace suggests two theological questions that may be ripe for reconsideration in our contemporary context. One question is for Aquinas: How much sense does it make theologically and ethically to distinguish humanity's natural and supernatural ends, and the natural and theological virtues? This technical distinction is not made by Augustine, for whom there is only one human end, love of God as the highest good, and one true virtue, charity and its derivative dispositions. The other is for Augustine: Is it right to insist, as "orthodox" Christianity has done ever since Augustine's battle with Pelagius, that nothing of the offer or acceptance of grace is our own, for all is grace, and purely so? Or that it is limited to the faithful? As Augustine says, "The love of God is shed abroad in our hearts, not by the free choice whose spring is in ourselves, but through the Holy Spirit which is given us."[5] (Aquinas agrees, as far as the theological virtues are concerned [I–II.113.3 and 7].)

In reply to Aquinas, the "Augustinian" Herdt seems to say that we experience our longing and striving for God as one continuous process, because by nature we are made for God "and our heart is restless until it rests in [God]."[6] Yet in reply to the anti-Pelagian Augustine, the Aquinas-informed Herdt implies that our efforts are relevant to flourishing's success, for she stresses that by cultivating humility we will be more "open" to the inflow of grace (82, citing *ST* 161.5.ad2; but see I–II.114.2). She does not explicitly limit this grace to Christians.

Human responsibility and initiative are important, not only from the standpoint of individual spirituality, but also from that of Christian education and moral formation. Augustine acknowledges as much, not only in his sermons, but also when he lambastes his parents for their overly permissive attitudes toward his teenage sexual experimentation.[7] Parents, teachers, and ecclesial communities put a good deal of effort into, and invest much importance and value in, an active commitment to moral formation. They provide children especially and adult members as well with instruction, liturgies, and examples that hold up and inspire Christian virtue. Christian versions of virtues like humility and magnanimity are not constructed on top of, but holistically subsume, through an integrated life, our human capacities and virtues.

In fact, Aquinas himself suggests (like Herdt) that our acquired virtues and vices can help or hinder what Herdt calls our "openness" to grace, for the theological virtues may not immediately result in changed behavior if habits of acquired vice stand in the way (I–II.65.3). Furthermore, in the process of conversion and sanctification, Aquinas indicates a sort of "synergy" between the natural and supernatural by proposing that, along with charity, there are infused *moral* virtues (I–II.65.3 and 5) that better align and conform nature with grace, as well as gifts of the Holy Spirit that continually inspire our occasional responses (I–II.68.8).

In fact, joy is one of those gifts (following St. Paul) (I–II.70.3; cf. II–II.28.1). Aquinas does not imagine joy as arising except as the consequence of charity. The implication, clearly, is that there is no purely "natural" kind of joy. Yet this does seem counterfactual, unless we hypothesize (with Karl Rahner) that while "pure nature" is a theoretical construct, real nature is always already de facto the recipient of the grace by which *all* are indeed called to union with God in Christ.[8]

Similarly Herdt: "The perfectly humble-and-magnanimous" are "participating in the *reditus* of creation to God." They are "called into a circle of fellowship that invites in the stranger and the enemy, befriending others into endlessly reverberating joy" (93). My guess is that Herdt intends her renditions of the virtues of humility and magnanimity, as well as of joy, primarily to express and enhance Christian faith and theology for the church. Yet on a larger horizon, Herdt seems to envision the joyful destiny of humanity as such, not excluding the humble, magnanimous, and loving multitudes who do not confess Christ. If so, I agree. Yet our common vision then goes beyond both Augustine and Aquinas; it is a salutary Christian reconstruction that our contemporary experience of faith and of the virtues demands.

• • •

REPLY TO LISA SOWLE CAHILL

Jennifer A. Herdt

Can I truly claim to have offered a Thomistic account of the virtue of humility? Is my account not perhaps more Augustinian, insofar as I do not distinguish between our natural and supernatural ends? And do I not depart from both Aquinas and Augustine in refusing to see grace as limited to the faithful? These, I take it, are the core questions posed to me by Lisa Cahill's gracious yet probing response to my essay. At stake is whether humility is to be understood as an acquired or an infused virtue, whether it is directed toward natural or supernatural flourishing, and whether humility can be possessed by non-Christians. Most centrally, however, the question is whether any defensible Christian virtue ethic requires reconstruction rather than simple fidelity to either Thomas or Augustine.

Space being tight, I will focus on Aquinas, while happily acknowledging the Augustinian flavor of my account. Humility is for Thomas a "part" of the cardinal virtue of temperance. Hence, it might seem to be a simple matter to determine that humility ought to be considered an acquired rather than an infused virtue. Yet matters are not so straightforward, since Thomas holds not only that the theological virtues of faith, hope, and charity are infused, but also that Christians receive infused moral virtues and so infused counterparts of each of the cardinal virtues. Insofar as Aquinas in his extended discussions of the cardinal virtues in the *Secunda Secundae* is offering an account not of the pagan virtues but rather of the virtues in Christians, it is sensible to assume that he is discussing the infused moral virtues except insofar as he specifies otherwise. With this assumption in place, it is not surprising, as it otherwise might be, to find Aquinas claiming that humility denotes subjection to God. We understand Thomas' account of humility most fully, I have argued, when we think of humility as exemplified by Jesus Christ, since Jesus is always for Aquinas the perfect exemplar of human virtue, both receiving divine grace most fully and most fully acknowledging and relying on that grace. Yet I have argued at the same time that it is coherent on this Thomistic account to make sense of a virtue of humility among those who do not acknowledge God or their dependence on God. How can this be?

On Thomas' account, it is possible in the absence of infused charity to acquire virtues that are properly termed true and even perfect in some senses: they are habits, enabling particular operations to be completed with ease and facility; they are good and cause their possessor to do good and to become good; they conduce to human flourishing and happiness in this life. At the same time, only the infused virtues, directed toward the ultimate good of beatitude, are *simply* true and perfect. The infused virtues are both necessary and sufficient to conduce to beatitude; the acquired virtues are neither. Thomas takes Christians normally to possess *both* acquired and infused virtues.[1] What would be the final end of the acquired virtues, were these the sole virtues possessed by the agent, now becomes a proximate end ordered to a further end that is now the final end.

In his discussion of the way in which distinct virtues are defined by distinct formal objects (human reason, for acquired virtues; the divine rule, for infused virtues), Thomas highlights not just the fact that acquired and infused virtues are different species but that they issue in different acts, acts that are at least sometimes apparently incompatible with one another. For instance, he underscores that the divine rule mandates asceticism, "chastising the body and bringing it into submission," while reason mandates care for bodily health (*ST* I–II.64.4). It is thus not evident how a single agent, possessing both acquired and infused temperance, can pursue the mean fixed by human reason while ordering that to the mean fixed by the divine rule. In light of this point, it is important to acknowledge that the infused virtues do for Thomas thoroughly transform the acquired virtues. When what has previously served as final end (say, the political common good) is now grasped as a proximate end directed to the further final end of friendship with God, nothing remains the same. This means that we should not expect perfect agreement between the justice, temperance, or fortitude of those possessing only the acquired virtues and those who have been given the infused virtues. On the other hand, just because the acquired and infused virtues properly speaking always have different proximate ends does not mean they cannot *often* be close functional analogues of one another. "Christians are, for instance, not called to behave badly with respect to human affairs, just because they are called to behave well in respect of being fellow-citizens with the saints and the household of God. . . . Thomas affirms that the act of acquired virtue can be meritorious, generating an act ordered to a higher end, by means of infused virtue's referral of that act (*De virtutibus in communi* 10 ad 4). This can only be the case if there are acts of acquired virtue that are *not* in tension with acts of infused virtue."[2] There is plenty of room for cooperation, then, among Christians and non-Christians, even if technically speaking they never perform the same acts.

Thomas can thus affirm both acquired and infused humility—the former directed toward natural human flourishing, and the latter directing this toward the end of friendship with God. Both acknowledge the dependent character of human achievement; the latter gratefully acknowledges dependence on divine grace. My account is fully compatible with this. I do not, however, follow Aquinas in all respects.

Thomas holds that children receive grace and the infused virtues at baptism, since they are united with Christ. Otherwise, they would not come to eternal life were they to die immediately following baptism. While some earlier thinkers were willing to countenance the damnation of unbaptized infants, Thomas takes it for granted that this would be an unacceptable consequence of such a position (*ST* III.69.6). Infused grace is both necessary and sufficient for salvation, regardless of whether anything Aristotle would deem virtue is present. Were infants and idiots to be damned, God's justice would be called into question. Aquinas does not, though, think that God's justice is similarly called into question if pagans (whether vicious or virtuous) are damned. I am not persuaded. I do not conclude that acquired virtue is sufficient for salvation, since this would be to fall into a works righteousness that Aquinas rejects no less unequivocally than did the Protestant reformers. It is always grace that effectively directs us to our final end in God. Does it follow that my account is not truly Thomistic, insofar as it amounts to reconstruction rather than strict fidelity? Yes; but I take it that it thereby follows Thomas' own example. His respect even for the greatest of teachers and *auctoritates* took the form not of simple deference but rather of dialogical engagement.

• • •

Notes to Chapter 3
(Jennifer A. Herdt)

1 I am grateful to the multiple audiences and readers who have offered thoughtful feedback on successive versions of this essay: the faculty research roundtable at Biola's Center for Christian Thought, February 24, 2017; the Center for Christian Thought's sixth annual meeting, "Humility: Moral, Religious, Intellectual," May 6–7, 2017; the Yale Center for Faith and Culture's consultation on Humility and Joy, April 28, 2017, part of the Center's project on the Theology of Joy and the Good Life, supported by a grant from the John Templeton Foundation; and participants in the Project Leadership Team meeting for Theology of Joy and the Good Life, August 5–7, 2017. I am also indebted to Bob Roberts for his helpfully detailed comments on an earlier draft of this essay.
2 Robert C. Roberts, *Spiritual Emotions* (Grand Rapids: Eerdmans, 2007), 116. Miroslav Volf's definition is close to this: "We can define joy as emotional attunement between the self and the world—usually a small portion of it—experienced as blessing" ("The Crown of the Good Life: A Hypothesis," in *Joy and Human Flourishing*, ed. Miroslav Volf and Justin Crisp [Minneapolis: Fortress, 2015], 130).
3 Roberts, *Spiritual Emotions*, 118.

4   Volf therefore differentiates joy from "true joy": "True joy presumes proper relation to some actual good" ("Crown of the Good Life," 135).
5   The *locus classicus* here is Valerie Saiving's "The Human Situation: A Feminine View," *Journal of Religion* 40, no. 2 (1960): 100–112.
6   Benedict, *The Rule of St. Benedict*, rev. ed., trans. Justin McCann (London: Sheed and Ward, 1976).
7   As related in Thomas Aquinas, *Summa Theologiae*. English translations are taken from *Summa Theologica*, trans. Fathers of the English Dominican Province (New York: Benziger Brothers, 1948), II–II Q.161.6 ad3.
8   David Hume, *Enquiry concerning the Principles of Morals* (Oxford: Clarendon, 1998), §9, ¶3.
9   Augustine, *De Virginit.* 31, quoted in *ST* 161.6 ad 2; see also *Enarr. in Ps.*, *Corpus Christianorum, Series Latina* (Turnhout: Brepols, 1981), 38:239.
10 One might, of course, identify magnanimity instead as a virtuous *form* of pride. In Aquinas' terms, however, pride is a vice, not a virtue.
11 I discuss Aquinas' account of magnanimity more fully, in relation to debates over Aristotelian magnanimity, in "Strengthening Hope for the Greatest Things: Aquinas's Redemption of Magnanimity," in *The Measure of Greatness: Philosophers on Magnanimity*, ed. Sophia Vasalou, 70–85 (Oxford: Oxford University Press, 2019). In defense of a dialectical reading of Aristotelian magnanimity, see René Gauthier, *Magnanimité* (Paris: J. Vrin, 1951), 116–17; Jacob Howland, "Aristotle's Great-Souled Man," *Review of Politics* 64, no. 1 (2002): 31; Howard Curzer, "A Great Philosopher's Not So Great Account of Great Virtue: Aristotle's Treatment of 'Greatness of Soul,'" *Canadian Journal of Philosophy* 20, no. 4 (1990): 517–38; Harry Jaffa, *Thomism and Aristotelianism* (Chicago: University of Chicago Press, 1952), 130, 133, 139, 141; on Aquinas in relation to Aristotelian magnanimity, see David Horner, "What It Takes to Be Great: Aristotle and Aquinas on Magnanimity," *Faith and Philosophy* 15, no. 4 (1998): 428; Mary M. Keys, "Aquinas and the Challenge of Aristotelian Magnanimity," *History of Political Thought* 24 (2003): 37–65, reprinted in *Aquinas, Aristotle, and the Promise of the Common Good* (Cambridge: Cambridge University Press, 2006), 143–72; Rebecca Konyndyk DeYoung, "Aquinas' Virtues of Acknowledged Dependence: A New Measure of Greatness," *Faith and Philosophy* 21 (2004): 214–27; and Tobias Hoffmann, "Albert the Great and Thomas Aquinas on Magnanimity," in *Virtue Ethics in the Middle Ages: Commentaries on Aristotle's Nicomachean Ethics, 1200–1500*, ed. Istvan Bejczy (Leiden: Brill, 2007), 101–29.
12 See Brian Shanley, "Aquinas's Exemplar Ethics," *Thomist* 72, no. 3 (2008): 353–54; and Joseph Wawrykow, "Jesus in the Moral Theology of Thomas Aquinas," *Journal of Medieval and Early Modern Studies* 42, no. 1 (2012): 13–34. Shanley points to a number of other scholars who note Christ's exemplar causality for Thomas: L.-B. Gillon pointed out the significance of imitation of Christ in Thomas' preaching and Scripture commentaries, a point that has been underscored more recently by Jean-Pierre Torrell. L.-B. Gillon, "L'imitation du Christ et la morale de saint Thomas," *Angelicum* 36 (1959): 263–86; Jean-Pierre Torrell, "Imiter Dieu come des enfants bien-aimé," in *Recherches thomasiennes* (Paris: J. Vrin, 2000), 325–35. Even in the *Summa*,

Thomas insists that all of Christ's actions are meant to serve as instruction for us. See Richard Schenk, "*Omnis Christi actio nostra est instructio*: The Deeds and Sayings of Jesus as Revelation in the View of Thomas Aquinas," in *La doctrine de la revelation divine de saint Thomas d'Aquin*, ed. Léon Elders, Studi Tomistici 37 (Rome: Libreria Editrice Vaticana, 1990), 104–31.
13 Roberts, *Spiritual Emotions*, 82.
14 Roberts, *Spiritual Emotions*, 82.
15 Roberts, *Spiritual Emotions*, 83.
16 Roberts, *Spiritual Emotions*, 88–89.
17 Robert C. Roberts and W. Jay Wood, "Humility and Epistemic Goods," in *Intellectual Virtue*, ed. Michael DePaul and Linda Zagzebski (Oxford: Clarendon, 2007), 261.
18 Roberts and Wood, "Humility and Epistemic Goods," 262.
19 Roberts and Wood, "Humility and Epistemic Goods," 262.
20 Hence, humility is not simply to be identified with gratitude, for humility is specifically a matter of having an appropriate attitude toward oneself, while gratitude has to do with an appropriate attitude toward those to whom one is indebted. Yet the two virtues are closely related and mutually reinforcing.
21 Julia Annas helpfully suggests that a person engaged in virtuous activity experiences what psychologist Mihalyi Csikszentmihalyi describes as "flow," the "enjoyable performance of activity which requires engagement and expertise," one feature of which is a loss of self-consciousness (*Intelligent Virtue* [Oxford: Oxford University Press, 2011], 71–72). Humility, then, is aware of the gifts that enable one's virtuous activity, while magnanimity is focused on the great vocation one has been enabled to undertake.
22 This is close to what Roberts and Wood claim: "We propose that the concern for status is swamped or displaced or put on hold by some overriding virtuous concern" ("Humility and Epistemic Goods," 261).
23 See, e.g., Gregory Vlastos' discussion of "spiritualized egocentrism"; the "true beauties" that are brought forth are not chosen to "enrich the lives of persons who are themselves worthy of love for their own sake" (Gregory Vlastos, "The Individual as Object of Love in Plato," in *Platonic Studies*, 2nd ed. [Princeton: Princeton University Press, 1981], 3–42). This objection becomes the basis for Martha Nussbaum's critique of Platonic ascent in *Upheavals of Thought: The Intelligence of Emotions* (Cambridge: Cambridge University Press, 2001), 496–500; Plato, *Symposium*, ed. K. Dover (Cambridge: Cambridge University Press, 1980), 113; G. M. A. Grube, *Plato's Thought* (London: Methuen, 1935), 87–119; Nussbaum, *Fragility of Goodness* (Cambridge: Cambridge University Press, 1986), 178–79.
24 But see Kevin Corrigan, "Love of God, Love of Self, and Love of Neighbor: Augustine's Critical Dialogue with Platonism," *Augustinian Studies* 34, no. 1 (2003): 97–106; as Corrigan argues, "Augustine, like Plotinus, as well as Aristotle and Plato, sees the question of self-relatedness as essentially a function of other-relatedness" (105). That is, loving the Supreme Good

decisively transforms all of our other loves, rather than being an ultimate fulfillment of a prior love of self.
25 Vlastos, "Individual as Object of Love," xx.
26 Ralph Waldo Emerson, *Emerson: Essays and Lectures*, ed. Joel Porte (New York: Library of America, 1983), 491; quoted in Jeffrey Stout, *Democracy and Tradition* (Princeton: Princeton University Press, 2004), 38.
27 Roberts' discussion is penetrating. See *Spiritual Emotions*, 86–87.
28 Anna Williams, *The Ground of Union: Deification in Aquinas and Palamas* (Oxford: Oxford University Press 1999), 71–82; Olivia Blanchette, *The Perfection of the Universe according to Aquinas* (University Park: Penn State University Press, 1992), 292.

NOTES TO CHAPTER 3 RESPONSE
(LISA SOWLE CAHILL)

1 See Augustine, *Mor. eccl.* 15.
2 See, for example, Lisa Fullam, *The Virtue of Humility: A Thomistic Apologetic* (Lewiston, N.Y.: Edwin Mellen, 2009); Stephen E. Pardue, *The Mind of Christ: Humility and the Intellect in Early Christian Theology* (London: T&T Clark, 2013); Gerald W. Schlabach, "Augustine's Hermeneutic of Humility: An Alternative to Moral Imperialism and Moral Relativism," *Journal of Religious Ethics* 22, no. 2 (1994): 299–330; and Brian Dunkle, "Humility, Prophecy, and Augustine's Harmony of the Gospels," *Augustinian Studies* 44, no. 2 (2013): 207–25.
3 Pope Francis, *Evangelium gaudium (The Joy of the Gospel)*, 2013, http://w2.vatican.va/content/francesco/en/apost_exhortations/documents/papa-francesco_esortazione-ap_20131124_evangelii-gaudium.html.
4 Augustine, "Letter 118, To Dioscorus," in *Letters of St. Augustine*, ed. Philip Schaff (Peabody, Mass.: Hendrickson, 1994), 437–38.
5 Augustine, *The Spirit and the Letter*, I.5, in *Later Works*, ed. John Burnaby (Philadelphia: Westminster, 1955), 198.
6 Augustine, *Confessions*, I.1.i., in *Confessions*, ed. Henry Chadwick (Oxford: Oxford University Press, 1991), 3.
7 Augustine, *Confessions*, II.iii.5–8.
8 Karl Rahner, *Foundations of Christian Faith: An Introduction to the Idea of Christianity*, trans. William V. Dych (New York: Crossroad, 1978), 127, on the "supernatural existential" as present to all human beings.

NOTES TO CHAPTER 3 REPLY
(JENNIFER A. HERDT)

1 I here part ways with the unification theorists, who argue that Christians cannot possess acquired virtues, since acquired virtues are ordered to natural happiness as last end, whereas Christians are directed to supernatural happiness as last end. See Angela McKay Knobel, "Two Theories of Christian Virtue," *American Catholic Philosophical Quarterly* 84, no. 3 (2010): 599–618, for an account of the debate between unification theorists and coexistence theorists; and William Mattison for a recent restatement of

the unification theory, a minority stance but one that has had its eminent defenders, notably Gilson; William Mattison, "Can Christians Possess the Acquired Cardinal Virtues?" *Theological Studies* 72 (2011): 558–85. An excellent recent defense of the position that Aquinas regards Christians as typically possessing both acquired and infused virtues is given by David Decosimo in *Ethics as a Work of Charity: Thomas Aquinas and Pagan Virtue* (Stanford: Stanford University Press, 2014).

2 See Jennifer Herdt, "Aquinas and Democratic Virtue: An Introduction," *Journal of Religious Ethics* 44, no. 2 (2016): 233–45.

CHAPTER BIBLIOGRAPHY

Annas, Julia. *Intelligent Virtue*. Oxford: Oxford University Press, 2011.

Augustine. *Confessions*. Edited by Henry Chadwick. Oxford: Oxford University Press, 1991.

———. *Enarr. in Ps.*, Corpus Christianorum, Series Latina. Turnhout: Brepols, 1981.

———. *Later Works*. Edited by John Burnaby. Philadelphia: Westminster, 1955.

———. *Letters of St. Augustine*. Edited by Philip Schaff. Peabody, Mass.: Hendrickson, 1994.

Benedict. *The Rule of St. Benedict*. Rev. ed. Translated by Justin McCann. London: Sheed and Ward, 1976.

Blanchette, Olivia. *The Perfection of the Universe according to Aquinas*. University Park: Penn State University Press, 1992.

Corrigan, Kevin. "Love of God, Love of Self, and Love of Neighbor: Augustine's Critical Dialogue with Platonism." *Augustinian Studies* 34, no. 1 (2003): 97–106.

Curzer, Howard. "A Great Philosopher's Not So Great Account of Great Virtue: Aristotle's Treatment of 'Greatness of Soul.'" *Canadian Journal of Philosophy* 20, no. 4 (1990): 517–38.

Decosimo, David. *Ethics as a Work of Charity: Thomas Aquinas and Pagan Virtue*. Stanford: Stanford University Press, 2014.

DeYoung, Rebecca Konyndyk. "Aquinas' Virtues of Acknowledged Dependence: A New Measure of Greatness." *Faith and Philosophy* 21 (2004): 214–27.

Dunkle, Brian. "Humility, Prophecy, and Augustine's Harmony of the Gospels." *Augustinian Studies* 44, no. 2 (2013): 207–25.

Emerson, Ralph Waldo. *Emerson: Essays and Lectures*. Edited by Joel Porte. New York: Library of America, 1983.

Fullam, Lisa. *The Virtue of Humility: A Thomistic Apologetic*. Lewiston, N.Y.: Edwin Mellen, 2009.

Gauthier, René. *Magnanimité*. Paris: J. Vrin, 1951.

Gillon, L.-B. "L'imitation du Christ et la morale de saint Thomas." *Angelicum* 36 (1959): 263–86.

Grube, G. M. A. *Plato's Thought*. London: Methuen, 1935.

Herdt, Jennifer. "Aquinas and Democratic Virtue: An Introduction." *Journal of Religious Ethics* 44, no. 2 (2016): 233–45.

———. "Strengthening Hope for the Greatest Things: Aquinas's Redemption of Magnanimity." In *The Measure of Greatness: Philosophers on Magnanimity*, edited by Sophia Vasalou, 70–85. Oxford: Oxford University Press, 2019.

Hoffmann, Tobias. "Albert the Great and Thomas Aquinas on Magnanimity." In *Virtue Ethics in the Middle Ages: Commentaries on Aristotle's Nicomachean Ethics, 1200–1500*, edited by Istvan Bejczy, 101–29. Leiden: Brill, 2007.

Horner, David. "What It Takes to Be Great: Aristotle and Aquinas on Magnanimity." *Faith and Philosophy* 15, no. 4 (1998): 415–44.

Howland, Jacob. "Aristotle's Great-Souled Man." *Review of Politics* 64, no. 1 (2002): 27–56.

Hume, David. *Enquiry concerning the Principles of Morals*. Oxford: Clarendon, 1998.

Jaffa, Harry. *Thomism and Aristotelianism*. Chicago: University of Chicago Press, 1952.

Keys, Mary M. "Aquinas and the Challenge of Aristotelian Magnanimity." *History of Political Thought* 24 (2003): 37–65. Reprinted in *Aquinas, Aristotle, and the Promise of the Common Good*, 143–72. Cambridge: Cambridge University Press, 2006.

Knobel, Angela McKay. "Two Theories of Christian Virtue." *American Catholic Philosophical Quarterly* 84, no. 3 (2010): 599–618.

Mattison, William. "Can Christians Possess the Acquired Cardinal Virtues?" *Theological Studies* 72 (2011): 558–85.

Nussbaum, Martha. *Fragility of Goodness*. Cambridge: Cambridge University Press, 1986.

———. *Upheavals of Thought: The Intelligence of Emotions*. Cambridge: Cambridge University Press, 2001.

Pardue, Stephen E. *The Mind of Christ: Humility and the Intellect in Early Christian Theology*. London: T&T Clark, 2013.

Plato. *Symposium*. Edited by K. Dover. Cambridge: Cambridge University Press, 1980.

Rahner, Karl. *Foundations of Christian Faith: An Introduction to the Idea of Christianity*. Translated by William V. Dych. New York: Crossroad, 1978.

Roberts, Robert C. *Spiritual Emotions*. Grand Rapids: Eerdmans, 2007.

Roberts, Robert C., and W. Jay Wood. "Humility and Epistemic Goods." In *Intellectual Virtue*, edited by Michael DePaul and Linda Zagzebski, 257–79. Oxford: Clarendon, 2007.

Saiving, Valerie. "The Human Situation: A Feminine View." *Journal of Religion* 40, no. 2 (1960): 100–112.

Schenk, Richard. "*Omnis Christi actio nostra est instructio*: The Deeds and Sayings of Jesus as Revelation in the View of Thomas Aquinas." In *La doctrine de la revelation divine de saint Thomas d'Aquin*, edited by Léon Elders, 104–31. Studi Tomistici 37. Rome: Libreria Editrice Vaticana, 1990.

Schlabach, Gerald W. "Augustine's Hermeneutic of Humility: An Alternative to Moral Imperialism and Moral Relativism." *Journal of Religious Ethics* 22, no. 2 (1994): 299–330.

Shanley, Brian. "Aquinas's Exemplar Ethics." *Thomist* 72, no. 3 (2008): 345–69.

Stout, Jeffrey. *Democracy and Tradition*. Princeton: Princeton University Press, 2004.

Thomas Aquinas. *Summa Theologica*. Translated by the Fathers of the English Dominican Province. New York: Benziger Brothers, 1948.

Torrell, Jean-Pierre. "Imiter Dieu come des enfants bien-aimé." In *Recherches thomasiennes*, 325–35. Paris: J. Vrin, 2000.

Vlastos, Gregory. "The Individual as Object of Love in Plato." In *Platonic Studies*, 2nd ed., 3–42. Princeton: Princeton University Press, 1981.

Volf, Miroslav. "The Crown of the Good Life: A Hypothesis." In *Joy and Human Flourishing*, edited by Miroslav Volf and Justin Crisp. Minneapolis: Fortress, 2015.

Wawrykow, Joseph. "Jesus in the Moral Theology of Thomas Aquinas." *Journal of Medieval and Early Modern Studies* 42, no. 1 (2012): 13–34.

Williams, Anna. *The Ground of Union: Deification in Aquinas and Palamas*. Oxford: Oxford University Press 1999.

4

Creaturely Humility

Placing Humility, Finding Joy

Norman Wirzba

In the beginning, before the first human being had yet to make an appearance upon the earth, there was a divine Gardener intoxicated with soil. This gardening God loved soil, played with it, even kissed it. With knees on the ground and hands immersed, this God lifted up handfuls of soil and breathed into it the form, fertility, and fecundity that created the first human being, and the first plants, birds, and animals. Soil is no trifling thing. It was created and intended by God as the generative matrix through which life comes, in which it daily abides, and to which it will eventually return upon death. No hospitable soil, no divine animating breath, no intermingling of creatures . . . no life. Simple as that.

The diversity of forms, the vitality of life, the potential for fertility and fruit—all are features of each creature's entanglements with soil, with others, and with God. Lest these entanglements be forgotten, perhaps even despised, the gardening God instructed the first human to join in the divine gardening work that creates and nurtures life. The work was not presented as optional or a punishment. It was, instead, the indispensable apprenticeship in which humans could learn to understand God, themselves, the world, and their place in it. No gardening work, no love of soil and its creatures, no honoring of the animating field in which life moves . . . and life falls apart. Simple as that.

It is tempting to dismiss this biblical story as archaic and out of step with contemporary ways of knowing and being. As most every demographic indicator shows, to be modern or postmodern is to be postagricultural, liberated from what Karl Marx once called "the idiocy of rural life."[1] To think that life makes sense in terms of a gardening God, or that life achieves clarity and fulfillment in the vocation of gardening, is to be stuck in a worldview and anthropology that have been left behind.

But what if this story witnesses to truths about the world and our condition that are not only honest but indispensable for the ways we imagine and implement a distinctly human life? What if we need it, and the anthropology it recommends, to understand the nature of humility and advocate for its authentic realization? And what if the humility birthed in a gardening sensibility is a key element in the experience of joy?

In this essay I will argue that when people acknowledge their *life in*, *dependence on*, and *responsibility for* soil, the recognition of *humility as a fundamental human posture* emerges not as something added to a human life but as that life's most honest realization. To express humility is to witness[2] to the complex, demanding, intimate bonding between humans and humus.[3] Facing honestly, and giving one's life to, soil puts people in a position and posture where they can perceive with unmatched clarity the contours of human life as entangled within and benefited by countless creatures and ecosystem processes large and small. By honoring their entanglements—most basically by being attentive and responsive to the creatures with which they are entangled—people position themselves so they can experience joy as the reception of the help and blessing of others. In other words, humility is rooted in the knowledge that we live only by the countless lives and deaths of others, while joy is born in the grateful acknowledgment of the divine blessing that others—often in the immediacy of their touch—can be to us.

Humble people are marked by their refusal of the hubris that would elevate humanity above soil, exempt them from creaturely responsibilities, and position them to do with life whatever they want, because they know through the testimony of their tongues and stomachs that without soil their life is impossible. Joyful people, in turn, are marked by the freedom with which they acknowledge and receive the gifts that others provide and are. To turn away from the matrix of soil, and the vast diversity of life it encompasses and supports, or to despise it, is to break with our own humanity. It is also to forfeit the knowledge of humility and joy.

It is not clear that today's readers are in an optimal position to interpret Scripture's garden story. Insofar as most people now inhabit an urban, consumerist world, they also inhabit a sensibility and a metaphysic that make it difficult for them to perceive the story's significance or appreciate the insights it is trying to communicate. What does the person growing his or her own food understand about the garden story that the shopper of food simply cannot? In our approach to this story it is crucial that we pay attention to and place under scrutiny the habits of being and systems of valuation that inform our lives and ways of interpretation. How does our consumer placement in the world—we all live by shopping!—and the commodification of things that is its correlate shape the ways we think about life, the meaning of humility, and the prospects for joy?

The thought that a human being (*adam*) is inextricably bound to the soil (*adamah*) and experiences its life in terms of it, the idea that animals and birds might be helpers and kin to human beings, and the vocational sensibility that appreciates care of land and creatures as fundamental, perhaps even nonnegotiable—these positions reflect a sensibility and sensitivity from an unrecognizable era. For those inhabiting a modern, industrial food system, soil signifies as ground to be mined for its nutrients, or as a production platform upon which people exercise their ambition. For the ancient Israelites, however, and other agrarian cultures like them, soil was a moral agent that participates in the judgment of human wrongdoing (Gen 4:10), a medium that speaks truth (Isa 29:4), and a creature that mourns because of the devastation that has been exacted upon it (Joel 1:10). For these people, soil was clearly understood to be a vital, contributing, communicating member of a vast community of creation.[4]

Why attend to soil? Put directly, to misunderstand soil is to misunderstand the human being that arises out of and is bound to it. *Adam* and *adamah* go together, as do *humanity* and the organically rich layer of soil called *humus*, because the life of humanity is impossible and makes no sense apart from the life of soil. The fate of humanity, and by this I mean the nutrition, energy, and health of persons and societies, is inextricably tied to the health and vitality of soils. Soil is not simply the ground *upon which* people stand and move. Soil is forever moving *in and through* our bodies and the geo-eco-bio-physiological matrices that make human life possible, which is why it must be constantly borne in mind and stomach and heart.[5] Soil is a fundamental site of orientation for an embodied human life, which is why people must constantly face it, take their measure from it, and find their inspiration in it.

Environmental historians have long observed that the abuse of the land and its people go hand in hand. One cannot despise soil and not also at the same time despise the creatures that draw their life from it. Put positively, this means that attending to and respecting the earth will have profound implications for how we understand human worth and the processes of identity formation. bell hooks has described this insight powerfully by observing how the histories of slavery (which taught African Americans to despise agricultural work), and then postemancipation urbanization (which physically removed African Americans from the land), enabled racism and white supremacy to become the ultimate factors determining the fate of black people. She argues that African Americans must recover an empowering relationship to the land and find in that relationship an affirmation of their dignity and value that is founded upon the grace of the Creator. She argues, "To tend earth is always to tend our destiny, our freedom and our hope. . . . To live in communion with the earth, fully acknowledging nature's power with humility and grace, is a practice of spiritual mindfulness that heals and restores."[6]

Rethinking Humanity's Place in the World

Access to humility and joy depend on people positioning themselves in the world in particular sorts of ways. Their positioning, in turn, depends on what people understand themselves and the world to be. As we have now to see, the philosophical assumptions that inspire and guide our practical being in the world are not eternally given, fixed, or even (potentially) conducive to the cultivation of a humble humanity. Does not the degradation and violent destruction of many of the world's lands and communities—all evidence of a culture's supposed progress and economic success—testify to a refusal of humility as deeply embedded within the dominant metaphysical picture of our time?

How should we think of the world? How should we describe human beings and their place within it?

Since the time of Aristotle, one of the most common ways to characterize our being in the world has been to use the image of an object in a container. The world is like a massive container that "holds" its inhabitants. It provides the space for things to be and to become. It gives them a location to occupy and a position to stand. With this characterization it is important to underscore that a container does not factor significantly in the constitution or reality of the things it contains. As Aristotle put it in his *Physics* (210b27–30), "The vessel is no part of what is in it." Though things necessarily exist in places—here Aristotle was following the maxim of Archytas, his older contemporary, who said that "to be is to be in place"—they have their reality independent of them. Containers do not determine the things they contain because they only *surround* them. The things contained have their own independent, internally sourced reality. The stone in the pot does not need the pot to substantiate its reality. It would be the same stone any place else because the stone's meaning is derived from *within* rather than from without.[7]

This picture of the world as a container of things, and the stance of separation it presupposes, has been enormously influential. It assumes a world that preexists the things it contains and is more or less static (Aristotle maintained that a place is an "unchangeable limit/motionless boundary" [*Phys.* 212a20–21]). It assumes that there is no intrinsic, mutually constitutive relationship between the container and the things it contains, because things are what they are independent of the places that situate them.

Given these assumptions, it is easy to see how later philosophers would describe the world as a "stage" holding up diverse pieces of furniture that can then be moved around to suit the needs of the various human dramas being played upon it, or as a "production platform" that supports the various extractive and constructive activities of human invention, or as a "store" or "warehouse" that contains multiple commodities that exist ready for the consumer purchase. Though people are *in* the world like an object in a container, they are nonetheless *separate* from it because they do not depend on it for their identity. To be sure, people use the world to satisfy their needs and wants, but in their use they communicate their transcendence above it. The world is a place that gives us a location—a place to stand, move, explore, manipulate, mine, and purchase—but it does not draw us deeply into itself, nor does it get deep into us and shape us from the inside. The identity and vocation of human beings are worked out independently of the world in which they move—which is why it is possible to damage the world without thinking that one has also damaged oneself. The bond between *adam* and *adamah*, between humanity and humus, has been severed.

The metaphor of the world as a container has as its corollary the idea of human life as more or less self-contained. Think, for instance, of today's ideal urban apartment or suburban home, equipped with every modern convenience, as described by the anthropologist Tim Ingold.

> We live in a world turned outside in—what I shall call an inverted world—in which all that moves and grows, shines or burns, or makes a noise has been reconstructed within as a simulacrum or image of the exterior. Real living animals, from mice to spiders, are banished or eradicated to make way for their sculptural counterparts, ornamental plants are placed in pots, picture windows afford a view not unlike that which might be projected on a television screen, artificial light is engineered to simulate the rays of the sun, concealed radiators give off heat from

invisible sources while an imitation coal fire, electrically lit, burns in the grate, and speakers, tastefully placed around the walls, emit recorded sound that could be wind sighing in the trees or waves breaking upon the shore.... Where the earth is, heaven knows—somewhere deep down that we would rather not think about, accessible only to the utility men who come in when the defenses that hold our lives in containment have been breached.[8]

In contexts like these the world is kept *outside*, while much of what we do and value happens *inside* the spaces over which we have firm control. Moving about in climate- and sound-controlled automobiles, we can, if we have a GPS system, get to where we want to go, entirely oblivious to the places through which we move. We can, without having to leave the comforts of the couch, see all or only what we want to see of the world by changing the TV channel or moving to another website. The whole world can be previewed and made ready for purchase simply by clicking the "Submit Your Order" button on the screen of a laptop or smartphone.

Clearly, not all people experience their world this way. Many lack the money and the access to such a world. Even so, the desire to have the world "on demand" or with the ease of a credit card swipe is a fundamental aspiration that inspires politicians and marketers to frame the world in the ways that they do. People, it seems, prefer to live in the world without sympathy or responsibility for it. They want to enjoy it without having to know it or care for it.[9] Like a god, they want to be the transcendent and sovereign choosers who, being anywhere and floating above and about at will, can have anything they want and on their own terms.

The need to know intimately or care practically for the world evaporates when it has been framed as a "resource" and rendered so easily available. To live in a commodified, virtual world, one hardly needs to face it or give one's work or love to it, because *convenience* has replaced *care* and *entertainment* has replaced *engagement* as the primary modes of our being in the world. When shopping becomes the dominant means of our involvement with the world, and when this shopping happens in a global, anonymous economy in which the histories of products and production are unknown, then it is likely that people will misunderstand the world in which they live. In fact, and the mountains of data notwithstanding, they will become the most ignorant, unsympathetic humans the world has ever known with respect to the material contexts of livelihood. They will fail to appreciate the world's fragility and fertility, and its potential and limits. They will be unable to see why care of places matters or what this care practically entails. In this failure, people will also misunderstand themselves and refuse the tasks they most need to do, because the rightness of a life and its flourishing have become self-chosen, individually tailored affairs.[10] They will display a normal, nonmalicious, naïve arrogance.

In contexts like these it is almost impossible to cultivate a disposition of humility because there is no measure of a human life other than the measure we give ourselves, and no felt dependence on or responsibility for the fragile lives of others and the (potential) blessing they might be to us. Nor can there be much joy because the opportunities for people to experience others *as gifts* (rather than purchased commodities), or as sites of nurture and help, have mostly evaporated. Like a stone in a container, we have become atomized units in a world that has become optional. If we do not like where we are or who we are with, we can simply move on or retreat to the virtual worlds of our own making. If we do not like the choices made available to us, we can simply switch to another site on the World Wide Web. Forgetting our embodied entanglements to earth and others, we have fancied ourselves to float above and beyond them.

The everyday metaphysic inscribed in today's consumer culture, and the positioning of humanity in the world it encourages, stand in striking contrast to how most premodern people thought of the world and their place within it. To begin, it is important to note that indigenous and agrarian people do not think of the world as outside or separable from their own life. Nor do they think of human life as self-contained and transcending earth. Land and creatures permeate however they think of themselves and their work. We might say that for these people expectation, desire, and happiness are calibrated to the collective need and potential of places and people that, together with all the creatures there, form *communities* of kinship and shared fate. Human identity and vocation simply do not make sense in isolation from fellow creatures and the material worlds in which people move, because life happens through our entanglements and engagements with them. For traditional, landed folks, places and the creatures they support go deep inside and shape human identity and vocation from within.

It is this complex, *embodied* intertwining of people, places, and fellow creatures that has prompted Tim Ingold to describe human life as a "meshwork." As we now have to see, meshwork thinking reflects a dramatically different metaphysic and ontology in which relationships with and dependencies on others do not simply *occur* but *constitute* the being of whatever is. This meshwork metaphysical picture makes possible an articulation of humanity in which humility registers as the truth of humanity (rather than simply a disposition one may elect to take up) and joy as a genuine possibility. It is a picture that stands in striking contrast to the dominant economic and political forms of our time.

The key to thinking meshwork life is to think with verbs much more than with nouns. This is difficult to do because we have grown accustomed to the idea of the world as a collection of discrete, separable substances that can be classified, ordered, or manipulated to serve various ends.[11] To think with verbs is to call into question the boundaries that keep things separate, because what things *are* is a feature of their entanglements with and movement alongside others. Identities are not fixed or permanent because things are always related to other things in fields of mutual involvement that are constantly changing. The challenge is to conceptualize a field of dynamic interaction and development that does not close in upon itself but remains *open*: "In a world that is truly open there are no objects as such. For the object, having closed in on itself, has turned its back on the world, cutting itself off from the paths along which it came into being, and presenting only its congealed, outer surfaces for inspection. The open world . . . has no such boundaries, no insides or outsides, only comings and goings. Such productive movements may generate formations, swellings, growths, protuberances and occurrences, but not objects."[12]

Nothing in this world exists in and for itself because for anything to be at all it must have already been in relationship with a vast field of others and processes that enable its coming to be. The verbal character of life means that we must not ever lose sight of a thing's *coming-to-be* and its continuing *being-with-others*. The implication that follows is that there must be a narrative dimension to our understanding of the life of things. To know what something "is," we must attend to the many processes and entanglements with others that tell the story of how that thing came to be the thing that it now is. The idea of a self-standing, self-moving, self-determining thing is not only arrogant. It is a fundamental misrepresentation, a distortion, because a thing can only "be" because of its *coming-to-be-with-others*.

To adopt a meshwork metaphysic is difficult because many of us are held captive by what Ingold calls the "logic of inversion." According to this well-established and entrenched logic, the life of things is internal to them. Upon observing a living being, life is most often characterized as an *internal* power or essence working itself *out* (think here of Plato's famous analogy of the interior, invisible hand/soul finding expression in the external, visible glove/body). If this is the case, then it is apparent that the relationships that join living beings to each other, though important, are not constitutive. What a living thing *is* can be thought apart from the gathering of others it finds itself with, because the truth or essence of the thing is internally derived. Having been established internally first, relationships come after: "The establishment of relations *between* these elements—whether they be organisms, persons, or things of any other kind—necessarily requires that each is turned in upon itself prior to its integration into the network. And this presupposes an operation of inversion."[13] Inversion works by turning a thing "in on itself so that its lines and movements of growth become boundaries of containment."[14] People are thus understood to live within their bodies, because life is contained within the boundaries of their skin.

Meshwork thinking undoes the inversion by saying that *things are their relations*. Things have no existence, no life, no meaning apart from the relations that entangle them in a bewildering array of lines of development. Rather than being self-contained like a circle or blob, and then entering into relationship, things are more like open-ended lines that continually make contact with and cling to other things similarly undergoing development. "Organisms and persons, then, are not so much nodes in a network as knots in a tissue of knots, whose constituent strands, as they become tied up with other strands, in other knots, comprise the meshwork."[15] Without this interlacing and knotting—made especially visceral every time we eat—it would be impossible for anything to live. Life is not a property or power internal to a body. Life is our entanglements within a field of beings and movements. If this is true, then *bonds* rather than *boundaries* make life possible. According to Ingold, this is the key insight of animism.

Animism is easily misunderstood, and perhaps too quickly dismissed, as reflecting a primitive sensibility. It is often characterized as the attribution of life, spirit, soul, or agency to objects that are otherwise believed to be inert. Ingold differs, and argues that animism is not about adding to things "a sprinkling of agency but of restoring them to the generative fluxes of the world of materials in which they come into being and continue to subsist."[16] In other words, the dismissal of animism reflects the logic of inversion that assumes life to be within things rather than things within life. "Things are alive and active not because they are possessed of spirit—whether *in* or *of* matter—but because the substances of which they are comprised continue to be swept up in circulations of the surrounding media that alternately portend their dissolution or—characteristically with animate beings—ensure their regeneration. Spirit is the regenerative power of these circulatory flows which, in living organisms, are bound into tightly woven bundles or tissues of extraordinary complexity."[17]

This way of speaking is puzzling to people who have adopted an observational or consumer modality that focuses on discrete objects in space. Such modalities are mostly oblivious to the field of relations in which things in their action and development are constantly bringing each other into varying stages of existence. But if we appreciate that things—whether visibly animate or not—come to be as the things they are because of a history of entanglements with others and with developmental processes, then it becomes evident that animacy is prior to whatever differentiation into things that follows from such entanglement: "Life in the animic ontology is not an emanation but a generation of being, in a world that is not preordained but incipient, forever on the verge of the actual."[18] Drawing on the work of Maurice Merleau-Ponty, a trenchant critic of disembodied notions of perception, Ingold argues that sentient, embodied beings are stitched into the world such that they could not be alive if the world itself were dead.

The stitching characteristic of meshwork life does not simply place us alongside others in external ways, as when surfaces touch. Life is more interdependent, more intimate, than that. To convey this intimacy, it is necessary to adopt the language of sympathy. "Like lines of polyphonic music, whose harmony lies in their alternating tension and resolution, the parts possess an inner feel for one another and are not simply linked by connections of exteriority."[19] In a sympathetic relationship, the members cannot be what they are apart from each other, because who they are is a feature of their togetherness coming to be. In their being they carry the memory, the taste, and the feeling touch, of all those others that have intersected with and contributed to their own development.

The Nature of Humility

Why this rather lengthy discussion of meshwork thinking and the entanglements of things? My point is not simply to differentiate one ontology (substance) from another (meshwork) but to bring in to view the bodily positioning, and the practices and habits of being, that both inspire and reflect these ontologies. A form of life in which people understand themselves to be more or less self-contained and separable from others differs dramatically from a form of life in which people understand themselves to be intimately bound to and constituted by others. Insofar as people inhabit the former, it is much less likely that they will understand humility or bear witness to it in their living. Why? Because to know humility is to know oneself as literally nothing apart from the blessings received from, and the responsibilities owed to, the wide range of others that make one's life possible.[20]

The idea that human beings are self-standing, autonomous, even autarchic beings has become entrenched. People aspire to be apart and in control or, failing such control, at least be exempt from the lives of others and the messy, often violent contexts in which they move. There is a kind of comfort in believing oneself able to retreat into an inviolable self when the weight of the world becomes too much. This desire, however expressed, is a deception. We have never been alone or self-standing. Nor could we be. In fact, the "I" has never been "one." Each "you" is a "zoo" because, to give one example, each human being is quite literally host to the billions of microorganisms that constitute the biome that is our gut.[21]

Clearly this emergent and irreducibly social account of human life calls into question characterizations of agency and responsibility that presuppose an individuated self. But it does not mean moral responsibility has come to an end. What has happened, instead, is a diversification and complexification of the action of response that is now understood to be moving within a world much larger (and smaller) than we had expected. In this context, the ideals of certainty and control will be humbled, and in this humbling a space created for patient attention, faithful commitment, and merciful engagement with others. Humble agency and responsibility do not hesitate to ask for forgiveness and help.

Modern and postmodern forms of life—as reflected in phenomena as diverse as individualism, the quests for autonomy and anonymity, urbanization, industrialism, wage-labor, consumerism, everyday boredom, the pursuit of a techno-utopia—have made humility difficult because they are the expression of the urge to separate, deny dependence, and refuse responsibility. They express the desire to have life conveniently, cheaply, and on one's own terms. The desire here expressed need not be malicious or Promethean. It can just as well be a bored or fearful retreat into isolation so we will not be bothered by the demands of others or troubled by the violent histories of our life together. In contexts of separation like these, verbal professions of humility are bound to sound hollow or false, because they are voiced by people who, in their practical forms of life, consider themselves to be the centers of meaning and value. Though others appear, they do not register as gifts or blessings that call forth our care and celebration.

The misunderstanding and lack of humility are hardly recent phenomena. If we return to the biblical story with which this essay began, it becomes clear that the desire to resist the sympathies and responsibilities of creaturely entanglement has been with humanity from the beginning.[22]

Life in the garden paradise was beautiful, but it was not without its temptations. Foremost among these was the desire to be master of one's life. Did the divine Gardener really say that there are things these human earthlings should and should not do? Why should humans allow themselves to be so limited? And so it occurred to the first humans that they might erase all limits, all need for restraint or responsibility, by simply consuming the fruit of the knowledge of good and evil. By consuming this fruit, the distinction between what should or should not be done was erased as well, and with this erasure humans could think themselves to be free to live the unfettered life they want. Like an imagined god, these earthbound creatures elevated themselves above the ground so as to assume a sovereign position over it. No restraint, no responsibility, no respect . . . a carefree life. Simple as that.

In his commentary on this story, Dietrich Bonhoeffer describes the eating of the forbidden fruit as a *rebellion* against our creaturely condition. "The word *disobedience* fails to describe the situation adequately. It is rebellion, the creature's stepping outside of the creature's only possible attitude, the creature's becoming creator, the destruction of creatureliness, a defection, a falling away from being safely held as a creature."[23] Bonhoeffer argues that a creature is defined by its need to accept life as a gift coming from beyond itself. Indeed, before the Fall, Adam perceived others as a gift because he knew that he lived by grace rather than by the power of his own might. Divine grace is the perpetual giving of what the creature needs to live, while joy is born in the grateful acknowledgment and cherishing of the gifts received.

To reject others as gifts, and to refuse responsibility for them, is to bring about a kind of death. When God declared that the consumption of the forbidden fruit would precipitate death (Gen 2:17), the death talked about was not biological cessation (humans are created as mortal beings) but a deranged, degrading, damaging form of life. To live this deathly life is to desire to live from out of oneself, to assume the posture of a self-moving, self-determining being that no longer needs to acknowledge or respect others.[24] This way of life, and the erosion of sympathies it presupposes, is both dishonest and damaging because it (a) denies that we daily depend on others and God for life and (b) transforms a world of gifts to be gratefully received into an arena of competitive grasping. To rebel against creatureliness is to refuse one's entanglements with and responsibilities for others. It is to take flight from our shared vulnerability. It is to disavow the knowledge that life can only succeed insofar as these entanglements are welcomed and embraced as the meshwork that constitutes and nurtures every creature. The undoing of humility begins here.[25]

The welcome of others as gracious gifts from God is difficult. The issue is not only the admission of one's self-*insufficiency* and the realization that we need others, above all the gift-giving God, to live at all. One must also inhabit dispositions like curiosity and interest that perceive others as compelling and worthy of our attention, effort, and concern. One must presuppose that our welcome and nurture of others is always rooted in the prior realization that we have already been welcomed and nurtured by them.[26] The temptation, however, is to adopt a psychology of separation that involves fear, apathy, boredom, or laziness.

Scott Cairns has pointed to this dimension in his poem "The Entrance of Sin," where he describes Adam and Eve walking about in the garden paradise. He writes that "sin made its entrance long before the serpent spoke." "Rather, sin had come in the midst of an evening stroll, when the woman had reached to take the man's hand and he withheld it." The temptation was not to do something wicked or forbidden or arrogant. The temptation was to *turn away* from a gift offered. "The beginning of loss was this: every time some manner of beauty was offered and declined, the subsequent isolation each conceived was irresistible."[27] Why turn away? Could it be that people hope to find safety or security within themselves, or believe that life really is more manageable without others? What is this *anxiety of creatureliness* that prevents us from cherishing others as the potential sources of our life and joy?

It is customary to define sin as pride and as the arrogant attempt to become a god. As such, sin is the refusal of humility. Bonhoeffer spoke this way when he described humanity's fallen life as the desire to live *sicut deus*. But if the above analyses are correct, then we need to go deeper to witness the drive to separation that turns us inward and away from others as more fundamental. This is why Bonhoeffer, following Martin Luther, also described sin as the heart curved in upon itself (*cor curvum in se*).[28] Using the language of Ingold, we can say that sin takes root insofar as people inhabit and act out of the logic of inversion that presumes life to be a reality interior to themselves. The sinful self, rather than finding its life "outside" itself in its participation in the flows of life going on all around, looks to itself as the place of safety, power, and meaning. What we need to appreciate is that this whole manner of turning or curving inward, besides being a distortion of humanity's being-in-the-world, is fundamentally a forgetting of the self-offering God who, in the body and ministries of Jesus Christ, gives himself to others for the life of the world. God exists not in splendid isolation or from some imperious height but in a communion that is hospitable and outward bound for the sake of others.

Recall in the story that the rebellion against creatureliness is also described as the desire to be like God, *sicut deus*. The presumption in this position is to think that the life of a god consists in being carefree, unfettered, and floating apart from the world. But what if divine life is not like that at all? That it is not is clearly communicated by the Genesis story, where we find the Giver of life to also be the Gardener of life. Gardening is hardly a disinterested or disengaged affair, which is why Scripture says that God looks after the land and that "[t]he eyes of the LORD your God are always on it, from the beginning of the year to the end of the year" (Deut 11:12, NRSV). It is why the psalmist writes that God continually faces each creature, filling it with good things, because the moment God turns away, or withholds the life-giving breath/spirit that holds them in life, they return to their dust (Ps 104:27-30). Again and again we see that the God of life, the God who creates and sustains and saves life, is the God who is dedicated to a self-offering mode of being that is without end. In the life of God there is no turning away from others, no turning inward to retreat from the demands of care. Put another way, the logic of the divine life has no room for the logic of inversion.

Nowhere do these themes come together more clearly than in the Christ-hymn of Philippians. Here Paul describes the life of Christ as a life of humility and service and self-emptying. His mode of being testifies again and again to a meshwork world. Divine life is not the sort of life that floats above the hurt and need of the world. Instead, the practical ministries of Jesus—feeding, befriending, healing, exorcising, and reconciling others—reveal God's way of being as being-with and being-for others. In God there is no pulling away, no separating from, no retreat inward. Instead there is always the outbound movement that finds its most practical expression in a life of service to others. In this service there is no holding back. There is only complete self-emptying and complete giving, the sort of service that extends to the point of one's own death (Phil 2:5-8).

Paul exhorts Christians to live into this self-emptying, self-offering life—"Let the same mind be in you that was in Christ Jesus" (2:5, NRSV)—because *outbound life is the truth of life*. A life of selfish ambition or conceit, a life that puts self-interest first, is fundamentally a distortion of what life is because it is a life that, by turning inward, denies the gifts of God all around and thus also banishes the prospect of genuine joy. Moreover, by turning inward, people make themselves unable to truly perceive others as being in need, in pain, or as worthy of celebration. Again and again, what we see in the life of Christ is one who is turned to others, available to them, and wanting to be with them. His is a sympathetic life that is attuned and responsive to others. Insofar as people participate in his humble, kenotic, self-offering life, they have the opportunity to experience life's fullness.

Turning outward to others has never been a simple or risk-free endeavor. To put oneself at the disposal of others is also to make oneself vulnerable to their rejection or abuse. It is significant, therefore, that Christian life is defined in ecclesial terms as life lived as an organic body (headed by Christ) in which people are members with each other. The love we offer to each other and to the world is not accomplished alone. It is carried out under the inspiration of the Holy Spirit that inspires the whole membership to support and build each other up. Insofar as Christians feel themselves to be encouraged and helped by the membership of Christ's body to live the humble, self-offering life of Christ, they experience in the gifts of friendship and support yet further sources of joy.

What we can now see is that humility, far from being simply an attitude that people may adopt from time to time, is the expression of a life attuned to others, and the acknowledgment that life alone is a contradiction in terms. In this attunement people are opened up so that they can perceive others in their need and in all their potential and wonder. The perception of others that Jesus invites is of a particular sort because it is directed and focused by a lens of love. What I mean is that when people are inhabited by Christ—as when Paul says, "it is no longer I who live, but it is Christ who lives in me" (Gal 2:20, NRSV), and that by being in Christ others cease to be seen from a simply human point of view but have instead become "new creation" (2 Cor 5:16-18)—they no longer perceive others in terms of what they can do for that self. Instead, they perceive others to be gifts of God and the embodied expression of the love of God that creates and sustains them in their life.

This new form of perception in which people encounter and engage others as the material expressions of divine love is what makes a life of joy possible. Joy is not an attitude that is willed upon the world. Instead it is the recognition that the world in which we live, though often degraded and hurt, is fundamentally a scene of God's gift-giving, and a field in which divine love moves. To enter into the experience of joy, however, presupposes humility, because without humility people are unable to recognize the integrity and sanctity of others as being a blessing to their life and as calling forth in us the twin works of care and celebration. The care we show to others indicates that we appreciate their lives, though vulnerable, as being of inestimable, sacred value, and therefore worthy of being cherished, nurtured, and protected. And when we celebrate their lives we communicate to them and to others how precious the love of God is that is being realized in them.

Joy is found in the realization that we are surrounded in myriad ways with the love of God. There can be no joy, however, apart from the humble realization that life is always together and never alone, and the affirmation that our lives are never our own. Humility is the truth of a human life, because in its expression we witness to the good of our dependence on and need of others. And joy is life's flower, because in it we sense and savor the divine love that seeks to meet our need.

* * *

RESPONSE TO NORMAN WIRZBA

Jane Foulcher

There is much to ponder in Norman Wirzba's rich chapter: soil, as the proper starting place for thinking about humility; how we construe our ontology (substance or meshwork) as determining whether our relationships (human, world, God) are either exploitative or cooperative; the recognition that dependence, and interdependence, are the sources of creaturely flourishing, not a shameful failure of the human project; the acceptance, and offering, of gift as the ultimate source of joy; and finally, humility as comprising less an attitude than a way of being with others.

By beginning with soil, Wirzba draws attention, perhaps inadvertently, to the *material* resonances of humility. Such resonances have been largely lost to the Western Christian tradition as humility was incorporated into various schemes of virtues. In monastic traditions, by contrast, the notion of humility often retains the sense of material lowliness that it held in early Christianity. Monasticism has an inherent interest in the practice of Christian life; above all it is motivated by a desire to follow the lowly way of Christ. So monastic writings offer surprisingly fruitful ground for contemporary engagement with humility. And they often take us back to the soil, to the earth. Consider the words of the "Mellifluous Doctor," Bernard of Clairvaux: "Woods and stones will teach you what you can never hear from any master."[1]

These words come from a letter to one of Bernard's protégés, Henry Murdac. A well-educated Yorkshire nobleman, Henry joined the Cistercian community at Clairvaux at Bernard's invitation, turning down a position at York Cathedral. In 1134, Henry was amongst the small group of monks sent to found the Abbey of Vauclair, in a river valley just south of Laon, the fifteenth foundation made from Clairvaux of the rapidly expanding Cistercian order. He was subsequently appointed abbot of Vauclair, then abbot of Fountains Abbey back in his home territory, and, more controversially, archbishop of York.[2]

From Bernard's letter we can infer that Henry was experiencing a spiritual crisis: he had got himself lost "reading the Prophets." Bernard points Henry to the Gospels and to Christ, and, in his characteristically lyrical fashion, begins to paint a vivid, sensual picture of all that his young friend is missing by having his head stuck in books:

> Like a bridegroom from his bridal bed he [Christ] has leapt from the shady coverts of the mountain sides and run into the open pastures of

the Gospels. . . . How gladly would I share with you the warm loaves which, still piping hot, fresh, as it were, from the oven, Christ of his heavenly bounty so often breaks with his poor! Would that when God sweetly deigns to shed on his poor servant a drop of that heavenly dew which he keeps for his chosen, I might presently pour it forth on you and in turn receive from you what you feel![3]

In the very act of pointing his friend toward Christ's presence in the Gospels, Bernard finds that Christ's presence escapes the bounds of the written word. The Word, we might say, leaps off the page, and instead is "made flesh" and found in the embrace of a physical place: the monastery at Citeaux. Metaphor is suddenly incarnated. You can just about catch the aroma of the monastery bakery. Bernard is, like the divine Gardener, "intoxicated with soil." He continues:

> Believe me who have experience, you will find much more labouring amongst the woods than you ever will amongst books. Woods and stones will teach you what you can never hear from any master. Do you imagine you cannot suck honey from the rocks and oil from the hardest stone; that the mountains do not drop sweetness and the hills flow with milk and honey; and that the valleys are not filled with corn?[4]

The dating of this letter is uncertain, but the address, simply to Henry Murdac, rather than Brother Henry, strongly suggests that this is part of Bernard's campaign to sell Cistercian monastic life to his friend. And of course, he succeeds. But if Henry read this as an invitation to find God in a rural idyll, as we might do, Bernard might well be accused of false advertising. We need to read between the lines of this letter to understand the texture of Cistercian life—and its relation to soil and humility.

The Cistercian movement was above all a reform movement, committed to a more faithful living out of the *Rule of St. Benedict* (which in turn, is simply a way of faithfully following Christ). While recent scholarship has cast doubt over the picture of Cistercians taming dank wildernesses across Europe, their commitment to manual work, especially in the early years, would have meant a radical change in the lives of noble-born monks like Henry and Bernard. The monks did indeed labor "amongst the woods." Bernard imagined the monastery as a sort of earthly paradise, a new Eden, where men worked alongside the divine Gardener. Work was viewed not merely as the means of supporting an otherworldly or spiritual agenda but as foundational to the monks' way of life. In the *Rule of St. Benedict*, the Latin word for work (*opus*) is used in relation to manual work (*opera manuum* or *labore manuum*) as well as the work of the oratory (the *opus dei*, or work of God).[5] There is a necessary physicality about this way of life.

While cast in the glow of its literary purpose (to secure Bernard's beatification), William of St. Thierry's description of the early Cistercian community of Clairvaux captures this weaving together of what we generally categorize separately, as either physical or spiritual work. Here they are of a piece:

> The first thing those who came down from the hills surrounding Clairvaux would see was *God in these houses* [Ps 47.4]. This silent valley spoke to them of the simplicity and humility in the buildings, mirroring the simplicity and humility of those living there. Then, in that valley full of men, where none was at rest, where all were toiling at their work and each one had a job assigned to him, at midday and at midnight they found silence all round them, save for the sound of work, save for the brothers occupied in the praise of God.[6]

Work, prayer, simplicity, humility. There is an ecology here that resonates with Wirzba's mapping of humility in the context of an understanding of human life as "meshwork." Monastic life is not a *container* for some other purpose, a stage for the spiritual journey of the individual, but rather a meshwork in which relationships are reordered. Bernard invites Henry to step outside, away from the containment of books and his library, and to become part of the Cistercian ecosystem, to notice his creatureliness, to discover his "entanglement" with soil.

Much of the Christian monastic tradition has kept in view the connections, often at risk, between humility, the material world, and social life. In early Christianity these connections were much more apparent. Humility in the Greco-Roman context was not a virtue but rather primarily a condition of the socially inferior, the lowly, those whose servile status and dependence on physical labor precluded them from public (virtuous) life.[7] While more ethical understandings of humility (the lowering of the self before God or another) are apparent in the Old Testament–Jewish tradition,[8] the social resonances of the Greco-Roman understandings are not only present in early Christianity but signal the radical social implications of love of neighbor.[9] To love one's neighbor requires a renunciation of status, a radically countercultural move in an honor-driven society.

To become a Christian in the Greco-Roman world was to join an alternative community, a countercultural ecosystem, in which relationships are reordered according to its central story, the story of the humble, humiliated Christ. The story of the conversion of Victorinus, related by Augustine in his *Confessions*, illustrates this nexus between humility, conversion, and its social consequences beautifully. Victorinus, a professor of rhetoric and hitherto a defender of Roman cultic practice, had become privately convinced of the truth of the gospel, but it is only when he makes his profession public and joins the church, through baptism, that his friend Simplicianus recognizes him as a Christian. Victorinus risks his privileged place in Roman society in what Augustine identifies as an act of humility: "He was not ashamed to be the child of Christ and to become an infant at your font, submitting his neck to the yoke of humility and bowing his head before the ignominy of the Cross."[10]

It is probably no accident that after Constantine, as Christianity becomes enmeshed in the power structures of late antiquity, various forms of Christian monasticism emerge in pursuit of an ecosystem that will enable the living out of this way of humility. Monasticism, in its many forms, always involves renunciation of status and the embrace of material simplicity.

In the Cistercian monastery the stripping back of material life to its bare essentials sharpens the monk's perception of their "entanglements"—with soil, with creatures human and nonhuman, and with the divine creator. Grounded in a vow of stability and an ordered life of work and prayer, the monk commits himself or herself to this particular place, this soil, and to this particular group of people, this monastic community. Entanglements remain entanglements, with all the complexity that this word implies, but in the workspace of the monastery, the slow and often painful work of healing or reordering this complex web of relationships is given priority (and, it should be noted, is expected to take a lifetime). All this begins, as Wirzba suggests, "by being attentive and responsive to the creatures with which they are entangled" (108).

From this perspective humility can be neither a possession nor a moral virtue. The French Cistercian Christian de Chergé (1937–1996) suggests that "Christian humility appears primarily to be a climate, which is not human, but upon which man is dependent if he wants to breathe freely."[11] Humility is simply part of the atmosphere, the given of the divine climate. When one breathes God, one breathes humility. This idea sits happily, I think, with Wirzba's conception of humility, and joy, arising from "life attuned to others" (121).

• • •

Reply to Jane Foulcher

Norman Wirzba

Jane Foulcher's quotation from Bernard of Clairvaux's letter to Henry Murdac bears repeating: "Believe me who have experience, you will find much more laboring amongst the woods than you will ever find amongst books. Woods and stones will teach you what you can never hear from any master." Woods and stones as teachers? Laboring in the woods as a higher form of learning?

Imagine yourself being told to go into the woods to work. Few among today's college-educated citizens would know *what* there is to do or *how* to do it. Even fewer would know how to listen to the trees and the land and take their instruction from them. The issue is not simply that we are habituated to take our learning from books and screens, as if learning is primarily a cerebral affair. More deeply, the evidence of bewilderment in a forest (or field or garden) signals a profound rupture between people and the places that sustain them, a rupture that deprives people of a genuine encounter with fellow creatures and the Spirit of God moving through and among them. Deprived of genuine encounter, people also lose the felt appreciation of this world as a sacred place in which they belong.

The rupture between people and places communicates many things: a fundamental ignorance of and discontent with the geophysical places of our life; a devaluation, if not a despising, of physical labor; a general distrust of bodies and embodied forms of knowing; and a yearning for a life that is easy, convenient, and on one's own terms. These are hardly the ideal conditions in which something like an honest and humble estimation of humanity's place in the world, with others, can occur. But what if we cannot properly know *who* we are, or what we should do, if we do not understand *where* we are and those we are *with*? As numerous anthropologists have noted, the practical forms of contemporary life—anonymous shopping, constant mobility, screen fixation, impersonal communication, boredom—encourage us to move *through* the world, often at a frantic pace, but not really *into* it.[1]

In an essay exploring his homeplace in Henry County, Kentucky, Wendell Berry said this about the importance of knowing *where* he is:

> Until we understand what the land is, we are at odds with everything we touch. And to come to that understanding it is necessary, even now, to leave the regions of our conquest—the cleared fields, the towns and cities, the highways—and re-enter the woods. For only there can a man

> encounter the silence and the darkness of his own absence. Only in this silence and darkness can he recover the sense of the world's longevity, of its ability to thrive without him, of his inferiority to it and his dependence on it. Perhaps then, having heard that silence and seen that darkness, he will grow humble before the place and begin to take it in—to learn *from it* what it is. As its sounds come into his hearing, and its lights and colors come into his vision, and its odors come into his nostrils, then he may come into *its* presence as he never has before, and he will arrive in his place and will want to remain. His life will grow out of the ground like the other lives of the place, and take its place among them. He will be *with* them—neither ignorant of them, nor indifferent to them, nor against them—and so at last he will grow to be native-born. That is, he must reenter the silence and the darkness, and be born again.[2]

The suggestion that human beings, like plants, "grow out of the ground," or that we must learn to come into the presence of leaves, bark, sunlight, soil, morning dew, worms, and centipedes, in such a way that their presence *enters into us* so deeply that we do not want to leave or forsake them—this all goes against the grain of well-established teaching that affirms the superior, even exceptional, status of human beings relative to other animals, plants, and soil. Nonetheless, Berry expresses the truth of our being. Every time we eat we give evidence to the fact that we are *rooted* in the earth, *bound* together with other creatures, large and microscopic, in a *shared* life that daily finds its inspiration and nourishment in the life-creating, life-sustaining Spirit of God. To forget this most fundamental truth is not only dishonest. When we forget it, we will likely become negligent, even destructive.

> There appears to be a law that when creatures have reached the level of consciousness, as men have, they must become conscious of the creation; they must learn how they fit into it and what its needs are and what it requires of them, or else pay a terrible penalty: the spirit of creation will go out of them, and they will become destructive; the very earth will depart from them and go where they cannot follow.[3]

People and places the world over are now paying the penalty in sickly and anxious bodies, degraded and depleted waters, and wasted lands and communities.

Christians bear considerable responsibility for this sad state. Having disowned the very learning that Bernard and Berry recommend, they have instead been captivated by dualisms of body and soul, earth and heaven, and so have encouraged spiritualities of otherworldly flight. It is not hard to understand why. Dualism speaks powerfully to the horror we feel at the pain, suffering, and violence that so many bodies experience. We do not need to go to a battlefield or prison to experience it. A hospital or nursing home will suffice. While we live on earth, there may be flourishes of embodied pleasure and delight. But we also know that our bodies will change, weaken, and wear down. You and I will die. All creatures die. Together, all the flesh of this world decomposes into the ground. This is why the desire for escape from bodies and places is strong. Though people may be less inclined to frame their flight in Socratic terms, today's transhumanist vision of a techno-utopia, in which minds are reduced to information patterns uploaded into machines that can, in principle, be maintained and multiplied forever, is keeping the dream alive.[4] The goal is not to enter a forest or linger among stones. It is to find a lab that is engineering the virtual worlds and the indestructible bodies that will be more to our liking.

Dualism has long been a temptation for Christians. So has docetism, a kind of cousin to dualism. Docetism is one of Christianity's earliest and most enduring heresies. It says that Jesus Christ did not have a real or natural body. If he did, that would mean that divinity mingled with all the imperfections and pains of embodiment. Docetists could not imagine that God would humble Godself, become flesh, and become a servant. To encounter Jesus was, therefore, to meet a person who only seemed (from the Greek *dokein*, which means "to seem") to have a body. Not surprisingly, docetism was espoused by Gnostics, who believed embodiment to be evil. The path to salvation, on their view, was cerebral and through the acquisition of esoteric knowledge (*gnosis* in Greek). It most definitely was not through physical labor or the care and cherishing of any creature or place.

Bernard's advice to Henry, and Berry's counsel to us, are a far cry from the dualist and docetic urges I have briefly described. To understand them, we should recall the early Christian hymn recorded in the Letter to the Colossians, where we are told that in Jesus of Nazareth "all the fullness of God was pleased to dwell" (1:19, NRSV). Not a piece or fraction of God, but God's fullness! And lest we think that this divine fullness resided only in Jesus' soul, the letter later makes clear, "For in him the whole fullness of deity dwells bodily" (2:9, NRSV). The embodied life of God is at the heart of the Gospel. Though bodies suffer, they are never evil, never to be despised, and never to be abandoned. Jesus demonstrates this continuously in his ministries that are devoted to the healing, feeding, exorcising, reconciling, and befriending of bodies. Though Jesus regularly speaks to others, his ministries presuppose the intimacy of touch and the skill of physical labor. Jesus moves among bodies in a tactile, fully embodied way. We could say, the healing work of Jesus happens when his body, animated by the fullness of God's love, responds to and liberates the divine love that is being blocked, frustrated, or violated in the bodies of others.

Creaturely bodies, and the places that nurture and inspire them, are of the profoundest significance and value. They deserve our constant attention and care, because they are the embodied expression of God's love. This means that no place or thing in this world is irrelevant or superfluous. Every creature and every place is God's love variously made tactile, visible, fragrant, audible, and nutritious. To want to turn away from any of it, or worse, to despise, condemn, or abandon any of it, is an act of the greatest wickedness. It is why God promises to destroy those who destroy the earth (Rev 11:18).

In his First Letter to Timothy, Paul says, "For everything created by God is good, and nothing is to be rejected, provided it is received with thanksgiving; for it is sanctified by God's word and by prayer" (1 Tim 4:4-5, NRSV). Though I do not know exactly what Bernard meant when he said that woods and stones will teach Henry more than any master can teach, my guess is that Bernard understood every tree, every stone, and every creature to be first and foremost a gift from God, and the embodiment of God's love, all gratefully to be received. This is why we should want to give our love and labor to them. To submit to their instruction, one first has to come into their presence and experience the complex grace that brings them and holds them in their being.[5] All of this takes time and detailed attention. But in giving one's concentration and care, one does not simply encounter a thing. One also encounters the power of God moving through it. This is the honey that resides within the hardest stone, and the sweetness that drips from the mountain.

It is hard to know the world deeply or as God's creation apart from the physical labor that draws us into it. Foulcher's observation that Benedictine work was not otherworldly or "spiritual," but first and foremost manual labor, is an important reminder to our cerebral, spectator world that would rather watch others (on the screens that give us stylized, cropped, and airbrushed versions of others). What we know by looking or by the casual glance does not compare with the knowing that happens through the intimacy of touch and the many practical skills of the senses. In all of this, the life of Jesus is our model. Jesus did not merely look upon the world and on others. He moved and dwelled among them, came close enough so as to enter into their pain and confusion. He worked with them and for them, and in his work bore witness to the love of God everywhere around.

Not enough people experience their work in this way. For many, work has been reduced to a job that pays the bills. It is not an opportunity to encounter the grace and the love of God working itself out in places and fellow creatures. It is not an invitation to develop and apply one's skills to the healing and beautification of the world. This is an existential and a theological problem, because it means that people are prevented from knowing intimately and viscerally how they are dependent on and benefited by the lives of others. In contexts like these, God appears more as an abstract idea than as a sensed and felt reality.

What should we do? I think Bernard's and Berry's advice still holds. Go to the woods. Go to the fields. Encounter the soil. Commit to the care of a tomato plant. Give your attention to rocks. Spend time with a neighbor. Help someone in their need. Make something beautiful. Discover how to join the love of God embodied in you to the love of God embodied in another or in a place. The bewilderment we will feel, as averse to it as we might be, is important, because it will remind us that God's creation is not reducible to what we want to make of it for ourselves. We have much to learn from monastic traditions that instruct us in the arts of prayer and attention, kenosis and rootedness.[6] But we can also learn from indigenous and agricultural traditions that emphasize the importance of committing to places and communities. The knowledge and the skill we need to work well depend on communities of insight that have learned from past mistakes.

The world is in pain. Creatures are being violated. If we are to witness to the love of God in contexts like these, we will need to get to work, like Jesus, and humble ourselves in service to others and the world. This is what the work of humility is all about.

• • •

NOTES TO CHAPTER 4
(NORMAN WIRZBA)

1. Karl Marx, *The Communist Manifesto*, ed. Frederic L. Bender (New York: W. W. Norton, 1988), 59.
2. The category of the "witness" is important when speaking of humility, because humble people regularly acknowledge that they cannot comprehend, let alone adequately express in words, the multitude of ways in which life is inspired and enabled by others. As witnesses to the gifted character of life and the world, humble people gesture and point to a grace that exceeds their comprehension. When giving one's detailed attention to the bewildering array of gifts of life, some of which are experienced as painful, one eventually comes to the realization that there is in the expression of humility an acknowledgment of a basic incomprehension at the heart of an honest human life. A witness does not live from within a secure grasp of the world.
3. The focus of this essay is the bond between humanity and soil, and the work of attention and care that emerges there. Gardening and farming, however, are not the only sites where the work generative of humility

occurs. Art, various forms of craft, parenting, teaching, ministry, even sport (to name a few), can be sites for the learning of humility, because they too, in varying ways, initiate people into disciplines that foster sympathy and care and that acknowledge interdependence and need.

4 This way of speaking will alarm some readers of Scripture who worry that the attribution of agency to nonhuman creatures leads to pagan animism or nature worship. We will return to the question of animism later in this essay. For a groundbreaking analysis of nonanimal creaturely agency in Scripture, see the recent Ph.D. dissertation by Mari Jørstad entitled "The Life of the World: The Vitality and Personhood of Non-animal Nature in the Hebrew Bible" (Duke University, 2016).

5 Agrarians ranging from Hesiod and the Hebrew prophets Amos and Hosea, all the way to Sir Albert Howard and Wendell Berry, have argued for the centrality of soil in human life and culture. More recently, scientists and historians have shown how the degradation of soil health goes hand in hand with the demise of civilizations and the sickening of humanity. See in particular David R. Montgomery's *Dirt: The Erosion of Civilizations* (Berkeley: University of California Press, 2007) and (with Anne Biklé) *The Hidden Half of Nature: The Microbial Roots of Life and Health* (New York: W. W. Norton, 2016) for analyses on the macro and micro levels.

6 bell hooks, *Belonging: A Culture of Place* (New York: Routledge, 2009), 117, 119.

7 My treatment of the meaning of place in Aristotle and his Greek context has been greatly helped by Edward S. Casey's *The Fate of Place: A Philosophical History* (Berkeley: University of California Press, 1997). Casey summarizes Aristotle this way: "As a vessel holds water or air within it, so a place holds a body or bodies within it in a snug fit" (55).

8 Tim Ingold, *The Life of Lines* (London: Routledge, 2015), 41.

9 The history of settlement practices demonstrates that many have thought of the world's places as so many sites to be mined. When land has been exhausted and forests felled, people have simply moved on to fresh, "virgin territory" where the patterns of exploitation can be repeated. The impulse to remain in a place and to work for the health of the place and its many creatures, or to cultivate what Wendell Berry has variously described as a nurturing and sympathetic mind, has been eclipsed by a rapacious and extractive economy. For elaboration on the many dimensions of faithful and careful settlement, see *The Art of the Commonplace: The Agrarian Essays of Wendell Berry*, ed. Norman Wirzba (Washington, D.C.: Counterpoint, 2002).

10 In *The Great Derangement: Climate Change and the Unthinkable* (Chicago: University of Chicago Press, 2016), Amitav Ghosh argues that the central, animating spirit of modernity has been to shrink the human imagination to the narrow scope of the individual, often disembodied, self. The pursuit of an emancipatory (and thus clearly noble) agenda has had as its corollary a vision of humans as transcending the constraints of material, embodied, and interdependent life. Hence the inability of today's artists,

intellectuals, and politicians to understand, let alone meaningfully engage, the challenge that climate change poses to humanity and the world. Having despised attachments to place, and having neglected their responsibilities for soil, "this era, which so congratulates itself on its self-awareness, will come to be known as the time of the Great Derangement" (11).

11 Aristotle has certainly been a key philosophical figure in the framing of a substance ontology where the being of things is a feature of their distinction from other things. Primary substances make sense in terms of their isolation from anything else. In the modern period Descartes reinforced this individualizing ontology when he defined an ideal substance as "nothing other than a thing which exists in such a way as to depend on no other thing for its existence" (*Principles of Philosophy* 1.51, in *The Philosophical Writings of Descartes*, vol. 1, trans. John Cottingham, Robert Stoothoff, and Dugald Murdoch [Cambridge: Cambridge University Press, 1985], 210). What things *are* is determined by properties that are *internal* to the thing being thought. Though substances may be in relationship with others, relationality is not constitutive.

12 Tim Ingold, *Being Alive: Essays on Movement, Knowledge and Description* (London: Routledge, 2011), 117.

13 Ingold, *Being Alive*, 70.

14 Ingold, *Life of Lines*, 74.

15 Ingold, *Being Alive*, 70.

16 Ingold, *Being Alive*, 29.

17 Ingold, *Being Alive*, 29.

18 Ingold, *Being Alive*, 69.

19 Ingold, *Life of Lines*, 23.

20 To speak of "nothingness" is in no way to disparage things or creatures. Critics of humility often argue that the mention of our nothingness amounts to the diminishment of persons. Nothing could be further from the truth. Insofar as the created world is precious, a conclusion we must arrive at if we believe God's creation to be *ex amore*, all the life that occurs within it is also precious. The mistake is to assume that a person's life is self-contained or a private possession. Individual nothingness is meant to convey the inescapable dependence on others that every person lives through. As such, it is the honest expression of our entanglements with others.

21 For a popular treatment on the science behind this observation, see Ed Yong, *I Contain Multitudes: The Microbes within Us and a Grander View of Life* (New York: Ecco, 2016).

22 It is important to underscore this point lest one think that agrarian and indigenous peoples have been uniformly humble. This has clearly not been the case. My claim is that agrarian and indigenous ways of life and habits of being make the cultivation of humility a priority, and a more likely possibility, because they teach and reinforce *the good of our need*.

23 Dietrich Bonhoeffer, *Creation and Fall* (Minneapolis: Fortress, 1997), 120.

24 Bonhoeffer describes the new human situation this way: "Humankind is now *sicut deus* [like God]. It now lives out of its own resources, creates its own life, is its own creator; it no longer needs the Creator.... Adam is no longer a creature. Adam has torn himself away from his creatureliness" (*Creation and Fall*, 115).
25 For a more detailed treatment of this story, see chap. 4, "The Human Art of Creaturely Life," in my *From Nature to Creation: A Christian Vision for Understanding and Loving Our World* (Grand Rapids: Baker Academic, 2015).
26 Given more space, it would be valuable to develop God's own creation as the work of hospitality—God "making room" for others to be, and then offering them the nurture they need to thrive—and creation itself as a vast and diverse site of hospitality in which my body makes room for others (as in the microbiome that is our gut) and the bodies of others make room for me. Hospitality is clearly a scriptural ideal. Histories of violence and exploitation, however, reveal a world in which particular bodies, owing to their race, ethnicity, gender, sexual orientation, and class, have been systematically abused and exploited. In contexts like this, where bodies have not been welcomed and nurtured, the work of healing and justice must first take effect so that joy might come within sight. For a discussion of humility in the contexts of oppression, see the essay by Stacey Floyd-Thomas in this volume.
27 Scott Cairns, "The Entrance of Sin," in *The Collected Poems* (Brewster, Mass.: Paraclete, 2015), 139–40.
28 For an extended philosophical treatment of sin in light of Luther's insight, see Brian Gregor, *A Philosophical Anthropology of the Cross: The Cruciform Self* (Bloomington: Indiana University Press, 2013).

Notes to Chapter 4 Response
(Jane Foulcher)

1 Bernard of Clairvaux, *The Letters of St. Bernard of Clairvaux*, trans. Bruno Scott James (Stroud: Sutton, 1953; repr., Kalamazoo, Mich.: Cistercian, 1998), letter 107.
2 Janet Burton, "Henry Murdac," in *Oxford Dictionary of National Biography*.
3 Bernard of Clairvaux, *Letters*, 107.
4 Bernard of Clairvaux, *Letters*, 107.
5 Timothy Fry, ed., *RB 1980: The Rule of St. Benedict in English* (Collegeville, Minn.: Liturgical, 1981). See for example chaps. 47 and 48.
6 William of Saint-Thierry, Arnold of Bonneval, and Geoffrey of Auxerre, *The First Life of Bernard of Clairvaux*, trans. Hilary Costello (Collegeville, Minn.: Cistercian, 2015), 41.
7 Klaus Wengst, *Humility: Solidarity of the Humiliated; The Transformation of an Attitude and Its Social Relevance in Graeco-Roman, Old Testament-Jewish and Early Christian Tradition*, trans. John Bowden (London: SCM Press, 1988), 4–15. Wengst's study of the word groups *tapeinos* (Gk.) and *humilis* (Lat.) denoting humble and humility in Greco-Roman texts makes this clear.

8 Wengst, *Humility*, 16–35.
9 Wengst, *Humility*, 36–53; cf. Gerd Theissen, *A Theory of Primitive Christian Religion*, trans. John Bowden (London: SCM Press, 1999), 63–80.
10 Augustine, *Confessions* 8.2, trans. R. S. Pine-Coffin (Harmondsworth: Penguin, 1961), 159.
11 Christian de Chergé, *Dieu pour tout jour: Chapitres de Père Christian de Chergé à la communauté de Tibhirine (1985–1996)*, 2nd ed. (Montjoyer: Abbaye Notre-Dame d'Aiguebelle, 2006), 260. "L'humilité chrétienne me paraît d'abord être un CLIMAT qui n'est pas de l'homme, mais auquel l'homme ne saurait échapper s'il veut respirer librement."

Notes to Chapter 4 Reply
(Norman Wirzba)

1 See Marc Augé's description of this transformation of practical life in *Non-places: An Introduction to Supermodernity*, 4th ed. (London: Verso, 2008). To live in a "non-place" is to be situated somewhere in such a way that one's location has little discernible effect on how one lives or understands oneself. To be genuinely *placed* is to have one's life and identity shaped decisively by the many relationships that are happening there.
2 Wendell Berry, "A Native Hill," in *The Art of the Commonplace: The Agrarian Essays of Wendell Berry*, ed. Norman Wirzba (Washington, D.C.: Counterpoint, 2002), 27.
3 Berry, *Art of the Commonplace*, 19.
4 For an engaging exploration of the various dreams of techno-utopia being pursued today, see Mark O'Connell's *To Be a Machine: Adventures among Cyborgs, Utopians, Hackers, and the Futurists Solving the Modest Problem of Death* (New York: Doubleday, 2017).
5 In *The Forest Unseen: A Year's Watch in Nature* (New York: Penguin, 2013), David Haskell gives his attention for one year to one square meter of forest. He describes how much there is to learn and how much we still do not know. It is an exercise in patience, humility, and devotion, and an exercise that yields profound insights and evokes gratitude and praise.
6 Douglas E. Christie gives a profound and beautiful account of what this learning might look like today in *The Blue Sapphire of the Mind: Notes for a Contemplative Ecology* (New York: Oxford University Press, 2013).

Chapter Bibliography

Augé, Marc. *Non-places: An Introduction to Supermodernity*. 4th ed. London: Verso, 2008.
Augustine. *Confessions*. Translated by R. S. Pine-Coffin. Harmondsworth: Penguin, 1961.
Bernard of Clairvaux. *The Letters of St. Bernard of Clairvaux*. Translated by Bruno Scott James. Stroud: Sutton, 1953. Reprint, Kalamazoo, Mich.: Cistercian, 1998.

Berry, Wendell. *The Art of the Commonplace: The Agrarian Essays of Wendell Berry*. Edited by Norman Wirzba. Washington, D.C.: Counterpoint, 2002.

Bonhoeffer, Dietrich. *Creation and Fall*. Minneapolis: Fortress, 1997.

Cairns, Scott. "The Entrance of Sin." In *The Collected Poems*, 139–40. Brewster, Mass.: Paraclete, 2015.

Casey, Edward S. *The Fate of Place: A Philosophical History*. Berkeley: University of California Press, 1997.

Chergé, Christian de. *Dieu pour tout jour: Chapitres de Père Christian de Chergé à la communauté de Tibhirine (1985–1996)*. 2nd ed. Montjoyer: Abbaye Notre-Dame d'Aiguebelle, 2006.

Christie, Douglas E. *The Blue Sapphire of the Mind: Notes for a Contemplative Ecology*. New York: Oxford University Press, 2013.

Descartes, René. *The Philosophical Writings of Descartes*. Vol 1. Translated by John Cottingham, Robert Stoothoff, and Dugald Murdoch. Cambridge: Cambridge University Press, 1985.

Fry, Timothy, ed. *RB 1980: The Rule of St. Benedict in English*. Collegeville, Minn.: Liturgical, 1981.

Ghosh, Amitav. *The Great Derangement: Climate Change and the Unthinkable*. Chicago: University of Chicago Press, 2016.

Gregor, Brian. *A Philosophical Anthropology of the Cross: The Cruciform Self*. Bloomington: Indiana University Press, 2013.

Haskell, David. *The Forest Unseen: A Year's Watch in Nature*. New York: Penguin, 2013.

hooks, bell. *Belonging: A Culture of Place*. New York: Routledge, 2009.

Ingold, Tim. *Being Alive: Essays on Movement, Knowledge and Description*. London: Routledge, 2011.

———. *The Life of Lines*. London: Routledge, 2015.

Jørstad, Mari. "The Life of the World: The Vitality and Personhood of Non-animal Nature in the Hebrew Bible." Ph.D. diss., Duke University, 2016.

Marx, Karl. *The Communist Manifesto*. Edited by Frederic L. Bender. New York: W. W. Norton, 1988.

Montgomery, David R. *Dirt: The Erosion of Civilizations*. Berkeley: University of California Press, 2007.

Montgomery, David R., and Anne Biklé. *The Hidden Half of Nature: The Microbial Roots of Life and Health*. New York: W. W. Norton, 2016.

O'Connell, Mark. *To Be a Machine: Adventures among Cyborgs, Utopians, Hackers, and the Futurists Solving the Modest Problem of Death*. New York: Doubleday, 2017.

Theissen, Gerd. *A Theory of Primitive Christian Religion*. Translated by John Bowden. London: SCM Press, 1999.

Wengst, Klaus. *Humility: Solidarity of the Humiliated; The Transformation of an Attitude and Its Social Relevance in Graeco-Roman, Old Testament-Jewish and Early Christian Tradition*. Translated by John Bowden. London: SCM Press, 1988.

William of Saint-Thierry, Arnold of Bonneval, and Geoffrey of Auxerre. *The First Life of Bernard of Clairvaux*. Translated by Hilary Costello. Collegeville, Minn.: Cistercian, 2015.

Wirzba, Norman. *From Nature to Creation: A Christian Vision for Understanding and Loving Our World*. Grand Rapids: Baker Academic, 2015.

Yong, Ed. *I Contain Multitudes: The Microbes within Us and a Grander View of Life*. New York: Ecco, 2016.

II
Methodology

Introduction to Part 2

As we discussed in the introduction to part 1, this book comprises two sets of conversation: the explicit ones within the chapter–response–reply structure and the implicit ones between the chapters themselves. The two parts of the book are divided according to the main themes of those second, implicit conversations.

The driving set of questions for part 2 concerns methodology in the broadest of terms. What sources and standards should we use to identify humility and its relation to flourishing life—and how might different scholarly methods carry with them implicit substantive commitments on these questions? So we find *Don E. Davis and Sarah Gazaway* with *Jane Foulcher*, debating whether humility, along with any other moral construct, is suitable for conceptualization and analysis in primarily secular or empirical terms (Davis and Gazaway's position), or primarily in light of its particular history—theological, cultural, and so forth (Foulcher's view).

This explicit exchange echoes across the other chapters in different ways. One might read *Jason Baehr* and *Kent Dunnington* as engaged in a similar debate. Baehr aims to clarify what humility means by appealing to common intuitions, providing what he hopes to be a sufficiently precise tool for reflecting on our moral lives. This suggests that the first step in discerning the true nature of humility and its place in flourishing life is rational (i.e., providing a definition of humility that, without flagrantly disregarding conventional usage, is above all else logically sound and semantically coherent). In contrast, Dunnington suggests that Christian humility provides a striking foil to the kind of humility envisioned in much contemporary analytic philosophy, which, being "not historically attuned to how much [its] conceptual analysis depends on intuitions shaped by a mishmash of conflicting perspectives," yields attenuated accounts of humility. By pursuing Christian humility under the counsel of Benedict and other wise forbearers, Dunnington concludes that contemporary Christians are sure to discover the difference Jesus makes to everyday life.

A third construal of this implicit methodological question is present in the explicit exchange between *Elizabeth J. Krumrei-Mancuso* and *Everett L. Worthington Jr.* on Krumrei-Mancuso's chapter exploring the significance of humility for "servant leadership." Among other things, their discussion explores the significance of Christian tradition for psychological research. What emerges appears to be an agreement between the two that psychological research in general, and on humility in particular, should *not* take the normative history of the construct as foundational for its intelligibility. Yet the fact that research constructs are "grounded in contemporary research findings" need not exclude their being "informed by historic theological and philosophical writings" (Worthington, 257). On this view, humility, like other ethical norms or constructs, can be accurately understood independent of its particular history, though such histories can add color to them.

Of course, the variations on this theme also point back to the relationship between the first and second parts of the book as a whole, characterized as they are by theological approaches that foreground the normativity of humility as it has been conceived in Christian tradition(s) (part 1) and by philosophical and psychological approaches that are chiefly empirical, analytic, or historical in nature (part 2). Similarly, part 1's implicit orientation around Floyd-Thomas' emancipatory critique of humility also poses pressing questions for the authors of part 2, as Davis and Gazaway's chapter explicitly acknowledges. In this sense, the division of this book into two parts—one interested in the normativity of humility and one interested in methodological analysis and application of humility—might be understood as an attempt not to corral two distinctly different kinds of discourses into isolated pens but to differentiate between them so that they might more clearly, and perhaps more forcefully, engage one another.

5

Observing Humility

Relational Humility and Human Flourishing

Don E. Davis and Sarah Gazaway

Psychological research on humility has almost exclusively focused on potential benefits for individuals, relationships, and systems.[1] From these empirical studies, we can potentially examine the degree to which humility promotes flourishing in people's lives. (We operationalize flourishing with widely studied constructs such as life satisfaction, meaning in life, or relationship satisfaction in valued relationships [e.g., between romantic partners].) On the other hand, some scholars from philosophy or theology have questioned whether humility is in fact a virtue on various grounds. An interdisciplinary discussion provides an opportunity to take stock of and scrutinize the initial evidence of the benefits of humility. In the current chapter, we consider theories about when humility may have a dark side. Based on these ideas, we seek to refine a theory about when (i.e., under what conditions) and how humility leads to optimal flourishing.

We first provide an overview of how scholars have defined and measured humility. Second, we summarize preliminary efforts to explore possible benefits of humility and discuss some of the important limitations of this work. Third, we extend current theory on relational humility to consider when humility judgments (perceptions of another person's degree of humility) might undermine flourishing in individuals, relationships, or systems. Our primary thesis is that people use humility language (and judge humility in others) in order to negotiate the fair allocation of resources (e.g., physical, financial, or psychological). In order to accurately judge humility, people must rely on situations that provide unambiguous information about a person's tendency to keep their own interests in appropriate balance with the needs of other relationships. A variety of situations can cause egoistic motives. In this chapter, we focus especially on how surprising levels of generosity can provide information about a target person's level of humility. In such situations, we suggest that people seen as more humble tend to generate margin—that is, they produce gains that outweigh the costs of their actions. Then they share that margin with others within a relationship or social system. This way of thinking about humility begins to clarify some of the contexts in which humility language can contribute to injustice. Scholars who considers humility to be a virtue may want to embed some of these contextual factors their thinking.

Toward a Definition and Measurement Strategy

Definitions of humility in psychology have tended to converge toward emphasis on intrapersonal qualities: humble people have an accurate view of their strengths and limitations—not too high or low.[2] Definitions diverge when it comes to whether to include interpersonal qualities as core to the construct, with some teams conceptualizing the construct as entirely intrapersonal and viewing interpersonal sequelae as correlative but not constitutive of the construct, and with other teams viewing the construct as especially situated within the tensions and negotiations that occur within interpersonal relationships, including establishing trust and seeking to maintain a strong reputation.

We adopt the latter perspective and view humility as a construct that is judged (and therefore situated) within interpersonal relationships. A variety of situations may provide information about someone's degree of humility (e.g., power struggles, conflicts, and opportunities to share credit or resources). In this way, humility is broader than constructs such as gratitude (which pertains to recognizing benefits or gifts) or forgiveness (which pertains to how one handles interpersonal offenses). As a pragmatic strategy, some researchers have begun to focus on different types or subdomains of humility, such as intellectual humility, political humility, religious humility, or cultural humility. The qualifier in each of these cases constrains the types of situations in which humble behavior is being evaluated, and it is possible that people may act humbly in some situations but not others. For example, a mother who is also a CEO may tend to express a different degree of humility in her role as a mother than in her role as a CEO.

The fact that humility judgments are always contextualized within a perspective and a relationship is what we have meant by "relational humility" in our previous work. Similar to trust or commitment, the perception of humility has a contextual history, and even one behavior can possibly exert massive influence on that perception—for example, consider a marriage in which years of fidelity are suddenly abruptly ended by a discrete act of infidelity and subsequent defensiveness. In this example, the severe rupture of trust would likely lead to a major shift in humility judgment by the relationship partner, but the perception might recover over time, as trust and commitment are reestablished within the relationship.

The Stringent Era

Measurement of humility has had two distinct phases, a "stringent era" characterized by skepticism about the ease and reliability of measuring humility and a "relaxed era" characterized by a breezy confidence in the efficacy of measurement tools. Marking the beginning of the stringent era, Tangney published a seminal theory paper describing the challenges of advancing a research program on humility.[3] Researchers seriously considered whether a construct such as humility (especially the part associated with having an accurate view of self) could be studied with traditional self-report methods. The modesty effect hypothesis suggests that the higher people's actual humility, the more likely they would underreport their humility on self-reports. Indeed, people tend to self-enhance some; narcissists may self-enhance a lot; truly humble people may answer accurately or even self-deprecate. The concern led researchers to explore various alternatives to self-report, such as comparing oneself to others,[4] implicit measures,[5] or other-reports.[6]

The Relaxed Era

Then something dramatically changed—it was as if the clouds parted and the sun began to shine on humility scholarship for a few years. Measures and empirical studies began to proliferate. Researchers published a flurry of scale-development papers.[7] Surprisingly, given the earlier concerns about self-report, most of the measures were self-report. We see three key factors that temporarily decreased scrutiny of self-reports.

First, no one ever published a strong paper demonstrating evidence of the modesty effect problem. In fact, as intuitive as the modesty effect seemed to humility scholars, researchers began to point out the lack of direct evidence for the problem.[8]

Second, several teams adopted a pragmatic stance toward interpreting self-reports that incorporated the biased nature of the construct itself. Drawing on theory on personality judgment,[9] researchers treated self-reports of humility as subjective and inherently perspectives of one's social reputation used to navigate relationships. This tradition treats other-reports as primary (i.e., people judge virtues to predict and communicate reputational information about how a person is likely to act within relationships) and self-reports as a complex case of other-reports in which the person is both judge and target. For example, a hiring committee might decide not to make an offer for a candidate who has a couple of ambiguous words in a letter of recommendation or displays a moment of conceitedness while interacting with departmental staff. People use such signals of humility (or lack thereof) to make decisions about how much to commit to and trust relationships. From this perspective, people with strong social skills ought to have relatively accurate perceptions of their own humility, because distortions might quickly accumulate interpersonal offenses.

Third, interdisciplinary initiatives—particularly on intellectual humility—introduced a greater variety in how humility was conceptualized, especially as scholars began to think about the potential need to focus on particular contexts that may strain the practice of humility, and whether these contexts point to a general humility (analogous to intelligence or self-efficacy, which can be empirically tested) or a variety of different constructs. Is behavior sufficiently consistent across subdomain contexts (e.g., cultural humility, intellectual humility) in a way that allows us to study a general humility (akin to g in the intelligence field)? The other possibility is that, for most people, humility is contextualized to certain relationships, roles, or systems. A person who is very humble within a family could display a high degree of arrogance in leadership roles (e.g., as a coach or military leader). Likewise, does external pressure affect how we view humility, or is the same behavior seen as equally humble across contexts (e.g., consider the same account of an individual's success delivered within a collectivist context and within an individualist context, with the different valuations of modesty operative therein). General humility may be exceedingly rare if we require a person to express optimal humility across all their social contexts, including contexts that place competing demands on a person (e.g., a political speech delivered to a pluralistic public).

Toward Consolidating Definitions and Measures

The surplus of measures points to growing scholarly interest in humility. For this activity to generate scientific growth, the field must begin to consolidate (or at least clearly and consistently distinguish) diverging definitions and constructs. To that end, in their review of measures, McElroy et al. (2018) made three suggestions. (1) Breaking rank with some prior work, they suggested that modesty, understood as behaving in ways that align with social norms regarding drawing attention to positive aspects of the self, be incorporated into the definition as a subdomain of humility, because its content pervades almost all existing measures, even when researchers attempted to do otherwise.[10] (2) They suggested incorporating teachability as an interpersonal manifestation of having an accurate view of self, which also aligns with philosophical work emphasizing that humility involves not just an awareness of limitations but a demonstrated ability to exhibit ownership of (or responsiveness to) that knowledge.[11] (3) They also explicitly dilated on the need to address the outstanding debate regarding whether humility also involves an orientation to the betterment of others (argued forcefully in Worthington and Allison's *Heroic Humility*).[12]

This latter suggestion dovetails with the taxonomy of definitions by McAnnally-Linz of philosophical and theological approaches to defining humility.[13] After reviewing various ways of cashing out a humble view of self (which highlights the lack of sophistication in current measures and the need to draw from methods of studying self-knowledge),[14] he eventually argues for a Christian conception of humility focused on devotion to God's work in the world. His thinking aligns well with ours, if we allow room for cultures to contextualize the object of devotion (e.g., God's work in the world might stand in place for an articulation of the highest good within a relational system). Taken together, we define humility as involving not just an accurate view of self (one might have superior capabilities) or submission to modesty norms with one's behavior (one could act humbly, but with a deceitful heart), but also a commitment to the good of others.

Overview of Initial Research on Humility and Flourishing

Benefits to the Individual

Before we consider contexts that may optimize the benefits of humility, we first want to provide a general overview of initial scientific findings about the benefits of humility for individuals, relationships, and systems. The most straightforward way of looking at this research question provides weak (or at least inconclusive) evidence that humility promotes flourishing for individuals. Our team is currently conducting a meta-analysis of all the correlates of humility, and studies that examine the correlation of humility with constructs associated with personal well-being, such as life satisfaction, meaning in life, psychological well-being, or health, have demonstrated only weak to moderate positive (and sometimes weakly negative) correlations. For example, initial estimates of the relationship between humility and life satisfaction (a common indicator of flourishing in psychological studies) range from −0.24 to 0.28 (i.e., around 4 percent of the variance in life satisfaction scores).[15] These findings—if not somehow obscured by problems of self-report—suggest that a variety of other factors are stronger and more proximal predictors of flourishing.

Benefits within Relationships

Research on how humility affects constructs associated with relationship quality (e.g., relationship satisfaction, commitment, or trust) appears more likely to support the thesis that humility promotes flourishing. Apparently, we like it when our relational partners are humble.[16] The *social bonds hypothesis* states that people judge humility in other people to regulate bonds that cause those judging humility to act as if the needs of another person (or the relationship) are tantamount to their own needs.[17] Social bonds require precise regulation, because people are prone to exploitation if a relational partner takes advantage of a strong social bond but does not reciprocate. This hypothesis has received empirical support in the contexts of romantic relationships, married couples, and interethnic couples.[18] Furthermore, humility has been linked with prosocial qualities (or negatively correlated with antisocial qualities).[19] For example, studies have linked humility with greater helping[20] and generosity.[21] Cohen et al. used latent profile analyses (clustering technique that examines configurations of scores to put people into groups) to determine people with high, medium, and low "morality," or prosociality.[22] Humility was one of the stronger determinants of morality, and which group a person was categorized in then predicted a variety of outcomes associated with prosocial and antisocial behaviors in the workplace.

Humility has also been linked with forgiveness, which, like humility, indicates an investment in a social bond. Forgiveness arrests the escalation of conflict and provides an opportunity for trust to grow to the degree that the offender apologizes, makes amends, and works to avoid future offenses. Both partners can come to trust that the other person values the relationship for reasons extending beyond their own self-interest, which enhances their commitment to the relationship. When partners both consistently engage in behaviors that signal high value and commitment, this ought to consolidate a stable view of one's partner as humble in disposition, which ought to buffer the relationship from stressors. Viewing one's partner as humble has also been linked with forgiveness after an offense.[23]

In addition to research on couples, researchers have also replicated the social bonds hypothesis within the context of multicultural counseling. Several studies have documented that clients who view their therapist as culturally humble (i.e., taking a humble stance toward a marginalized gender or racial identity) also report a stronger working alliance (agreement about the tasks and approach to therapy and a strong bond with the therapist) and, as a result, better therapy outcomes.[24] Although most of these initial studies have focused on individual relationships, one study aggregated ratings for a therapist across clients and found that humility regarding salient cultural identities served a protective role for therapy relationships.[25] When clients said their therapists missed opportunities to explore their salient marginalized identities, they also reported worse outcomes; however, for therapists who were viewed as culturally humble, this link between missed cultural opportunities and client outcomes was decreased. These results also provide support for what we have called the *social oil hypothesis*, which suggests that humility acts like a social lubricant and protects relationships from the wear-and-tear of potential conflict.

Humility in Larger Systems

Psychological scientists have also explored more systemic benefits of humility, particularly within business organizations. Hypotheses generally dovetail with the social bond and social oil hypotheses. Humility has been linked with leadership styles associated with trustworthiness and integrity (i.e., ethical leadership) as opposed to simply focusing on performance goals (i.e., task-oriented leadership).[26] Consistent with the social bond hypothesis, subordinates are more likely to forgive a leader viewed as humble.[27] Consistent with the social oil hypothesis, humility buffered (i.e., reduced) the negative relationship between perceived office politics and negative outcomes.[28]

Brad Owens and colleagues have spearheaded a programmatic line of research within the management field. Their team developed a measure based on qualitative interviews of actual leaders. It includes three subscales (teachability, self-awareness, and giving credit to others) associated with interpersonal expression of humility within a leadership context.[29] In three studies, they provided evidence for the *humility contagion hypothesis*, which suggests that leaders model a way of relating (e.g., appreciating and spotlighting contributions, being receptive to feedback and other ideas) that sets the tone for humility to recreate itself in the relationships among team members.[30] In related work, humility promoted greater distribution of leadership among teams (shared leadership), which in turn led to greater team performance.[31] The link between humility and shared leadership was stronger as team members had more proactive personality traits; likewise, the link between shared leadership and performance was stronger as team members had greater performance abilities (i.e., competence). Similarly, initial evidence suggests that humility of leaders promotes greater "psychological capital" (a construct involving having confidence, making positive attribution, persevering toward goals, and bouncing back from adversity), which leads to greater performance.[32]

Taken together, research on humility in leaders has primarily focused on aggregates of other-reports and has generally found benefits for leaders who manage to be seen as humble by subordinates. The reliance on one method does raise questions about whether these benefits may partially relate to something akin to a halo effect, in which general relationship satisfaction conveys also to perceptions of humility.

Is a Major Course Correction on the Horizon?

Whereas all these storylines are generally positive, the fact remains that these studies suggest humility is only weakly related to measures of individual flourishing. Therefore, it seems scientifically prudent to consider the strongest critiques of the hypothesis that humility regularly leads to human flourishing. To do so, we need to consider other relational contexts than those treated in the studies discussed above. For reasons we will share, we anticipate earlier concerns about the measurement of humility resurfacing (mainly those focused on the potential paradox of describing oneself as humble, which could sometimes come across as bragging), but perhaps in a new and surprising way. The problem has surfaced in recent work on intellectual humility within psychology.

Intellectual humility involves being fair-minded when negotiating ideas and has implications for public discourse around religion and politics. Definitions vary and have also led to a variety of measures.[33] Studying the role of intellectual humility, especially within politics or religion, requires careful scrutiny. It would be easy for researchers to inadvertently embed their own ideological preferences and biases about what intellectual humility is into item content. If measures included ideological bias, then this could undermine the validity of inferences in studies comparing different political or religious groups (e.g., liberals versus conservatives; religious people versus atheists). It would be misleading if a measure of intellectual humility inadvertently conflated the construct with the content of conviction (e.g., "My views about _____ are just as likely to be wrong as other views").³⁴ Moreover, before we interpret the initial work showing moderate, positive correlation between intellectual humility and political orientation, it is important to ensure that the item content does not conflate humility with political or religious ideology. For example, imagine how a theologically conservative person might answer the following question to the degree that their source of knowledge is a sacred text (e.g., "My sources for information about _____ might not be the best").³⁵ It would also be a problem if items gave people credit for intellectual humility when really they adopted a strategy of avoiding strong convictions on potentially divisive ideas, which is one explanation of curvilinear effects found in initial work on intellectual humility toward specific ideas.

Some initial data from our team heightened our concern about potential bias in self-reports of humility. In two samples of religious leaders, we conducted latent profile analyses (clustering techniques that place people into categories based on the configuration of their scores) using several measures of humility, moral values, and intratextual fundamentalism, which conceptualizes fundamentalism based on the degree to which people develop a closed interpretive system as opposed to allowing other sources of knowledge, such as science, to influence how they understand the world.³⁶ The group with the highest intellectual humility also scored highest on intratextual fundamentalism. These findings certainly contradict the typical social psychology portrayal of religious fundamentalists.³⁷

Granted, these participants could have engaged in severe self-enhancement; however, a more straightforward interpretation would be that humility judgments (of self or others) may involve embedded values and assumptions about what constitutes "good evidence." For example, perhaps people high in intratextual fundamentalism view Scripture (and a particular tradition of interpreting it) as the highest quality of evidence; maybe those low in fundamentalism ascribe to some other authority (e.g., progressive narratives about privilege; scientific method). If we are right that humility is contextualized within a perspective (and thus within embedded values and assumptions for evaluating humility), then we may need to carefully interpret findings when some people have wildly different standards for evaluating their own humility that others do. Indeed, from a scientific perspective, we may want to take the variability in normative standards into account in order to study and compare intellectual humility across groups with different norms for evaluating evidence.

Taken together, we are suggesting that humility scholars will need to carefully scrutinize their assumptions about humility. For example, some people will tend to have more theologically conservative views about how to evaluate humility (e.g., is this person humble before God and the religious tradition); whereas others will tend to have more theologically liberal views (e.g., is this person aware of the abuses of power and hierarchy), and it would be easy for researchers to embed their own values and biases into measures of humility. As interdisciplinary scholars view psychological research on humility, it is important to keep in mind that researchers are still negotiating how to disentangle judgments of humility from assumptions about what constitutes quality evidence. In our view, the most difficult form of humility involves not just coming across as humble to people within one's own cultural community but having an ability to express humility across very different cultural contexts. This type of humility across contexts requires a complex form of flexibility to maintain integrity to one's own values and identity while also being able to show respect for the humility norms of other groups.

A Componential Extension of Humility Theory

Given this potential problem, we sought to elaborate on prior theorizing on humility. In earlier work, we noted that humility is especially important and observable (i.e., evident for evaluation by a third-party) in contexts that tend to enhance egoistic behavior.[38] Furthermore, we noted that hierarchical relationships can enhance egotism without further elaboration. To this point, many humility researchers have viewed the most commonly used measure of humility (i.e., the honesty-humility subscale of the HEXACO) as perhaps only tangentially related to humility—particularly the subscale associated with avoidance of greed. Davis et al. reevaluated the de facto dismissal based on purely theoretical reasons when they found evidence of substantial empirical overlap between the subscales of Modesty and Greed-Avoidance and other measures of humility.[39] Our goal in this section is to see if we could offer an account that would bring this work into greater conceptual alignment. We suggest that, in addition to other subdomains (i.e., contexts that tend to evoke egoistic behavior), the allocation of resources (i.e., one's tendency to express greedy versus generous behavior) is a major opportunity to evaluate a person's degree of humility (i.e., whether a person has an accurate view of themselves versus having an inflated sense of self, such as a sense of superiority, expressed as a tendency to feel entitled to more than one's fair share of limited resources).

According to Ashton et al., honesty-humility is a domain of personality that regulates altruistic behavior when a person has the power to exploit relationships, in contrast to agreeableness, which regulates altruistic behavior when a person is vulnerable to exploitation within relationships.[40] Based on the HEXACO tradition, and the lexical approach on which it is founded, humility pertains especially to the regulation of interpersonal superiority (Modesty subscale; e.g., "I am an ordinary person who is no better than others") and hoarding of resources (Greed-Avoidance subscale; e.g., "Having a lot of money is not especially important to me") when one has the power to exploit others.

Components of a Humility Judgment

To explore whether humility judgments assume embedded values, it might help to systematically consider the components that inform a humility judgment. First, the judge has some ideal expectation for how the target person ought to have allocated the valued resources (e.g., talking, credit, or honor) in a particular context of interests, goals, roles, and relational histories. The ideal behavior would be an action motivated by character traits that cause a person to consistently take only what they need and use their influence to work for the good of the collective, whether it be a relationship, group, or social system. Second, the judge evaluates the degree to which the actual behavior fell short of the ideal allocation. Judges have a certain internal sense of probability. It is relatively rare for someone not only to generate "margin"—a surplus of one or another good—but also readily and generously to share that surplus for the good of a relationship. Third, the judge evaluates the causes of the behavior, including the motives of the target person (e.g., benevolent or exploitive), as well as the degree to which the behavior was caused by internal versus external factors. Accordingly, the judge estimates the degree to which the behavior was caused by a character that consistently acts humbly despite circumstances that would tend to cause egoistic behavior.

This componential elaboration supplies previously unspecified logic for scholars who have examined humility in situations also used to study forgiveness or gratitude. According to theorizing on the injustice gap,[41] after offenses, victims and offenders negotiate their respective stories about an offense. Relative to offenders, victims tend to appraise offenses as more hurtful and more likely to be caused by stable, internal qualities of the offender.[42] When this negotiation does not satisfy the parties, victims and offenders tend to use humility language to malign the reputation of the other within their social networks.[43] For example, consider an employee who has worked for a particular boss for five years but was recently passed over for a promotion. The employee might abruptly shift her perspective of the boss' humility, telling everyone who will listen that the boss was arrogant and egotistical in the process. In this case, the humility language serves to provide information about how one can expect to be treated within a relationship with the target person, and people with access to this information can weigh the motives and perspective of the judge.

Regarding gratitude, resource allocation is also at stake. When a person receives honor or recognition, this puts the person in the spotlight in a way that requires the honoree to mitigate the potential for envy. The same components apply, as relationship partners (e.g., colleagues or teammates) consider the relationship between ideal behavior and what actually happened and also attempt to infer internal and external causes of the behavior, including the degree to which the behavior was caused by stable internal qualities of the target person. Someone expressing moderate humility would simply conform to modesty norms for the context (e.g., thanking key contributors and appropriately distributing credit). Someone expressing exceptional humility would demonstrate a surprising degree of commitment to sharing equally in the joy of achievement rather than using the spotlight to gain unfair personal advancement.

Ideas for Scientific Testing

Considering the components of a humility judgment may clarify when and how humility can promote flourishing. First, our extension clarifies that humility judgments involve at least two aspects that are surprising: (1) a target person uses ability and competitive traits to create margin; and (2) the target person shares generously out of devotion to the good of the relationship or collective. This thinking leads to the following testable hypotheses.

The "peacock hypothesis" of humility. Power may increase people's potential to be seen as humble. Therein lies a possible paradox: being seen as humble requires surprising generosity, but having the ability to express generosity may often occur because a person has exceptional abilities at creating margin, which can sometimes involve exploitation of subordinates. Indeed, it is difficult to take and share at the same time, which may be part of why exceptional humility is so rare and surprising. Perhaps this paradox also explains the weak link between humility and well-being for the individual. For many people, the generosity aspect of humility may put people at risk of exploitation. Perhaps humility showcases a certain abundance in the relevant valuable resource (e.g., money, emotional investment).

Development. Expectations influencing humility judgments ought to change over time based on the target person's maturity or role within a relationship or system. Some indirect evidence suggests that men and women are socialized to express humility differently. To this point, there is some developmental work on modesty norms in children, but it is important to explore when and how men and women may receive and internalize different messages related to the expected expression of humility.

Power. Humility judgments also depend on a target person's relative power within a system. In order to understand how humility relates to the flourishing of individuals and communities, more work is needed to explore how one's position within layered hierarchies influences perspectives of humility.

Our main idea in the current chapter is that *situations involving the allocation of resources tend to promote egoistic behavior, but when people act in surprisingly generous ways, it provides a signal of the person's humility.* Consider an example of an academic department allocating funding for doctoral students and how positionality within this hierarchical system might influence humility judgments. This department has three primary sources of funding (college budget, revenue from fees for online courses, and grants) and three doctoral programs. Normally, they pool resources so that all three of their doctoral programs fund the same number of students. Now imagine the various responses when one faculty member decides to reallocate $100k in grant funds from doctoral students to providing course releases to two assistant professors within his program. From the perspective of the doctoral students, the behavior has no influence on humility judgments, because their stipends remained exactly the same. Faculty members in the same program view the behavior as extremely generous (i.e., and other-oriented), which leads to inferences of humility of the target person. The chair is happy to support the decision, because the reallocation aligns with her goals and she likes that she was consulted in the process. In stark contrast, other faculty feel very upset and frame the behavior as a violation of department norms; they view the behavior and process as low in humility. The dean views the reallocation as neither particularly humble nor arrogant; however, once she realizes the department had surplus resources, she reduces the contribution of the college to the department the following year. Based on our theorizing, these various perspectives ought to lead to systematically different perspectives of the target person's degree of humility.

The dark side of humility. This scenario demonstrates that hierarchy likely affects how people view humility. People higher in a hierarchy may benefit from reinforcing humility norms at subordinate levels, if these norms allow them to take margin generated by subordinates. The dean's perspective illustrates this possible "dark side" of humility—she benefits from the operation of humility norms at a subordinate level. Leaders might exploit subordinates by promoting humility norms and then seizing the margin generated at a subordinate level.

Of course, there are counterforces to such exploitation. Declining trust decreases cooperation, and subordinates may engage in undermining (e.g., loafing) or retaliatory behaviors (e.g., damaging the reputation of the leader, which hurts opportunities for promotion) that hurt productivity of the system. Indeed, various theories of leadership allude to such tensions. A nefarious view is that some leaders may learn to reduce salary costs through paying people with a sense of meaning or the opportunity to work for a company that promotes a strong culture and sense of community.

To anticipate the critique that humility makes people vulnerable to exploitation, we must somehow address the contextual factors that make humility vulnerable to exploitation. Our model clarifies what some of these contextual factors might be—namely, situational factors in which humility judgments might contribute to inequalities in relationships or social systems and the fact that what orients the influence of such contextual factors on humility judgments are speculative assessments concerning generosity of behavior.

First, within a similar level of a hierarchy (e.g., a male and female assistant professor within a department), humility norms could easily contribute to inequalities if expectations differ for people considered to operate at the same level within a system. For example, if a department chair expects applicants to stubbornly negotiate salary throughout their careers and to be much more willing to seek and execute a counteroffer, and such behaviors are typically more likely in males than in females, then male candidates have a systematic advantage at both creating margin and being perceived as sharing that margin generously. The same actual behavior (getting a counteroffer) would be seen as less humble for females relative to males.

Second, at different levels of hierarchy, a leader could reinforce humility norms in subordinates (give me as much margin as you can and trust me to handle the margin fairly) and then squander the public trust to allocate resources wisely for the good of the community. We might then consider various ways that subordinates might accuse a leader of squandering resources. For example, the leader might make investments that are unsustainable and that decline in value over time, leaving increasingly less flexibility for future leadership to adjust to future opportunities. The leader also might show favoritism in various ways (invest in certain subgroups over others, which eventually undermines cohesion and causes groups to consider whether being part of the collective is sufficiently valuable).

Third, sometimes groups or larger systems may reduce conflict through putting pressure on what people want or expect from a system. Consider an academic department that needs faculty to both teach courses and get grants. Perhaps in a perfect world, the system could allow people focused on teaching to have their first choice of courses. The department might allow those getting grants to have greater choice of when they teach in order to prioritize their time. In this case, competition is reduced because people have the capacity to pursue their interests within the system. Of course, the specialization might not seem fair, to the degree that teaching roles are given less privilege (e.g., pay or autonomy over time) than are roles focused on securing external funding. A theory of humility could consider tradeoffs within a system that may function to decease competition over scarce resources.

Taken together, our theorizing highlights the contextual nature of humility judgments. They always happen from a biased perspective that includes the values and relational history of the judge, as well as any tendencies to view relevant evidence through a self-interested lens. Although these biases are certainly present within individual relationships (e.g., parent-child, teacher-student, or partner-partner in a romantic relationship), they may be especially amplified within larger systems. There is a potential for the powerful view of humility to function in an oppressive fashion. Thus, in systems that are especially apt to be exploitive (e.g., families, business, teams, or schools), there is a potential for striving to undermine the flourishing of individuals. Humility would only promote flourishing in a system and in individuals when some degree of justice is achieved in the allocation of resources.

Future Research

There are at least two primary implications of our thinking for the future science of humility. First, we have renewed reason to take a second look at how to interpret self-report measures of humility. From the context that considers power and hierarchies, leaders have an incentive to appear more humble than they really are. At least within business, leaders are often promoted based on their ability to optimize outcomes and profit for companies. This would select for traits associated with drawing out margin from subordinates while also minimizing the degree to which one must share resources; at the same time, appearing unfair or greedy will hurt the leader's reputation and deteriorate team performance. Future research could explore ways that leadership systems may institutionalize the leader's ability to extract margin without suffering reputational damage by locking in norms and expectations for resource sharing. Furthermore, personal qualities of leaders (e.g., "paying people with meaning" or other psychological needs) may also allow leaders to excel at their role.

Second, to this point, we have seen very little empirical scholarship exploring the potential damage that occurs when groups or societies apply humility norms differently to different individuals. We can adduce indirect evidence that women may suffer from such dynamics within the business context, but such humility-related penalties likely occur across a range of identities or roles. For sure, norms related to virtue function to promote cooperation, but they can also function to create and maintain inequalities if differentially applied based on roles, identities, or any other means of holding people to different standards of conduct. This idea could be tested with basic research that manipulates roles or identities and then demonstrates that humility is perceived differently if perhaps seemingly slight contextual factors are changed. We could also begin to capture some of the mechanisms implied by our model, such as the appraisal process associated with the injustice gap.

Conclusion

Given the currently weak evidence that humility promotes benefits for the practitioner of humility, we set out to expand theorizing on how humility may be related to negotiation of resource allocation within relationships or larger systems. Considering these dynamics ought to help articulate a stronger theory about when and how humility can promote (and sometimes undermine) human flourishing. For a larger community to thrive, it needs members to seek to (a) give more than they require (b) for as long as they can; it also needs (c) leaders who invest in the good of the community, including tending to the needy, rather than investing primarily in their own interests. (d) Systemically, a thriving system must address two challenges to justice. First, it must generate enough margin to share with those who cannot take care of their own needs while also limiting incentives to take advantage of resource sharing (free rider problem). Second, it must temper the ability of leaders to exploit subordinate systems without investing effectively in the good of the collective (exploitation problem). The strongest systems attend to both aspects of "unjust" allocation of resources. Finally, a thriving system must (e) regulate the undercurrent of competition that threatens to undermine cooperation within human relationships. Larger collectives have a major challenge of ensuring that local identification reduces intergroup competition. The potential for greed and attempts at exploitation is a threat to humility. Notice that modern humility language draws on spatial metaphors (e.g., having a big ego). An arrogant person consistently consumes more than they contribute to relationships. One of the great challenges of modern societies is to develop larger systems that encourage humility rather than egotism in their members and leaders. Groups that can accomplish such humble cultures will surely have an advantage.

* * *

RESPONSE TO DON E. DAVIS AND SARAH GAZAWAY

Jane Foulcher

Is humility a good thing? Don E. Davis and Sarah Gazaway pose a critical question regarding humility: "Does humility promote human flourishing?" Humility has famously been dismissed as a "monkish virtue" (David Hume) or as arising from a "slave morality" (Friedrich Nietzsche) and thus leading to the impoverishment rather than flourishing of human life. Twentieth-century second-wave feminists came to a similarly negative conclusion, viewing humility as unhealthy self-abnegation or submission in the context of patriarchal power systems. The renewed interest in and growth of research into humility, and its relation to human well-being, might therefore come as a surprise. The backdrop to this revived interest in humility has a least two components: the revival of philosophical virtue ethics in the late twentieth century[1] and the development of positive psychology in the early twenty-first century.[2] Christian theologians have engaged solidly with philosophical virtue ethics, particularly following the publication of Alasdair MacIntyre's *After Virtue* in 1981. Not surprisingly, given its relatively recent emergence, theological engagement with positive psychology is still in its infancy.[3] Interdisciplinary discussion between psychology, philosophy, and theology regarding humility has only just begun—indeed, this book is an early fruit. I need to say all this in order to situate my response to the Davis and Gazaway chapter: I come to this subject as a theologian. This means that my engagement with the material is essentially as an outsider looking in to the discipline of psychology. I can make some observations and offer some alternative perspectives from (a corner of) my discipline. No more.

First, it is impossible to avoid questions of definition. In Davis and Gazaway's chapter we enter an intradisciplinary conversation regarding definition and measurement that is well underway. The chapter begins by charting the main contours of the territory that scholars in the discipline of psychology have been traversing in relation to measuring humility. Concerns around the reliability of self-report constituted an early impediment to empirical research: researchers were rightly concerned that the "modesty effect" might confound self-assessments of humility. More significantly, though unsurprisingly, research within empirical psychology has struggled with defining humility. What exactly is being measured and why? What, why, and how questions have continued to be debated as "the science of humility" has developed over the last two decades. The Davis and Gazaway chapter sketches some of this debate, but for those outside the fold of empirical psychology it is worth dipping further into the literature, especially recent review articles, to observe the extent and nature of this work.[4] In *Heroic Humility*, for example, Worthington and Allison propose a three-part definition of humility, drawn from the now-sizable body of work being produced by a group of scholars including Everett Worthington Jr., Don Davis, Joshua Hook, and others, much of it funded through the Templeton Foundation.[5] They suggest that there is a level of consensus (among empirical psychologists) regarding two aspects of humility: accurate self-assessment and modesty. Accurate self-assessment involves an understanding of one's strengths, weaknesses, and limits, together with an openness to learning and change—"teachability."[6] Modesty concerns one's "self-presentation" to others, neither "too high" nor "too low."[7] Worthington and Allison propose a third feature around which there is less agreement but which they believe is essential for "true humility": other-orientation, "holding an abiding attitude oriented towards benefiting others."[8] Davis and Gazaway, at the end of their discussion of definition and measurement, define humility in a similar threefold way (see 143).

Philosophers and theologians too have struggled with conceptualizing humility, although scholars in these disciplines would probably not consider it measurable or indeed wish to measure it. In my own work, in Christian monastic traditions, I often found myself qualifying "humility" with further descriptors: material and social humility, ontological or existential humility, and so on. In the twelfth century, Bernard of Clairvaux found it necessary to make a distinction between cold humility, which has to do with honest self-assessment, and warm humility, humility transformed by divine love.[9]

Indeed, humility, in Christian thinking, has a long and complicated history. One element of that complexity is humility's entanglement with the classical virtues tradition. It is worth understanding a little of how this came about and some of the consequences of this entanglement.

The notion of virtue itself is not unproblematic in the Christian theological tradition. Although the language of virtue is almost completely absent from the Hebrew and Christian Scriptures, early Christian theology developed within the Roman Empire and necessarily engaged with Greco-Roman philosophical and ethical thought, including its virtues tradition. But while the language of virtue enters Christian theological discourse, we also find a radical critique of the shape and purpose of the virtuous life. No longer is virtue accumulated for the sake of human glory. For Augustine, for example, human flourishing (*eudaimonia*) is founded on the knowledge of God, and the goal of end of human life (*telos*) is "the enjoyment of God."[10] For Christian theologians "human flourishing" can never sit as a separate construct, untethered from God, the source of all life. Rather, human flourishing always concerns humanity's relationship to God, and specifically how Jesus Christ, the "God-man," opens a new way of being human. Glory has a very different flavor in a Christian worldview: a glory that finds its source and true nature in the life, death, and resurrection of Jesus.[11]

Where does humility sit in relation to this reshaping of virtue? There is not space here to fully map the changing fortunes of humility in Christian discourse.[12] But the starting point is important. Klaus Wengst's study of the word groups *tapeinos* (Gk.) and *humilis* (Lat.) in Greco-Roman texts indicates that humility is not a virtue but rather primarily a condition of the socially inferior, whose servile status and dependence on physical labor precluded them from participation in public life, the pursuit of honor, and therefore virtue.[13] In early Christianity and through much of the Western monastic tradition, humility retains social and material resonances. To become Christian entailed a reordering of one's relationships with God, self, and others. And the template, and vehicle, for this reordering was Christ himself, who had "emptied himself, taking the form of a slave," and had "humbled himself and become obedient to the point of death—even [a humiliating] death on a cross" (Phil 2:7-8, NRSV). Humility here is assuredly not the same as temperance or moderation. It is notable that humility (*humilitas*) is not found in Augustine's influential scheme of seven virtues (the three "infused" or theological virtues: faith, hope, and charity; and four classically derived cardinal virtues: prudence, temperance, fortitude, and justice).[14] And while Augustine does call humility a virtue, he always understands it as a manifestation of divine life, linked with grace: "The way of humility comes from no other source; it comes only from Christ. It is the way originated by him who, though most high, came in humility. What else did he teach us by humbling himself and becoming obedient even to death, even to the death on the cross?"[15] Humility cannot be understood outside Christ.

By the time we get to Thomas Aquinas' engagement with Aristotle, though, humility seems irrevocably wedded to temperance and moderation. Of course, it is no use bemoaning humility's entanglement with the virtues, but this history may, at least in part, explain why empirical psychology (along with philosophy) has had to grapple, at length, with conceptualizing humility. Its complex evolution has made it a multifaceted, sometimes paradoxical, notion. Defined in one way, it immediately seems to require a caveat, an addition, another angle. Humility seems to require multiple takes, if you like; which is exactly what one can see in the development of the "science of humility."

A second aspect of Davis and Gazaway's chapter invites comment. The work of Davis and others reflects a shift from thinking about humility as an intrapersonal to an interpersonal quality: highlighting, for example, the significance of humility as a "social oil" that enables relationships to weather rivalry and conflict. In this chapter Davis and Gazaway push this work further, theorizing that "people use humility language (and judge humility in others) in order to negotiate the fair allocation of resources," so that "people seen as more humble tend to generate margin—that is, they produce gains that outweigh the costs of their actions. Then they share that margin with others within a relationship or social system" (140). One of the advantages of conceptualizing humility in this way, Davis and Gazaway argue, is that it "begins to clarify some of the contexts in which humility language can contribute to injustice" (140).

Within Christian traditions the relational nature of humility has been a persistent theme, but it has also long recognized the dangers around humility judgments—in relation both to the self and to others. There is a sense in which Christian theology's realism regarding human nature helps us here. While imitation is essential to our development as human beings, it is also the basis of human rivalry. And humility judgments are easily turned into mimetic rivalry.[16] A negative example will help here. In an early monastic rule known as the *Rule of the Master*, a source for the influential sixth-century *Rule of St. Benedict*, the Master encourages what amounts to a humility competition! While the monastery is conceived as an essentially egalitarian society, social ordering, as in all human communities, is critical to the practical functioning of the community: roles, leadership, the ordering of seating in chapel and at table—all become matter for consideration. The Master's approach to social ordering involves the elimination of all ranks (aside from his own as abbot) in the monastic community:

> The abbot must take care never to appoint anyone second to himself, nor to assign anyone to third place. Why? So that by not causing anyone to become proud of the honor and by promising the honor of being his successor to someone who lives a holy life, he may make all eager to rival one another in doing what is good and in humility, just as the Lord judged the apostles quarreling over first place when "he brought a child into their midst and said: 'Let anyone who wants to be great among you be like this, and let anyone who wants to be first among you be your servant.'"[17]

While the Master's objective is to cultivate humility, the result of this abolition of rank is a competition—in fact a competition "to generate margin" (to pick up Davis and Gazaway) between oneself and other, rival, monks. Monks are constantly required to judge their own humility performance against others. There is, potentially, an unholy rush to the bottom: much like the jostling of an ecclesiastical procession, where proximity to last place is intended to signify humility ("the first shall be last") but in fact signals superior rank. Significantly, in the compilation of his rule Benedict did not follow the *Rule of the Master* on this point, instead opting for a system based on date of entry to the monastery, thus entirely avoiding the need for judgments regarding humility (or any other spiritual attributes).

In the Christian monastic tradition, self-forgetfulness is often seen as constitutive of humility. Judgments of others are considered corrosive, to both the self and the community. Bernard of Clairvaux describes the fall from humility vividly:

> The first step of pride is curiosity. How does it show itself? You see one who up to this time had every appearance of being an excellent monk. Now you begin to notice that wherever he is, standing, walking or sitting, his eyes are wandering, his glance darts right and left, his ears are cocked. . . . These symptoms show his soul has caught some disease. He used to watch over his own conduct; now all his watchfulness is for others. . . .
>
> The monk who observes others instead of attending to himself will begin before long to see some as his superiors and others as his inferiors; in some he will see things to envy, in others, things to despise. The eyes have wandered and the mind soon follows. It is no longer steadily fixed on its real concerns and is now carried up on the crest of the waves of pride, now down in the trough of envy. One minute the mind is full of envious sadness, the next childishly glad about some excellence he sees in himself.[18]

For Bernard this wandering of the eyes sets the monk on a slippery slope away from truth about the self, away from Christ (who embodies and calls us to truth), away from humility: these all cohere. For Bernard, like Augustine, humility has is beginning and end in Christ.

In embarking on an interdisciplinary conversation, I wonder if we are comparing apples and apples, or apples and pears? Is Christian humility really comparable with the construct labeled "humility" being explored in the field of positive psychology? And can it really be cultivated as a virtue? I am yet to be convinced. Modesty, accurate self-assessment, and other-orientation are, perhaps, able to be clearly defined and measured. But for the Christian theologian, humility is, ultimately, a divine rather than human virtue—one that can never be caught or bagged but only manifested as a sort of byproduct of divine-human encounter.

• • •

Reply to Jane Foulcher

Don E. Davis and Sarah Gazaway

Foulcher ended her response with an important question: Is there sufficient overlap in the discourse systems of Christian theology and empirical psychology regarding humility for a point of contact? Are we trying to compare "apples to pears"? Perhaps there is little room for anything more than parallel play. Indeed, if our methodologies are too different, perhaps the wisest thing we can do, after noticing that we use the same word, is to agree that we are talking about very different things. To assess this possibility, we decided to read Foulcher's recent book in order to explore the possibility for fruitful collaboration.[1] In response, we sought to imagine some potential benefits of accepting influence from each other across these disciplinary lines, as well as to find prospects for common ground.

Opportunity to appeal to the living. A first important area of common ground seems to be implicit or explicit attempts to appeal to the living—making our knowledge relevant to how our contemporaries live their lives. Even in the most esoteric areas of our disciplines, by putting words on a page, it would seem there is an implicit argument of relevance to someone else's life. Why should a university give us lectionary space? Do any of our ideas have the power to transform how people live their lives and the kinds of people they become? An adapted saying from St. Bernard of Clairvaux notes this potential overlap of efforts within the context of humility: "There are many who seek knowledge for the sake of knowledge: that is curiosity. There are others who desire to know in order that they may themselves be known: that is vanity. But there are some who seek knowledge in order to serve and edify others: and that is humility."[2]

Our team is currently developing ideas of how to promote humility in therapeutic settings. Foulcher's book has many examples of people attempting to build humility into the structures of their lives. Reading how prior cultures build humility into the structures of their daily life provided several important correctives.

First, individuals in Foulcher's book were refreshingly unpreoccupied with the paradox of trying to grow in humility. Rather, many people strove to form communities that would "interiorize" a culture of humility. This included renouncing their prior identities, sharing work that limits hierarchy, and developing ways of handling power and authority that limit competition (e.g., processes such as using seniority rather than performance as a key criterion, as Foulcher mentions regarding Benedict of Nursia in her comment on our chapter).

Second, monastic communities took great care to renounce sources of greed. This point aligns with our chapter. Regulation of greed needs much more attention within the psychological literature on humility. Only one measure of humility includes regulation of greed as a key component. We hope to explore this aspect of humility much more in our future work. What is it like for people to live in less greedy cultures? What if more humble communities generate less profit but also generate less overconsumption? Maybe the environmental issues we face are also a physical manifestation of an inner state.

Opportunity to align measures. A second area we hope to accept influence from Foulcher is in the area of measurement. As we read her book, we imagined what she might have to say if she were part of our team, as we consider the state of existing measures.[3] Her approach of tracking the evolution of humility raised some crucial questions for our team. For example, are the current measures of humility somehow culturally biased and restricted in their range of content? What hidden assumptions of universality may pose problems for studying humility cross-culturally? Clearly, we cannot study ancient societies (e.g., Romans) using psychological research methods and are limited to studying the diversity that exists among the living. However, reading Foulcher made us strongly question how culture may influence people's understanding and practice of humility—indeed, whether it makes sense to think of humility being the same "thing" across different contexts.

Opportunity for systematic literature reviews. A third way we can accept influence from Foulcher, and theologians in general, is to include them in the work of conducting systematic literature reviews of psychological science. Just as anyone can critique a definition, the source for theories can come from anywhere. Good theories are in conversation with existing empirical work, but the intuitions people use to tell stories about data are human process—not proprietary to psychological scientists. Many of Foulcher's keen intuitions would get included in theories about why and how humility promotes social and psychological benefits. An occupational hazard of psychology is that our definitions, in order to imply clear measurement strategies, cannot handle a variety of contextual moderators or qualifications. So, for pragmatic reasons, and for better or worse, we must push contextual qualifiers into broader theories about when and how a construct ends up leading to positive or negative outcomes in a person's life.

Conclusion. After our reading, we certainly sympathize with the reaction that we may not have much room for common ground. We do have very different methodologies. But perhaps the most expansive area of common ground is not what we know, based on our respective disciplines, but the fact that both our disciplines eventually run into a vast expanse of mystery. Perhaps this is where we can best help each other—making sure that we hold each other accountable not to claim more than is warranted by the methods within our discipline. Indeed, theology and psychology are both human systems, subject to all the limitations of competition and cultural blind spots that distort awareness of truth. After both have gone as far as human minds can imagine, they still get lost in a great veil that is the mystery of the unknown. Both eventually fade into a space at the limits of what can be known about God and creation.

For psychologists, our set of rules makes us quite cautious drawing many inferences about things we cannot fit into our current methods of observation. This caution has many benefits, but it can sometimes devolve into a problem of assuming that ideas that are not scientifically falsifiable are therefore bad ideas in general. Many of humanity's greatest discoveries involved going beyond the current limits. Speaking to fellow psychologists: we need not moralize our caution—it makes for good science but may hamper our ability to engage existential questions. We are more than what we can see and hear. Fully thriving as humans may require allowing ourselves to ask questions that we may never answer. In this sense, intellectual humility may require more than what science can provide.

We want to conclude by appealing to something like the mission that inspired Christian, the Trappist monk featured at the end of Foulcher's book. In his many lectures on humility, Christian referred to something like existential humility (the ability to sit in uncertainty with hope) within the vision that God might do something new within a community. These ideas appeared to give him (and others) the courage to live out his commitment to remain in Algeria, knowing that death was imminent. He held a deep commitment to pray and practice alongside Muslim neighbors in the hope that God would create something new as they prayed alongside each other. For psychologists and theologians of faith, and those who view their work as an acting out of a calling, I wonder what might happen as we do our work "alongside each other" with confidence that something new could happen between us.

• • •

Notes to Chapter 5
(Don E. Davis and Sarah Gazaway)

1 For reviews, see D. E. Davis, C. DeBlaere, J. Owen, J. N. Hook, D. P. Rivera, E. Choe, D. R. Van Tongeren, E. L. Worthington Jr., and V. Placeres, "The Multicultural Orientation Framework: A Narrative Review," *Psychotherapy* 55, no. 1 (2019): 89–100.

2 S. E. McElroy-Hetzel, D. E. Davis, J. N. Hook, E. L. Worthington Jr., and C. DeBlaere, "Assessing Humility: A Critical Review of Measures" (2017). Manuscript submitted for publication.
3 J. P. Tangney, "Humility: Theoretical Perspectives, Empirical Findings and Directions for Future Research," *Journal of Social and Clinical Psychology* 19 (2000): 70–82.
4 W. C. Rowatt, A. Ottenbreit, K. P. Nesselroade Jr., and P. A. Cunningham, "On Being Holier-than-Thou or Humbler-than-Thee: A Social-Psychological Perspective on Religiousness and Humility," *Journal for the Scientific Study of Religion* 41 (2002): 227–37.
5 W. C. Rowatt, C. Powers, V. Targhetta, J. Comer, S. Kennedy, and J. Labouff, "Development and Initial Validation of an Implicit Measure of Humility Relative to Arrogance," *Journal of Positive Psychology* 1 (2006): 198–211.
6 D. E. Davis, J. N. Hook, E. L. Worthington Jr., D. R. Van Tongeren, A. L. Gartner, D. J. Jennings II, and R. A. Emmons, "Relational Humility: Conceptualizing and Measuring Humility as a Personality Judgment," *Journal of Personality Assessment* 93 (2011): 225–34; B. P. Owens, M. D. Johnson, and T. R. Mitchell, "Expressed Humility in Organizations: Implications for Performance, Teams, and Leadership," *Organization Science* 24 (2013): 1517–38.
7 For a review of over twenty measures, see S. E. McElroy, K. G. Rice, D. E. Davis, J. N. Hook, P. C. Hill, E. L. Worthington Jr., and D. R. Van Tongeren, "Intellectual Humility: Scale Development and Theoretical Elaborations in the Context of Religious Leadership," *Journal of Psychology and Theology* 42 (2014): 19–30.
8 For a review, see M. C. Ashton, K. Lee, and R. E. de Vries, "The HEXACO Honesty-Humility, Agreeableness, and Emotionality Factors: A Review of Research and Theory," *Personality and Social Psychology Review* 18 (2014): 139–52.
9 D. C. Funder, "On the Accuracy of Personality Judgment: A Realistic Approach," *Psychological Review* 102, no. 4 (1995): 652–70.
10 D. E. Davis, S. E. McElroy, K. G. Rice, E. Choe, C. Westbrook, J. N. Hook, D. R. Van Tongeren, C. DeBlaere, P. Hill, V. Placares, and E. L. Worthington Jr., "Is Modesty a Subdomain of Humility?" *Journal of Positive Psychology* 11 (2016): 439–46.
11 D. Whitcomb, H. Battaly, J. Baehr, and D. Howard-Snyder, "Intellectual Humility: Owning Our Limitations," *Philosophy and Phenomenological Research* 94 (2015): 509–39.
12 E. L. Worthington Jr. and S. T. Allison, *Heroic Humility: What the Science of Humility Can Say to People Raised on Self-Focus* (Washington, D.C.: American Psychological Association, 2018).
13 R. McAnnally-Linz, "An Unrecognizable Glory: Christian Humility in the Age of Authenticity" (Ph.D. diss., Yale University, 2016).
14 For example, T. D. Wilson, "Know Thyself," *Perspectives on Psychological Science* 4 (2009): 384–89.
15 N. Aghababaei, S. Mohammadtabar, and M. Saffarinia, "Dirty Dozen vs. the H Factor: Comparison of the Dark Triad and Honesty-Humility

in Prosociality, Religiosity, and Happiness," *Personality and Individual Differences* 67 (2014): 6–10; Rowatt et al., "Development and Initial Validation."

16 For a review, see D. E. Davis, J. N. Hook, R. McAnnally-Linz, E. Choe, and V. Placeres, "Humility, Religion, and Spirituality: A Review of the Literature," *Psychology of Religion and Spirituality* 9, no. 3 (2017): 242–53.

17 D. E. Davis, E. L. Worthington Jr., J. N. Hook, R. A. Emmons, P. C. Hill, R. A. Bollinger, and D. R. Van Tongeren, "Humility and the Development and Repair of Social Bonds: Two Longitudinal Studies," *Self and Identity* 12 (2013): 58–77.

18 J. E. Farrell, J. N. Hook, M. Ramos, D. E. Davis, D. R. Van Tongeren, and J. M. Ruiz, "Humility and Relationship Outcomes in Couples: The Mediating Role of Commitment," *Couple and Family Psychology: Research and Practice* 4 (2015): 14–26; S. E. McElroy-Heltzel, D. E. Davis, C. DeBlaere, J. N. Hook, M. Massengale, E. Choe, and K. G. Rice, "Cultural Humility: Pilot Study Testing the Social Bonds Hypothesis in Interethnic Couples," *Journal of Counseling Psychology* 65, no. 4 (2018): 531–37; A. S. Peters, W. C. Rowatt, and M. K. Johnson, "Associations between Dispositional Humility and Social Relationship Quality," *Psychology* 3 (2011): 155–61.

19 Ashton, Lee, and de Vries, "HEXACO Honesty-Humility."

20 J. P. LaBouff, W. C. Rowatt, M. K. Johnson, J.-A. Tsang, and G. McCullough, "Humble People Are More Helpful than Less Humble Persons: Evidence from Three Studies," *Journal of Positive Psychology* 7 (2012): 16–29.

21 J. J. Exline and P. C. Hill, "Humility: A Consistent and Robust Predictor of Generosity," *Journal of Positive Psychology* 7 (2012): 208–18.

22 T. R. Cohen, A. T. Panter, N. Turan, L. Morse, and Y. Kim, "Moral Character in the Workplace," *Journal of Personality and Social Psychology* 107, no. 5 (2014): 943.

23 P. Carmody and K. Gordon, "Offender Variables: Unique Predictors of Benevolence, Avoidance, and Revenge?" *Personality and Individual Differences* 50 (2011): 1012–17; D. E. Davis, J. N. Hook, E. L. Worthington Jr., D. R. Van Tongeren, A. L. Gartner, D. J. Jennings II, and R. A. Emmons, "Relational Humility: Conceptualizing and Measuring Humility as a Personality Judgment," *Journal of Personality Assessment* 93 (2011): 225–34; Farrell et al., "Humility and Relationship Outcomes"; C. Powers, R. K. Nam, W. C. Rowatt, and P. C. Hill, "Associations between Humility, Spiritual Transcendence, and Forgiveness," *Research in the Social Scientific Study of Religion* 18 (2007): 75–94; K. E. Sheppard and S. D. Boon, "Predicting Appraisals of Romantic Revenge: The Roles of Honesty-Humility, Agreeableness, and Vengefulness," *Personality and Individual Differences* 52 (2012): 128–32.

24 For a review, see Davis et al., "Humility, Religion, and Spirituality."

25 J. Owen, M. M. Leach, B. Wampold, and E. Rodolfa, "Client and Therapist Variability in Clients' Perceptions of Their Therapists' Multicultural Competencies," *Journal of Counseling Psychology* 58 (2011): 1–9.

26 R. E. de Vries, "Personality Predictors of Leadership Styles and the Self-Other Agreement Problem," *Leadership Quarterly* 23 (2012): 809–21.
27 T. E. Basford, L. R. Offermann, and T. S. Behrend, "Please Accept My Sincerest Apologies: Examining Follower Reactions to Leader Apology," *Journal of Business Ethics* 119 (2014): 99–117; McElroy et al., "Intellectual Humility."
28 J. Wiltshire, J. S. Bourdage, and K. Lee, "Honesty-Humility and Perceptions of Organizational Politics in Predicting Workplace Outcomes," *Journal of Business and Psychology* 29 (2014): 235–51.
29 Owens, Johnson, and Mitchell, "Expressed Humility in Organizations."
30 B. P. Owens and D. R. Hekman, "How Does Leader Humility Influence Team Performance? Exploring the Mechanisms of Contagion and Collective Promotion Focus," *Academy of Management Journal* 59 (2016): 1088–1111.
31 C.-Y. (C.) Chiu, B. P. Owens, and P. E. Tesluk, "Initiating and Utilizing Shared Leadership in Teams: The Role of Leader Humility, Team Proactive Personality, and Team Performance Capability," *Journal of Applied Psychology* 101 (2016): 1705–20.
32 A. Rego, B. Owens, K. C. Yam, D. Bluhm, M. P. Cunha, T. Silard, L. Gonçalves, M. Martins, A. V. Simpson, and W. Liu, "Leader Humility and Team Performance: Exploring the Mechanisms of Team PsyCap and Task Allocation Effectiveness," *Journal of Management* 45, no. 3 (2017): 1009–33.
33 McElroy-Heltzel et al., "Cultural Humility."
34 R. H. Hoyle, E. K. Davisson, K. J. Diebels, and M. R. Leary, "Holding Specific Views with Humility: Conceptualization and Measurement of Specific Intellectual Humility," *Personality and Individual Differences* 97 (2016): 165–72.
35 Hoyle et al., "Holding Specific Views with Humility."
36 P. Williamson, R. W. Hood Jr., A. Ahmad, M. Sadiq, and P. C. Hill, "The Intratextual Fundamentalism Scale: Cross-Cultural Application, Validity Evidence, and Relationship with Religious Orientation and the Big 5 Factor Markers," *Mental Health, Religion and Culture* 13 (2010): 721–47.
37 D. L. Hall, D. C. Matz, and W. Wood, "Why Don't We Practice What We Preach? A Meta-analytic Review of Religious Racism," *Personality and Social Psychology Review* 14 (2010): 126–39.
38 Davis et al., "Humility and the Development and Repair of Social Bonds."
39 D. E. Davis, X. Yang, C. DeBlaere, S. E. McElroy, D. R. Van Tongeren, J. N. Hook, and E. L. Worthington Jr., "The Injustice Gap," *Psychology of Religion and Spirituality* 8 (2016): 175–84.
40 Ashton, Lee, and de Vries, "HEXACO Honesty-Humility."
41 J. J. Exline, E. L. Worthington Jr., P. Hill, and M. E. McCullough, "Forgiveness and Justice: A Research Agenda for Social and Personality Psychology," *Personality and Social Psychology Review* 7 (2003): 337–48.
42 Davis et al., "Injustice Gap"; Exline et al., "Forgiveness and Justice."
43 Ashton, Lee, and de Vries, "HEXACO Honesty-Humility."

NOTES TO CHAPTER 5 RESPONSE
(JANE FOULCHER)

1 The pioneers of this movement include Elizabeth Anscombe, Philippa Foot, and Iris Murdoch.
2 Davis et al., "Humility, Religion, and Spirituality," 242.
3 See, for example, Gillies Ambler, Matthew P. Anstey, Theo D. McCall, and Mathew A. White, eds., *Flourishing in Faith: Theology Encountering Positive Psychology* (Eugene, Ore.: Cascade, 2017).
4 A more substantial orientation is offered, for example, in Davis et al., "Humility, Religion, and Spirituality."
5 Worthington and Allison, *Heroic Humility*.
6 Worthington and Allison, *Heroic Humility*, 25.
7 Worthington and Allison, *Heroic Humility*, 24.
8 Worthington and Allison, *Heroic Humility*, 24–25.
9 Bernard of Clairvaux, *Sermons on the Song of Songs*, trans. Kilian Walsh, CF7 (Kalamazoo, Mich.: Cistercian, 1976), sermon 42.
10 Gerard J. P. O'Daly, *Augustine's Philosophy of Mind* (Berkeley: University of California Press, 1987), 5.
11 See the helpful exposition of this in McAnnally-Linz, "Unrecognizable Glory."
12 See Pierre Adnès, "Humilité," in *Dictionnaire de spiritualité*, vol. 7 (Paris: Beauchesne, 1969); Jane Foulcher, *Reclaiming Humility: Four Studies in the Monastic Tradition* (Athens, Ohio: Cistercian, 2015); André Louf, *The Way of Humility*, trans. Lawrence S. Cunningham (Kalamazoo, Mich.: Cistercian, 2007).
13 Klaus Wengst, *Humility: Solidarity of the Humiliated; The Transformation of an Attitude and Its Social Relevance in Graeco-Roman, Old Testament-Jewish and Early Christian Tradition*, trans. John Bowden (London: SCM Press, 1988), 4–15.
14 George J. Lavere, "Virtue," in *Augustine through the Ages: An Encyclopedia*, ed. Allan D. Fitzgerald (Grand Rapids: Eerdmans, 1999), 871–74.
15 Augustine, *The Works of Saint Augustine*, part 3, vol. 15, *Expositions of the Psalms (1–32)*, trans. Maria Boulding (Hyde Park, N.Y.: New City, 2000), exposition 2 Psalm 31:6b in sec. 18, pp. 380–81.
16 The work of René Girard is pertinent here.
17 *The Rule of the Master*, trans. Luke Eberle, CS 6 (Kalamazoo, Mich.: Cistercian, 1977), 92.1–5.
18 Bernard of Clairvaux, *The Steps of Humility and Pride*, trans. M. Ambrose Conway, CF 13A (Trappist, Ky.: Cistercian, 1973), 57.

NOTES TO CHAPTER 5 REPLY
(DON E. DAVIS AND SARAH GAZAWAY)

1 Jane Foulcher, *Reclaiming Humility: Four Studies in Monastic Tradition* (Athens, Ohio: Cistercian, 2015).

2. M. Srokosz, "Humility: A Neglected Scientific Virtue?" *Science and Christian Belief* 25, no. 2 (2013): 101–12. Srokosz adapted the saying from a sermon by St. Bernard of Clairvaux on Song of Songs 36:3 in which he omitted a portion of the middle of the statement and changed the last word of the saying from "love" to "humility."
3. S. E. McElroy-Heltzel, D. E. Davis, C. DeBlaere, E. L. Worthington Jr., and J. N. Hook, "Embarrassment of Riches in the Measurement of Humility: A Critical Review of 22 Measures," *Journal of Positive Psychology* 14, no. 3 (2018): 1–12.

CHAPTER BIBLIOGRAPHY

Adnès, Pierre. "Humilité." In *Dictionnaire de spiritualité*, vol. 7, 1136–87. Paris: Beauchesne, 1969.

Aghababaei, N., S. Mohammadtabar, and M. Saffarinia. "Dirty Dozen vs. the H Factor: Comparison of the Dark Triad and Honesty-Humility in Prosociality, Religiosity, and Happiness." *Personality and Individual Differences* 67 (2014): 6–10.

Ambler, Gillies, Matthew P. Anstey, Theo D. McCall, and Mathew A. White, eds. *Flourishing in Faith: Theology Encountering Positive Psychology*. Eugene, Ore.: Cascade, 2017.

Ashton, M. C., K. Lee, and R. E. de Vries. "The HEXACO Honesty-Humility, Agreeableness, and Emotionality Factors: A Review of Research and Theory." *Personality and Social Psychology Review* 18 (2014): 139–52.

Augustine. *The Works of Saint Augustine*. Part 3, vol. 15, *Expositions of the Psalms (1–32)*. Translated by Maria Boulding. Hyde Park, N.Y.: New City, 2000.

Basford, T. E., L. R. Offermann, and T. S. Behrend. "Please Accept My Sincerest Apologies: Examining Follower Reactions to Leader Apology." *Journal of Business Ethics* 119 (2014): 99–117.

Bernard of Clairvaux. *Sermons on the Song of Songs*. Translated by Kilian Walsh. CF 7. Kalamazoo, Mich.: Cistercian, 1976.

———. *The Steps of Humility and Pride*. Translated by M. Ambrose Conway. CF 13A. Trappist, Ky.: Cistercian, 1973.

Carmody, P., and K. Gordon. "Offender Variables: Unique Predictors of Benevolence, Avoidance, and Revenge?" *Personality and Individual Differences* 50 (2011): 1012–17.

Chiu, C.-Y. (C.), B. P. Owens, and P. E. Tesluk. "Initiating and Utilizing Shared Leadership in Teams: The Role of Leader Humility, Team Proactive Personality, and Team Performance Capability." *Journal of Applied Psychology* 101 (2016): 1705–20.

Cohen, T. R., A. T. Panter, N. Turan, L. Morse, and Y. Kim. "Moral Character in the Workplace." *Journal of Personality and Social Psychology* 107, no. 5 (2014): 943–63.

Davis, D. E., C. DeBlaere, J. Owen, J. N. Hook, D. P. Rivera, E. Choe, D. R. Van Tongeren, E. L. Worthington Jr., and V. Placeres. "The Multicultural Orientation Framework: A Narrative Review." *Psychotherapy* 55, no. 1 (2019): 89–100.

Davis, D. E., J. N. Hook, R. McAnnally-Linz, E. Choe, and V. Placeres. "Humility, Religion, and Spirituality: A Review of the Literature." *Psychology of Religion and Spirituality* 9 (2017): 242–53.

Davis, D. E., J. N. Hook, E. L. Worthington Jr., D. R. Van Tongeren, A. L. Gartner, D. J. Jennings II, and R. A. Emmons. "Relational Humility: Conceptualizing and Measuring Humility as a Personality Judgment." *Journal of Personality Assessment* 93 (2011): 225–34.

Davis, D. E., S. E. McElroy, K. G. Rice, E. Choe, C. Westbrook, J. N. Hook, D. R. Van Tongeren, C. DeBlaere, P. Hill, V. Placares, and E. L. Worthington Jr. "Is Modesty a Subdomain of Humility?" *Journal of Positive Psychology* 11 (2016): 439–46.

Davis, D. E., E. L. Worthington Jr., J. N. Hook, R. A. Emmons, P. C. Hill, R. A. Bollinger, and D. R. Van Tongeren. "Humility and the Development and Repair of Social Bonds: Two Longitudinal Studies." *Self and Identity* 12 (2013): 58–77.

Davis, D. E., X. Yang, C. DeBlaere, S. E. McElroy, D. R. Van Tongeren, J. N. Hook, and E. L. Worthington Jr. "The Injustice Gap." *Psychology of Religion and Spirituality* 8 (2016): 175–84.

de Vries, R. E. "Personality Predictors of Leadership Styles and the Self-Other Agreement Problem." *Leadership Quarterly* 23 (2012): 809–21.

Exline, J. J., and P. C. Hill. "Humility: A Consistent and Robust Predictor of Generosity." *Journal of Positive Psychology* 7 (2012): 208–18.

Exline, J. J., E. L. Worthington Jr., P. Hill, and M. E. McCullough. "Forgiveness and Justice: A Research Agenda for Social and Personality Psychology." *Personality and Social Psychology Review* 7 (2003): 337–48.

Farrell, J. E., J. N. Hook, M. Ramos, D. E. Davis, D. R. Van Tongeren, and J. M. Ruiz. "Humility and Relationship Outcomes in Couples: The Mediating Role of Commitment." *Couple and Family Psychology: Research and Practice* 4 (2015): 4–26.

Foulcher, Jane. *Reclaiming Humility: Four Studies in Monastic Tradition*. Athens, Ohio: Cistercian, 2015.

Funder, D. C. "On the Accuracy of Personality Judgment: A Realistic Approach." *Psychological Review* 102, no. 4 (1995): 652–70.

Hall, D. L., D. C. Matz, and W. Wood. "Why Don't We Practice What We Preach? A Meta-analytic Review of Religious Racism." *Personality and Social Psychology Review* 14 (2010): 126–39.

Hoyle, R. H., E. K. Davisson, K. J. Diebels, and M. R. Leary. "Holding Specific Views with Humility: Conceptualization and Measurement of Specific Intellectual Humility." *Personality and Individual Differences* 97 (2016): 165–72.

LaBouff, J. P., W. C. Rowatt, M. K. Johnson, J.-A. Tsang, and G. McCullough. "Humble People Are More Helpful than Less Humble Persons: Evidence from Three Studies." *Journal of Positive Psychology* 7 (2012): 16–29.

Lavere, George J. "Virtue." In *Augustine through the Ages: An Encyclopedia*, edited by Allan D. Fitzgerald, 871–74. Grand Rapids: Eerdmans, 1999.

Louf, André. *The Way of Humility*. Translated by Lawrence S. Cunningham. Kalamazoo, Mich.: Cistercian, 2007.

McAnnally-Linz, R. "An Unrecognizable Glory: Christian Humility in the Age of Authenticity." Ph.D. diss., Yale University, 2016.

McElroy, S. E., K. G. Rice, D. E. Davis, J. N. Hook, P. C. Hill, E. L. Worthington Jr., and D. R. Van Tongeren. "Intellectual Humility: Scale Development and Theoretical Elaborations in the Context of Religious Leadership. *Journal of Psychology and Theology* 42 (2014): 19–30.

McElroy-Heltzel, S. E., D. E. Davis, C. DeBlaere, J. N. Hook, M. Massengale, E. Choe, and K. G. Rice. "Cultural Humility: Pilot Study Testing the Social Bonds Hypothesis in Interethnic Couples." *Journal of Counseling Psychology* 65, no. 4 (2018): 531–37.

McElroy-Heltzel, S. E., D. E. Davis, C. DeBlaere, E. L. Worthington Jr., and J. N. Hook. "Embarrassment of Riches in the Measurement of Humility: A Critical Review of 22 Measures." *Journal of Positive Psychology* 14, no. 3 (2018): 1–12.

McElroy-Hetzel, S. E., D. E. Davis, J. N. Hook, E. L. Worthington Jr., and C. DeBlaere. "Assessing Humility: A Critical Review of Measures." 2017. Manuscript submitted for publication.

O'Daly, Gerard J. P. *Augustine's Philosophy of Mind*. Berkeley: University of California Press, 1987.

Owen, J., M. M. Leach, B. Wampold, and E. Rodolfa. "Client and Therapist Variability in Clients' Perceptions of Their Therapists' Multicultural Competencies." *Journal of Counseling Psychology* 58 (2011): 1–9.

Owens, B. P., and D. R. Hekman. "How Does Leader Humility Influence Team Performance? Exploring the Mechanisms of Contagion and Collective Promotion Focus." *Academy of Management Journal* 59 (2016): 1088–1111.

Owens, B. P., M. D. Johnson, and T. R. Mitchell. "Expressed Humility in Organizations: Implications for Performance, Teams, and Leadership." *Organization Science* 24 (2013): 1517–38.

Peters, A. S., W. C. Rowatt, and M. K. Johnson. "Associations between Dispositional Humility and Social Relationship Quality." *Psychology* 3 (2011): 155–61.

Powers, C., R. K. Nam, W. C. Rowatt, and P. C. Hill. "Associations between Humility, Spiritual Transcendence, and Forgiveness." *Research in the Social Scientific Study of Religion* 18 (2007): 75–94.

Rego, A., B. Owens, S. Leal, A. I. Melo, M. Pina e Cunha, L. Gonçalves, and P. Ribeiro. "How Leader Humility Helps Teams to Be Humbler, Psychologically Stronger, and More Effective: A Moderated Mediation Model." *Leadership Quarterly* 28, no. 5 (2017): 639–58.

Rego, A., B. Owens, K. C. Yam, D. Bluhm, M. Pina e Cunha, T. Silard, L. Gonçalves, M. Martins, A. V. Simpson, and W. Liu. "Leader Humility and Team Performance: Exploring the Mechanisms of Team PsyCap and Task Allocation Effectiveness." *Journal of Management* (2017). Advance online publication.

Rowatt, W. C., A. Ottenbreit, K. P. Nesselroade Jr., and P. A. Cunningham. "On Being Holier-than-Thou or Humbler-than-Thee: A Social-Psychological Perspective on Religiousness and Humility." *Journal for the Scientific Study of Religion* 41 (2002): 227–37.

Rowatt, W. C., C. Powers, V. Targhetta, J. Comer, S. Kennedy, and J. Labouff. "Development and Initial Validation of an Implicit Measure of Humility Relative to Arrogance." *Journal of Positive Psychology* 1 (2006): 198–211.

The Rule of the Master. Translated by Luke Eberle. CS 6. Kalamazoo, Mich.: Cistercian, 1977.

Sheppard, K. E., and S. D. Boon. "Predicting Appraisals of Romantic Revenge: The Roles of Honesty-Humility, Agreeableness, and Vengefulness." *Personality and Individual Differences* 52 (2012): 128–32.

Srokosz, M. "Humility: A Neglected Scientific Virtue?" *Science and Christian Belief* 25, no. 2 (2013): 101–12.

Tangney, J. P. "Humility: Theoretical Perspectives, Empirical Findings and Directions for Future Research." *Journal of Social and Clinical Psychology* 19 (2000): 70–82.

Wengst, Klaus. *Humility: Solidarity of the Humiliated; The Transformation of an Attitude and Its Social Relevance in Graeco-Roman, Old Testament-Jewish and Early Christian Tradition*. Translated by John Bowden. London: SCM Press, 1988.

Whitcomb, D., H. Battaly, J. Baehr, and D. Howard-Snyder. "Intellectual Humility: Owning Our Limitations." *Philosophy and Phenomenological Research* 94 (2017): 509–39.

Williamson, P., R. W. Hood Jr., A. Ahmad, M. Sadiq, and P. C. Hill. "The Intratextual Fundamentalism Scale: Cross-Cultural Application, Validity Evidence, and Relationship with Religious Orientation and the Big 5 Factor Markers." *Mental Health, Religion and Culture* 13 (2010): 721–47.

Wilson, T. D. "Know Thyself." *Perspectives on Psychological Science* 4 (2009): 384–89.

Wiltshire, J., J. S. Bourdage, and K. Lee. "Honesty-Humility and Perceptions of Organizational Politics in Predicting Workplace Outcomes." *Journal of Business and Psychology* 29 (2014): 235–51.

Worthington, E. L., Jr., and S. T. Allison. *Heroic Humility: What the Science of Humility Can Say to People Raised on Self-Focus*. Washington, D.C.: American Psychological Association, 2018.

6

Defining Humility
The Scope of Humility
Jason Baehr

According to one familiar way of thinking about humility, it comprises a certain attitude or orientation toward one's limitations. Minimally, a humble person is aware of, rather than oblivious to or in denial about, her limitations. But such awareness is not sufficient for humility, for a person could be aware of but chronically irritated by or defensive about her limitations. As such, she would be less than humble. Accordingly, humility also involves accepting or "owning" one's limitations.[1]

While the scope of humility evidently includes one's limitations and weaknesses, some have argued that it should be understood in broader terms. In particular, it is sometimes claimed that humility involves a fitting awareness and responsiveness, not just toward one's limitations and weaknesses, but also toward one's *abilities* and *strengths*. Jeanine Grenberg, for example, contends that humility is comprised of a "meta-attitude" that includes a "proper perspective" on oneself as "dependent and corrupt" but also a *"capable and dignified* rational agent."[2] Similarly, Ian Church has recently defended a view of intellectual humility according to which it is marked by an "appropriate attention to and ownership of intellectual limitations *and intellectual strengths.*"[3]

Call the first view—according to which humility involves an orientation toward one's limitations and weaknesses—the "narrow view" of humility, and the second view—according to which it also involves an orientation toward one's strengths and abilities—the "wide view." The wide view has some plausibility. This becomes apparent when considering certain familiar, but ultimately problematic, conceptions of humility. The following call to humility is from the fourteenth-century English mystic Walter Hilton: "You should consider yourself more vile than any living creature, so that you can hardly endure yourself, so great will be your consciousness of inward sin and corruption."[4] Such conceptions of humility have a long history in philosophical and theological writings about humility. However, for those who regard humility as a healthy and admirable trait, that is, as a genuine personal *virtue*, these views are objectionable. They suggest that the humble person necessarily has a *skewed* or *distorted* view of her moral status—that humility requires thinking of oneself as *worse* than one really is.

One natural response to such conceptions is to insist that the humble person has a proper appreciation, not just of her weaknesses and limitations, but also of her strengths and abilities. We will take a closer look at this reasoning toward the end of the chapter. In the meantime, my aim is to argue in support of the narrow view of humility. I do so, first, by raising two objections to the wide view. I then offer a pair of error theories aimed at explaining whatever initial appeal the wide view might enjoy. Finally, I consider and respond to several objections to the narrow view. My hope is that the discussion, in addition to laying bare the relative strengths and weaknesses of the wide and narrow views, will shed light on the overall structure of humility and its relationship to other morally significant qualities like servility, arrogance, and proper pride.

Two preliminary points are in order. First, the present chapter is not intended as a comprehensive defense of the narrow view of humility. Rather, it is intended merely as a defense of the narrow view over and against the wide view. Thus, I will not be taking a stand on whether the scope of humility can or should be broadened in other respects—for example, whether it should be broadened to incorporate not just a certain self-focus but also a certain focus or orientation toward others. That said, I will note in passing that the narrow view does not entail, or even make probable, that humble persons will be objectionably self-focused. On the contrary, we should expect humble persons, being free to admit their limitations and failures, to look beyond themselves in ways that self-focused and self-involved persons tend not to.

Second, while admittedly a quasi-technical concern, the difference between the narrow and wide views of humility is not without consequence. To illustrate, suppose one is interested in developing a valid psychological measure of humility. When it comes to formulating or assessing potential scale items, it will make no small difference whether one is thinking of humility as demanding a certain attitude toward one's limitations and weaknesses only, or as also demanding a certain awareness or responsiveness to one's abilities and strengths. Alternatively, suppose one is attempting to cultivate humility in oneself or others (e.g., in one's children, students, or parishioners). Here as well it is likely to matter—in terms of the sorts of things one focuses on or the activities one undertakes—whether humility is conceived of in narrower or broader terms. These reasons for caring about the comparative merits of the narrow and wide views of humility are in addition to a purely theoretical reason. Humility, properly conceived, is a deep and admirable personal excellence. On this basis alone, a proper understanding of its essential or defining features is a worthwhile intellectual pursuit.

Problems with the Wide View

My first argument against the wide view centers around a principle that pertains generally to virtue-theoretic attempts to specify the defining character of a virtue: if, when considering whether a given activity A is a defining feature of some particular virtue V, we find that A is already a defining feature of some *other* virtue W that is clearly *distinct* from V, we should resist identifying A as a defining feature of V.[5]

Suppose, for instance, that someone defines curiosity, conceived of as an intellectual virtue, as a disposition to wonder, ask questions, and consider issues from multiple perspectives. This definition might elicit the following objection. While curiosity does involve wondering and asking questions, the claim that it is *also* a matter of considering multiple perspectives packs too much into the concept. For considering multiple perspectives is the work of a related but distinct intellectual virtue: namely open-mindedness. While curious people might tend to be open-minded, we should not run these two virtues together. Wondering and asking questions is the business of curiosity; considering multiple perspectives is the business of open-mindedness.[6]

My contention is that the wide view makes a comparable error. For the relevant orientation toward one's *strengths and abilities* is already the business of a virtue other than humility. Specifically, *proper pride* is widely regarded as involving a disposition to own one's strengths, abilities, achievements, and the like. To illustrate, suppose an extremely capable student with whom I am well acquainted comes to me expressing doubt about her ability to do graduate-level work in philosophy. In response, I am likely to say something like, "While I understand your concern, you needn't be worried. You're more than prepared to excel in a graduate program. In fact, I think it's time for you to begin acknowledging and owning the remarkable abilities you've demonstrated throughout your undergraduate career. You ought to be *proud* of how capable you are and of how much you've accomplished."

It appears, then, that the wide view is guilty of trying to shoehorn an "ownership" of one's abilities and strengths into its conception of humility, thereby conflating humility with the distinct but no less important virtue of proper pride. I return to this mistake below.

A second argument against the wide view builds on the first. It is aimed at showing that the wide view has manifestly implausible implications when applied to particular cases. If the wide view is correct, then when my capable but diffident student communicates her self-doubt, it should make sense for me to respond by saying something like, "You're being too hard on yourself. You should try to be a little *more humble* and start owning your strengths." For, on the wide view, strengths-owning is a quality a sufficient amount of which is necessary for "hitting the mean" or possessing the virtue of humility. My student clearly does not possess a sufficient amount of this quality: she fails to see or appreciate her strengths. It follows from the wide view that she needs to become more humble.[7]

But this seems like exactly the wrong diagnosis. There would not appear to be any aspect of humility with respect to which the student is deficient (in the relevant quantitative sense). Rather, her shortcoming is that she is excessively humble. The narrow view makes perfect sense of this. The student is ascribing limitations or weaknesses to herself that she does not possess. Therefore, on the narrow view, she is being *servile*, not humble.

To get a better sense of the problem, note that on the wide view, humility exists along two primary dimensions: limitations-owning and strengths-owning. A virtuously humble person is said to hit the mean between excess and deficiency along *both* of these dimensions. My student, while excessive in limitations-owning, is deficient in strengths-owning (she has considerable philosophical strengths, which she does not appreciate). Therefore, according to the wide view, she needs to become more humble along one of the two main dimensions of humility. But, again, from an intuitive standpoint, there does not appear to be any sense in which her humility needs to increase. It is excessive, period. What she needs is proper pride.

Another way to come at this point is to compare the following two people, who exhibit opposite limitations and strengths: (1) person A has an accurate view of and owns her *limitations*, but she struggles to see or appreciate her *strengths*; (2) person B has an accurate view of and owns her *strengths*, but she struggles to see and own her limitations. If the wide view is correct, then (*ceteris paribus*) person A and person B will be *equally* (if both imperfectly) humble. Person A hits the mean along the limitations-owning (but not the strengths-owning) dimension of humility, whereas person B hits the mean along the strengths-owning (but not the limitations-owning) dimension. However, from an intuitive standpoint, these persons are *not* equally humble. Surely person A, who has an accurate view of and owns her limitations, exhibits greater humility than person B, who consistently fails to see and own her limitations.

In a recent defense of the wide view of intellectual humility, Church responds to something like this objection by arguing that the wide view does *not* entail that persons like my unconfident student need to become more humble. He comments: "[J]ust as we say that the servile person lacks intellectual humility only insofar as they have *too much* of it, we can say the same thing about the person who under-attends to and under-owns their intellectual strengths: that in under-attending to and under-owning their intellectual strengths, they lack humility, but only insofar as they have too much of it and have missed the virtuous mark of the mean."[8] This line of response raises several questions: Can a defender of the wide view really maintain that persons like my unconfident student are *too humble* (vs. not humble enough)? If so, how? Furthermore, supposing the wide view can explain the sense in which such persons are too humble, can it really escape the conclusion that they *also* are not humble enough?

In response to the first question, I think an affirmative answer is in order, albeit not without qualification. If my student is entirely inattentive to and agnostic about her strengths—that is, if she is not ascribing limitations to herself where in fact she should be recognizing strengths—then it is unclear on what grounds a defender of the wide view might deem her "too humble." However, if she is (erroneously) ascribing limitations to herself, then there is a clear sense in which she is "too humble," even according to the wide view. Notably, this is a function of the *overlap* between the wide view and the narrow view. The wide view agrees with the narrow view that humility is at least partly a function of appropriate limitations-owning. Accordingly, because the person in question is ascribing limitations to herself that she does not actually have, it follows from the wide view that she is excessively humble.

The more important question is whether this is all that follows from the wide view. Church's response suggests that it is. He makes clear that on his view, proponents of the wide view need not think of persons like the unconfident student as insufficiently humble. However, as indicated above, if the wide view is true, then strengths-owning is a positive, defining feature of humility, a feature of which the humble person must have "enough but not too much." The problem is that the person in question does not have enough of this quality. Again, she needs more humility along the strengths-owning dimension of this virtue. If so, then while, with respect to the limitations-owning dimension of humility, she is "too humble," it remains, with respect to the strengths-owning dimension, that she is "not humble enough." I conclude that the wide view cannot escape the counterintuitive implication.

Explaining (Away) the Appeal of the Wide View

We have considered a pair of arguments in support of the narrow view over and against the wide view. The second of these arguments seems especially telling against the wide view. What, then, has attracted proponents of the wide view? How to explain its appeal?

At the outset of the chapter, we noted that the wide view holds out a solution to accounts of humility that skew negative, portraying humility as involving an *overemphasis* on or *exaggeration* of one's weaknesses or limitations. Again, such conceptions are not uncommon. They can lead to an acceptance of the wide view in the following way. One natural way of excluding the relevant distortion is to insist that humility requires an *accurate* (vs. a disparaging) view of oneself. In fact, in the philosophical, psychological, and theological literature on humility, accurate self-assessment is often identified as one of its central features, and apparently for this reason. June Tangney, for instance, identifies as a "key element" of humility an "accurate assessment of one's abilities and achievements (*not* low self-esteem, self-deprecation)."[9]

Accordingly, someone might see fit to argue in the following way: Humility involves accurate self-assessment. A person's "self" includes her limitations and weaknesses *but also her abilities and strengths*. Therefore, humility involves an accurate assessment of one's abilities and strengths.[10]

This way of thinking about humility averts the problems faced by objectionably negative construals of humility. However, it also inherits all of the problems with the wide view identified above. Therefore, prior to accepting this view, we should consider whether there might be a *different* way of building an accuracy requirement into an account of humility, a requirement that would make humility *inconsistent* with self-denigration and the like, but without requiring an accurate assessment of abilities and strengths.

The narrow view, suitably formulated, does precisely this. In its most general form, it identifies humility with an "appropriate" awareness of and responsiveness to one's limitations and weaknesses. One natural way of fleshing out what it is for such an awareness to be "appropriate" is in terms of *accuracy*.[11] Indeed, according to one prominent conception, humility centrally involves having an accurate view of one's limitations. Nancy Snow, for instance, says the following: "Humility can be defined as the disposition to allow the awareness of and concern about your limitations to have a realistic influence on your attitudes and behavior. At the heart of this realism is a perspective gained through *accurate appraisal* of your limitations and their implications for your circumstances, attitudes, and behavior."[12] Similarly, Norvin Richards identifies humility with "having an *accurate* sense of oneself, sufficiently firm to resist pressure toward incorrect revisions," adding that "here the pressures are to think too *much* of oneself, rather than too little."[13] In other words, the humble person has an accurate view of herself in the sense that she does not think too highly of herself—she is aware of and acknowledges her limitations and flaws.

My claim, then, is that the wide view represents a kind of overcorrection vis-à-vis objectionably negative accounts of humility. In an attempt to avoid thinking of humility in servile or self-abasing terms, one might be led to conclude that humility requires having an accurate view of one's limitations *and strengths*. We have seen, however, that the inclusion of strengths within the accurate perspective proper to humility is at once problematic and unnecessary. The narrow view, by contrast, threads the needle between the problems that beset the wide view, on the one hand, and an overly negative characterization of humility, on the other.

A second error theory begins with a familiar fact about character virtues: namely, that they often *complement* or *balance* each other. Courage is balanced by caution. Justice is tempered by mercy. Open-mindedness is constrained by intellectual perseverance. Some philosophers have held the even stronger view that complementary virtues are "unified" in the sense that it is impossible to possess one without possessing the other. Note, however, that both of these views are entirely consistent with the possibility that complementary or unified virtues are conceptually distinct from each other. They do not support defining one such virtue in terms of the characteristic features of another (e.g., defining courage in terms of caution, or vice versa). Indeed, doing so would erase any meaningful distinction between the virtues in question.[14]

My suggestion is that a failure to appreciate this point can make the wide view seem more plausible than it is. The idea that humility is (at least partly) constituted by appropriate limitations-owning is highly plausible. So is the idea that proper pride is (at least partly) constituted by appropriate strengths-owning. It is also reasonable to think that appropriate limitations-owning is bound up with appropriate strengths-owning, such that: if a person is good at assessing and owning her strengths, she will (at least) be less likely to attribute to herself weaknesses that she does not really possess; and if she reliably owns her weaknesses and limitations, she will (at least) be more likely to make a proper estimation of her strengths.

In light of this, it can be tempting to reason as follows: To be a virtue, humility needs to be accompanied by proper pride. Proper pride involves appropriate strengths-owning. Therefore, humility is partly a matter of appropriate strengths-owning.

But, again, such reasoning is invalid. While humility and proper pride complement and fortify each other, it does not follow that one should be defined in terms of the other—that is, that humility should be defined (even partly) in terms of appropriate strengths-owning. Indeed, to the extent that it is plausible to think of humility and proper pride as distinct traits, we should be wary of this inclusion.

Objections to the Narrow View

We have considered several reasons for embracing the narrow view of humility over the wide view. We have also sought to "explain away" at least some of the initial motivation for the wide view. How might a proponent of the wide view respond to our argument? One objection to the narrow view is as follows: Overestimating or exaggerating one's strengths or abilities can indicate of a *lack* of humility. Therefore, humility itself must range not merely over limitations and weaknesses but also over strengths and abilities. And, therefore, the narrow view must be mistaken.

I agree with the main premise of this argument but deny that it poses a problem for the narrow view. How, then, is the fact that a person can fail to be humble on account of overestimating or exaggerating her strengths and abilities consistent with the narrow view? The answer is straightforward: when a person overestimates or exaggerates her abilities, she thereby fails to acknowledge certain of her *limitations*—namely, the limitations of her abilities.

Limitations pervade our existence. We are limited morally, intellectually, physically, metaphysically, spiritually, and otherwise. Even our strengths and abilities are limited. Humility, according to the narrow view, is the virtue that equips us to be properly attentive to and accepting of our limitations. As such, it involves noting and "owning" *even the limitations of our abilities*. The humble athlete, for instance, while perhaps recognizing her extraordinary ability on the field, also recognizes that her physical or athletic dominance does not entail her *moral* superiority, and so does not view herself as better or more important than her peers or fans from a moral standpoint. There is, then, a limited respect in which, according to the narrow view, the scope of humility extends to our abilities: it extends to our abilities *as limited*. Although an overestimation of abilities can indicate a failure of humility, this does not lend any special support to the wide view.

A similar argument against the narrow view might go as follows: *Arrogance* is a deficiency of humility. Exaggerating one's abilities can *as such* (not merely qua failure of limitations-owning) be an expression of arrogance. Therefore, contra the narrow view, humility *as such* requires not exaggerating one's abilities.[15]

Even if this argument were cogent, it would not quite support the wide view. The wide view stipulates that humility requires a positive awareness of one's abilities. If successful, the present argument shows that not exaggerating one's abilities is a requirement of humility. The problem is that one can avoid an exaggerated or inflated view of one's abilities without having a positive awareness of them—for example, by simply *not paying attention to or forming beliefs about* one's abilities.

There is another, deeper problem with the argument. Recall that while arrogance is a deficiency of humility, it is also an *excess of proper pride*. Figure 6.1 illustrates the relationship between pride, humility, arrogance, and servility:

FIGURE 6.1. Relationship between Pride, Humility, Arrogance, and Servility

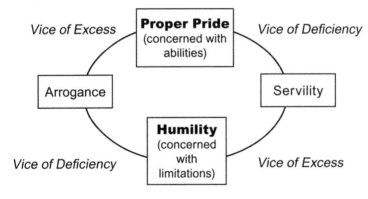

According to the figure, and as described above, proper pride is concerned with an appropriate attentiveness to and ownership of one's abilities and strengths, while humility is concerned with an appropriate attentiveness to and ownership of one's limitations and weaknesses. While different in this way, pride and humility terminate in a common pair of vices: arrogance includes both an excess of proper pride and a deficiency of humility; and servility ranges over a deficiency of proper pride and an excess of humility. What the model makes clear is that to explain the fact that exaggerating one's abilities can *as such* be an expression of arrogance, we need not view exaggeration of one's abilities as manifesting a deficiency of humility and therefore need not view humility as ranging over abilities as well as limitations. For the fact that exaggerating one's abilities can manifest arrogance is explainable in terms of the claim that arrogance is (partly) an excess of proper pride.[16]

A third argument against the narrow view is from Church, who argues that this view "allows for cases where someone . . . can be at once and within the same domain intellectually humble and 'intellectually servile.'"[17] His reasoning is that, on the narrow view, a person could be appropriately aware of and responsive to their intellectual limitations while failing to "appropriately attend to and own their intellectual strengths enough," which in turn would make the person intellectually servile. Church claims that it is "deeply counterintuitive" to suggest that someone could be both servile and humble within the same domain.[18]

By way of response, it is important, first, to be clear that even on the narrow view, certain forms of servility are incompatible with humility. For instance, if one is ascribing weaknesses to oneself in areas where one in fact is strong, then one would be *servile*, not humble, according to the narrow view. We can refer to servility of this sort as "strong servility." Strong servility is distinct from "weak servility," which consists (merely) of *not* being sufficiently aware or appreciative of one's strengths. We will return to this distinction momentarily.

While the narrow view of humility excludes the co-instantiation of humility and strong servility, it leaves open the possibility that a person might exhibit an appropriate awareness and responsiveness toward her limitations while failing to recognize or appreciate her strengths. That is, she might be humble with respect to her limitations while being (weakly) servile with respect to her strengths. However, this is hardly "deeply counterintuitive." Indeed, it may not be counterintuitive at all. Recall that humility is but one virtue among many. A merely or predominantly humble person might still be far from perfect. Therefore, it should not be surprising that such a person, while appropriately attuned to her limitations, might have a hard time appreciating her strengths. Nor does it seem counterintuitive or otherwise objectionable that, in having a hard time appreciating her strengths, she might *in a sense* or *with respect to certain of her qualities* be (weakly) servile. I conclude that the sense in which humility is compatible with servility on the narrow view does not pose a significant problem for this view.

We turn now to a fourth and final argument against the narrow view. On one venerable and reasonably intuitive way of thinking about humility, it is a matter of occupying one's proper place within the broader order of things. This way of thinking about humility has enjoyed special resonance within the Jewish-Christian theological and intellectual traditions, with God at the top of the order of things and human beings somewhere down below (albeit not as far below as other living creatures). Aquinas, for instance, says: "The virtue of humility consists in this, that a man keeps to his own place."[19]

This conception of humility poses a problem for the narrow view *provided* that "keeping to one's place" involves acknowledging that, say, while relative to certain points or locations within the broader order, one is limited or occupies a low position, relative to other points or locations, one is *capable* or occupies a *high* position (e.g., as humans, we are less exalted than the angels, but greater than the lowly worm). For, on this conception, humility ranges over abilities as well as limitations.

It is doubtful, however, that many of the thinkers who have conceived of humility as a matter of occupying our "proper place" in the broader order of things have had in mind not merely our tendency to think too much of ourselves but also a tendency to think too little of ourselves. This is especially so within the Jewish-Christian tradition, where humanity's struggle with pride and its drive to usurp God's position are front and center in the dominant theological narrative. On a more plausible interpretation of this conception, humility is a matter of "occupying one's proper place in the broader order of things" in the sense that it involves not attempting to occupy a *higher* or *greater* place within this order than is fitting for one. In short, it is a matter of keeping an eye on and resisting the impulse to *transcend* one's limitations. Indeed, when Aquinas describes a humble person as one who "keeps to his own place," he immediately qualifies this statement by saying that the humble person "does not reach out to things above him" (vs. that he remains above things that are below him).[20]

None of this is to deny, of course, that it is a good thing for humans to be mindful of their strengths and abilities. The mistake is thinking of such activity as definitive or expressive of humility, rather than of some related virtue like proper pride. In keeping with this, we can imagine a person, similar to the diffident student described above, who fails to occupy her place within the broader order of things by regularly *demoting* herself—that is, by thinking of herself as *more* limited and *less* capable than she really is. Again, if humility is partly a matter of attending to and owning one's strengths, if strengths-owning is one "quantity" that the possession of humility requires having "enough but not too much" of, then it should make sense to say of this person: "She needs to become more humble; she needs to own her strengths." But here as well this seems like profoundly inapt advice. Instead we should say something like: "She is excessively humble. She ought to recognize, own, and be proud of her abilities."

Nor is the problem merely with what it would be appropriate or inappropriate to *say* to such a person. Again, it seems wrong to think that this person is, in any interesting respect, deficient in humility. To be sure, she is servile and so lacks proper or virtuous humility. This is very different from claiming that there is an aspect or ingredient of humility—a proper appreciation of one's *strengths*—that she lacks a sufficient quantity or amount of. But this, again, is precisely what the wide view of humility would have us say.

Conclusion

We have found that the wide view faces some formidable objections and that while it may have some initial appeal, this appeal does not arise from any distinct advantage of the wide view vis-à-vis the narrow view. This conclusion notwithstanding, I close by briefly revisiting the question of what humility, as depicted by the narrow view, demands in terms of an orientation toward one's strengths and abilities. Two main points merit attention.

First, we have seen that there is a sense in which humility thus conceived can extend to a person's abilities and strengths. Again, this is because our abilities and strengths themselves are *limited*. In fact, it is not implausible to think that limitations of our strengths are among the limitations that it is easiest for us to lose sight of or ignore. If so, it is not surprising that a concern with strengths and abilities has found its way into theoretical models of humility. The mistake has been to conclude that humility is concerned with strengths and abilities *as such*.

Second, there is a further, subtler reason to think of humility as connected with a person's orientation toward her abilities and strengths. Many people have a hard time appreciating or "owning" their strengths. This is evident in their inability to accept or feel comfortable with praise for these strengths. What lies at the bottom of such resistance? My suggestion is that in a nontrivial number of cases, the persons in question are hung up on—they have not yet "owned" or come to terms with—one or more of their limitations. Their discomfort with or shame about their limitations, weaknesses, or mistakes prevents them from seeing or accepting praise for their strengths. To illustrate, consider a person who seems incapable of accepting compliments on his formidable skill and accomplishments in some domain D. While strong in D, this person might be hung up on ways in which his abilities or accomplishments in D are less than perfect. His preoccupation with these (perhaps quite minimal or trivial) limitations might prevent him from appreciating or owning his (formidable) strengths in D.[21] Accordingly, a person who is *comfortable* with and can freely *acknowledge* his limitations will be free of one potential obstacle to attending to and owning his strengths and abilities. This is an additional reason to expect a positive correlation between humility, understood as a proper orientation toward one's limitations, and a proper awareness of and responsiveness to one's strengths.[22]

• • •

Response to Jason Baehr

Robert C. Roberts

In his wonted careful, methodical way, Jason Baehr disputes a "wide" view of humility according to which it is essentially a matter of accepting and "owning" *both* one's limitations and one's strengths. He thinks it counterintuitive to call the trait of owning one's strengths humility. Would that not be better called pride? And he appeals to an important principle of virtue individuation: that virtues differ in large part by specific functions in the life of their possessor, and that it is confusing to try to pack more than one basic function into a trait-concept, especially where the two functions are such that a person may have one and lack the other, or possess them in different measure. Baehr wants to reserve "humility" for the owning of one's limitations and to assign the function of properly "owning" one's strengths to the virtue of pride. I will take the present occasion to think about the relationships between, on the one side, humility and pride in their virtuous and vicious forms and, on the other, human strengths and limitations.

Baehr says, "a humble person is aware of, rather than oblivious to or in denial about, her limitations. But such awareness is not sufficient for humility, for a person could be aware of but chronically irritated by or defensive about her limitations. As such, she would be less than humble. Accordingly, humility also involves accepting or 'owning' one's limitations" (173). Does a person who is "chronically irritated by or defensive about her limitations" necessarily lack humility? This will depend, I think, on what we mean by "irritated" and "defensive"—or perhaps better, what the psychological source of the irritation or defensiveness is.

Consider first a case in which the irritation clearly indicates a lack of humility. Joe enjoys comparing himself, morally, with people whose moral flaws are greater than his. The comparison makes him feel good about himself. He likes to consider and talk about other people's faults. So it irritates him no end when he himself is caught in a fault—especially when other people are looking on. He then becomes defensive and rationalizes and seeks to demean the other person. This particular irritation and defensiveness about his limitations seems to have its roots in Joe's self-righteousness, vanity, and envy, and these traits seem clearly incompatible with humility.

Now consider Florence, who is also "irritated," though in a different sense, by her limitations. Florence is a glutton for challenges. Her "thing" is overcoming limitations. She finds limitations exhilarating, and her exhilaration comes from her *not* accepting or owning these limitations. She never met a limitation she did not welcome—as an adversary. She sees it as an alien presence but savors it as a call to battle. She "defends" herself against her limitations but is not defensive in anything like the way Joe is defensive about his moral faults. She is not complacent about her limitations; she always strives to get the better of them. We might even say that a person who, while fully aware of her limitations, is complacent about them has *vicious* humility, perhaps the one that I call defeatist lethargy in my response to Floyd-Thomas (this volume). The lethargic defeatist accepts and owns his limitations, but not in the right way for virtuous humility. Something's amiss in his agency. He lacks the kind of pride that I call aspiration. It seems to me that Florence's attitude toward her limitations, while it is not itself humility, does not bespeak a lack of humility, even though it is, in a sense, an attitude of nonacceptance.

Must the humble person be aware, rather than oblivious, of her limitations? I venture that we are all oblivious of many of our limitations. We have not thought about, or tested, or discovered them. Maybe Baehr should revise his formula to this: humility is acceptance of the limitations we are aware of. This would probably not be adequate, since conceited, grandiose, and vain people often fail to see their limitations *because* of these vices. The formula would protect such vices against recognition insofar as they are sources of ignorance about limitations. The fact that unawareness of many of our limitations, and thus our failure to "own" them, is unavoidable for finite human beings implies that virtuous humility cannot be defined as owning *all* of our limitations. So the question becomes, which of our limitations are relevant to humility?

I suggest that any limitation *can* be relevant, though my last paragraph suggests that not all limitations are in fact relevant. And the limitations I am unaware of are not the only ones that are not relevant. Many of the limitations of which I am aware are not relevant. For example, I know that I cannot jump six feet in the air, straight up. I accept it, and it is integrated into my life (so perfectly so that I never even try!), but it is no virtuous achievement of my humility that I own *that* limitation. I also know very little about carnivorous plants. I am aware of and perfectly comfortable with that limitation, but my being so is hardly an achievement of virtuous humility.

So, among our many limitations, what is the difference that makes some of them relevant to humility and others not? Consider Joe again. He gets irritated when he has to face one of his moral limitations because, comparing himself morally with others, he feels that he is in competition with them. He enjoys beholding other people's limitations because the comparison makes him feel important, and when he has to face his own moral limitations, he feels diminished. The kind of importance or diminishment that he feels is one that we might call *narcissistic*. He enjoys narcissistic expansion when he compares advantageously to someone else, and feels narcissistic diminishment when he compares unfavorably. Notice the difference between this and genuine moral concern. If his concern is moral, he will feel diminished by his sins, but the diminishment will not be narcissistic.

I submit that limitations are relevant to humility when they are ones that human beings take to be narcissistically diminishing. The concerns characteristic of vices like envy and self-righteousness are concerns for *narcissistic importance*.

What is narcissistic concern for importance as persons? It is to be contrasted with the genuine importance of persons, which comes from being integrated into a community that loves and respects one and from making a contribution to such a community. Central to narcissistic concern for importance is the concern to be *more* important than some other persons who are seen as members of one's sphere. *Self-righteousness*, for example, is the concern to be morally better than others. *Arrogance* is the concern to have more privileges and entitlements than others. *Envy* is a negative or frustrated response to the sense that one is less important than one's rivals (less beautiful, less interesting, less intelligent, etc.). *Invidious triumph* is the positive response based on the same concern to be more important than others. *Vanity* is the concern to be important by being seen to be important by others, and often has the same comparative character as the other vices. Other vices in the same family are *conceit, domination, snobbery, pretension, hyperautonomy, racism, refractoriness,* and *grandiosity*.

Human limitations irritate us and make us defensive insofar as we think of them as diminishing our narcissistic importance as persons. Joe is threatened by his moral inferiority to others in his sphere because he is self-righteous—that is, concerned to be morally better than others so as to be more important than they. (His irritation may be based on a real desire for righteousness, in which case his irritation would not indicate a lack of humility.) The racist is threatened by the excellence of a member of the despised race because he is concerned that he and his own race be superior and thus more important. And Florence, though she is "irritated," in a sense, by her limitations, can be humble nevertheless because they do not threaten her sense of narcissistic importance.

Jeanine Grenberg and Ian Church both think that humility is a correct attitude, not only toward one's limitations, but also toward one's strengths. Stated in this abstract way, Grenberg and Church are right. Baehr considers and rejects the thesis that humility is a correct assessment and acceptance of one's strengths. I think he is right about that. What then *is* the humble attitude toward one's strengths? To answer this question, it will be helpful to consider what is the characteristic *un*humble attitude toward one's strengths. Consider Cecil, who, because of his superior intelligence, sees himself as fundamentally better than other people; he condescends to them in a variety of ways that say, as it were, "I am more important than you," and they respond by labeling him *conceited*. Closely related to conceit is the vice of *arrogance*. Arthur is a television star, and his unusual talent has become the "justification" for Arthur's feeling that he has special privileges of sexual access to women; he may treat them as other men may not, because he is "special." Donald is very wealthy and enjoys domineering over subordinates because it makes him feel large and important. He suffers from the vice of *domination*. In these three cases, the humble counterpart of unhumility would be the person who possesses the strengths in question (high intelligence, acting talent, and wealth), yet without taking them as an occasion for conceit, arrogance, or domination.

So Church and Grenberg are right that humility applies to cases of strengths as well as weaknesses. But they think that the humble attitude toward one's strengths is that of accepting and owning them. That seems off target. The humble attitude that would correspond to conceit, arrogance, and domination on the basis of one's strengths would be *not* to think oneself better than others because of one's greater strength, *not* to arrogate illicit "privileges" to oneself on that basis, and *not* to use one's strengths as an occasion for pushing other people around. But even more fundamentally than this, humility would be the *lack of concern* for the kind of personal importance that seems to the unhumble to come from superior strengths—the concern for what I have been calling narcissistic personal importance.

The point is that strengths and limitations are relevant to humility and the vices of pride only because, in human social nature, they are such important occasions for narcissistic concern. They are so important, indeed, that when we come across a person who, despite having great strengths or weaknesses, does not see them in terms of threatening or satisfying her narcissistic concern, we ascribe to her the virtue of humility. In the formula "appropriate attitude" toward one's limitations or strengths, the appropriateness is not to be concerned about their relevance to one's narcissistic importance. Humility ranges over strengths and limitations only because and to the extent that they are important as issues for narcissistic concern.

I will conclude with a couple of small critical points about Baehr's essay. The first point is about the word "servility." Servility is one of the vices of humility. (For some thoughts about humility as a vice, see my comments on Floyd-Thomas' chapter.) The Merriam-Webster online dictionary gives two senses of "servility," the first designating a social status, "of or befitting a slave or a menial position," and the second describing a trait, "meanly or cravenly submissive : abject." The vice of servility is the reciprocal of the vice of domination. A dominates B, and B responds in kind by submitting abjectly to A's domination. But Baehr uses "servility" for an attitude of chronic self-deprecation or underestimation. These two vices are connected in ways that would be interesting to explore, but they are not the same.

My second point is about Baehr's use of Aristotle's doctrine of the mean. He says the student who underestimates her abilities is "excessively humble," and that arrogance is "an *excess of proper pride*" (italics in original). In my opinion, it would be better to avoid the doctrine of the mean altogether in thinking about virtues and vices, but Aristotle is right when he says there can be no excess of virtue. "There is no excess or deficiency of temperance or courage because what is intermediate is in a sense an extreme . . . for in general there is neither a mean of excess and deficiency, nor excess and deficiency of a mean."[1] You cannot have too much of virtuous humility or pride, and you cannot have too little of vicious humility or pride.[2]

• • •

Reply to Robert C. Roberts

Jason Baehr

I am grateful to Roberts for his thoughtful and incisive remarks on my chapter, which touch on several deep issues related to humility, pride, weaknesses, and strengths. By way of reply, I will (1) offer a brief and partial defense of the "limits-owning" (LO) account of humility against Roberts' main objections, (2) raise a worry about the alternative account of humility proposed by Roberts, and (3) address the pair of "small critical points" he raises toward the end of his remarks.

According to the LO account, humble persons are uninclined to be *defensive* or *irritated* about their limitations. Against this claim, Roberts presents the case of Florence, who is obsessed with overcoming her limitations, but whose obsession is not motivated by arrogance, vanity, or any other vices of pride. Florence is, in a sense, irritated by and defensive about her limitations; however, her irritation and defensiveness would not seem to prevent her from being humble.

This case does not pose a serious problem for the LO account, for it can accommodate the judgment that Florence might be humble. This account does not say that a person is humble only if she "owns" her limitations in *every* possible sense; nor that humble persons are never, in *any* sense, irritated or defensive about their limitations. Indeed, according to the LO account, owning one's limitations is inconsistent with being complacent about them. Provided that the limitations are significant and malleable, owning them is partly a matter of trying to *weed them out* or *mitigate their influence*.[1] This is something Florence does in spades. While not a forceful objection to the LO account, the Florence case does underscore an important question: namely, what forms of irritation or defensiveness about one's limitations are inconsistent with humility and which are permitted by it? I return to this question below.

Roberts also raises a good question about *which* limitations humble persons characteristically own. Is a person deficient in humility if she fails to own limitations of which she is entirely unaware? What about limitations that are mundane or seemingly unimportant, such as (to use Roberts' examples) one's lack of a six-foot vertical leap or ignorance of an exotic plant species?

To see how a proponent of the LO account might answer these questions, suppose we think of humility as a *corrective* virtue; in particular, as a virtue with the function of mitigating the vice or vices of human pride.[2] And suppose we think of pride as a deep tendency to ignore, deny, conceal, transcend, or similarly resist our manifold limitations—and, importantly, to do so when we should not or when doing so is likely to undermine our own or others' flourishing.[3] In keeping with this view, a defender of the LO account might say that humility "corrects" for pride in the sense that it mitigates deep human tendencies to improperly deny or resist our limitations. It does this by making us appropriately attentive to and disposed to own these limitations.

Formulated in this way, the LO account suggests the following replies to Roberts' questions. First, it suggests that irritability or defensiveness about one's limitations is inconsistent with having "owned" them only if this irritability or defensiveness stems from the sort of prideful orientation just noted. Where an irritability or defensiveness about one's limitations arises from a different source, it is compatible with humility. Florence's humility is of the latter sort: it does not arise from a prideful denial or rejection of her limitations. Therefore, as Roberts rightly notes, her resistance of her limitations does not bespeak a deficiency of humility. This is entirely consistent with the LO account.

As to *which* limitations humble persons characteristically own, the first (and necessarily brief) part of my response is: limitations of which the person *is aware or ought to be aware*. This principle does justice to two insights noted by Roberts. The first is that a person's being unaware of a limitation that is, for nonculpable reasons, difficult to identify need not entail that the person is deficient in humility. Suppose, for instance, that an aspiring fiction writer is educated by mediocre instructors and surrounded by fellow students with subpar literary skills. Such a person might, with good reason, fancy himself a much better writer than he is. Given the circumstances, this person's failure to recognize his limitations as a writer might not count against his humility (he might have good reason to think he is a better writer than he is). Accordingly, if a person is unaware of his limitations on account of their being (nonculpably) difficult to identify, this need not signal a deficiency in humility. The second insight is that although pride or arrogance can blind a person to his limitations (e.g., by making him think he is much more capable than he is), this should not prevent us from thinking of such persons as lacking humility. In scenarios like this, it ordinarily will be the case that the person ought to be aware of his limitations. If so, the principle noted above entails that the person's failure to own his limitations is an indication of his lack of humility.

What about limitations that are mundane or seemingly insignificant? When a person "owns" the fact that he does not have a six-foot vertical leap or that he does not know about some exotic plant species, does this make him more humble? The above characterization of humility suggests that the answer to these questions depends on whether the limitations are such that the person is disposed to pridefully resist them. People do not normally exhibit prideful resistance to limitations that are mundane or trivial. Therefore, they normally are not humble on account of owning such limitations. But imagine a person who feels like he needs to know everything. This person might pretend to know much more than he does, conceal his ignorance from others, and respond defensively when his ignorance is exposed. If so, then what most of us are likely to consider a mundane limitation *would* be relevant to whether the person should be considered humble.

My suggestion, then, is that thinking of humility as corrective of vicious pride supplies answers to Roberts' questions about what "owning" a limitation does and does not preclude and about the sorts of limitations an ownership of which is relevant to humility. Again, a person's owning of a limitation is relevant to an assessment of the person's humility only if (a) the person is aware of or should be aware of this limitation and (b) the person's owning of the limitation is corrective of a tendency in the person to pridefully resist it.[4]

I turn now to a worry about the alternative account of humility proposed by Roberts. Similar to the account just sketched, Roberts' "no-concern" view of humility is parasitic on an account of vicious pride. However, instead of characterizing humility as a way of coping with or mitigating the vices of pride, Roberts portrays it as a mere *absence* of such. He also claims that the vices of pride have their basis in a *single* motivation: namely, a "narcissistic concern" for personal greatness, which centrally involves a "concern to be *more* important than some other persons who are seen as members of one's sphere."

While there is much that seems right to me about Roberts' account of humility, I think it construes the motivational basis of pride too narrowly, resulting in an objectionably broad and permissive account of the target concept. For Roberts, if a person's characteristically prideful behavior (e.g., his treatment of others as inferior or his chronic unwillingness to admit his flaws) is rooted in anything *but* a narcissistic concern for personal importance, then it cannot be expressive of vicious pride, and therefore (given the view that humility is the absence of vicious pride) must be consistent with virtuous humility. The problem is that humility-negating pride, while perhaps often rooted in a concern for personal superiority, can have its basis in other motives as well.

Imagine, for instance, a person who was denied basic love and respect at a critical developmental stage early in his life. As an adult, he habitually acts in arrogant and conceited ways toward his peers in an effort to reassure himself of his basic dignity and worth. Alternatively, consider a person who cannot bear the thought of being exposed as morally broken or fragile. As a consequence, she is seemingly incapable of admitting any mistake or wrongdoing. Finally, imagine someone with an unrelenting drive toward self-sufficiency and autonomy. He avoids close relationships so as to escape the kinds of commitments and obligations they tend to generate. He does everything he can to avoid depending on anyone for anything.

These cases, while admittedly sketchy, point in the direction of forms of humility-negating pride that are not motivated by a narcissistic concern for personal greatness or superiority. The first person is prideful on account of his efforts to reassure himself of his basic dignity and worth by habitually treating others in an arrogant and conceited manner. At bottom, he is insecure rather than egotistical. The second person is prideful because of her chronic defensiveness, which in turn is a function of her moral invulnerability. This vulnerability is not an expression of any superiority complex on her part. Rather, the prospect of being exposed as morally imperfect or defective is simply more than she can bear. The third person manifests a form of pride on account of his drive for radical self-sufficiency and autonomy. While his pursuit of these unrealistic goals may betray an outsized view of his abilities (he cannot possibly achieve the kind of radical freedom he seeks), it need not involve a concern for self-importance in Roberts' sense.

The problem, again, is that Roberts' account of humility rules incorrectly with respect to these cases. The persons in question are not motivated by a narcissistic concern for personal importance. Therefore, his view leaves wide open the implausible possibility that these people might not in any respect be deficient in humility.[5]

I close with brief replies to the "small critical points" Roberts raises in the final section of his remarks. First, he suggests that a defender of the LO account should not think of servility as the vice of excess corresponding to humility. I am of two minds about this. On the one hand, it seems entirely possible that if one's behavior is "befitting of a menial position" or "meanly or cravenly submissive" (the dictionary definitions of servility), this behavior might have at its core an attribution to oneself of limitations one does not really have, and therefore count as excessively humble according to the LO view. On the other hand, I think Roberts is correct to suggest both that vicious servility need not involve a misattribution of limitations to oneself and that excessive humility need not take the form of servility. Indeed, I think defenders of the LO account might do better, if forced to identify just a single vice of excess corresponding to humility, to focus on something like self-denigration or self-disparagement. I am grateful to Roberts for helping me to see this point.

The notion of "excessive humility" leads to Roberts' second smaller criticism. Roberts points out, correctly in my view, that if humility is a genuine virtue, then it cannot admit of excess. I did not mean to suggest otherwise. When I refer to an "excess of humility," or an excess of any other virtue-relevant trait, I am intending to pick out an excess not of a *virtue* but rather of the sorts of actions and attitudes—the raw psychological materials—out of which the virtue is built. To illustrate, take the activity of limitations-owning. According to the LO account, the *virtue* of humility consists of a disposition to engage in this activity at the right time, in the right amount, for the right reason, and so on. By contrast, someone who attributes to himself limitations that he does not have or who owns his limitations too frequently would be *excessively* (not virtuously) humble.

Of course, one can deny that the latter sort of person should be considered humble in *any* sense. But this move has untoward consequences, especially when generalized on. It would seem tendentious to insist, for instance, that the "brutally honest" person is not *really* honest (vs. that his honesty is not a virtue) or that the person who "waits patiently" for a badly dysfunctional relationship to improve is not *really* patient (vs. that she is patient to a fault). Again, the more plausible view is that traits like humility, honesty, and patience may or may not be virtuous. In their "perfected" or "rationally infused" form, they are virtues; otherwise they are not.

• • •

Notes to Chapter 6
(Jason Baehr)

1 For a recent defense of this view applied to *intellectual* humility, see Dennis Whitcomb, Heather Battaly, Jason Baehr, and Daniel Howard-Snyder, "Intellectual Humility: Owning Our Limitations," *Philosophy and Phenomenological Research* 94, no. 3 (2017): 509–39. For related treatments, see Nancy Snow, "Humility," *Journal of Value Inquiry* 29 (2017): 203–16; James Spiegel, "Open-Mindedness and Intellectual Humility," *Theory and Research in Education* 10 (2012): 27–38; and Gabrielle Taylor, *Pride, Shame, and Guilt* (New York: Oxford University Press, 1985). Thomas Aquinas also defends a view along these lines. He says, of the humble person, that "he must know his disproportion to that which surpasses his capacity. Hence knowledge of one's deficiency belongs to humility, as a rule guiding the appetite" (*Summa Theologiae* II–II.161.2, trans. Fathers of the English Dominican Province).
2 Jeanine Grenberg, *Kant and the Ethics of Humility* (New York: Cambridge University Press, 2005), 133 (emphasis added).
3 Ian Church, "The Limitations of the Limitations-Owning Account of Intellectual Humility," *Philosophia* 45, no. 3 (2017): 1083 (emphasis modified). Alan Hazlett's account of intellectual humility, while doxastically focused, also appears to be "wide" in the relevant sense (see Allan Hazlett, "Higher-Order Epistemic Attitudes and Intellectual Humility," *Episteme* 9 [2012]: 205–23). As does the account in Jasper Kallestrup and Duncan Pritchard, "Intellectual Pride and Intellectual Humility," in *The Moral Psychology of Pride*, ed. J. Adam Carter and Emma Gordon (Lanham, Md.: Rowman and Littlefield, 2017), 69–78.
4 Walter Hilton, *Ladder of Perfection* (London: Penguin Group, 1988), 18.
5 It is important that V and W be clearly distinct; otherwise, the principle could run aground in cases in which one virtue is a species of another. For

instance, Nathan King ("Perseverance as an Intellectual Virtue," *Synthese* 191 [2014]: 3501–23) argues convincingly that intellectual courage is a species of intellectual perseverance. If so, then without the caveat in question, the principle would entail that if persisting in the face of danger is characteristic of intellectual courage, we should not treat it as characteristic of intellectual perseverance (which would be a mistake given that intellectual courage is a type of intellectual perseverance). By contrast with intellectual courage and perseverance, humility and proper pride seem clearly to be distinct (i.e., it is not intuitively plausible to think of humility, say, as a species or type of proper pride like it is to think of courage as a species or type of perseverance).

6 It is not uncommon for theoretical discussions of particular virtues to lose sight of this principle. One often finds attempts to specify the defining character of a given virtue V encroaching on other putative virtues that are distinct from, if closely related, to V. See, for example, the account of intellectual humility in Samuelson et al., which pretty clearly ranges over a wide variety of intellectual virtues, including but not at all limited to intellectual humility. See Peter L. Samuelson, Matthew J. Jarvinen, Thomas B. Paulus, Ian M. Church, Sam A. Hardy, and Justin L. Barrett, "Implicit Theories of Intellectual Virtues and Vices: A Focus on Intellectual Humility," *Journal of Positive Psychology* 10, no. 5 (2015): 389–406.

7 For a similar case and point, see Whitcomb et al., "Intellectual Humility."

8 Church, "Limitations of the Limitations-Owning Account," 7 (emphasis added).

9 J. P. Tangney, "Humility: Theoretical Perspectives, Empirical Findings and Directions for Future Research," *Journal of Social and Clinical Psychology* 19 (2000): 70–82, 497 (emphasis in original).

10 This is a more precise rendering of the kind of reasoning mentioned at the outset of the essay. That reasoning moved directly from the skewed picture of humility to a picture that incorporates strengths; it did not invoke the notion of accuracy. The present line of reasoning, I take it, has greater initial plausibility.

11 I do not here intend to distinguish between an *accurate* perspective and a perspective that is highly *reasonable* or *well-supported* by one's evidence but ultimately mistaken. The present point is intended to be neutral with respect to this distinction.

12 Snow, "Humility," 210 (emphasis added).

13 Norvin Richards, "Is Humility a Virtue?" *American Philosophical Quarterly* 25 (1988): 254 (emphasis added).

14 The idea that "complementary" virtues are *not* distinct is consistent with an extreme (and less than popular) version of the unity thesis that traces back to Socrates in the *Protagoras*, according to which terms like wisdom, justice, and courage pick out a "single thing." See Gregory Vlastos, "The Unity of the Virtues in *Protagoras*," *Review of Metaphysics* 25, no. 3 (1972): 415–58 for a discussion.

15 I owe this argument to Nate King.

16 This argument takes for granted that an action can manifest a particular vice V by manifesting only one dimension (rather than the whole) of V. This strikes me as an unproblematic assumption, so I will not pause to defend it here.
17 Church, "Limitations of the Limitations-Owning Account," 7.
18 Church, "Limitations of the Limitations-Owning Account," 8.
19 *Summa Contra Gentiles* (New York: Benziger Brothers, 1929), book 4, chap. 55, p. 214.
20 *Summa Contra Gentiles*, book 4, chap. 55, p. 214. Notably, as Aquinas himself makes clear, keeping to one's place can have a robustly *social* dimension: it can include, for instance, a recognition that one is not superior to or more important than others, that one's freedom is limited by the rights and well-being of others, and so on.
21 No less plausibly, he might find it difficult to own his strengths in D on account of being preoccupied with or ashamed about his (perhaps significant) limitations in some *other* domain E.
22 I am grateful to Drew Collins and Ryan McAnnally-Linz for incisive comments on an earlier draft of this essay (and on my reply to Roberts). Work on the essay benefited from the generous support of the John Templeton Foundation, Grant No. 60622, "Developing Humility in Leaders."

Notes to Chapter 6 Response
(Robert C. Roberts)

1 Aristotle, *Nicomachean Ethics*, trans. W. D. Ross, ed. and rev. J. L. Ackrill and J. O. Urmson (Oxford: Oxford University Press, 1980), 2.6, 1107a22–27, pp. 39–40.
2 This essay was written with the support of the Templeton Religion Trust, by way of the Self, Motivation, and Virtue Project at the Institute for the Study of Human Flourishing at the University of Oklahoma. The opinions expressed in it are those of the author, and not necessarily of the Templeton Religion Trust.

Notes to Chapter 6 Reply
(Jason Baehr)

1 Whitcomb et al., "Intellectual Humility," 9–10.
2 This view has been widely defended among philosophers and theologians. See Craig Boyd, "Pride and Humility: Tempering the Desire for Excellence," in *Virtues and their Vices*, ed. Kevin Timpe and Craig Boyd (Oxford: Oxford University Press, 2014), 245–66.
3 There are, in fact, a range of possible explanations of what is wrong or bad or inappropriate about pride. I am not here endorsing any particular view on this matter.
4 Humility might be corrective of pride in more than one way: e.g., it might mitigate a person's current prideful tendencies; or it might have eliminated

such tendencies at some point in the past. For a related discussion, see Baehr, *Inquiring Mind*, chap. 9.

5 This problem could be fixed if Roberts were to broaden his view of the motivational basis of vicious pride to include the sorts of motives just sketched. Furthermore, if Roberts were to conclude that these persons are deficient in humility but are not viciously prideful, an alternative solution would be to give up the view that humility can be equated with the mere absence of pride.

Chapter Bibliography

Aristotle. *Nicomachean Ethics*. Translated by W. D. Ross. Edited and revised by J. L. Ackrill and J. O. Urmson. Oxford: Oxford University Press, 1980.

Baehr, Jason. *The Inquiring Mind: On Intellectual Virtues and Virtue Epistemology*. Oxford: Oxford University Press, 2011.

Boyd, Craig. "Pride and Humility: Tempering the Desire for Excellence." In *Virtues and their Vices*, edited by Kevin Timpe and Craig Boyd, 245–66. Oxford: Oxford University Press, 2014.

Church, Ian. "The Limitations of the Limitations-Owning Account of Intellectual Humility." *Philosophia* 45, no. 3 (2017): 1077–84.

Grenberg, Jeanine. *Kant and the Ethics of Humility*. New York: Cambridge University Press, 2005.

Hazlett, Allan. "Higher-Order Epistemic Attitudes and Intellectual Humility." *Episteme* 9 (2012): 205–23.

Hilton, Walter. *Ladder of Perfection*. London: Penguin Group, 1988.

Kallestrup, Jasper, and Duncan Pritchard. "Intellectual Pride and Intellectual Humility." In *The Moral Psychology of Pride*, edited by J. Adam Carter and Emma Gordon, 69–78. Lanham, Md.: Rowman and Littlefield, 2017.

King, Nathan. "Perseverance as an Intellectual Virtue." *Synthese* 191 (2014): 3501–23.

Richards, Norvin. "Is Humility a Virtue?" *American Philosophical Quarterly* 25 (1988): 253–59.

Samuelson, Peter L., Matthew J. Jarvinen, Thomas B. Paulus, Ian M. Church, Sam A. Hardy, and Justin L. Barrett. "Implicit Theories of Intellectual Virtues and Vices: A Focus on Intellectual Humility." *Journal of Positive Psychology* 10, no. 5 (2015): 389–406.

Snow, Nancy. "Humility." *Journal of Value Inquiry* 29 (1995): 203–16.

Spiegel, James. "Open-Mindedness and Intellectual Humility." *Theory and Research in Education* 10 (2012): 27–38.

Summa Contra Gentiles. New York: Benziger Brothers, 1929.

Tangney, J. P. "Humility: Theoretical Perspectives, Empirical Findings, and Directions for Future Research." *Journal of Social and Clinical Psychology* 19 (2000): 70–82.

Taylor, Gabrielle. *Pride, Shame, and Guilt*. New York: Oxford University Press, 1985.

Vlastos, Gregory. "The Unity of the Virtues in *Protagoras*." *Review of Metaphysics* 25, no. 3 (1972): 415–58.

Whitcomb, Dennis, Heather Battaly, Jason Baehr, and Daniel Howard-Snyder. "Intellectual Humility: Owning Our Limitations." *Philosophy and Phenomenological Research* 94, no. 3 (2017): 509–39.

7

Employing Humility

The Role of Humility in Servant Leadership

Elizabeth J. Krumrei-Mancuso

Abuse of power is by no means a new phenomenon, yet greater access to information about corruption scandals in business and politics, police brutality, and sexual harassment in the workplace has resulted in many people becoming disillusioned with those in positions of power.[1] The 2017 Edelman Trust Barometer, a global trust and credibility survey, reported that the general population around the world is showing an "implosion" of trust in four key institutions—business, government, NGOs, and media.[2] The report described a "pitifully low level of confidence" in the leaders of business and government, with global credibility of CEOs at 37 percent and credibility of government officials and regulators at 29 percent.[3] More than two-thirds of the general population did not have confidence that their current leaders could address their country's challenges. Further, trust in NGOs had fallen to nearly the same level as trust in businesses. This raises serious concerns about and for those who lead others. In fact, the data show that "a person like yourself"[4] is now seen as being as credible as an academic or technical expert, and far more credible than a CEO or government official, implying that the traditional pyramid of influence and authority has toppled. The executive summary of the Trust Barometer concluded that institutions must recognize that: relationships are integral to building trust, they must treat employees and customers well, and they must adopt an approach that begins with listening and engaging others before taking action. The executive summary calls for leadership that places people squarely at the center of everything leaders do.[5]

Fortunately, there is a fairly extensive base of theories and research on a variety of forms of leadership that move in the direction of the needs expressed in Edelman's global report. The current chapter focuses on one of these models, servant leadership, and asks what role humility plays in facilitating this form of leadership.

There has been a growth in interest in servant leadership in recent years, perhaps because leaders' self-serving behaviors have been viewed as foundational to unethical practices and abusive choices that have resulted in a lack of trust in those in leadership. For the same reason, there has been a growth in interest in the concept of humility in organizational research, given that unbridled egos and the self-importance of corporate executives have been pinpointed in corporate scandals.[6] Given that leaders have power conferred on them, they have the autonomy to decide if and when to put the needs of others first. This makes servant leadership an intriguing concept, one that contrasts with general stereotypes of leaders being power hungry.

Even outside of the context of leadership, language surrounding service, including servant, servitude, and servanthood, may conjure up images of humility. This raises the question of whether the inclination to serve others is to some extent predicated on a person's ability to be humble. In the context of leadership, humility may be particularly crucial to service, given the power differential that exists between leaders and followers. Humility may be one of the hinges on which servant leadership operates, given that humility has the opportunity to counteract the tendency for hierarchical relationships to become unhealthy and abusive.[7] The current chapter explores these concepts in greater depth, examining theory and outcomes surrounding servant leadership and how humility relates to implementing this form of leadership. Although servant leadership is selected as a specific case, no assumptions are made about whether humility operates similarly or differently in other forms of leadership.

Defining and Operationalizing Servant Leadership

One way to define the essence of servant leadership would be that it involves the leader being in a nonfocal position and seeking to fulfill the interests of others rather than maximize personal ambition.[8] Qualities of servant leadership have been modeled and described for centuries. They are often attributed to the leadership of Christ[9] and have been described in writings such as the sixth-century *Rule of St. Benedict*. In the context of current scholarship, the term "servant leadership" is traced to Robert Greenleaf, who, after being director of management research at AT&T, founded the Center for Applied Ethics in 1964 (now the Robert K. Greenleaf Center for Servant Leadership) and published a seminal essay on the topic of servant leadership in 1970. Virtually all current scholarship on servant leadership draws on Greenleaf's writings in formulating a definition of the construct.

According to Greenleaf, a defining feature of servant leadership is that the leader's focus is on other people's highest-priority needs being served, rather than on the needs of the leader, or even the needs of the organization, for that matter.[10] Servant leaders encourage followers to attain their fullest potential. Greenleaf suggested that the best test of servant leadership is whether those served grow as people, become healthier, wiser, freer, more autonomous, and more likely themselves to become servants. Greenleaf believed that focusing on serving others and putting the needs of followers above one's own results in a ripple effect of followers developing a desire to serve others. If this is true, servant leadership might impact the least privileged in society: they will benefit, or at least not be further deprived, when servant leadership is in place.

Greenleaf suggested that the servant leader is servant *first*. Servant leadership begins with the natural feeling that one wants to serve and *then* the aspiration to lead. This process is distinct from choosing to serve after leadership is established. The person who is leader first is more likely to serve out of his or her conscience or in conformity with normative expectations. In contrast, the servant-first leader is more likely to persevere in attempts to meet others' highest priority needs. Servant leaders act by transcending their own interests and lead by example and through persuasion. Power is used to create opportunity and alternatives so that others can have choice and build autonomy.

Larry Spears, a successor of Greenleaf as CEO of the Robert K. Greenleaf Center for Servant Leadership, summarized ten nonexhaustive attributes of servant leadership found in Greenleaf's writing, including listening, empathy, healing, awareness, persuasion, conceptualization, foresight, stewardship, commitment to the growth of people, and building community.[11] Subsequently, many theorists and researchers have developed similar, but varied, lists of attributes of servant leadership.[12] In addition, a number of researchers have made efforts to operationalize the concept of servant leadership in the form of measures assessing servant leadership behaviors and/or traits (see table 7.1 on p. 212). These measures employ both self-report or observant-report methods, which is important given that servant leadership can be understood as consisting of intensions of the leader, behaviors of the leader, and/or interpretation of leadership by followers.

Although servant leadership shows some commonalities to other forms of leadership, research indicates that servant leadership is a distinct form of leadership.[13] The unique features that differentiate servant leadership from other models of leadership include that the role of the leader is to serve followers, with the goal of promoting personal growth and development among followers, which in turn betters society.[14]

Outcomes of Servant Leadership

Greenleaf acknowledged that there may be a real contradiction in the idea of the servant as leader and that the expected outcomes of servant leadership are difficult to assess.[15] Some have argued that servant leadership's primary altruistic focus on subordinates' well-being with secondary attention to organizational concerns may conflict with efficiency and the attainment of organizational goals.[16] If servant leaders are motivated by service to subordinates and community needs without consideration of how this impacts organizations' finances, this may detract from financial outcomes of organizations.[17] These critiques raise questions about the effectiveness of servant leadership. Fortunately, there is a respectable body of research on servant leadership, of which a fair amount draws on multiple raters (leaders and followers) and/or multiple time points of assessment. The research is limited in scope, focusing mostly on leadership in organizations, but offers variety in terms of the types of organizations and their locations. The research cited in this chapter alone spans more than eighteen different types of organizations as well as general, representative samples of employees in more than sixteen different countries in North America, Europe, Africa, and Asia, including the Middle East.

Many studies confirm that servant leadership, consistent with its focus, is associated with stronger relationships between leaders and followers.[18] Servant leadership is also related to benefits to followers on both professional and personal levels. It is associated with a greater sense of fairness in the workplace,[19] need satisfaction in the areas of autonomy, competence, and relatedness,[20] mental toughness,[21] psychological empowerment,[22] job satisfaction,[23] and even life satisfaction.[24] Servant leadership has also been associated with less job stress and daily work strain[25] and less burnout.[26]

These benefits to employees seem to benefit companies as well. Relevant to the issues of our times highlighted by the Edelman Trust Barometer,[27] servant leadership has been related to greater trust in leaders and in organizations.[28] Servant leadership has also been linked to greater organizational identification and commitment[29] and decreased follower disengagement and turnover intentions.[30] Beyond minimizing negative effects, servant leadership has been linked to positive employee work behaviors, including greater work engagement[31] and task orientation,[32] more intrinsic motivation,[33] greater efforts to bring about constructive change within a work unit,[34] inclination to seek critical feedback,[35] more creative behavior,[36] and overall better work performance.[37] Further, there is a substantial body of research that links servant leadership to organizational citizenship behavior, which refers to employees' behaviors that contribute to their organization beyond their formal job requirements. Servant leadership is associated with followers engaging in more helping behavior to benefit coworkers or more conscientious behavior to benefit their organization as a whole.[38]

The effects of servant leadership seem to extend beyond individual employees to work teams as well. Servant leadership has been related to more collective team behavior, better exchange of information, and better joint decision-making,[39] greater employee confidence in one's team's general capabilities,[40] and better team effectiveness and performance.[41]

Research is also beginning to examine how service leadership in organizations impacts outcomes for those served by the organization. So far, it has been linked to greater customer orientation,[42] greater patient satisfaction in hospitals,[43] and greater contribution to communities.[44]

In response to the concern that a service focus would negatively impact a company's bottom line,[45] research thus far seems to indicate that servant leadership is associated with better organizational effectiveness and performance, including greater return on assets.[46]

Thus, by and large, the research literature indicates that servant leadership has positive effects in the workplace; however, limited research has directly examined how the outcomes of servant leadership compare to those of other forms of leadership, including transformational leadership, transactional leadership, and initiating structure leadership. Transformational leadership is a leadership style that emphasizes the collective purpose of a group or organization by articulating an externally focused sense of purpose, inspiring followers to be innovative, and motivating followers to work toward a common good.[47] There is some indication that servant leadership is more predictive of better work performance,[48] team performance,[49] organizational performance,[50] organizational commitment,[51] and positive impact on the community[52] in comparison to transformational leadership, but that servant leadership is less effective in promoting organizational learning than transformational leadership.[53] Transactional leadership is a model that operates through routine and focuses on maintaining the status quo of an organization. It measures success on the basis of an organization's established system of rewards and penalties. Where transformational leadership is about motivation and inspiration, prioritizing overall group progress, transactional leadership is about positive and negative reinforcement, appealing to the self-interest of followers. When compared to both transformational leadership and transactional leadership, servant leadership accounts for incremental variance in follower satisfaction, performance, organizational citizenship behaviors directed toward colleagues and toward customers, and corporate social responsibility attitudes, and these findings cannot simply be attributed to followers' increased levels of satisfaction with servant leadership.[54] Finally, servant leadership has been compared to initiating structure leadership, which emphasizes the importance of specifying tasks and how they are to be done, defining relationships and lines of responsibility, and clarifying roles. Initiating structure leadership is transactional in nature in that it emphasizes expectations and consequences for followers. Servant leadership has been shown to be more effective at promoting helping behaviors and creative behaviors than initiating structure leadership, but initiating structure has been more effective at promoting work performance and less deviant behavior than servant leadership.[55]

As might be expected, the mechanisms by which servant leadership functions to promote outcomes are unique from the mechanisms through which other forms of leadership exert their influence.[56] A fair amount of research has examined mediation models, indicating that the outcomes of servant leadership often occur through the cultivation of a positive relationship between leader and followers,[57] meeting the needs of followers,[58] fair treatment in the workplace,[59] and a service climate.[60]

The Role of Humility in Servant Leadership

Based on the many benefits of servant leadership supported by the literature, it is worth exploring what qualities and characteristics enable and promote servant leadership. The current chapter focuses specifically on exploring how humility relates to the construct of servant leadership. Humility has been defined as the ability to transcend oneself, including being able to keep in perspective one's abilities, accomplishments, and limitations.[61] The hallmarks of humility have been described as a secure, accepting identity, freedom from distortion within one's perceptions of self in either self-enhancing or self-debasing ways, openness to new information, other-focus, and egalitarian beliefs.[62] Owens et al. provided a conceptualization of humility within the context of leadership, focusing specifically on observable behaviors that demonstrate humility.[63] They defined this expressed humility as an interpersonal characteristic involving a manifested willingness to view oneself accurately, a displayed appreciation of others' strengths and contributions, and teachability. In the context of servant leadership specifically, van Dierendonck defined humility as understanding one's strong and weak points, keeping one's accomplishments and talents in perspective, and admitting one's fallibility and mistakes.[64] Thus, recent literature has contained fairly consistent definitions of humility, particularly in the study of leadership, including servant leadership.

Research has demonstrated the benefits of humility to the outcomes of leadership in general,[65] but here the focus is specifically on servant leadership. What follows is an exploration of how humility relates to Greenleaf's original conceptualization of servant leadership and then an exploration of humility within more contemporary research and writing on servant leadership. On these bases, the chapter will highlight a proposed conceptualization of how humility relates to servant leadership.

The relevance of humility to Greenleaf's original conceptualization of servant leadership. Remarkably, Greenleaf did not use the term "humility" in describing servant leadership; nevertheless, humility seems crucial to his ideas about leading as a servant, like an unspoken thread underlying the themes of his writing.[66] First is his emphasis on the concept of *primus inter pares*, or the idea that a leader is first among equals.[67] This may offer a response to the call in the executive summary of the 2017 Trust Barometer for leadership to move beyond "for the people" to "with the people."[68] Greenleaf's operationalization of *primus inter pares* seems to be that servant leaders work through persuasion rather than coercive power.[69] Because leaders have the power and capability to place themselves at the top of the pyramid, choosing to view themselves as equals among others and to lead through persuasion rather than force may require the presence of humility. Further, Greenleaf's suggestion that servant leadership always *begins* with the desire to serve prior to an aspiration to lead presumes that a servant leader's motivation cannot involve self-centered desires, thereby assuming a certain level of humility.

Greenleaf's writings also point to a number of servant leader behaviors that can be hypothesized to require humility. Central to Greenleaf's conceptualization of servant leadership is the emphasis on promoting growth and wholeness in subordinates. Greenleaf believed that empathy for others and acceptance of who people are enables them to grow into something greater. Expressing unqualified acceptance and empathy requires a tolerance of the imperfections found in all followers. Research has shown that being able to accept fallibility in others often depends on one's humility to recognize one's own fallibility.[70] Further, Greenleaf emphasized that something subtle but important is communicated to those being led when there is an understanding that the search for wholeness is something shared by the servant leader.[71] The admission that the leader is in search of the same thing as the follower—that is, wholeness or growth—tends to minimize separateness between the leader and subordinate, which requires a certain amount of leader humility. The result of this process is that a stronger connection is forged between the leader and the follower, which has been highlighted as key to the positive outcomes of servant leadership.

Greenleaf also highlighted listening as a crucial servant leadership behavior. He believed the approach of the servant leader must be to listen to those they want to communicate to, requiring that the leader's desire to understand outweighs his or her desire to be understood. Building on this, Greenleaf believed that servant leaders automatically respond to problems by listening first, whereas other types of leaders have the tendency to try to place blame, rather than admitting they need others' insights and potential solutions. Presumably, admitting a need to understand and the desire to benefit from others' expertise requires leader humility. Greenleaf's later writings further noted that seeking strength requires the humility to seek a confidant who can be a sounding board and offer perspective on oneself.[72]

Finally, Greenleaf described the servant leader behavior of standing aside and waiting when necessary, emphasizing that the best way to serve others may be to give others the time to define their own needs and state how they want to be served.[73] This would require servant leaders to have the humility to relinquish their own notions of how to serve others, in order to serve in ways defined by others.

Contemporary theories and research about how humility relates to servant leadership. There is a consensus in contemporary theory that humility is highly relevant to servant leadership. This is supported empirically as well. For example, in a small narrative inquiry study of top executives who had been identified as servant leaders by subordinates and colleagues, humility emerged as a theme of leadership across all sectors (education, corporate, and government), even though the interview questions were based on five dimensions of servant leadership that did not explicitly refer to humility.[74] This suggests that humility is common to servant leaders, but does not reveal the exact interrelation of humility and servant leadership. A number of distinct conceptualizations can be distilled from the literature about how humility relates to servant leadership. A pertinent question is whether humility is part of the core definition of servant leadership or exists as an ancillary quality.

Those who include humility as part of the core definition of servant leadership[75] do so because they believe leaders keeping their own accomplishments in proper perspective (i.e., humility) is a measure of the extent to which a leader will put the interests of others first and serve them (i.e., servant leadership). Even though a good number of servant leadership measures include a direct assessment of humility,[76] slightly more measures do not explicitly assess humility as part of the conceptualization of servant leadership.[77]

Methodologies used in the development of these measures offer some insight into various conceptualizations of the interrelationship of servant leadership and humility. Typically, numerous survey items are developed to assess the latent variable of servant leadership, which is not directly measured but inferred on the basis of the individual survey items. Factor analyses are then used to collapse the large number of individual items into one or more interpretable underlying factors that have similar patterns of responses. Most measures of servant leadership are multidimensional in nature,[78] where humility may or may not be one of the factors contributing to servant leadership. Interestingly, some researchers have found humility items to load onto a higher-order factor representing servant leadership,[79] which would support the idea of humility being integral, together with other concepts, to the conceptualization of the latent construct of servant leadership. However, it should be noted that somewhat stronger fit tends to be associated with multidimensional factor models than models with all factors interrelated.[80] Further, Hale and Fields demonstrated in two independent samples that a model with two separate factors for service and humility fit the data better than a model of servant leadership combining service and humility together.[81] Thus, the factor structure of servant leader measures seems to offer the most support for viewing humility as a distinct component in relation to other components of servant leadership, even if it is considered definitional.

Unfortunately, the approach of building humility into the core definition of servant leadership contributes to a frequently recognized problem in the literature on servant leadership: a lack of measurement clarity.[82] Even though some argue that humility should be viewed as a distinct backbone of servant leadership,[83] it has also been pointed out that humility is a characteristic of a number of leadership styles besides servant leadership, including supportive leadership, level 5 leadership, transformational leadership, and authentic leadership.[84] Of course, servant leaders *can* characteristically exhibit traits such as humility that overlap with other leadership styles; further, servant leadership may party be defined on the basis of a trait shared with other forms of leadership. However, when the definitional degree of overlap between servant leadership and other forms of leadership is extensive, a problem we face is that of distinctiveness. Defining servant leadership on the basis of leadership qualities that are common to other forms of leadership builds measurement overlap into research, obscuring the discriminant and construct validity of servant leadership.[85] This poses challenges to research examining the outcomes of servant leadership and how they are unique from the outcomes of other forms of leadership. Specifically, previous research has shown that when measures of servant leadership incorporate dimensions that are core features of servant leadership along with dimensions less specific to servant leadership, these measures can tap into other forms of leadership when respondents score high on characteristics of servant leadership that overlap with other leadership approaches and low on base conditions of servant leadership.[86] In such instances, variance in outcomes of interest can be influenced by other leadership approaches when leaders score high on domains that are relevant, but not exclusive to servant leadership. This makes it difficult to study servant leadership empirically.

Grisaffe, VanMeter, and Chonko classified two qualities as unique distinctives of servant leadership that differentiate this form of leadership from other forms of leadership: (1) serving first and (2) selflessly focusing on others' needs.[87] This concurs with the writings of Greenleaf as well as the review in this chapter that the most consistently assessed component of servant leadership is altruistically serving followers and putting their needs first (see table 7.1 on p. 212). Thus, the most parsimonious core definition of servant leadership may be a leadership modality that operates by the leader selflessly serving followers and putting their needs first.

This is not to diminish the importance of humility to servant leadership. Important, nondefinitional conceptualizations of humility in relation to servant leadership include that humility functions as a precursor, operating mechanism, or moderator in relation to servant leadership. As a precursor, humility can be thought of as a trigger for servant leadership. The low self-focus and low self-serving tendencies involved in humility may give way to prioritizing the needs and goals of others through servant leadership. Some of the proponents of conceptualizing humility as central to the definition and measurement of servant leadership[88] have also acknowledged that humility may be better conceptualized as a virtuous attitude that *underlies* servant leadership behavior toward followers.[89] That is, Van Dierendonck and Patterson differentiated humility as being less central to the definition of servant leadership and more in a position of being a precursor to servant leader behaviors. Others have also classified humility[90] and low narcissism[91] as antecedents to servant leadership.

Another very closely related option is that humility can be conceptualized as an operating mechanism through which servant leaders function.[92] Humility may be the vehicle through which someone comes to see others as worthy of care and compassion.[93] Common ideas are that humility is the operating mechanism for a host of core servant leadership qualities, including being motivated primarily by the desire to serve and empower followers rather than by the desire to be in power, giving priority to the interests of followers rather than oneself, forging strong relationships with followers, listening to and desiring to understand followers, and admitting one's own limitations and therefore respecting and acknowledging others' contributions and seeking others' expertise.[94] Unfortunately, very little research has examined these hypotheses directly. There is some indirect indication that leader humility is associated with a greater tendency to engage in servant leadership in general, given that data gathered over multiple points revealed a negative relationship between CEO narcissism and servant leadership.[95] Further, qualitative data have supported the idea that humility counteracts self-interest, paving the way for servant leaders to focus on serving others,[96] and that humility allows servant leaders to build trust and successfully resolve conflicts in the workplace.[97] Finally, Hanse et al. have offered evidence that humility is one of the servant leadership domains that predicts better-quality relationships between a leader and his/her subordinates, including more loyalty, professional respect, mutual trust, and good communication.[98]

There are a number of hypotheses about how humility as an operating mechanism of servant leadership contributes to the positive outcomes of servant leadership previously reviewed in this chapter. For example, Sousa and Van Dierendonck proposed that because humility helps leaders prioritize the needs of others above themselves, it creates space for increased helping behaviors among followers.[99] In addition, because humility facilitates leaders acknowledging the contributions of others, it facilitates the quantity of information exchange within an organization. Finally, humble inquiry by leaders instills a culture of dialogue and genuine interest in mutual understanding, which fosters creativity and innovative thinking among followers.

Research on the role of humility in the outcomes of servant leadership is sparse but slightly more expansive than the research examining humility as an operating mechanism of servant leader behaviors directly. First, there is cross-cultural evidence that people view humility to be positively related to leadership effectiveness in the context of servant leadership.[100] In addition, performance orientation values among middle managers from organizations across cultures have been correlated with a greater emphasis on humility in servant leadership among these leaders,[101] suggesting that servant leadership is compatible with task accomplishment and achievement. Further, the limited research available tends to indicate that leader humility is a fairly robust predictor of many positive work qualities in followers, but that it may not directly predict work performance. Servant leader humility has been related to outcomes of interest in followers, including vitality, engagement, job satisfaction, and organizational commitment.[102] In fact, leader humility was the most robust servant leader predictor of extra-role behavior among followers.[103] Similarly, Sousa and van Dierendonck found that humility, like other aspects of servant leadership, contributed to work engagement among followers, involving more vigor, dedication, and absorption related to work.[104]

In an examination of shared servant leadership within a group setting, leader humility related to many outcomes of interest, including collective team behavior, information exchange, and joint decision-making, whereas some, but not all, of the other domains of servant leadership predicted the same outcomes.[105]

Finally, some indirect evidence has been offered by Sousa and van Dierendonck,[106] who found that psychological empowerment of subordinates was strongest among leaders who rated themselves as being lower on servant leadership than the level of servant leadership attributed to them by their subordinates. Sousa and van Dierendonck interpreted this discrepancy in ratings as servant leaders underestimating their effectiveness as leaders in comparison to the evaluation they received from followers, considering this a sign of leader humility.[107] Although this interpretation is questionable, if it is accepted, this study would further support the idea that humility among servant leaders is associated with positive outcomes, in this case followers' perceptions that they were psychologically empowered. Psychological empowerment involved having an intrinsic motivation toward their work based on a sense of meaning, competence, self-determination, and impact.

However, it should be noted that some studies have found that leader humility, unlike some of the other domains of servant leadership, was not predictive of work performance.[108] In addition, some research has not found evidence that any of the domains of servant leadership, including humility, were directly predictive of team performance.[109]

A final model to consider is whether humility acts as a moderator of links between servant leadership and its outcomes. This option has not frequently been examined in the literature, but partial support was offered by Sousa and van Dierendonck,[110] who hypothesized that leader humility would amplify the relationship between other servant leader qualities and follower work engagement. They did not observe this for their sample as a whole, but they found a small three-way interaction in which the humility component of servant leadership strengthened the effects of the other aspects of servant leadership on work engagement for leaders with higher hierarchical power positions in their organization. Among leaders with less powerful positions, those lower in humility were able to compensate for their lack of humility by displaying more of the other qualities of servant leadership in order to achieve greater follower engagement.

Conclusions about the conceptualization of humility in relation to servant leadership. Core characteristics of servant leadership are that the leader takes on the position of a servant and focuses on meeting the needs of others, including helping followers to develop, grow, and flourish. This requires that the leader not focus on self and not be motivated by self-interest. Humility may be one of the essential ingredients that allows servant leaders to transcend the self in a way required for taking an *other-*, rather than a *self-*, orientation in leadership. Although it is theoretically sound to reason that humility is closely associated with servant leadership, incorporating humility into the definition of servant leadership is problematic for measurement reasons, and therefore creates more problems than benefits in advancing the science of servant leadership. A better option is to consider humility an ancillary condition that makes servant leadership possible, a necessary but not sufficient condition that precedes servant leadership and functions as an operating mechanism for servant leadership behaviors (see figure 7.1 on p. 213). This conceptualization may offer a solution to concerns that have been raised about ambiguity in the current definitions of servant leadership, with regard to whether it represents a trait theory or a theory of leadership as behavior.[111] In the current conceptualization, qualities such as humility are traits of leaders that are necessary but not sufficient for servant leadership behaviors to take place. It should be noted that, naturally, humility is not the only trait necessary for servant leadership. It exists among other characteristics of leaders such as authenticity, integrity, and empathy that together pave the way for leaders to engage in characteristic servant leader behaviors.

Directions for Future Research on the Role of Humility in Servant Leadership

Examining the role of humility in servant leadership brings together two areas of research that each face unique challenges. In the study of servant leadership, there have been some discrepancies between leader and follower reports of servant leadership and leadership effectiveness.[112] This may be further compounded when trying to also isolate humility, a variable that is notoriously difficult to assess.[113] In light of these challenges, more research will be needed in order to draw strong conclusions about how humility functions in servant leadership. Not much of the research on servant leadership presents findings separately for humility and other dimensions or conditions of servant leadership in order to evaluate how humility specifically relates to servant leader traits, behaviors, and outcomes.

TABLE 7.1 Commonly Assessed Domains of Servant Leadership

Domains assessed	Measures								
	Barbuto and Wheeler, "Scale Development"	Dennis and Bocarnea, "Development of the Servant," "Servant Leadership Assessment Instrument"	Ehrhart, "Leadership and Procedural Justice Climate"	Laub, "Assessing the Servant Organization"	Liden et al., "Servant Leadership"	Reed, Vidaver-Cohen, and Colwell, "New Scale"	Sendjaya, Sarros, and Santora, "Defining and Measuring"	Sousa and van Dierendonck, "Introducing a Short Measure"	Van Dierendonck and Nuijten, "Servant Leadership Survey"
Servant leadership behaviors									
Altruistically serving followers; putting followers' interests first	X	X	X	X	X	X	X	X*	X
Empowering followers (e.g., to engage in decision-making)		X	X		X		X	X	X
Working toward a positive impact on the larger community	X		X			X	X		X
Helping followers grow and succeed			X	X	X	X			
Leading through shared vision and persuasion	X	X			X			X	
Taking an egalitarian approach to leadership					X		X	X	
Leading with knowledge, awareness, and foresight	X		X		X				
Forming relationships with followers			X	X					
Valuing and loving followers		X		X					

Domains assessed	Measures								
	Barbuto and Wheeler, "Scale Development"	Dennis and Bocarnea, "Development of the Servant," "Servant Leadership Assessment Instrument"	Ehrhart, "Leadership and Procedural Justice Climate"	Laub, "Assessing the Servant Organization"	Liden et al., "Servant Leadership"	Reed, Vidaver-Cohen, and Colwell, "New Scale"	Sendjaya, Sarros, and Santora, "Defining and Measuring"	Sousa and van Dierendonck, "Introducing a Short Measure"	Van Dierendonck and Nuijten, "Servant Leadership Survey"
Servant leadership behaviors									
Being responsive to followers' emotional needs	X				X				
Holding followers accountable for their work								X	X
Trusting followers (their morality and competence)		X							
Forgiving followers for mistakes/offenses									X
Servant leader traits									
Integrity (morality, honesty)			X		X	X	X		
Humility		X						X	X
Authenticity				X			X		X
Courage									X
Spirituality							X		

*Sousa and van Dierendonck focused on shared servant leadership, and emphasized acting in the interest of the group/whole. See Sousa and van Dierendonck, "Introducing a Short Measure."

FIGURE 7.1. Conceptualization of Humility in Relation to Servant Leadership

Regardless of whether humility is considered to be a sufficient condition for servant leadership or not, simply qualifying it as a necessary condition raises potential questions about its implications for the cultivation of servant leadership. Greenleaf's starting point seems to be that servant leaders are by *nature* servants. In crediting Hesse's *Journey to the East* for his ideas about servant leadership, Greenleaf describes the key figure of the story in the following way: "His servant nature was the real man, not bestowed, not assumed, and not to be taken away."[114] This is consistent with the idea that servant leadership is built on the traits of a leader, such as humility. This is supported by limited empirical work indicating that personality characteristics of a leader can promote or discourage servant leadership.[115] Yet Greenleaf left open the possibility that nonservant leaders can be transformed into servant leaders through the arduous discipline of cultivating servant leader mechanisms such as listening. Presumably, the same applies for humility. Although the question has not often been examined, there is some evidence that humility can be cultivated.[116] Therefore, it would be beneficial for future research to consider whether servant leadership training programs might benefit from incorporating humility interventions.

Another limitation in the current research on humility in servant leadership is the narrow slice of contexts in which servant leadership has been studied, those being almost exclusively organizations and businesses. There is a need to examine humility in the many other macro and micro areas where servant leadership may be taking place, for example in the leadership provided in societies by public figures and social influencers and in the many instances of leadership taking place in communities, social groups, and family units. As Greenleaf (1970) acknowledged, a great leader may be the head of a vast organization or a mother in her home.

A final area of research that must be expanded in order to fully understand the implications of humility for servant leadership is how views of the role of humility in leadership differ across cultures. There is some indication that servant leadership is experienced differently across cultures.[117] Furthermore, the importance of humility as a component of servant leadership is endorsed differently across cultures, with comparatively high endorsement of humility in Southern Asia and low endorsement of humility in Nordic Europe.[118] Some have hypothesized that humility is appreciated as a leader quality and contributes to trust in cultures characterized by lower power distance between leaders and followers, whereas humility is less consistent with leadership norms in cultures that promote greater power distance between leaders and followers.[119] In the latter case, humility among leaders may confuse followers and result in perceptions of a leader being less effective. Thus, in studying the role of humility in servant leadership, it is necessary to consider the cultural interpretations of humility within a given society and the implications thereof for servant leader effectiveness.

• • •

Response to Elizabeth J. Krumrei-Mancuso

Everett L. Worthington Jr.

In her review of both servant-leadership and humility, with special consideration to their intersection, Krumrei-Mancuso has done two things excellently. First, she has summarized the literature on servant leadership. In doing so, she notes that (1) servant leadership is defined by a primary focus on subordinates with the intent to elevate them and without a focus on elevating oneself and (2) humility might also involve other-orientation. With that commonality in mind, she has considered many possibilities of how humility might relate to servant leadership. Her tentative conclusion is, "A better option is to consider humility an ancillary condition that makes servant leadership possible, a necessary but not sufficient condition that precedes servant leadership and functions as an operating mechanism for servant leadership behaviors. . . . This conceptualization may offer a solution to concerns that have been raised about ambiguity in the current definitions of servant leadership, with regard to whether it represents a trait theory or a theory of leadership as behavior" (211).

First, Krumrei-Mancuso's review of the servant leadership literature is complete and educational. It is a valuable heuristic contribution to have the summaries of research and writing on servant leadership gathered in one place.

A second helpful contribution is her evaluation of the current assessment instruments and which components of servant leadership each instrument claims to assess. This gives an insight into the way researchers understand the components needed to make up servant leadership.

Third, her chapter collects the references on assessment of servant leadership. That collection makes them accessible to researchers and can thus promote research on servant leadership in general and specifically on the roles of different types of humility in servant leadership.

Fourth, she zeroes in on the other-orientation of servant leadership and a comparable other-orientation of humility. The similarities suggest that there might be some type of connection theoretically, and she spends the last half of the chapter considering various possibilities. She suggests that, according to Greenleaf, the main defining feature of servant leadership is that the leader focuses on other people's highest-priority needs being served, not on the interests of the leader, or even the interests of the organization.[1] Grisaffe, VanMeter, and Chonko classified two qualities as unique distinctives of servant leadership that differentiate this form of leadership from other forms of leadership: (1) serving first and (2) selflessly focusing on others' needs.[2] Krumrei-Mancuso evaluates the major measuring instruments seeking to assess servant leadership, which is a nice contribution to the literature in itself. She finds that the most consistently assessed component of servant leadership was altruistically serving followers and putting their needs first. She concludes, "Thus, the most parsimonious core definition of servant leadership may be a leadership modality that operates by the leader selflessly serving followers and putting their needs first" (208).

The fifth contribution Krumrei-Mancuso makes to the literature is bringing together the investigations that sought to examine the ways that humility and servant leadership intersect. She does a masterful job of considering a variety of these intersections (i.e., humility as correlated with servant leadership, humility as a precursor to servant leadership, and humility as necessary but not sufficient to produce servant leadership) and evaluating them using contemporary research.

In light of these contributions, I might note a few minor criticisms of her chapter. These fall under the debate over definitions.

Definition of servant leadership. I am not keen on the definition of servant leadership. She suggests that, according to Greenleaf, the defining feature of servant leadership is that the leader's focus is on other people's highest-priority needs being served, not on the interests of the leader, or even the interests of the organization.[3] These characteristics might be the *distinctive* defining characteristic of servant leadership, but that may only be because servanthood is what differentiates servant leadership from other models of leadership, such as supportive leadership, level 5 leadership, transformational leadership, and authentic leadership. I think in following Grisaffe, VanMeter, and Chonko's line of reasoning, Krumrei-Mancuso is confusing *distinctive* characteristics that differentiate servant leadership from other types of leadership with a *definition* of servant leadership. Servant leaders are indeed servants. But they also are leaders, and there is no indication in Krumrei-Mancuso's definition about how they lead.

Use of Jesus as exemplar of servant leadership. There is a definitional uncertainty regarding humility. She notes, for example, that "[q]ualities of servant leadership have been modeled and described for centuries. They are often attributed to the leadership of Christ[4] and have been described in writings such as the sixth-century *Rule of St. Benedict*" (200–201).

I would probably suggest steering clear of using Jesus as the exemplar of servant leadership if she wishes to maintain her definition of servant leadership. There are four reasons.

First, in Philippians 2:3-11 (NIV), Paul uses Jesus as a model for other-oriented humility: "Rather, in humility value others above yourselves, not looking to your own interests but each of you to the interests of the others" (Phil 2:3b-4). Thus, Paul describes humility as being other-oriented. This is, in fact, a distinctive feature of Christian humility, as Davis, Hook, McAnnally-Linz, Choe, and Placeres have observed.[5] Worthington and Allison have stated that psychologists have generally agreed that humility must be characterized by (1) accurate self-assessment; (2) a willingness to learn ways to strengthen weaknesses, or teachableness; and (3) a modest self-portrayal.[6] However, Worthington and Allison also suggest that a fourth distinctive, other-orientation, is treated as essential by (arguably) over half of the psychologists and not as essential by the others. We might note that some Eastern religions and many psychologists influenced by individualistic cultural perspectives or Eastern philosophy (or both) might disagree that other-orientedness characterizes humility—though generally they might see it as a correlated trait that often shows up. Eastern philosophy and religion—the Zen versions perhaps more than compassionate Buddhism—and individualistic cultural perspectives emphasize a quiet ego as the core of humility. For both Buddhism and Hinduism, this is rooted in a belief that the fundamental nature of existence is unity and the goal of existence is unifying with the whole.[7] One route to unity is through meditation. One might meditate on nonlogical paradoxes (i.e., koans) or on compassion (or other things), but the ultimate goal is freedom from desire, from the ego, and from the illusion of self.[8]

Second, Krumrei-Mancuso states, "One way to define the essence of servant leadership would be that it involves the leader being in a nonfocal position and seeking to fulfill the interests of others rather than maximize personal ambition" (200). We might question whether "being in a nonfocal position" is indeed necessary. Jesus is one model of a servant leader, and yet he is head of the church. His is the name at which every knee shall bow and every tongue confess that he is Lord. This is far from a nonfocal position.

Third, we note too that the Christian-related model of humility as being other-oriented is not the same thing as being a model for servant-leadership. Paul says that Christ "made himself nothing by taking the very nature of a servant" (Phil 2:7), but the passage does not mention leadership—only humility. That humility was rewarded by God and will be rewarded by all of creation ultimately: "at the name of Jesus every knee should bow, in heaven and on earth and under the earth, and every tongue acknowledge that Jesus Christ is Lord, to the glory of God the Father" (Phil 2:10-11, NIV).

Fourth, Krumrei-Mancuso notes that servant leadership requires a leader's focus to be on other people's highest-priority needs being served, not on the interests of the leader, or even the interests of the organization. Again, I am not sure this is servant leadership if Christ is the exemplar of this. Jesus clearly did have interests besides other people. First, Jesus had God's kingdom interests in mind. That is, while he died for all people, Jesus' interest is not, I believe, as parochial as wanting to promote fulfilled individuals. Rather, as Paul says in Philippians 2:11, Jesus is focused on the glory of God the Father rather than the glory of created humans, in spite of their status as image-bearers of God.

Focus solely on meeting the needs of others as the defining condition for servant leadership. Similarly, I doubt that any CEO ever succeeded if he or she was not mindful of the needs of the organization. One forms an organization—whether a business or nonprofit or nongovernmental organization—to accomplish a purpose, and that main purpose is rarely (if ever) the promotion of the well-being of its employees. Clearly that can be an important objective, as organizations like Southwest Airlines have shown over the years, but the organization (and leader) must be attentive to organizational objectives if survival is to occur.

Servant focus does not necessarily imply humility. Krumrei-Mancuso claims that humility is a necessary but not sufficient condition for servant leadership. But it seems that people could be very servant-focused without being humble in the least. One could be oriented toward being a servant leader by enculturation, training, or upbringing. One could simply have poor self-esteem and think that all he or she is fit for is meeting the needs of others. Because of the orientation of many organizations toward fostering individual projects (or even team-directed projects), promoting someone to a leadership position because one expects his or her servitude and advocacy of individually or team-oriented goals might be a cultural norm. Thus, we see that one might be a servant-leader without being humble, which calls into question the claim that humility is a necessary but not sufficient condition for servant-leadership. In my mind, that assumption is tenuous at best. Krumrei-Mancuso lays out a strong argument in its behalf, so this begs for empirical investigation.

Questions about what servant leadership entails. Krumrei-Mancuso seems to take servant leadership as perhaps the best nonhierarchical leadership model (although this is more implied than claimed). There are, of course, other nonhierarchical leadership models, such as transformational leadership, which is a style of leadership aiming to inspire and teach followers to become leaders.[9] Even servant leadership might be a paradox, if not a self-contradiction. The person is servant, but is also leader. So both leadership and servanthood must be manifest. The model needs to flesh out how this paradox can occur. Can they be present at the same time in a person who is both leading and serving? Do they "power share"? Or "time share?" That is, do two different roles alternate, exist at the same time, derive one from the other (i.e., a person gains the authority to lead because he or she has served the organization)? In brief, how are leaders also simultaneously servants? And if they are sharing leaders' time, focus, and power, might there be other models of leadership that do this as well? The bottom line here is that many specifics of exactly what servant leadership is are not transparent and need further specification. We can observe great models—like Jesus. But Jesus' status within Christianity as fully man and fully God makes him more of an idealistic model than a realistic coping model.

The scholarly work present in Krumrei-Mancuso's chapter is impressive and will aid scholars and researchers in the future. I am not convinced, though, particularly of (a) the definition of servant leader she works with,[10] (b) the claim that humility is a necessary but not sufficient condition for demarking servant leadership, and (c) the use of Jesus as an exemplar of servant leadership[11] to the extent that the definition of servant leader is held to.

. . .

Reply to Everett L. Worthington Jr.

Elizabeth J. Krumrei-Mancuso

I am grateful to Worthington for his thoughtful response and his words about the contributions of my chapter. I am also particularly thankful for his critiques, which have given me the opportunity to rethink some of my prior assumptions and realize areas where my points can be clarified.

I will organize my reply by responding to each of the themes in Worthington's critique. Although Worthington is not necessarily in favor of Greenleaf's conceptualization of servant leadership as I presented it, I will maintain my focus on Greenleaf's work within my response, because this has been the most foundational model of servant leadership for extant definitions and research, which allows me to provide the most consistency with the servant leadership literature. All the Greenleaf references I use in my response are to his original 1970 essay.

Definition of servant leadership. Worthington insightfully points out that my chapter promotes some confusion regarding the distinctive characteristics of servant leadership versus the general definition of servant leadership. This likely stems from the chapter's emphasis on the research dilemma that occurs when there is a lack of discriminant validity between measures of servant leadership and other forms of leadership. When attempting to explore what is unique about servant leaders compared to other leaders or how servant leadership outcomes differ from the outcomes of other forms of leadership, it is necessary to have a good grasp of the distinctive characteristics of servant leadership. When operational definitions or assessment instruments substantially tap multiple forms of leadership, the research findings are ambiguous, and it is unclear what outcomes are unique to servant leadership versus representative of other or all forms of leadership.

Given the chapter's focus on how humility relates to servant leadership specifically, I seem to have overemphasized differentiating servant leadership from other forms of leadership at the cost of providing a thorough starting definition of servant leadership. In hindsight, I would have been clearer about the focus of the chapter being on the "distinctive defining characteristics" of servant leadership, as Worthington phrases it. I also would have been more precise in my wording that servant leadership is *a form of leadership* in which the leader's focus is on other's highest-priority needs being served.

I do not want to neglect Worthington's point that "servant leaders are indeed servants. But they also are leaders, and there is no indication in Krumrei-Mancuso's definition about how they lead" (216). I had described serving others as *a* defining feature of servant leadership according to Greenleaf, but Greenleaf certainly described a variety of leadership behaviors, including that leaders provide direction toward a goal, provide vision, initiate, provide ideas and structure, take risks, and build trust. However, it is important to note that Greenleaf argued that "the servant-leader *is* servant first" and "is sharply different from one who is *leader* first."[1] According to Greenleaf, the difference between those who are servant first and those who are leader first is in the care taken by the "servant-first" to make sure that other people's highest-priority needs are being served. This nicely summarizes Greenleaf's conceptualization that servant leadership involves both leading and serving, but that service takes precedence.

Use of Jesus as exemplar of servant leadership. Worthington highlights my comment that the qualities of servant leadership have often been attributed to the leadership of Christ. Although the following statement may seem evasive in terms of responding to Worthington's criticism of this point, my intent in this single reference was merely to show that servant leadership has a long history, as qualities of servant leadership have been attributed to historical leaders, including Christ. My focus was not on promoting the use of Christ as the exemplar of servant leadership.

Nevertheless, Worthington provides useful food for thought in this critique. Although I am not able to fully follow the first and third reasons for why there is an inconsistency with the idea of Jesus engaging in servant leadership, I generally appreciate Worthington's rationales against using Christ as an exemplar for servant leadership. I believe the biggest complicating factor in doing so is that Christ was not only human but also God. This brings elements that will never be fully consistent with any human roles. Jesus had the right, ability, and calling to do many things that were not meant to be emulated by others, meaning that the analogy of What Would Jesus Do? (for those who remember the once-popular bracelets) will always have its limits.

As a side note, I appreciate this opportunity to clarify the language Worthington picks up on in his second argument, regarding the servant leader being in a nonfocal position. I meant to emphasize that the servant leader *takes* a nonfocal position. I did not mean to imply that the leader is not in a focal leadership position, but rather that the leader, in making decisions, focuses on the best interests of others rather than self (i.e., other is focal, self is nonfocal in the servant leader's decision-making). This does not negate that the servant leader is in a central leadership position.

Focus solely on meeting the needs of others as the defining condition for servant leadership. Worthington notes that he doubts any CEO ever succeeded if he or she was not mindful of the needs of the organization. I agree that leaders must focus on the needs of their organizations. Further, I do not think Greenleaf advocated for neglecting the needs of the organization. However, Greenleaf did advocate for taking care of the needs of people being the first priority, and he seemed to believe meeting the needs of the organization would flow naturally from this. He wrote that the "*first order of business* is to build a group of people who, under the influence of the institution, grow taller and become healthier, stronger, more autonomous."[2] Further, he stated, "an institution starts on the course toward people-building with leadership that has a firmly established context of *people first*. With that, the right actions fall naturally into place."[3] Greenleaf offered further discussion of this idea in his paper "The Institution as Servant."[4]

Although Greenleaf's advocacy for focusing *first* on serving others is a bit less extreme than the idea of focusing *solely* on meeting the needs of others, it may still seem nonsensical. I do not have enough experience with servant leadership across a variety of settings to be able to speak to its success firsthand. My initial thought is that setting may matter. My own research on servant leadership has focused on examining this model among college student peer leaders who are hired to develop relationships with campus residents by engaging in peer counseling, providing spiritual support, and building a sense of community. The primary goal of their leadership positions is to promote the well-being of campus residents and the campus community. In such a setting, servant leadership seems like an ideal model. But what about business settings and other types of organizations? In business, it certainly sounds counterintuitive to focus on service more than on moneymaking. As noted in the chapter, a number of authors have questioned the efficiency of an organization that focuses primarily on subordinates' well-being with only secondary attention to organizational concerns,[5] echoing Worthington's critique.

However, if I defer to the empirical research on this matter, it seems the available data support that servant leadership is associated with a host of positive outcomes, even in businesses. It seems that servant leadership benefits organizations through many employee characteristics, including greater organizational identification and commitment, greater work motivation and engagement, better work performance, and greater contributions to the organization beyond formal job requirements (see chapter for review). Further, in response to the critique that a service focus would negatively impact an organization's ability to accomplish a purpose, research thus far seems to indicate that servant leadership is associated with better organizational effectiveness and performance, even including greater return on assets (see chapter for review).

More work is needed to compare servant leadership to other forms of leadership, but the available research indicates that servant leadership promotes positive organizational outcomes precisely because it cultivates positive relationships between leaders and followers, meets the needs of followers, increases employee well-being, promotes fair treatment in the workplace, and encourages a service climate among employees (see chapter for review). If this is the case, we might conclude that a servant leadership focus does not inhibit an organization from accomplishing its purpose.

Servant-focus does not necessarily imply humility. In my chapter, I concluded that rather than incorporating humility into the core definition of servant leadership, as many researchers have done, it is more appropriate to think of humility as an ancillary condition that makes servant leadership possible: a condition that precedes servant leadership and functions as an operating mechanism for servant leadership behaviors. Worthington goes a step further on this trajectory to suggest that humility is not, in fact, necessary for servant leadership. He lists a number of alternative mechanisms that might take the place of humility as I had conceptualized it functioning in servant leadership.

My thinking had been that (1) a true service orientation, as Greenleaf described it, requires a focus on others rather than on self, (2) leaders are in a position of power in which they can choose whether to focus on self or others, and, therefore, (3) leaders who choose a service orientation must have humility in order to shift focus from self to others. However, Worthington offers many insightful examples of ways in which a leader may function as servant absent humility. This provides me the opportunity to rethink my conceptualization. I believe Worthington is correct, as long as the examples he provided can meet the benchmark of a *people-first* service orientation (at least if we continue to use Greenleaf's conceptualization). For example, we might ask whether leaders who engage in servant leadership behaviors for the primary purpose of achieving the associated positive organization outcomes would still qualify as servant leaders. I believe Greenleaf would say no, given that such individuals have lost the emphasis on *people first*—as they are driven by profit, or some other organizational aim, first. Greenleaf's starting point was that servant leaders are by *nature* servants. He further distinguished between institutions that *use* people and institutions that *build* people. He believed institutions can achieve success through the intelligent *use* of people but that such success is not long-lasting. Thus, I would say the extent to which leaders can be true servants within this *people-first* conceptualization without requiring humility is the extent to which humility is unnecessary for servant leadership.

Questions about what servant leadership entails. I will not claim servant leadership as the best nonhierarchical leadership model, mostly because I do not have sufficient knowledge or experience pertaining to each leadership model to create a fair comparison. To Worthington's point that servant leadership might be a self-contradiction, I will add that even Greenleaf thought there might be a real contradiction in the servant as leader. His defense for the idea was that the notion of the servant as leader came not from conscious logic but from intuitive insight. His belief was that serving and leading are both mostly intuition-based concepts. As a more logical than intuitive person, my thought is that the proof is in the pudding. A fair amount of research supports servant leadership as a successful model. Unfortunately, not nearly enough research has compared servant leadership to other leadership models to be able to draw conclusions about which model is "best." I imagine the answer to that question depends on a number of factors, including leadership setting, context, and fit between leader and leadership model.

Notes to Chapter 7
(Elizabeth J. Krumrei-Mancuso)

1. This chapter was supported by a generous grant from the John Templeton Foundation, Grant No. 60622, Developing Humility in Leaders.
2. Edelman, *Trust Barometer Annual Global Study Executive Summary* (2017), 2, https://www.edelman.com/executive-summary/.
3. Edelman, *Trust Barometer*, 2.
4. Edelman, *Trust Barometer*, 3.
5. Edelman, *Trust Barometer*, 16.
6. B. P. Owens, M. D. Johnson, and T. R. Mitchell, "Expressed Humility in Organizations: Implications for Performance, Teams, and Leadership," *Organization Science* 24 (2013): 1517–38.
7. D. E. Davis, J. N. Hook, E. L. Worthington Jr., D. R. Van Tongeren, A. L. Gartner, D. J. Jennings II, and R. A. Emmons, "Relational Humility: Conceptualizing and Measuring Humility as a Personality Judgment," *Journal of Personality Assessment* 93 (2011): 225–34; D. E. Davis, E. L. Worthington Jr., J. N. Hook, R. A. Emmons, P. C. Hill, R. A. Bollinger, and D. R. Van Tongeren, "Humility and the Development and Repair of Social Bonds: Two Longitudinal Studies," *Self and Identity* 12 (2013): 58–77.
8. J. A. Morris, C. M. Brotheridge, and J. C. Urbanski, "Bringing Humility to Leadership: Antecedents and Consequences of Leader Humility," *Human Relations* 58 (2005): 1323–50.
9. For example, Y. S. Chung, "Why Servant Leadership? Its Uniqueness and Principles in the Life of Jesus," *Journal of Asia Adventist Seminary* 14, no. 2 (2011): 159–70.
10. R. K. Greenleaf, *The Servant as Leader* (South Orange, N.J.: Robert K. Greenleaf, 1970).
11. L. C. Spears, "Tracing the Growing Impact of Servant Leadership," in *Insights on Leadership: Service, Stewardship, Spirit, and Servant-Leadership*, ed. L. C. Spears (New York: John Wiley and Sons, 1998), 1–12.
12. J. J. Barbuto and D. W. Wheeler, "Scale Development and Construct Clarification of Servant Leadership," *Group and Organization Management* 31 (2006): 300–326; R. F. Russell and A. G. Stone, "A Review of Servant Leadership Attributes: Developing a Practical Model," *Leadership and Organization Development Journal* 23 (2006): 145–57.
13. Barbuto and Wheeler, "Scale Development"; M. G. Ehrhart, "Leadership and Procedural Justice Climate as Antecedents of Unit-Level Organizational Citizenship Behavior," *Personnel Psychology* 57 (2004): 61–94; R. C. Liden, S. J. Wayne, H. Zhao, and D. Henderson, "Servant Leadership: Development of a Multidimensional Measure and Multi-level Assessment," *Leadership Quarterly* 19 (2008): 161–77.
14. Barbuto and Wheeler, "Scale Development."
15. Greenleaf, *Servant as Leader*.

16 J. A. Andersen, "When a Servant-Leader Comes Knocking," *Leadership and Organization Development Journal* 30 (2009): 4–15.
17 A. Panaccio, M. Donia, S. Saint-Michel, and R. C. Liden, "Servant Leadership and Wellbeing," in *Flourishing in Life, Work and Careers: Individual Wellbeing and Career Experiences*, ed. R. J. Burke, K. M. Page, C. L. Cooper, R. J. Burke, K. M. Page, and C. L. Cooper (Northampton, Mass.: Edward Elgar, 2015), 334–58.
18 Barbuto and Wheeler, "Scale Development"; J. J. Hanse, U. Harlin, C. Jarebrant, K. Ulin, and J. Winkel, "The Impact of Servant Leadership Dimensions on Leader-Member Exchange among Health Care Professionals," *Journal of Nursing Management* 24 (2016): 228–34; C. Zhao, Y. Liu, and Z. Gao, "An Identification Perspective of Servant Leadership's Effects," *Journal of Managerial Psychology* 31 (2016): 898–913.
19 Ehrhart, "Leadership and Procedural Justice Climate"; D. M. Mayer, M. Bardes, and R. F. Piccolo, "Do Servant-Leaders Help Satisfy Follower Needs? An Organizational Justice Perspective," *European Journal of Work and Organizational Psychology* 17 (2008): 180–97.
20 Mayer, Bardes, and Piccolo, "Do Servant-Leaders Help?"; M. Chiniara and K. Bentein, "Linking Servant Leadership to Individual Performance: Differentiating the Mediating Role of Autonomy, Competence and Relatedness Need Satisfaction," *Leadership Quarterly* 27 (2016): 124–41.
21 M. Rieke, J. Hammermeister, and M. Chase, "Servant Leadership in Sport: A New Paradigm for Effective Coach Behavior," *International Journal of Sports Science and Coaching* 3 (2008): 227–39.
22 M. Sousa and D. van Dierendonck, "Servant Leaders as Underestimators: Theoretical and Practical Implications," *Leadership & Organization Development Journal* 38 (2017): 270–83.
23 Barbuto and Wheeler, "Scale Development"; M. L. Donia, U. Raja, A. Panaccio, and Z. Wang, "Servant Leadership and Employee Outcomes: The Moderating Role of Subordinates' Motives," *European Journal of Work and Organizational Psychology* 25, no. 5 (2016): 722–34; F. Jaramillo, D. B. Grisaffe, L. B. Chonko, and J. A. Roberts, "Examining the Impact of Servant Leadership on Sales Force Performance," *Journal of Personal Selling and Sales Management* 29 (2009): 257–75; M. J. Neubert, E. M. Hunter, and R. C. Tolentino, "A Servant Leader and Their Stakeholders: When Does Organizational Structure Enhance a Leader's Influence?" *Leadership Quarterly* 27 (2016): 896–910; D. van Dierendonck and I. Nuijten, "The Servant Leadership Survey: Development and Validation of a Multidimensional Measure," *Journal of Business and Psychology* 26, no. 3 (2011): 249–67.
24 K. Upadyaya, M. Vartiainen, and K. Salmela-Aro, "From Job Demands and Resources to Work Engagement, Burnout, Life Satisfaction, Depressive Symptoms, and Occupational Health," *Burnout Research* 3 (2016): 101–8.
25 Jaramillo et al., "Examining the Impact."
26 W. Rivkin, S. Diestel, and K. Schmidt, "The Positive Relationship between Servant Leadership and Employees' Psychological Health: A

Multi-method Approach," *Zeitschrift für Personalforschung* 28, nos. 1–2 (2014): 52–72; Upadyaya, Vartiainen, and Salmela-Aro, "From Job Demands."
27 Edelman, *Trust Barometer.*
28 E. E. Joseph and B. E. Winston, "A Correlation of Servant Leadership, Leader Trust, and Organizational Trust," *Leadership and Organization Development Journal* 26 (2005): 6–22.
29 Jaramillo et al., "Examining the Impact"; Liden et al., "Servant Leadership"; P. Saran, "Antecedents and Consequences of Organizational Citizenship Behavior among NGO Staff from Thailand, Myanmar, Laos and Cambodia," *International Journal of Behavioral Science* 11 (2016): 53–66; Zhao, Liu, and Gao, "Identification Perspective."
30 E. M. Hunter, M. J. Neubert, S. J. Perry, L. A. Witt, L. M. Penney, and E. Weinberger, "Servant Leaders Inspire Servant Followers: Antecedents and Outcomes for Employees and the Organization," *Leadership Quarterly* 24 (2013): 316–31; Zhao, Liu, and Gao, "Identification Perspective."
31 Van Dierendonck and Nuijten, "Servant Leadership Survey."
32 Rieke, Hammermeister, and Chase, "Servant Leadership in Sport."
33 Rieke, Hammermeister, and Chase, "Servant Leadership in Sport."
34 A. A. Chughtai, "Servant Leadership and Follower Outcomes: Mediating Effects of Organizational Identification and Psychological Safety," *Journal of Psychology: Interdisciplinary and Applied* 150 (2016): 866–80.
35 Chughtai, "Servant Leadership and Follower Outcomes."
36 M. J. Neubert, K. M. Kacmar, D. S. Carlson, L. B. Chonko, and J. A. Roberts, "Regulatory Focus as a Mediator of the Influence of Initiating Structure and Servant Leadership on Employee Behavior," *Journal of Applied Psychology* 93 (2008): 1220–33; Neubert, Hunter, and Tolentino, "Servant Leader and Their Stakeholders."
37 R. C. Liden, A. Panaccio, J. D. Meuser, J. Hu, and S. J. Wayne, "Servant Leadership: Antecedents, Processes, and Outcomes," in *The Oxford Handbook of Leadership and Organizations*, ed. D. V. Day (New York: Oxford University Press, 2014), 357–79; Rieke, Hammermeister, and Chase, "Servant Leadership in Sport."
38 Barbuto and Wheeler, "Scale Development"; Ehrhart, "Leadership and Procedural Justice Climate"; J. Hu and R. C. Liden, "Antecedents of Team Potency and Team Effectiveness: An Examination of Goal and Process Clarity and Servant Leadership," *Journal of Applied Psychology* 96 (2011): 851–62; B. Mahembe and A. S. Engelbrecht, "The Relationship between Servant Leadership, Organisational Citizenship Behaviour and Team Effectiveness," *South African Journal of Industrial Psychology* 40 (2014): 1–10; Neubert et al., "Regulatory Focus"; Neubert, Hunter, and Tolentino, "Servant Leader and Their Stakeholders"; Saran, "Antecedents and Consequences"; F. O. Walumbwa, C. A. Hartnell, and A. Oke, "Servant Leadership, Procedural Justice Climate, Service Climate, Employee Attitudes, and Organizational Citizenship Behavior: A Cross-Level Investigation," *Journal of Applied Psychology* 95 (2010): 517–29; Zhao, Liu, and Ghao, "Identification Perspective."

39 M. Sousa and D. van Dierendonck, "Introducing a Short Measure of Shared Servant Leadership Impacting Team Performance through Team Behavioral Integration," *Frontiers in Psychology* 6 (2016): 1–12.
40 Hu and Liden, "Antecedents of Team Potency."
41 Barbuto and Wheeler, "Scale Development"; Hu and Liden, "Antecedents of Team Potency"; J. Schaubroeck, S. K. Lam, and A. C. Peng, "Cognition-Based and Affect-Based Trust as Mediators of Leader Behavior Influences on Team Performance," *Journal of Applied Psychology* 96 (2011): 863–71; Mahembe and Engelbrecht, "Relationship between Servant Leadership"; Saran, "Antecedents and Consequences."
42 Jaramillo et al., "Examining the Impact."
43 Neubert, Hunter, and Tolentino, "Servant Leader and Their Stakeholders."
44 Liden et al., "Servant Leadership."
45 Andersen, "When a Servant-Leader."
46 Barbuto and Wheeler, "Scale Development"; J. Huang, W. Li, C. Qiu, F. H. Yim, and J. Wan, "The Impact of CEO Servant Leadership on Firm Performance in the Hospitality Industry," *International Journal of Contemporary Hospitality Management* 28 (2016): 945–68; S. J. Peterson, B. M. Galvin, and D. Lange, "CEO Servant Leadership: Exploring Executive Characteristics and Firm Performance," *Personnel Psychology* 65 (2012): 565–96.
47 B. M. Bass, *Leadership and Performance beyond Expectations* (New York: Free Press, 1985).
48 Liden et al., "Servant Leadership."
49 Schaubroeck, Lam, and Peng, "Cognition-Based and Affect-Based Trust."
50 Peterson, Galvin, and Lange, "CEO Servant Leadership."
51 Liden et al., "Servant Leadership."
52 Liden et al., "Servant Leadership."
53 A. I. Choudhary, S. A. Akhtar, and A. Zaheer, "Impact of Transformational and Servant Leadership on Organizational Performance: A Comparative Analysis," *Journal of Business Ethics* 116 (2013): 433–40.
54 D. B. Grisaffe, R. VanMeter, and L. B. Chonko, "Serving First for the Benefit of Others: Preliminary Evidence for a Hierarchical Conceptualization of Servant Leadership," *Journal of Personal Selling and Sales Management* 36 (2016): 40–58.
55 Neubert et al., "Regulatory Focus."
56 Neubert et al., "Regulatory Focus"; D. van Dierendonck, D. Stam, P. Boersma, N. de Windt, and J. Alkema, "Same Difference? Exploring the Differential Mechanisms Linking Servant Leadership and Transformational Leadership to Follower Outcomes," *Leadership Quarterly* 25 (2014): 544–62.
57 Schaubroeck, Lam, and Peng, "Cognition-Based and Affect-Based Trust"; Walumbwa, Hartnell, and Oke, "Servant Leadership"; Zhao, Liu, and Gao, "Identification Perspective."
58 Chiniara and Bentein, "Linking Servant Leadership"; Chughtai, "Servant Leadership and Follower Outcomes"; Mayer, Bardes, and Piccolo, "Do

Servant-Leaders Help?"; Schaubroeck, Lam, and Peng, "Cognition-Based and Affect-Based Trust"; Van Dierendonck et al., "Same Difference?"

59 Ehrhart, "Leadership and Procedural Justice Climate"; Walumbwa, Hartnell, and Oke, "Servant Leadership."

60 Huang et al., "Impact of CEO Servant Leadership"; Hunter et al., "Servant Leaders Inspire Servant Followers"; Walumbwa, Hartnell, and Oke, "Servant Leadership."

61 J. P. Tangney, "Humility: Theoretical Perspectives, Empirical Findings and Directions for Future Research," *Journal of Social and Clinical Psychology* 19 (2000): 70–82.

62 J. Chancellor and S. Lyubomirsky, "Humble Beginnings: Current Trends, State Perspectives, Hallmarks of Humility," *Social and Personality Psychology Compass* 7 (2013): 819–33.

63 Owens, Johnson, and Mitchell, "Expressed Humility in Organizations."

64 D. van Dierendonck, "Servant Leadership: A Review and Synthesis," *Journal of Management* 37 (2011): 1228–61.

65 For example, Owens, Johnson, and Mitchell, "Expressed Humility in Organizations"; and L. Reave, "Spiritual Values and Practices Related to Leadership Effectiveness," *Leadership Quarterly* 16 (2005): 655–87.

66 Greenleaf, *Servant as Leader*.

67 R. K. Greenleaf, *Servant Leadership: A Journey into the Nature of Legitimate Power and Greatness*, 25th anniversary ed. (New York: Paulist, 2002).

68 Edelman, *Trust Barometer*, 16.

69 Greenleaf, *Servant as Leader*.

70 J. J. Exline, R. F. Baumeister, A. L. Zell, A. J. Kraft, and C. O. Witvliet, "Not So Innocent: Does Seeing One's Own Capability for Wrongdoing Predict Forgiveness?" *Journal of Personality and Social Psychology* 94 (2008): 495–515; E. L. Worthington, "An Empathy-Humility-Commitment Model of Forgiveness Applied within Family Dyads," *Journal of Family Therapy* 20 (1998): 59–76.

71 Greenleaf, *Servant as Leader*.

72 R. K. Greenleaf, *On Becoming a Servant Leader*, ed. Don M. Frick and Larry C. Spears (San Francisco: Jossey-Bass, 1996).

73 Greenleaf, *Servant as Leader*.

74 R. Jit, C. S. Sharma, and M. Kawatra, "Servant Leadership and Conflict Resolution: A Qualitative Study," *International Journal of Conflict Management* 27 (2016): 591–612.

75 Van Dierendonck, "Servant Leadership."

76 R. S. Dennis and M. Bocarnea, "Development of the Servant Leadership Assessment Instrument," *Leadership and Organization Development Journal* 26 (2005): 600–615; R. S. Dennis and M. C. Bocarnea, "Servant Leadership Assessment Instrument," in *Handbook of Research on Electronic Surveys and Measurements*, ed. R. A. Reynolds, R. Woods, and J. D. Baker (Hershey, Pa.: Idea Group Reference / IGI Global, 2007), 339–42; S. Sendjaya, J. C. Sarros, and J. C. Santora, "Defining and Measuring Servant Leadership Behaviour in Organizations," *Journal of Management Studies* 45

(2008): 402–24; Sousa and van Dierendonck, "Introducing a Short Measure"; van Dierendonck and Nuijten, "Servant Leadership Survey."
77 Barbuto and Wheeler, "Scale Development"; Ehrhart, "Leadership and Procedural Justice Climate"; Joseph and Winston, "Correlation of Servant Leadership"; Liden et al., "Servant Leadership"; L. L. Reed, D. Vidaver-Cohen, and S. R. Colwell, "A New Scale to Measure Executive Servant Leadership: Development, Analysis, and Implications for Research," *Journal of Business Ethics* 101 (2011): 415–34.
78 Z. Zhang, J. C. Lee, and P. H. Wong, "Multilevel Structural Equation Modeling Analysis of the Servant Leadership Construct and Its Relation to Job Satisfaction," *Leadership and Organization Development Journal* 37 (2016): 1147–67.
79 S. Sendjaya and B. Cooper, "Servant Leadership Behaviour Scale: A Hierarchical Model and Test of Construct Validity," *European Journal of Work and Organizational Psychology* 20 (2011): 416–36; van Dierendonck and Nuijten, "Servant Leadership Survey."
80 For example, van Dierendonck and Nuijten, "Servant Leadership Survey."
81 J. R. Hale and D. L. Fields, "Exploring Servant Leadership across Cultures: A Study of Followers in Ghana and the USA," *Leadership* 3 (2007): 397–417.
82 Grisaffe, VanMeter, and Chonko, "Serving First"; D. L. Parris and J. W. Peachey, "A Systematic Literature Review of Servant Leadership Theory in Organizational Contexts," *Journal of Business Ethics* 113 (2013): 377–93; van Dierendonck, "Servant Leadership."
83 For example, M. Sousa and D. van Dierendonck, "Servant Leadership and the Effect of the Interaction between Humility, Action, and Hierarchical Power on Follower Engagement," *Journal of Business Ethics* 141 (2017): 13–25.
84 Grisaffe, VanMeter, and Chonko, "Serving First"; Sousa and van Dierendonck, "Servant Leadership."
85 Grisaffe, VanMeter, and Chonko, "Serving First."
86 Sousa and van Dierendonck, "Servant Leadership."
87 Grisaffe, VanMeter, and Chonko, "Serving First."
88 For example, van Dierendonck and Nuijten, "Servant Leadership Survey."
89 D. van Dierendonck and K. Patterson, "Compassionate Love as a Cornerstone of Servant Leadership: An Integration of Previous Theorizing and Research," *Journal of Business Ethics* 128 (2015): 119–31.
90 J. W. Graham, "Servant-Leadership in Organizations: Inspirational and Moral," *Leadership Quarterly* 2 (1991): 105–19.
91 Liden et al., "Servant Leadership."
92 Morris, Brotheridge, and Urbanski, "Bringing Humility to Leadership."
93 A. Comte-Sponville, *A Small Treatise on the Great Virtues* (New York: Henry Holt, 2001).
94 Jit, Sharma, and Kawatra, "Servant Leadership and Conflict Resolution"; Sousa and van Dierendonck, "Introducing a Short Measure"; van Dierendonck, "Servant Leadership."

95 Peterson, Galvin, and Lange, "CEO Servant Leadership."
96 S. Sachdeva and A. Prakash, "Journey to the Heart of Servant Leadership: Narratives in the Indian Context," *Journal of the Indian Academy of Applied Psychology* 43 (2017): 20–33.
97 Jit, Sharma, and Kawatra, "Servant Leadership and Conflict Resolution."
98 Hanse et al., "Impact of Servant Leadership Dimensions on Leader–Member Exchange among Health Care Professionals," *Journal of Nursing Management* 24 (2016): 228–34.
99 Sousa and van Dierendonck, "Introducing a Short Measure."
100 Hale and Fields, "Exploring Servant Leadership."
101 R. Mittal and P. W. Dorfman, "Servant Leadership across Cultures," *Journal of World Business* 47 (2012): 555–70.
102 Van Dierendonck and Nuijten, "Servant Leadership Survey."
103 Van Dierendonck and Nuijten, "Servant Leadership Survey."
104 Sousa and van Dierendonck, "Servant Leadership."
105 Sousa and van Dierendonck, "Servant Leadership."
106 Sousa and van Dierendonck, "Servant Leaders as Underestimators."
107 Sousa and an Dierendonck, "Servant Leaders as Underestimators."
108 Van Dierendonck and Nuijten, "Servant Leadership Survey."
109 Sousa and van Dierendonck, "Introducing a Short Measure."
110 Sousa and van Dierendonck, "Servant Leadership."
111 Andersen, "When a Servant-Leader."
112 Barbuto and Wheeler, "Scale Development."
113 For example, Davis et al., "Humility and the Development."
114 Greenleaf, *Servant as Leader*, 2.
115 Hunter et al., "Servant Leaders Inspire Servant Followers."
116 C. R. Lavelock, E. J. Worthington Jr., D. E. Davis, B. J. Griffin, C. A. Reid, J. N. Hook, and D. R. Van Tongeren, "The Quiet Virtue Speaks: An Intervention to Promote Humility," *Journal of Psychology and Theology* 42 (2014): 99–110.
117 Hale and Fields, "Exploring Servant Leadership."
118 Mittal and Dorfman, "Servant Leadership across Cultures."
119 Hale and Fields, "Exploring Servant Leadership."

Notes to Chapter 7 Response
(Everett L. Worthington Jr.)

1 Greenleaf, *Servant Leadership*.
2 Grisaffe, VanMeter, and Chonko, "Serving First."
3 Greenleaf, *Servant Leadership*. See also Grisaffe, VanMeter, and Chonko, "Serving First."
4 For example, Chung, "Why Servant Leadership?"
5 Davis et al., "Humility, Religion, and Spirituality."
6 Worthington and Allison, *Heroic Humility*.
7 For a review, see S. L. Porter, A. Rambachan, A. Vélez de Cea, D. Rabinowitz, S. Pardue, and S. Jackson, "Religious Perspectives on Humility,"

in *Handbook of Humility: Theory, Research, and Application*, ed. Everett L. Worthington Jr., Don E. Davis, and Joshua N. Hook (New York: Routledge, 2017), 75–96.
8   Porter et al., "Religious Perspectives on Humility."
9   H. Blane, *7 Principles of Transformational Leadership: Create a Mindset of Passion, Innovation, and Growth* (Wayne, N.J.: Career Press, 2017).
10 Greenleaf, *Servant Leadership*.
11 Chung, "Why Servant Leadership?"

Notes to Chapter 7 Reply
(Elizabeth J. Krumrei-Mancuso)

1   Greenleaf, *Servant Leadership*, 6.
2   Greenleaf, *Servant Leadership*, 22 (emphasis added).
3   Greenleaf, *Servant Leadership*, 22.
4   R. K. Greenleaf, *The Institution as Servant* (South Orange, N.J.: Robert K. Greenleaf, 1972).
5   Andersen, "When a Servant-Leader"; Panaccio et al., "Servant Leadership and Wellbeing."

Chapter Bibliography

Andersen, J. A. "When a Servant-Leader Comes Knocking." *Leadership and Organization Development Journal* 30 (2009): 4–15.

Barbuto, J. J., and D. W. Wheeler. "Scale Development and Construct Clarification of Servant Leadership." *Group and Organization Management* 31 (2006): 300–326.

Bass, B. M. *Leadership and Performance beyond Expectations*. New York: Free Press, 1985.

Blane, H. *7 Principles of Transformational Leadership: Create a Mindset of Passion, Innovation, and Growth*. Wayne, N.J.: Career Press, 2017.

Brown, K. W., and M. Leary, eds. *The Oxford Handbook of Hypo-egoic Phenomena*. New York: Oxford University Press, 2017.

Chancellor, J., and S. Lyubomirsky. "Humble Beginnings: Current Trends, State Perspectives, Hallmarks of Humility." *Social and Personality Psychology Compass* 7 (2013): 819–33.

Chiniara, M., and K. Bentein. "Linking Servant Leadership to Individual Performance: Differentiating the Mediating Role of Autonomy, Competence and Relatedness Need Satisfaction." *Leadership Quarterly* 27 (2016): 124–41.

Choudhary, A. I., S. A. Akhtar, and A. Zaheer. "Impact of Transformational and Servant Leadership on Organizational Performance: A Comparative Analysis." *Journal of Business Ethics* 116 (2013): 433–40.

Chughtai, A. A. "Servant Leadership and Follower Outcomes: Mediating Effects of Organizational Identification and Psychological Safety." *Journal of Psychology: Interdisciplinary and Applied* 150 (2016): 866–80.

Chung, Y. S. "Why Servant Leadership? Its Uniqueness and Principles in the Life of Jesus." *Journal of Asia Adventist Seminary* 14 (2011): 159–70.

Comte-Sponville, A. *A Small Treatise on the Great Virtues*. New York: Henry Holt, 2001.

Davis, D. E., J. N. Hook, R. McAnnally-Linz, E. Choe, and V. Placeres. "Humility, Religion, and Spirituality: A Review of the Literature." *Psychology of Religion and Spirituality* 9, no. 3 (2017): 242–53.

Davis, D. E., J. N. Hook, E. J. Worthington, D. R. Van Tongeren, A. L. Gartner, D. J. Jennings, and R. A. Emmons. "Relational Humility: Conceptualizing and Measuring Humility as a Personality Judgment." *Journal of Personality Assessment* 93 (2011): 225–34.

Davis, D. E., E. J. Worthington, J. N. Hook, R. A. Emmons, P. C. Hill, R. A. Bollinger, and D. R. Van Tongeren. "Humility and the Development and Repair of Social Bonds: Two Longitudinal Studies." *Self and Identity* 12, no. 1 (2013): 58–77.

Dennis, R. S., and M. Bocarnea. "Development of the Servant Leadership Assessment Instrument." *Leadership and Organization Development Journal* 26 (2005): 600–615.

———. "Servant Leadership Assessment Instrument." In *Handbook of Research on Electronic Surveys and Measurements*, edited by R. A. Reynolds, R. Woods, J. D. Baker, R. A. Reynolds, R. Woods, and J. D. Baker, 339–42. Hershey, Pa.: Idea Group Reference / IGI Global, 2007.

Dierendonck, D., and I. Nuijten. "The Servant Leadership Survey: Development and Validation of a Multidimensional Measure." *Journal of Business and Psychology* 26 (2011): 249–67.

Donia, M. L., U. Raja, A. Panaccio, and Z. Wang. "Servant Leadership and Employee Outcomes: The Moderating Role of Subordinates' Motives." *European Journal of Work and Organizational Psychology* 25, no. 5 (2016): 722–34.

Edelman. *Trust Barometer Annual Global Study Executive Summary*. 2017. https://www.edelman.com/executive-summary/.

Ehrhart, M. G. "Leadership and Procedural Justice Climate as Antecedents of Unit-Level Organizational Citizenship Behavior." *Personnel Psychology* (2004): 61–94.

Exline, J. J., R. F. Baumeister, A. L. Zell, A. J. Kraft, and C. O. Witvliet. "Not So Innocent: Does Seeing One's Own Capability for Wrongdoing Predict Forgiveness?" *Journal of Personality and Social Psychology* 94 (2008): 495–515.

Graham, J. W. "Servant-Leadership in Organizations: Inspirational and Moral." *Leadership Quarterly* 2 (1991): 105–19.

Greenleaf, R. K. *The Institution as Servant*. South Orange, N.J.: Robert K. Greenleaf, 1972.

———. *On Becoming a Servant Leader*. Edited by Don M. Frick and Larry C. Spears. San Francisco: Jossey-Bass, 1996.

———. *The Servant as Leader*. South Orange, N.J.: Robert K. Greenleaf, 1970.

———. *Servant Leadership: A Journey into the Nature of Legitimate Power and Greatness*. 25th anniversary ed. New York: Paulist, 2002.

Grisaffe, D. B., R. VanMeter, and L. B. Chonko. "Serving First for the Benefit of Others: Preliminary Evidence for a Hierarchical Conceptualization of Servant Leadership." *Journal of Personal Selling and Sales Management* 36 (2016): 40–58.

Hale, J. R., and D. L. Fields. "Exploring Servant Leadership across Cultures: A Study of Followers in Ghana and the USA." *Leadership* 3 (2007): 397–417.

Hanse, J. J., U. Harlin, C. Jarebrant, K. Ulin, and J. Winkel. "The Impact of Servant Leadership Dimensions on Leader-Member Exchange among Health Care Professionals." *Journal of Nursing Management* 24 (2016): 228–34.

Hu, J., and R. C. Liden. "Antecedents of Team Potency and Team Effectiveness: An Examination of Goal and Process Clarity and Servant Leadership." *Journal of Applied Psychology* 96 (2011): 851–62.

Huang, J., W. Li, C. Qiu, F. H. Yim, and J. Wan. "The Impact of CEO Servant Leadership on Firm Performance in the Hospitality Industry." *International Journal of Contemporary Hospitality Management* 28 (2016): 945–68.

Hunter, E. M., M. J. Neubert, S. J. Perry, L. A. Witt, L. M. Penney, and E. Weinberger. "Servant Leaders Inspire Servant Followers: Antecedents and Outcomes for Employees and the Organization." *Leadership Quarterly* 24 (2013): 316–31.

Jaramillo, F., D. B. Grisaffe, L. B. Chonko, and J. A. Roberts. "Examining the Impact of Servant Leadership on Sales Force Performance." *Journal of Personal Selling and Sales Management* 29 (2009): 257–75.

Jit, R., C. S. Sharma, and M. Kawatra. "Servant Leadership and Conflict Resolution: A Qualitative Study." *International Journal of Conflict Management* 27 (2016): 591–612.

Joseph, E. E., and B. E. Winston. "A Correlation of Servant Leadership, Leader Trust, and Organizational Trust." *Leadership and Organization Development Journal* 26 (2005): 6–22.

Laub, J. A. "Assessing the Servant Organization: Development of the Organizational Leadership Assessment (SOLA) Instrument." Ph.D. diss., Florida Atlantic University, 1999. *Dissertation Abstracts Online* 60 (1999): 308A (UMI No. 9921992).

Lavelock, C. R., E. J. Worthington Jr., D. E. Davis, B. J. Griffin, C. A. Reid, J. N. Hook, and D. R. Van Tongeren. "The Quiet Virtue Speaks: An Intervention to Promote Humility." *Journal of Psychology and Theology* 42 (2014): 99–110.

Liden, R. C., A. Panaccio, J. D. Meuser, J. Hu, and S. J. Wayne. "Servant Leadership: Antecedents, Processes, and Outcomes." In *The Oxford Handbook of Leadership and Organizations*, edited by D. V. Day, 357–79. New York: Oxford University Press, 2014.

Liden, R. C., S. J. Wayne, H. Zhao, and D. Henderson. "Servant Leadership: Development of a Multidimensional Measure and Multi-level Assessment." *Leadership Quarterly* 19 (2008): 161–77.

Mahembe, B., and A. S. Engelbrecht. "The Relationship between Servant Leadership, Organisational Citizenship Behaviour and Team Effectiveness." *South African Journal of Industrial Psychology* 40 (2014): 1–10.

Mayer, D. M., M. Bardes, and R. F. Piccolo. "Do Servant-Leaders Help Satisfy Follower Needs? An Organizational Justice Perspective." *European Journal of Work and Organizational Psychology* 17 (2008): 180–97.

Mittal, R., and P. W. Dorfman. "Servant Leadership across Cultures." *Journal of World Business* 47 (2012): 555–70.

Morris, J. A., C. M. Brotheridge, and J. C. Urbanski. "Bringing Humility to Leadership: Antecedents and Consequences of Leader Humility." *Human Relations* 58 (2005): 1323–50.

Neubert, M. J., E. M. Hunter, and R. C. Tolentino. "A Servant Leader and Their Stakeholders: When Does Organizational Structure Enhance a Leader's Influence?" *Leadership Quarterly* 27 (2016): 896–910.

Neubert, M. J., K. M. Kacmar, D. S. Carlson, L. B. Chonko, and J. A. Roberts. "Regulatory Focus as a Mediator of the Influence of Initiating Structure and Servant Leadership on Employee Behavior." *Journal of Applied Psychology* 93 (2008): 1220–33.

Owens, B. P., M. D. Johnson, and T. R. Mitchell. "Expressed Humility in Organizations: Implications for Performance, Teams, and Leadership." *Organization Science* 24 (2013): 1517–38.

Panaccio, A., M. Donia, S. Saint-Michel, and R. C. Liden. "Servant Leadership and Wellbeing." In *Flourishing in Life, Work and Careers: Individual Wellbeing and Career Experiences*, edited by R. J. Burke, K. M. Page, C. L. Cooper, R. J. Burke, K. M. Page, and C. L. Cooper, 334–58. Northampton, Mass.: Edward Elgar, 2015.

Parris, D. L., and J. W. Peachey. "A Systematic Literature Review of Servant Leadership Theory in Organizational Contexts." *Journal of Business Ethics* 113 (2013): 377–93.

Peterson, S. J., B. M. Galvin, and D. Lange. "CEO Servant Leadership: Exploring Executive Characteristics and Firm Performance." *Personnel Psychology* 65 (2012): 565–96.

Porter, S. L., A. Rambachan, A. Vélez de Cea, D. Rabinowitz, S. Pardue, and S. Jackson. "Religious Perspectives on Humility." In *Handbook of Humility:*

Theory, Research, and Application, edited by Everett L. Worthington Jr., Don E. Davis, and Joshua N. Hook, 75–96. New York: Routledge, 2017.

Reave, L. "Spiritual Values and Practices Related to Leadership Effectiveness." *Leadership Quarterly* 16 (2005): 655–87.

Reed, L. L., D. Vidaver-Cohen, and S. R. Colwell. "A New Scale to Measure Executive Servant Leadership: Development, Analysis, and Implications for Research." *Journal of Business Ethics* 101 (2011): 415–34.

Rieke, M., J. Hammermeister, and M. Chase. "Servant Leadership in Sport: A New Paradigm for Effective Coach Behavior." *International Journal of Sports Science and Coaching* 3 (2008): 227–39.

Rivkin, W., S. Diestel, and K. Schmidt. "The Positive Relationship between Servant Leadership and Employees' Psychological Health: A Multi-method Approach." *Zeitschrift für Personalforschung* 28, nos. 1–2 (2014): 52–72.

Russell, R. F., and A. G. Stone. "A Review of Servant Leadership Attributes: Developing a Practical Model." *Leadership and Organization Development Journal* 23 (2002): 145–57.

Sachdeva, S., and A. Prakash. "Journey to the Heart of Servant Leadership: Narratives in the Indian Context." *Journal of the Indian Academy of Applied Psychology* 43 (2017): 20–33.

Saran, P. "Antecedents and Consequences of Organizational Citizenship Behavior among NGO Staff from Thailand, Myanmar, Laos and Cambodia." *International Journal of Behavioral Science* 11 (2016): 53–66.

Schaubroeck, J., S. K. Lam, and A. C. Peng. "Cognition-Based and Affect-Based Trust as Mediators of Leader Behavior Influences on Team Performance." *Journal of Applied Psychology* 96 (2011): 863–71.

Sendjaya, S., and B. Cooper. "Servant Leadership Behaviour Scale: A Hierarchical Model and Test of Construct Validity." *European Journal of Work and Organizational Psychology* 20 (2011): 416–36.

Sendjaya, S., J. C. Sarros, and J. C. Santora. "Defining and Measuring Servant Leadership Behaviour in Organizations." *Journal of Management Studies* 45 (2008): 402–24.

Sousa, M., and D. van Dierendonck. "Introducing a Short Measure of Shared Servant Leadership Impacting Team Performance through Team Behavioral Integration." *Frontiers in Psychology* 6 (2016): 1–12.

———. "Servant Leaders as Underestimators: Theoretical and Practical Implications." *Leadership and Organization Development Journal* 38 (2017): 270–83.

———. "Servant Leadership and the Effect of the Interaction between Humility, Action, and Hierarchical Power on Follower Engagement." *Journal of Business Ethics* 141 (2017): 13–25.

Spears, L. C. "Tracing the Growing Impact of Servant Leadership." In *Insights on Leadership: Service, Stewardship, Spirit, and Servant-Leadership*, edited by L. C. Spears, 1–12. New York: John Wiley and Sons, 1998.

Stone, A. G., R. F. Russell, and K. Patterson. "Transformational versus Servant Leadership: A Difference in Leader Focus." *Leadership and Organization Development Journal* 25 (2004): 349–61.

Tangney, J. P. "Humility: Theoretical Perspectives, Empirical Findings and Directions for Future Research." *Journal of Social and Clinical Psychology* 19 (2000): 70–82.

Upadyaya, K., M. Vartiainen, and K. Salmela-Aro. "From Job Demands and Resources to Work Engagement, Burnout, Life Satisfaction, Depressive Symptoms, and Occupational Health." *Burnout Research* 3 (2016): 101–8.

van Dierendonck, D. "Servant Leadership: A Review and Synthesis." *Journal of Management* 37 (2011): 1228–61.

van Dierendonck, D., and I. Nuijten. "The Servant Leadership Survey: Development and Validation of a Multidimensional Measure." *Journal of Business and Psychology* 26, no. 3 (2011): 249–67.

van Dierendonck, D., and K. Patterson. "Compassionate Love as a Cornerstone of Servant Leadership: An Integration of Previous Theorizing and Research." *Journal of Business Ethics* 128 (2015): 119–31.

van Dierendonck, D., D. Stam, P. Boersma, N. de Windt, and J. Alkema. "Same Difference? Exploring the Differential Mechanisms Linking Servant Leadership and Transformational Leadership to Follower Outcomes." *Leadership Quarterly* 25 (2014): 544–62.

Walumbwa, F. O., C. A. Hartnell, and A. Oke. "Servant Leadership, Procedural Justice Climate, Service Climate, Employee Attitudes, and Organizational Citizenship Behavior: A Cross-Level Investigation." *Journal of Applied Psychology* 95 (2010): 517–29.

Worthington, E. L. "An Empathy-Humility-Commitment Model of Forgiveness Applied within Family Dyads." *Journal of Family Therapy* 20 (1998): 59–76.

Worthington, E. L., Jr., and S. T. Allison. *Heroic Humility: What the Science of Humility Can Say to People Raised on Self-Focus*. Washington, D.C.: American Psychological Association, 2018.

Zhang, Z., J. C. Lee, and P. H. Wong. "Multilevel Structural Equation Modeling Analysis of the Servant Leadership Construct and Its Relation to Job Satisfaction." *Leadership and Organization Development Journal* 37 (2016): 1147–67.

Zhao, C., Y. Liu, and Z. Gao. "An Identification Perspective of Servant Leadership's Effects." *Journal of Managerial Psychology* 31 (2016): 898–913.

8

Living Humility

How to Be Humble

Kent Dunnington

When Augustine was asked by an acolyte, "What are the instructions of the Christian religion?" he answered, "Always and only, 'humility'" (*Ep.* 118.3.22). Augustine's focus on humility as the center of Christian life has resounded in the lives and words of Christian saints in centuries since. And Christian Scripture supports such an emphasis, indicating that there is no surer way to God's mercy than humility. "God opposes the proud but gives grace to the humble" (Jas 4:6; 1 Pet 5:5 ESV). Given its centrality to the Christian life, much depends on an appropriate understanding of humility. Even more depends on wanting and trying to cultivate it.

There is no virtue whose fortunes track the sway of Christianity so well as humility. On one hand, the writings of the New Testament and of the church fathers transformed the Greek word describing the lowly and insignificant masses (the humble: *tapeinos*) into a Christian virtue (humility: *tapeinophrosunē*). On the other hand, the decline of the cultural dominance of Christianity was signaled in the early modern period by attacks on humility, which Hume ridiculed as a "monkish virtue" and Nietzsche as the essence of "slave morality."[1] Yet many post-Christian and post-religious persons continue to value humility, which raises a crucial question: How could a virtue so identified with the Jewish-Christian story remain significant to many who disregard that story?

The short answer is that humility remains culturally significant because its meaning has been attenuated, but this can be difficult to discern even for scholars, for at least two important reasons. First, the cultural influence of Christianity persists. Thus, many who are not Christian continue to have moral intuitions deeply responsive to Christian presuppositions about human frailty and the equal worth of every human person. Most secular philosophers, however, are not historically attuned to how much their conceptual analysis depends on intuitions shaped by a mishmash of conflicting perspectives, Christianity and political liberalism, for example.[2] But the second reason that it can be difficult to detect how contemporary accounts of humility are attenuated in comparison to Christian accounts is that there are not very many classic Christian *accounts* in the first place. With a few exceptions, Christians were more concerned to enjoin, teach, and narratively display humility than they were to define it or offer careful accounts of it. By contrast, contemporary philosophical writing about humility has been concerned almost exclusively to define it or at least to carefully delineate it conceptually.

This leaves contemporary Christians who have the admirable desire to pursue humility in a difficult position. Most contemporary accounts of humility are attenuated, and therefore it is not clear how efforts to exemplify the virtue as described will be devotionally useful. Furthermore, most of the older, sage counsels of humility have fallen into disuse and are no longer studied, especially by Protestant Christians. In the space remaining, I propose to help contemporary Christians get a better grasp on how to cultivate Christian humility by doing three things. First, I will simply run through the main competing accounts of humility that have been set forth over the last thirty years by philosophers. Second, I will offer a contemporary gloss on the most influential Christian guide to cultivating humility, the "ladder of humility" in chapter 7 of *The Rule of St. Benedict*. In a final section, I will offer an interpretation of the overlaps and gaps between contemporary accounts of humility and a venerable tradition of Christian training in humility. There are two upshots: first, Christian humility is distinguishable from more generic contemporary variants; second, and more importantly, by pursuing Christian humility under the counsel of Benedict and other wise forebears, contemporary Christians are sure to discover the difference Jesus makes to everyday life.

Contemporary Accounts of Humility

Since Elizabeth Anscombe's 1958 essay "Modern Moral Philosophy," philosophers have shown renewed interest in the ancient philosophical tradition of reflection on the virtues.[3] Two kinds of investigation emerged from this new interest: first, studies of the relevance of the category of virtue to moral and, more recently, epistemological theory; second, careful conceptual inquiry into a wide array of specific virtues. Among the latter are a series of essays—about thirty in the last thirty years—in which philosophers explore the question "What is humility?" As the literature has grown, a rich conversation among (mostly) analytic philosophers has developed around the concept of humility.

Summarizing the conversation is inevitably simplistic, but I think it fairly clear that five major views have emerged and, moreover, that one view has gained ascendancy. There are different ways of distinguishing the views, but two are most helpful. First, views can be distinguished based on whether they offer *descriptive* or *persuasive* definitions of humility. Descriptive definitions aim to elucidate the core meaning of the word "humility" as it is used by competent contemporary language-users. Persuasive definitions, on the other hand, aim to champion an understanding of "humility" that, although perhaps novel, better serves contemporary moral needs. Second, views can be distinguished based on whether they place primary emphasis on the affective, behavioral, or cognitive dimensions of humility. Almost no one denies that humility (like any virtue) will have affective, behavioral, and cognitive features (the ABCs of any virtue, so to speak), but typically one dimension is privileged as essential and as giving rise to the other dimensions. Is humility *fundamentally* about what you care about (affective), or about what you do (behavioral), or about what you think (cognitive)?

These distinctions help to map out the last thirty years of philosophical attempts to pin down humility. The "first wave" of attempts to conceptually pinpoint humility offered descriptive, cognitive-focused definitions of humility; the "second wave" offered persuasive, behavioral-focused definitions of humility and the "third wave" offered, and continues to offer, descriptive, affective-focused definitions of humility. There are exceptions to the trend, but that is the basic picture. Here, then, are the five major views. I will cite those whose articulation of the view in question has been most influential, and note subsequently those whose views are in the same ballpark.

Although hers was not the first contemporary attempt to philosophically clarify humility, Julia Driver's essay "The Virtues of Ignorance" invigorated the discussion and provided the point of departure for later efforts. In fact, Driver did not set out to address humility at all. Her essay was about modesty, and she clearly distinguished modesty from humility.[4] However, her definition of modesty has become so entrenched in the literature on humility that it deserves consideration as an important account of humility nevertheless.[5] On this account, humility is one of the so-called "virtues of ignorance," a virtue that requires an agent to believe something false about herself.

Underestimation account: Humility is the disposition to consistently underestimate your worth, skills, achievements, status, or entitlements.

Driver's underestimation account of humility has no supporters (besides Driver). It has two glaring problems. First, there is something confused about making a human defect—error in judgment—an essential component of a human excellence like a virtue. Second, if error in judgment is required for humility, then humility could only be cultivated through self-deception. Despite these obvious flaws, Driver's account is important because it puts center stage a curious feature of the virtue of humility, namely that there is something odd, if not paradoxical, about self-assertions of humility. After all, a humble person, on Driver's account, would need to underestimate her humility, and that seems right. It would be a point in its favor if an account of humility could explain what is odd about self-assertions of humility.

The other account of humility offered in the "first wave" of the humility conversation is still represented in the literature as the dominant or commonsense view of humility, despite the fact that it has only two defenders, Norvin Richards and Owen Flanagan.[6] Richards and Flanagan disagree with Driver's contention that humility requires ignorance, but they agree with her that humility is centrally a cognitive state. The humble person is defined by what she thinks of herself.

Non-overestimation account: Humility is consistent with accurate self-estimation; it consists of the disposition to consistently refuse the temptation to overestimate one's worth, skills, achievements, status, or entitlements.

Both the underestimation and the non-overestimation accounts prioritize the cognitive component of humility, and this feature opens both accounts up to obvious counterexamples. Roger is the best tennis player in the world, but he does not know it because his coach is always putting him down. He thinks he is about the tenth-best player in the world. He underestimates his tennis abilities. Still, his tennis game is all he thinks and talks about, and when someone does not acknowledge he is a top-ten player, he feels deeply insulted and obsesses over the perceived slight. Most people would deny Roger is humble, which indicates that underestimation does not adequately capture contemporary use of humility language. Suppose he gets a new coach who is less severe. He comes to realize he is in fact the best tennis player in the world. He is still obsessed with his tennis status and has even more opportunity to feel slighted. Suppose he is not overestimating his tennis game; he knows precisely how good he is. This fact does not seem to secure his humility with respect to tennis, which indicates that non-overestimation is not the essence of humility.[7] So it looks like emphasizing the cognitive dimension of humility misses what is essential in most commonsense notions of humility. It looks like Roger is "full of himself," and it looks like an account of humility needs to rule out such cases.

Or maybe not. Maybe the commonsense notion that humility is inconsistent with egocentrism of any kind is just a hangover from what Daniel Statman calls the "pessimistic view" of human nature, inherited by Western civilization from Jewish and Christian religion.[8] Statman argues such pessimism only makes sense given a low view of human worth in comparison to a God who alone is worthy of worship, and thus "humility is most intelligible within a religious frame of thought."[9] Does that mean humility is no longer a meaningful virtue outside of religious contexts? Statman answers: "Well, yes and no: yes, if one means by that a virtue consisting of a certain kind of (low) self assessment; and no, if one means a disposition towards a certain kind of behavior."[10] Accordingly, the "second wave" of humility accounts, offered by Statman, Aaron Ben Ze'ev, and Alex Sinha,[11] consists of persuasive definitions of humility aimed at reforming our notion of the virtue for contemporary, secular purposes. These accounts propose that how a person thinks of himself matters only insofar as it issues in behavior; thus humility should be understood as the virtue that prevents egocentric thoughts or attitudes from spilling over into egocentric behavior.

Egalitarian account: Humility is the disposition to refrain, despite one's accurate (high) self-assessment, from arrogant and boastful behavior, especially from acting as though one's (perhaps genuine) superiority grants one more extensive moral rights than anyone else.

The problem with these accounts (as is often the case with persuasive definitions) is that they appear to change the subject altogether. No one doubts the disposition described is a valuable one, but does it have anything to do with humility? Suppose we followed Richard Taylor's advice and abandoned humility. Would we be left without resources for naming the disposition to resist the temptation to treat oneself as morally more entitled than anyone else? Not at all. The virtue of justice includes just such a disposition.[12] The lesson here is clear: there are limits to how far a concept can be persuasively redefined. In the case of humility, the virtue has been historically entwined with the internal quest to subdue the ego. If such a quest is irrelevant or mistaken, then humility is probably not a virtue.

The "third wave" of accounts of humility has more ably located this essential feature of humility. There are a number of these accounts, but they share in common an attempt to offer a descriptive definition of humility that focuses on the affective. On these views, humility has to do primarily with what we care about. One such prominent view goes as follows:

Low-concern account: Humility is the disposition to have an unusually low concern about one's own worth, skills, achievements, status, or entitlements because of one's intense concern for other apparent goods.

There are a number of such accounts, and each would refine the definition above in ways that its author thinks most precisely articulates the virtue and avoids counterexamples. I have put the definition in terms of *concern*, an approach taken by Robert Roberts and Jay Wood, who offer arguably the most influential contemporary account of humility.[13] George Schlesinger offered the first low-concern account, but he spells out the virtue in terms of *attention* rather than concern, as does Nicholas Bommarito, the latest to offer a low-concern account.[14] G. F. Schueler and Michael Ridge describe the humble person as one who does not *care* about how much she is esteemed by others.[15] Ty Raterman, J. L. A. Garcia, and James Kellenberger also offer low-concern accounts; however, they think the emphasis should not be placed on a low concern about what *others* think but rather a reluctance or lack of interest to evaluate *oneself* in terms of one's goodness or excellence.[16] So there are lots of details and variety here. But what is clear is that low-concern accounts of some form have become the dominant contemporary philosophical view of humility.

A final account of humility, also part of the "third wave" focus on the affective dimension of the virtue, disagrees with low concern's *negative* construal of the virtue of humility. Low concern is a negative construal of humility because it construes humility as the *absence* of prideful concerns. In other words, for low concern, humility is present just so long as the wrong kind of prideful concerns is absent. But this final account thinks of humility as a positive virtue, as the presence of a certain kind of concern. What kind of concern? Nancy Snow argues that what is central to humility is not merely *lacking* the wrong kind of concerns about our worth, skills, achievements, and so on, but *possessing* the right kinds of concerns about our failures, limitations, and deficiencies.[17]

To understand Snow's perspective, consider Roger again. Suppose now that Roger has just become blissfully unconcerned about his status as a top-ten tennis player. He shows no penchant for bragging about his excellence, nor does he demur when others overlook him or minimize his accomplishments. But, despite this unconcern, he resists admitting when he plays poorly, he refuses to acknowledge the weaknesses in his game, and he is inclined to blame his coaches whenever he loses. Such a person (however psychologically odd) is not humble, Snow thinks, and this because he lacks the kinds of concerns he should have for his failures, limitations, deficiencies. "To be humbled," Snow argues, "we must acknowledge and care about our flaws."[18] Snow's account might be summarized as follows:

Limitations-owning account: Humility is the disposition to be attentive to, care about, and respond appropriately to one's failures, limitations, and deficiencies.

Specifically, Snow says we ought to "acknowledge" our failures, limitations, and deficiencies, "care about" them, "take them seriously," "be disturbed by having them," "feel sorrow or dejection because of" them, "deeply regret" them, "wish we didn't have" them, "do everything possible to be rid of" them, "do the best we can to control" them, "minimize [their] negative effects," and "regret yet accept" them.

St. Benedict's Guide to Humility

Suppose you were convinced by one of the aforementioned descriptions of the virtue of humility and wanted to try to develop the virtue so described. You would be hard-pressed to find any guidance. For instance, none of the articles cited above offer much by way of practical instruction about how to nurture the character trait of humility. That is not a limitation of any of the authors cited so much as it is a characteristic of contemporary analytic philosophy. By contrast, the Christian devotional tradition, and especially the Christian monastic tradition, is long on practical guides to humility. So in this section I will introduce the most popular and influential such guide in the Christian tradition, St. Benedict's "ladder of humility."

I have two aims in presenting Benedict's instructions. First, it should be insightful and challenging to anyone who would like to grow in humility, far more than anything I could come up with on my own. For that reason, I am going to gloss Benedict's instructions by trying to apply them to contemporary life. Benedict's instructions were aimed at cloistered monks, but I will re-present them in a manner more directly relevant for today. So that is the first purpose: basic instruction and edification. But, second, I also believe Benedict's instructions provide a striking foil to prevalent contemporary conceptions of the virtue of humility; that is why I started out by summarizing the most influential of those conceptions. I am hoping it will become apparent as we move through Benedict's instructions that he is homing in on a personal quality that differs from, or at least remains unaccounted for by, any of these contemporary philosophical perspectives on humility. I will develop that claim in the third and final section of the essay.

The "ladder of humility" in the seventh chapter of St. Benedict's *Rule* is unquestionably the most influential postscriptural Christian text on humility. The *Rule* itself is the most wide-reaching monastic rule in the Christian tradition, and the ladder of humility specifically is treated as authoritative in works such as Bernard of Clairvaux's *Steps of Humility and Pride* and Thomas Aquinas' *Summa Theologiae*. But Benedict did not invent the ladder from scratch; he was already drawing on a long tradition of monastic wisdom about humility, most particularly John Cassian's ten "indications" (*indiciis*) of humility.[19] Note that Cassian does not offer prescriptions for humility, but merely descriptions of its effects. Some have suggested this is the most that can be hoped for. Andrew Pinsent, for example, claims, "A self-help book entitled *How to Be Humble* or *Teach Yourself Humility* would miss the entire point—though, of course, within the history of Christianity there have been many attempts to systematize the stages in the acquisition of humility."[20] Pinsent says the point that would be missed by offering instructions for the acquisition of humility is that humility is a gift and thereby not "within our power to acquire." I take Pinsent's point, but it remains true that many in the Christian tradition—not just Benedict—have offered exactly such instruction. Benedict, for example, depicts the ladder of humility as akin to "the ladder which appeared to Jacob in his dream, by means of which angels were shown to him ascending and descending." The ladder, then, is our way to heaven, and Benedict states clearly that the rungs on the ladder are ones that "by our actions . . . we must mount" if we are to hope that the ladder will "by the Lord [be] lifted up to heaven."[21]

The second precaution Pinsent mentions is that Benedict's steps are not easily applicable to contexts more generic than the monastery. Surely there are limitations, but, as I hope to show, everything that Benedict says about how we leave pride behind and mount toward humility can be translated into mundane contemporary life. So, without throwing caution altogether to the wind, I will assume that Benedict still has something to say to us today. Benedict seemed to think the ordering of the steps mattered, as though you would need to master the earlier steps before you could tackle the later. But other commentators do not pay much attention to the order. Aquinas even reverses the order. So I will not make much of the order either. Here is Benedict's practical advice for how to grow in humility.

(1) *"The first degree of humility, then, is that a man always have the fear of God before his eyes (Ps 36:2), shunning all forgetfulness and that he be ever mindful of all that God hath commanded, that he always considereth in his mind how those who despise God will burn in hell for their sins, and that life everlasting is prepared for those who fear God."* The first step to humility is to resist sin. Why? Because sin is a transgression of God's commands, and submission to legitimate authority is a mark of humility. Suppose you claimed to be humble but could not submit to the demands of a legitimate superior. Benedict thinks you would be confused about humility. Refusal to submit to legitimate authority is a mark

of pride. Suppose you do not have such a frightening view of what awaits those who disobey God as Benedict does. Still, if you think it clear that God has given us directives for living well, how prideful would you have to be to prefer *your* wisdom over God's? Suppose, finally, you were skeptical about whether God *really* commands what the Bible or some religious authority claims God commands. Would it not be a mark of unwarranted self-confidence and self-assertion to trust your intuitions about these matters in the absence of very strong reasons? So the first step on the way to humility is to obey.

(2) *"The second degree of humility is, when a man loveth not his own will, nor is pleased to fulfill his own desires but by his deeds carrieth out that word of the Lord which saith: 'I came not to do My own will but the will of Him that sent Me' (Jn 6:38)."* The second step of humility is to adopt God's mission and objectives as more important than your own. We all have aspirations—to have a family, material security, meaningful work, the love of friends, and the respect of peers. There is nothing necessarily wrong with such aspirations, but they easily come into conflict with what we know to be God's aspirations. Often, for instance, we keep to ourselves far more money than we need while surrounded by those who are poor. But God's mission in the world, Christians believe, includes the creation of communities of *shalom* in which, at the very least, people do not starve or go without shelter.[22] We usually think of our failure to help such people as a mark of our lack of generosity, and it is. But Benedict thinks it is also a mark of pride just to the extent it reflects that we think our aspirations are more important than God's. So the second step of humility goes a bit further than obeying God's laws; it requires treating God's aspirations for the world as more important than our own.

(3) *"The third degree of humility is, that for the love of God a man subject himself to a Superior in all obedience, imitating the Lord, of whom the Apostle saith: 'He became obedient unto death' (Phil 2:8)."* By "Superior," Benedict means an abbot in a monastic order, but there is no reason to restrict his advice to the cloister. Benedict is pointing out that being ready to submit to other human beings on the basis of their role is a way of practicing humility. Is this not dangerous, since human beings are fallible? Yes, and there is no reason to think humility demands complete subservience to anyone other than God. Indeed, it is the distortion of directives such as these that has led to the disrepute of humility among many modern persons; humility has frequently been enjoined as a cover for patriarchal or other forms of oppressive power. But Benedict need not be read as advocating unquestioning submission. Rather, Benedict may simply be pointing out that one way of growing in humility is by practicing obedience to human superiors for the sake of suppressing our own willfulness. Imagine you have a boss who is not

an especially competent boss, and imagine she asks you to do something you do not think is a valuable use of your time. Benedict thinks that very often in such situations, when there is no injustice at stake, you should treat your boss' request as a way of learning not to take your own prerogatives too seriously. He recommends that we be on the lookout for opportunities to follow rather than lead, advice that is certainly strange given our current obsession with leadership.

(4) *"The fourth degree of humility is, that, if hard and distasteful things are commanded, nay, even though injuries are inflicted, he accept them with patience and even temper, and not grow weary or give up, but hold out, as the Scripture saith: 'He that shall persevere unto the end shall be saved' (Mt 10:22)."* One wishes Benedict would have said more here, again, because such a principle is ripe for abuse. In general, it is good to recall that these are principles meant to be undertaken voluntarily by one who wishes to ascend to God through humility, not principles meant to be enforced or even enjoined on others. I do not have space here to deal with the feminist critique that the Christian glorification of submission and suffering in the name of humility has disproportionately harmed women and other oppressed groups. The critique is lamentably accurate, but it is consistent with the claim that humility grows through bearing injury and suffering in the right way. Why should this be? Because injuries and suffering alike are attacks that threaten us with diminution and death. They reveal our fundamental limitation and fragility, and we naturally recoil against them. To learn to suffer injury or illness with patience is to learn to accept such limitation and fragility. To undergo hard and distasteful things without resentment or rebellion is to relinquish our claim to self-sufficiency and independence, the constitutive dispositions of pride. This is a hard saying. Cassian should be taken quite literally when he comments, "Humility cannot possibly be acquired without giving up everything" (*Institutes* 12.31).

(5) *"The fifth degree of humility is, when one hideth from his Abbot none of the evil thoughts which rise in his heart or the evils committed by him in secret, but humbly confesseth them. Concerning this the Scripture exhorts us, saying: 'Reveal thy way to the Lord and trust in Him' (Ps 37:5)."* Whereas the Scripture Benedict cites exhorts us to confess to God, Benedict instructs those who would be humble to confess to their abbot. We all know it is more humiliating to confess to another human being than it is to confess "privately" to God. From a certain perspective, this is irrational: Why should we prefer to expose our failures to a *perfect* God rather than an *imperfect* fellow human being? But, upon reflection, it is easy to make rational sense of the fact that we prefer private confession to God over confession to another human being. After all, when we confess to God, even if we do so sincerely (and often we do not), we are not *exposing* anything. We merely

acknowledge what God already knows about us. But when we tell our friend or our priest that we have lied, cheated, committed adultery, or stolen, we are very much exposing the gap between who we publicly portray ourselves to be and who we in fact are. It is the gap between who we pretend to be and who we are that makes us appear pathetic, and exposing this gap is humiliating. Benedict seems to be instructing us to take every advantage of such opportunities for humiliation. Again, this advice is countercultural in a society that privileges self-esteem. Contemporary writers on humility insist on a clear distinction between humiliation and humility, the former to be shunned, the latter embraced. But such a distinction is blurred in the monastic tradition of thinking about humility. Bernard of Clairvaux, for instance, says, "Humiliation is the only way to humility, just as patience is the only way to peace, and reading to knowledge. If you want the virtue of humility you must not shun humiliations. If you will not suffer yourself to be humbled, you can never achieve humility."[23] So an important step to becoming humble is intentionally exposing yourself to certain kinds of humiliation. Once again, this is dangerous counsel, subject to abuse by both paternalists and self-loathing individuals.

(6) *"The sixth degree of humility is, when a monk is content with the meanest and worst of everything, and in all that is enjoined him holdeth himself as a bad and worthless workman, saying with the Prophet: 'I am brought to nothing and I knew it not; I am become as a beast before Thee, and I am always with Thee' (Ps 73:22-23)."* Benedict is addressing the distribution of work assignments in the monastery. He is saying, "Be content doing the most insignificant work, rather than letting others know it is beneath your pay grade." Surely there are exceptions here. We should not *always* be content doing the most insignificant work. For instance, if you are the only paramedic in the room and someone is dying, you should not be content to hold the dying person's hand while some know-nothing attempts a rescue. In this situation, you really *should* let others know that hand-holding is beneath your pay grade. Why? Because the well-being of others desperately depends on you making your skills and abilities widely known. But the rarity of such occasions should set into relief the many other occasions where other motivations drive our concern to work at or above our pay grade. We know the work we do is among the most salient social indicators of our status. Here, Benedict is telling us to take advantage of opportunities to have our concerns about such status punctured. Benedict suggests we can prepare ourselves for such anonymous downward mobility by telling ourselves we are bad and worthless. But do we really need to *believe* we are bad and worthless?

(7) *"The seventh degree of humility is, when, not only with his tongue he declareth, but also in his inmost soul believeth, that he is the lowest and vilest of men, humbling himself and saying with the Prophet: 'But I am a worm and no man, the reproach of men and the*

outcast of the people' (Ps 22:7)." Oh no! Apparently if we are to grow in humility it is not enough to merely tell ourselves (or others) that we are bad and worthless, we have to *believe* it. This appears to be problematic in several ways. First, we do not have very direct control over what we believe. I cannot just decide to believe right now that the moon is made of green cheese. And second, if we are *not* really the lowest and vilest, then Benedict's instructions amount to a counsel of self-deception. And surely I am *not* the lowest and vilest! I may be bad, but I am not *that* bad. Can we make any sense of this? Dietrich Bonhoeffer follows the apostle Paul (1 Tim 1:15) in insisting that genuine contrition requires coming to see that it is *true* that we are the worst of sinners. "There can be no genuine acknowledgment of sin that does not lead to this extremity. If my sinfulness appears to me to be in any way smaller or less detestable in comparison with the sins of others, I am still not recognizing my sinfulness at all. My sin is of necessity the worst, the most grievous, the most reprehensible."[24] Why? Bonhoeffer suggests it is because I have privileged access to how my own sin is without excuse since I can see how it flows directly from my corrupt heart. I cannot know this about others, though. "Brotherly love will find any number of extenuations for the sins of others; only for my sin is there no apology whatsoever."[25] So perhaps Benedict is telling us that humility is required for this kind of soul-searching. Pride motivates us to compare our sinfulness to that of others, finding some measure by which we are not the worst. But humility allows us to abandon the self-protective strategy that is usually involved when we rank-order our sins in comparison with others in order to justify our sense that we are not the worst.

(8) *"The eighth degree of humility is, when a monk doeth nothing but what is sanctioned by the common rule of the monastery and the example of his elders."* Benedict tells the monks to stick to the program and not try to do anything different, unique, or remarkable. Benedict is targeting the temptation to be extraordinary. To describe the wish to be extraordinary as a temptation seems to be a mistake. We are encouraged to be extraordinary—to stand out from our peers in some way, to find our unique niche where we can excel and set ourselves apart. We fear that if we are not somehow extraordinary, we are a nobody. How else to explain our obsession with celebrities? What could be worse than being ordinary? Yet Benedict, and the monastic tradition generally, maintains that the desire to be extraordinary should usually be rejected. This need not be taken as a counsel of mediocrity. Benedict docs not say you cannot strive to be excellent. Rather, you must guard against the desire to be different, unique, or remarkable, because these desires have a rank-ordering impulse. The desire to be extraordinary is the desire to stand out in contrast to the ordinary others, to be seen as better than or at least in some sense more remarkable than the ordinary others. Benedict sees that

usually what motivates the rank-ordering impulse is pride. Even the wish to be *secretly* extraordinary is an expression of pride—in some ways even more insidious—because it reflects the ego's need for differentiation. We want to say to ourselves, "I'm not really like the rest of them." Of course, everyone needs differentiation at a young age in order to have an identifiable self at all. Benedict, however, thinks the ongoing wish for differentiation is devastating to our spiritual growth because it is an expression of an independence that is in tension with our origin and our destiny as utterly dependent creatures. Walker Percy was keenly aware of how advanced this step is on the ladder to humility. Commenting on one of his characters, Lancelot, Percy remarks, "All he had to do was solve the mystery of the universe, which may be difficult but is not as difficult as living an ordinary life."[26]

(9) *"The ninth degree of humility is, when a monk withholdeth his tongue from speaking, and keeping silence doth not speak until he is asked; for the Scripture showeth that 'in a multitude of words there shall not want sin' (Prov 10:19); and that 'a man full of tongue is not established in the earth' (Ps 140:12)."* Benedict understands that so much of our communication is a veiled attempt at self-promotion. We all know the dreaded "story-topper" who mistakenly thinks impressing others is the point of conversation, but there are subtler variations. My friend reports on her recent trip to Europe, and I can hardly wait to share that I have been there too—twice! I ask a question during a discussion, more interested in appearing smart than in discovering an answer. Even our statements of self-deprecation often conceal boasts, as in the "humblebrag": "I've lost so much weight these clothes look terrible on me!" The challenge is for us to discipline our speech away from such egoism, and Benedict thinks intentional silence just the tool. I was at a political town hall meeting with my friend Jonathan during the Iraq War. When Jonathan raised concerns about a candidate's prowar stance, that candidate responded, "I'm tired of people criticizing the war from the suburbs. Go put your life on the line in Iraq, then I'll take your quibbles seriously." But Jonathan and his wife *had* been in Iraq as part of a Christian peacemaking effort. In fact, they had nearly died risking their lives to nonviolently resist the evils of the Saddam Hussein regime. No one had more of a right than Jonathan to speak on this matter. Those of us in the crowd who knew Jonathan's story could hardly wait for this politician to get his comeuppance! But Jonathan said nothing. The crowd cheered the politician's quip, and Jonathan quietly returned the microphone. Although Jonathan had not taken a monastic vow of silence, his restraint exemplifies Benedict's exacting counsel of intentional silence.

(10) *"The tenth degree of humility is, when a monk is not easily moved and quick for laughter, for it is written: 'The fool exalteth his voice in laughter' (Sir 21:23)."* This is strange counsel if taken as a blanket rejection of laughter, for the

ability to laugh, especially at oneself, is a mark of humility. "Humility" and "humor" come from the same root word, after all. But Benedict is not counseling against laughter or humor in general. Rather, he warns us against laughter that is glib or frivolous. Such laughter serves only to distract us from our own neediness or from the suffering of others. It does not make us more human, as good humor can do. Bernard of Clairvaux says that "unseasonable or silly merriment" is the attempt to "shun sadness."[27] Obviously there are times when escapist humor is psychologically necessary for our survival. Even dark humor can be a way of entering into lament and sadness without being destroyed by it. One thinks here of the importance of humor to those who deal nobly with a significant illness—sometimes if we cannot laugh, there is nothing to do but cry. At other times humor provides the most fitting way of communally delighting in the gifts of friendship. Still, it is not hard to recognize in Benedict's warning the tendency we have to use joking and levity to perpetually delay confronting inadequacy, disappointment, or failure. And, as the previous steps indicate, Benedict thinks being confronted by such humiliation is our only hope for humility.

(11) *"The eleventh degree of humility is, that, when a monk speaketh, he speak gently and without laughter, humbly and with gravity, with few and sensible words, and that he be not loud of voice, as it is written: 'The wise man is known by the fewness of his words.'"* Practice restraint in communication. Take opportunities to refrain from speaking even when you think you have something to contribute. This is an art. Sometimes it would be unloving to withhold wisdom from the group. But usually what we have to say is not essential to the well-being or wisdom of others. More often, we speak to show our competence, expertise, wisdom, or depth. Be brief, be sensible, be discreet in your speech. Notice how long-windedness, abstruseness, and hyperbole are ways of making our thought-lives seem more weighty, interesting, or impressive than they really are. Practice reticence with the offering of advice, too. One of the most striking features of the stories of the Egyptian desert monks is their frequent refusal to offer advice to acolytes. This is an art, too. Occasionally people need our counsel. More often, though, they just need us to listen. Even when they do need advice, they usually need less than we are disposed to give. Benedict recognizes that most of our speech, including the advice we give, is really in service to ourselves.

(12) *"The twelfth degree of humility is, when a monk is not only humble of heart, but always letteth it appear also in his whole exterior to all that see him; namely, at the Work of God, in the garden, on a journey, in the field, or wherever he may be, sitting, walking, or standing, let him always have his head bowed down, his eyes fixed on the ground, ever holding himself guilty of his sins, thinking that he is already standing before the dread*

judgment seat of God, and always saying to himself in his heart what the publican in the Gospel said, with his eyes fixed on the ground: 'Lord, I am a sinner and not worthy to lift up mine eyes to heaven' (Lk 18:13); and again with the Prophet: 'I am bowed down and humbled exceedingly' (Ps 38:7-9; Ps 119:107)." The last rung on Benedict's ladder to humility is unclear. At least three main takeaways are available. First, that the crown of humility is the appearance of external modesty: do not just be humble of heart; appear humble in your "whole exterior." Second, that the crown of humility is consistency: the truly humble person is the one who is "always" humble. Monastic commentators rarely offer either of these two interpretations. Rather, the dominant interpretation has it that the crown of humility is the consistent refusal of curiosity. Accordingly, the most important feature of the humble monk depicted here is the bearing of his head and eyes: his head is bowed and his eyes are fixed on the ground. Benedict here is reminding us that the original sin was that of curiosity, Eve's wandering eyes fixing on the forbidden fruit and delighting in the serpent's offer of knowledge independent from God. This is the essence of the vice of *curiositas*, a desire to know about the world (propositional knowledge) and to know the world (knowledge by acquaintance) without having that knowledge mediated by God. Because Benedict sees this original sin as the root of pride, the crown of humility would be the recovery of an utterly different learning posture: one according to which we honor God as the source and *telos* of our search for knowledge and wisdom. In part because we have so little control over our mental life, the consistent refusal of curiosity would provide the clearest evidence of complete humility. If you want to go all the way, Benedict tells us, you must endeavor to have all of your "knowing" mediated by and dependent upon God—your self-knowledge, your intimate knowledge of others through personal relationship, and your intellectual knowledge of the created order.

Humility as Glad Acceptance of Dependence

Benedict has not given us an account of humility, which we could easily set alongside contemporary accounts to test for overlaps and gaps. Rather, Benedict has given us a set of practices and indicators of humility. The practices are the same as the indicators, as is often the case for the development of a habit. For instance, list the indicators for a skilled basketball player and you have also listed the things one would need to practice to become a skilled basketball player. It is the same here: the humble person is uninterested in being extraordinary; the person who wants to *become* humble must practice disinterest in being extraordinary. In this final section, I want to examine what we learn about Benedict's conception of humility from his list of practices and indicators of humility. For review, here is a summary of the list.

(1) Avoid sin

(2) Privilege God's aspirations

(3) Honor your boss

(4) Suffer well

(5) Confess sin

(6) Prize anonymity

(7) Know your dark heart

(8) Practice ordinariness

(9) Practice silence

(10) Avoid frivolity

(11) Avoid loquaciousness

(12) Avoid curiosity

As I ponder this list, there is a recurrent theme that stands out: the path to humility requires confronting our illusions of independence and self-sufficiency and coming to peace with our ultimate neediness. In one way or another, every rung on Benedict's ladder is an assault on the various strategies we use to avoid the weakness, inadequacy, fragility, poverty, sickness, insecurity, and fear at the core of who we are. Moreover, on Benedict's account we are not merely to confront these things; we are to adopt a certain posture in response to them. Namely, we are to learn to rest with, accept, even embrace our shortcomings as revelations of who we really are and of our desperate need for God. If Benedict were forced to offer an account of humility, I think he would propose something like the following.

Dependence account: Humility is the disposition to gladly accept our neediness and assume a posture of dependence.

How does an account like this compare with contemporary accounts? It clearly differs from non-overestimation accounts by privileging the affective dimension over the cognitive. Envision a scenario wherein a monk consistently resists temptations to overestimate his worth, skills, achievements, status, or entitlements. Will he thereby be in a position to gladly accept his neediness and assume a posture of dependence? Hardly. After all, he might resent the fact that his status (let "status" stand in for the longer list of things he should not overestimate) is what it is. He may be perfectly accurate in his appraisal of his status, but refuse to accept it, refuse to share it with others, refuse to let his behavior be shaped by his awareness of it, and so on. He may be perfectly accurate in his self-appraisal but continue to prefer recognition and distinction, and avoid being seen as ordinary or needy.

How about the low-concern account? Here I think we have an account that aligns much more closely with Benedict's vision. Like the dependence view, the low-concern view privileges the affective. What matters is that a person not *care* too much about his or her status. And certainly this is included in the Benedictine account I am suggesting. Consequently, the low-concern account can offer better explanations of many of the features of Benedict's ladder than can the non-overestimation account. But I think it still falls short; it does not fully capture the character trait that Benedict is encouraging the brothers to develop.

For instance, can the low-concern view explain why the humble person would prefer anonymity over recognition? Suppose Brother Morris epitomizes the low-concern view of humility. He absolutely could not care less about his status; he is so focused on other goods that his personal status holds no interest for him. Now the question: Would Brother Morris prefer anonymity over recognition? It is hard to see why he would. If he could not care less about his status, then he could not care less whether he gets recognized or not. Strangely, on the low-concern account, the monk who seeks anonymity is too self-concerned. Yet Benedict seems to clearly recommend the cultivation of such preferences.

A low-concern defender could offer the following response. Actually, there *is* a difference between practices that aim at humility and indicators of humility. It may be important to do things in the process of cultivating humility that the fully humble person him- or herself would not have to do, in the same way that there are things a beginning basketball player must do that a seasoned professional can disregard. And here is one such case. The would-be humble person must pursue anonymity as a strategy of suppressing her over-concern about her status. But when she becomes humble she will not need to do that anymore, precisely because she will have become genuinely free of those petty concerns about status. She will be equally comfortable with anonymity and recognition—and this would indicate she possesses humility in full.

I am persuaded by an argument like that. So I think we will have to look a little deeper to find why Benedict would not be fully satisfied with the low-concern view. Here is another possibility. Perhaps the problem with the low-concern view is that it lacks the theological dimension. After all, for Benedict our avoidance of humiliation, weakness, obscurity, and suffering has a theological aspect: we seek to deny our deep neediness as a way of avoiding God. Remember that the ladder of humility is, like Jacob's ladder, the way "speedily to arrive at that heavenly exaltation." So there is an irreducibly theological dimension to Benedict's understanding of humility. But there is a difference between unconcern about status and glad acceptance of our dependence upon God. After all, there are exemplars of the former who do not display the latter. G. E. Moore, for example, is reported by Roberts and Wood to have been profoundly unconcerned about his own status, yet there is no indication that Moore gladly accepted his dependence on God.[28] So maybe the low-concern account falls short because it does not own up to the fact that humility is irreducibly theological.

But here the defender of low concern might respond as follows: "Dependence on *God* is just as well (or better) ascribed to the virtue of faith rather than humility. Surely there is a distinction between humility and faith as virtues, even though in the overall Christian character they are intertwined. A person who has exemplary Christian faith also has humility, and the person who has Christian humility also has faith. What makes for *Christian* humility is its connection with trusting God in Jesus Christ."[29] In other words, do not conflate humility with Christian humility. Humility is low concern about status. Christian humility is what you get when that low concern is combined with trust in Jesus Christ. Benedict is obviously talking about Christian humility, but it would be a mistake to conclude from his presentation that the theological dimension of his depiction of the humble monk must be squeezed into a general account of humility.

I am sympathetic with that response, too. I do not want to restrict humility to Christians or theists only, in part because Scripture seems to suggest that being humble is one way to *come to know* God. But I still think Benedict's vision of humility includes more than what is included in the low-concern view. In fact, what low concern misses in the Benedictine wisdom is precisely what the limitations-owning account thinks is missing from low-concern accounts—namely, one could have low concern about one's status for all kinds of reasons, even noble reasons, without ever coming to peace with one's own limitations. Benedict seems to focus an awful lot on the monk's need to properly attend to his failures, deficiencies, and limitations. In other words, Benedict's view of humility seems to include *both* the absence of prideful concerns *and* the presence of proper attitudes about one's fundamental frailty and inadequacy.

So I think these two accounts, limitations-owning and low concern, both track important features of what Benedict seems to have in view. It is undeniable that Benedict thinks the proper confrontation of our fundamental limitations is required by humility, just as it is undeniable that Benedict thinks the humble person will display unconcern about her status. But these are meant to be stand-alone accounts of humility. Why think they should be brought together to offer an account that is adequate to Benedict's wisdom?

What brings these two accounts together is the monastic way of thinking about what *is* an appropriate response to the neediness and limitation that characterizes our lives. After all, even Aristotle thought it important to attend to, care about, and respond properly to one's limitations. Aristotle would be quite pleased, I suspect, with the kinds of responses to our limitations recommended by defenders of the limitations-owning view. Remember that Snow, for example, offers the following as appropriate responses to our limitations:

- "acknowledge" them
- "care about" them
- "take them seriously"
- "be disturbed by having them"
- "feel sorrow or dejection because of" them
- "deeply regret" them
- "wish we didn't have" them
- "do everything possible to be rid of" them
- "do the best we can to control [them] and minimize [their] negative effects"
- "regret yet accept" them.[30]

With the possible exception of the last bullet point, Aristotle would be on board with all of these recommendations for the appropriate response to limitation. But of course Aristotle was never a fan of humility! So I think that the limitations-owning account has something right formally—humility is partly about a certain kind of response to limitations—but misses one peculiar kind of response that is constitutive of humility. What was distinctive about the early Christian, and early monastic, valorization of humility was the insight, buttressed by Jewish-Christian anthropology, that the most appropriate response to fundamental human limitation and neediness is not regret, dismay, sorrow, dejection, or determination to overcome. Rather, the most appropriate response to human neediness and limitation is acceptance—and not just regretful acceptance, but glad acceptance, joyful acceptance, even embrace of our neediness as the truest and most important thing about us as creatures.[31] This attitude toward human frailty and neediness was at the heart of the offensiveness of the Christian moral vision to Romans, Greeks, Enlightenment liberals like Hume, and critics of "slave morality" like Nietzsche. And, of course, this peculiar attitude toward ultimate human neediness engenders the profound unconcern about status characteristic of the humble person. As you discover that the fundamental truth of your existence is your neediness and inadequacy, and as you learn gladly to accept and embrace the opportunity to enter more and more fully into dependence upon God and others, your own personal status recedes from view because it no longer reveals anything significant about who you take yourself to be. Conversely, unconcern about status makes it easy for the humble person to accept failure, inadequacy, and weakness. We have nothing to prove, no cherished vision of the self to establish as significant and important.

Such, I think, is the vision animating Benedict's ladder. Each rung on the ladder can be understood as a way of practicing peace, rest, joy, and trust while facing your own weakness, deficiency, and neediness head on. From a certain perspective, this is terrible advice. If our fulfillment as human persons depends finally on our personal power and achievement, humility is for fools. If, however, our fulfillment as human persons depends finally on our readiness to receive love and care from others, especially God, then humility is the path to our destiny. Benedict, the monks he instructed, and the Christian tradition as a whole see relationship, with God and one another, as our hope and salvation. To cultivate humility is to discover, through the glad acceptance of our neediness and the relinquishment of our concern for an independent and important self, that such a hope is good news indeed.

It is not surprising that significant dimensions of the Christian view of humility should survive in contemporary philosophical accounts of humility. For one thing, many philosophers who think about humility are Christian. For another, our culture, even if post-Christian, continues to be shaped by Christian perspectives about human nature. Still, I think something of the radical, even frightening, force of the early Christian acclamation of humility has been lost. Benedict pulls no punches. If you want to cultivate humility, you cannot avoid loss, humiliation, and suffering. Indeed, the Christian who would cultivate humility should see such woes as opportunities, and put them to holy use.

• • •

Response to Kent Dunnington

Everett L. Worthington Jr.

When a psychologist is asked to evaluate a philosopher's account of a virtue, disciplinary paradigms and shared exemplars, tools, and programs of research come into conflict.[1] One of the most important aspects of the different approaches by philosophy and psychology is the treatment of old and new sources of understanding. Philosophy often privileges old sources as having withstood the test of time; psychology privileges new data, new theory, and situational influences.

Dunnington does a superb job of summarizing five existing philosophical accounts of humility and then proposing a sixth (see table 8.1). After considering Benedict's twelve-step program to humility—an old source that he takes as a way of glimpsing deep Christian convictions that are criteria against which to measure six identified philosophers' accounts of humility—he prefers a glad-acceptance-of-dependence account for defining humility. He sees this account as addressing some quality not addressed by the underestimation, non-overestimation, egalitarian, and low-concern accounts of humility and being more closely allied with (yet still preferring it to) an owning of limitations account of humility. Whereas I can understand his clear logic, as a psychologist, I immediately think, *Why privilege Benedict as a standard against which to evaluate the accounts, dismissing accounts that do not accord with Benedict?* That Benedict rule is, after all, an old source.

Psychologists have also variously defined humility. Don E. Davis and his colleagues have provided reviews of and arguments for psychological definitions, most of which have been grounded in contemporary research findings though informed by historic theological and philosophical writings.[2] One obvious exception to psychology's new = good preference is Christian psychology, which does privilege theological understanding of Scripture along with contemporary data-plus-theory. Christian psychology does keep in mind that theology is a human enterprise and therefore not a criterion against which to measure psychology but rather a dialogue partner with psychology, or to use a metaphor I use in *Coming to Peace with Psychology: What Christians Can Learn from Psychological Science*, a dance partner.[3]

In *Heroic Humility: What the Science of Humility Can Say to People Raised on Self-Focus*,[4] the definition of humility that my colleagues and I initially put forth in our 2010 paper (cited above) is further refined, presenting humility as having three characteristics that are necessary but not independently sufficient to be humility—owning one's limitations, displaying modest actions, and having an other-enhancing perspective.[5] Four of the six definitions Dunnington offers are represented within the comprehensive definition in *Heroic Humility*. The underestimation and (to some extent) the low-concern accounts are not consistent with our definition. However, we emphasize that it is not enough merely to fail to overestimate one's strengths, to battle pride and arrogance, to cultivate low concern for one's status, to gladly accept one's dependence on God and others, or to be concerned about one's limitations in a way that engenders an appropriate response to them—even if we did all of these simultaneously.

Why are all of these not enough? Because they are all inherently self-focused. Even if this kind of self-focus might be laudable, such as in cultivating one's spiritual (and personal) betterment in the eyes of God or others or being actively concerned about the right thinking and feeling about our failures, limitations, and deficiencies, paradoxically, such self-focus is in some ways antithetical to humility. Humility is not merely an absence of something. It involves an absence of some things but also an active presence of some quality that makes it a virtue.

From the six philosophical accounts that Dunnington summarizes, it is not clear exactly what quality it is that makes humility to be humility. Refusing to overestimate one's strengths is hardly something positive. Nor is refraining from arrogant behavior or from being concerned with one's accomplishments or asserting what one lacks (i.e., a limitations-owning account). Perhaps the closest thing to something positive is indeed a grateful acceptance of limitations; at least gratitude is a positive emotion. But the Worthington and Allison definition,[6] while affirming these refusals, restraints, and refraining motives, does something positive: it suggests that humility requires active focus on elevating others. This is, after all, consistent with the Christian Scriptures. In Philippians 2:2-4, we see that Paul instructs the Philippians, "Do nothing out of selfish ambition or vain conceit. Rather, in humility value others above yourselves, not looking to your own interests but each of you to the interests of the others" (NIV). For Paul, humility is focus on building others up, not on his own heart attitude. The humility hymn that Paul recounts makes the same point for Jesus, "[w]ho being in very nature God, did not consider equality with God something to be used to his own advantage; rather, he made himself nothing, by taking the very nature of a servant" (Phil 2:6-7). Jesus is focused not on himself but on elevating others, on serving them ("to the glory of God the Father" [Phil 2:11]).

Two other points are worth considering. First, Dunnington frames humility as inherently spiritual. This, I believe, is a flaw that comes from not heeding situational pressures. Dunnington summarizes philosophers who seek to define "humility" in general and, in doing so, account for all of the subtypes. Psychologists tend to offer a general (omnibus) definition of humility (e.g., our refined definition). However, we then treat different subtypes of humility each as unique. For example, *relational humility* recognizes that humble supervisors and humble workers, humble wives and husbands, humble parents and humble children might not show humility the same way. Thus, relational humility needs to be specifically delineated depending on what kind of relationship is being considered. *Spiritual humility* recognizes that humility in the face of what one considers sacred might be different from humility in secular contexts.[7] In fact, humility in relation to God might differ from humility in relation to nature, humanity, or something transcendental. *Intellectual humility*, which involves response to different ideas about emotionally and value-laden ideas (i.e., about religion or politics), might be something altogether different from relational and spiritual humility. And furthermore, *religious humility* (i.e., responding humbly to religious ideas) would likely differ from *political humility* (i.e., responding humbly to political ideas) because religion and politics are not strictly intertwined, and for particular individuals the emotional importance of each might be weighted differently.

Second, just a quibble. Dunnington says, "If, however, our fulfillment as human persons depends finally on our *readiness to receive love and care from others*, especially God, then humility is the path to our destiny" (256; emphasis mine). But human fulfillment might depend also on being other-oriented in lifting others up, not putting others down—not merely on receiving love and care, but perhaps just as much on giving love and care to others. Clearly we are to be open to God and to receiving God's love and care, and we are relational, so receiving others' love and care is important. But so too is not being *merely* a receptive vessel. We are also to be conduits of God's love, giving it to others through a servant's heart (as Jesus is described in Phil 2:7).

Dunnington, I believe, has part of the equation. He makes a great, necessary, and new point not captured by the other five philosophical accounts of humility, the glad acceptance of dependence. But my reading is that the psychological definition Worthington and Allison suggest might accomplish something that none of the philosophical accounts does either—orient our service not just on God but also on lifting others up, on edifying others.

Many of these considerations I have outlined are really more about disciplinary differences between a philosophical approach and a psychological approach, though I am taking a Christian psychologist's approach.

Nevertheless, I hope that this critique makes clear that I appreciate Dunnington's rigor and his positive contribution of advancing a glad-acceptance-of-dependence approach. The positivity of describing humility as something rather than telling what it is not is a step clearly in the right direction.

TABLE 8.1. Dunnington's Summary of Accounts of Humility in Relation to Worthington and Allison's *Heroic Humility: What the Science of Humility Can Say to People Raised on Self-Focus*

Statement of the account of humility	Some major proponents	Relationship to the three points (in parentheses) of Worthington and Allison's (2018) definition of humility (for a quote, see the last entry in the left column)
First wave (cognitive)		
Underestimation account: humility is the disposition to consistently underestimate your worth, skills, achievements, status, or entitlements.	Julia Driver	(1) an accurate assessment of worth is sought, not an underestimation.
Non-overestimation account: humility is consistent with accurate self-estimation; it consists of the disposition to consistently refuse the temptation to overestimate one's worth, skills, achievements, status, or entitlements.	Norvin Richards; Owen Flanagan	(1) have an accurate sense of self, know their limitations, and are teachable.
Second wave (reform virtue for secular purposes)		
Egalitarian account: humility is the disposition to refrain, despite one's accurate (high) self-assessment, from arrogant and boastful behavior, especially from acting as though one's (perhaps genuine) superiority grants one more extensive moral rights than anyone else.	Daniel Statman; Aaron Ben Ze'ev; Alex Sinha	(2) present themselves modestly in ways that do not put others off by arrogance or by false, insincere modesty, or displaying weakness.
Third wave (affective)		
Low-concern account: humility is the disposition to have an unusually low concern about one's own worth, skills, achievements, status, or entitlements because of one's intense concern for other apparent goods.	Robert Roberts and Jay Wood; George Schlesinger; Nicholas Bommarito; G. F. Schueler; Michael Ridge	(1) people do care about their limitations, and they want to deal with them responsibly by learning how to overcome them—i.e., to be teachable.

Statement of the account of humility	Some major proponents	Relationship to the three points (in parentheses) of Worthington and Allison's (2018) definition of humility (for a quote, see the last entry in the left column)
Post-consideration of Benedict (right response to limitations—glad acceptance of essential dependence or right response to limitations)		
Dependence account: humility is the disposition to gladly accept our neediness and assume a posture of dependence.	Dunnington (suggesting Benedict would advocate)	(1) have an accurate sense of self, know their limitations, and are teachable; (2) present themselves modestly in ways that do not put others off by arrogance or by false, insincere modesty or displaying weakness.
Limitations-owning account: humility is the disposition to be attentive to, care about, and respond appropriately to one's failures, limitations, and deficiencies.	Nancy Snow; Dennis Whitcomb; Jason Baehr; Heather Battaly; Daniel Howard-Snyder	(1) have an accurate sense of self, know their limitations, and are teachable.
Limitations-owning, modest, and other-elevating account: humble people are those who (1) have an accurate sense of self, know their limitations, and are teachable; (2) present themselves modestly in ways that do not put others off by arrogance or by false, insincere modesty or displaying weakness; and (3) are especially oriented to advancing others and not through groveling weakness but through power under control, power used to build others up and not to squash them down (Worthington and Allison, *Heroic Humility*, 4).	Everett Worthington; Scott Allison; Don E. Davis; Joshua N. Hook; Daryl R. Van Tongeren	(3) are especially oriented to advancing others and not through groveling weakness but through power under control, power used to build others up and not to squash them down.

• • •

Reply to Everett L. Worthington Jr.

Kent Dunnington

Everett Worthington's thoughtful commentary on my essay raises several interesting questions. I will focus on three, saving what I take to be the most revealing line of questioning for last.

First, Worthington claims that my Benedict-inspired account of humility, along with the other accounts I canvassed, are all missing a crucial piece of the humility puzzle. All have failed to see that "humility requires active focus on elevating others." I think this is a mistake. It is true that humble people strongly tend to focus on others, but this is because of the way that humility clears the way for love to be more fruitful. There is a virtue whose essence is a focus on the well-being of others, but it is called benevolence, not humility.

Second, Worthington says I am wrong to frame humility as inherently spiritual. He thinks, instead, that I should treat "different subtypes of humility each as unique" (259). Spiritual humility, relational humility, and intellectual humility are the unique types that Worthington names. I would like to better understand why Worthington thinks this is the right methodological approach. Why not, for instance, think there is one virtue of humility that will be differently expressed in different domains? For instance, why not think that the scholar who is intellectually humble, the devotee who is spiritually humble, and the child who is relationally humble are all just being humble in their relevant circumstances? Worthington says this way of thinking "comes from not heeding situational pressures" (258). Situationists argue that there really are no deep, cross-situationally sensitive character traits *at all*, and therefore they tend to want to move away from virtue-language altogether as a helpful moral category. Is Worthington's method a compromise between classical virtue theory and situationism? I would like to better understand what is to be gained by thinking there really are multiple unique virtues of humility.

I find Worthington's observations about our disciplinary differences most interesting. Worthington thinks that philosophers tend to privilege older sources of understanding whereas psychologists privilege newer ones. As a generalization, I think that is false. Much contemporary analytic philosophy is intentionally ahistorical, leaning on nothing so much as contemporary intuition. But it is true that the field of philosophical virtue theory is often historically oriented, and this is because the idea that virtues/vices are the key to the well-lived human life is an ancient idea, one that was largely sidelined by modern moral thought.

Worthington asks, "*Why privilege Benedict as a standard against which to evaluate the [competing] accounts [of humility], dismissing accounts that do not accord with Benedict?* That Benedict rule is, after all, an old source" (257). In response, I write about Benedict, not because I think he is undoubtedly right about the true nature of humility, but simply in order to set into relief the distance between early Christian and contemporary definitions of humility. I began thinking about humility because the John Templeton Foundation was funding a number of research fellowships on the virtue of humility. At the first symposium, where the research fellows were sharing our various humility-related projects, I discovered that most of the projects (which, remember, had won out over many other proposals) were focused on humility as a virtue that helps limit self-serving cognitive bias. For instance, a humble person is supposedly less likely to think he knows something he does not in fact know. I found this odd because Jesus and the Christian tradition have held up children as a paradigm of humility, yet I have been around children enough to know they are not exemplary in this respect. I began to suspect that Templeton was interested in leveraging humility in the service of epistemic modesty. Such a concern, however, is hardly on the radar of the many early Christians who placed a premium on humility. They wanted to leverage humility for different purposes, mostly for the purpose of growth in friendship with God.

My point is that new sources of understanding are susceptible to cultural control every bit as much as old ones. A historical approach that treats the past as a repository of wisdom can protect us from confusing contemporary intuitions with "truth." For instance, one of the ways psychologists try to define humility is by asking folks what comes to their mind when they think of a humble person. But why would we trust contemporary intuitions? As a historically minded philosopher, I have a high degree of skepticism about the value of such intuitions. There is, of course, a worthwhile project of trying to systematize these intuitions into a manageable account, but it is not clear to me that this is something we really need. At least, I am convinced we *also* need accounts of humility that display the contingency of our contemporary intuitions.

I suspect what may be behind Worthington's question is a difference between us about why virtue theory is an important area of research. Some are sanguine about virtue theory as a tool of moral formation. What is important for such an approach is to get a workable definition of a virtue, one that jibes with contemporary intuitions, and then reverse-engineer it to figure out what practices can inculcate it. This is an admirable goal; it is pretty clearly how Aristotle used virtue theory. We are not, however, in anything like the social or political context in which Aristotle was operating, and therefore I suspect virtue theory is of limited use in trying to supply broadly available methods of moral formation.

My interest in virtue theory is different. I am interested in the virtues primarily as a way of trying to think about the modern, of trying to figure out, that is, just what exactly has happened to bring us into what is sometimes called the secular age. The virtues provide a powerful tool for this kind of investigation because they are a primary site of contestation about shifting commitments. Just think, for instance, about the theoretical battles that have been waged over humility: Aristotle dismissed it; Jesus championed it; the monastic tradition revered it; Machiavelli, Nietzsche, and Hume reviled it; Kant tried to rehabilitate it; and now the John Templeton Foundation wants to enliven it. Thus, humility is a window into a deeper set of conflicts, and my interest in it is largely an interest in that deeper set of conflicts. I tried in my essay to set Benedict alongside contemporary accounts of humility, not because I trust him unwaveringly, but because I distrust contemporary motivations and I need some way of probing why.

• • •

Notes to Chapter 8
(Kent Dunnington)

1 David Hume, *Enquiries concerning Human Understanding and concerning the Principles of Morals*, 3rd ed. (Oxford: Clarendon, 1975), 270; Friedrich Nietzsche, *The Anti-Christ* (Harmondsworth: Penguin, 1968), 26.

2 Richard Taylor is one of the few contemporary philosophers who recognizes that a rejection of Abrahamic religion entails a rejection of a suite of virtues that are interdefined by Abrahamic presuppositions about human nature and destiny. Otherwise, "philosophers, with the exception of those who take religion very seriously, are apt to talk nonsense when addressing matters of ethics" (*Ethics, Faith, and Reason* [Englewood Cliffs, N.J.: Prentice-Hall, 1985], 2). Taylor recommends leaving humility behind and retrieving Aristotelian proper pride.

3 Elizabeth Anscombe, "Modern Moral Philosophy," *Philosophy* 33, no. 124 (1958): 1–19.

4 Julia Driver, "The Virtues of Ignorance," *Journal of Philosophy* 86, no. 7 (1989): 378n5.

5 Whereas Driver made a clear distinction between humility and modesty, others have claimed the two concepts are interchangeable. The modesty/humility distinction is a mess in the literature. For example, Driver, Flanagan, Ben Ze'ev, and Nuyen all offer accounts of modesty to be distinguished from accounts of humility, yet their views are treated by others as accounts of humility. I will follow suit. It will not make much of a difference here since, whether they intended so or not, each of these author's accounts

is now treated in the literature as a contending account of humility. See Driver, "Virtues of Ignorance"; Owen Flanagan, "Virtue and Ignorance," *Journal of Philosophy* 87, no. 8 (1990): 420–28; Aaron Ben-Ze'ev, "The Virtue of Modesty," *American Philosophical Quarterly* 30, no. 3 (1993): 235–46; and A. T. Nuyen, "Just Modesty," *American Philosophical Quarterly* 35, no. 1 (1998): 101–9.

6   Norvin Richards, "Is Humility a Virtue?" *American Philosophical Quarterly* 25, no. 3 (1988): 253–59; Flanagan, "Virtue and Ignorance."

7   Non-overestimation defenders might retort that Roger still overestimates the *value* of his standing as the best tennis player, and it is *that* overestimation that explains his clear lack of humility, but even that seems insufficient. After all, Roger might know and understand that, all things considered, tennis is not that important, without that knowledge doing anything to lessen his concern about being highly esteemed as a great tennis player.

8   Daniel Statman, "Modesty, Pride and Realistic Self-Assessment," *Philosophical Quarterly* 42, no. 169 (1992): 430.

9   Statman, "Modesty, Pride," 431.

10 Statman notes that Richard Taylor (*Ethics, Faith, and Reason*) offers an unequivocal "no" to the question whether there is still a place for humility outside religious contexts. Taylor joins his voice to Nietzsche, Hume, Montaigne, and many other modern critics of humility. It is interesting that Richards is such a lonely voice in the contemporary scene.

11 Statman, "Modesty, Pride"; Ben-Ze'ev, "Virtue of Modesty"; Alex Sinha, "Modernizing the Virtue of Humility," *Australasian Journal of Philosophy* 90, no. 2 (2012): 259–74.

12 To be more precise, I should say: *Given an egalitarian view of human worth*, the virtue of justice includes such a disposition. Such caveats are required to get any definite behavioral entailments from virtues, because virtues are always embedded in larger perspectives that determine their import.

13 Robert C. Roberts and Jay Wood, "Humility and Epistemic Goods," in *Intellectual Virtue: Perspectives from Ethics and Epistemology*, ed. Michael DePaul and Linda Zagzebski (Oxford: Oxford University Press, 2003), 257–79.

14 George Schlesinger, "Humility," *Tradition* 27, no. 3 (1993): 4–12; Nicolas Bommarito, "Modesty as a Virtue of Attention," *Philosophical Review* 122, no. 1 (2013): 93–117.

15 G. F. Schueler, "Why Modesty Is a Virtue," *Ethics* 107, no. 3 (1997): 467–85; Michael Ridge, "Modesty as a Virtue," *American Philosophical Quarterly* 37, no. 3 (2000): 269–83.

16 Ty Raterman, "On Modesty: Being Good and Knowing It without Flaunting It," *American Philosophical Quarterly* 43, no. 3 (2006): 221–34; J. L. A. Garcia, "Being Unimpressed with Ourselves: Reconceiving Humility," *Philosophia* 34, no. 4 (2006): 417–35; James Kellenberger, "Humility," *American Philosophical Quarterly* 47, no. 4 (2010): 321–36.

17 Nancy Snow, "Humility," *Journal of Value Inquiry* 29, no. 2 (1995): 203–16. Whitcomb et al. offer an account of *intellectual humility* that is analogous to Snow's account of humility (Dennis Whitcomb, Jason Baehr, Heather

Battaly, and Daniel Howard-Snyder, "Intellectual Humility: Owning Our Limitations," *Philosophy and Phenomenological Research* 94, no. 3 [2017]: 509–39).
18 Snow, "Humility," 207.
19 For a model study of humility in the monastic tradition, one that is both scholarly and morally enriching, read Jane Foulcher, *Reclaiming Humility: Four Studies in Monastic Tradition* (Athens, Ohio: Cistercian, 2015).
20 Andrew Pinsent, "Humility," in *Being Good: Christian Virtues for Everyday Life*, ed. Michael Austin and R. Douglas Geivett (Grand Rapids: Eerdmans, 2011), 263.
21 These and all subsequent citations from chap. 7 of Benedict's *Rule* are taken from the 1949 translation by Boniface Verheyen OSB, available at http://www.ecatholic2000.com/benedict/rule8.shtml.
22 I will not try to make the biblical case for such a claim here. I think it would be hard to read the Bible without gaining this clear impression, but if you need to substitute some other clear divine mission, that should work, too.
23 Quoted in Foulcher, *Reclaiming Humility*, 233.
24 Dietrich Bonhoeffer, *Life Together* (New York: Harper and Row, 1954), 96.
25 Bonhoeffer, *Life Together*, 96.
26 Walker Percy, *Lancelot* (New York: Farrar, Straus and Giroux 1977), 100.
27 Bernard of Clairvaux, *The Twelve Degrees of Humility and Pride*, trans. Barton Mills (New York: Macmillan, 1929), 72.
28 Robert C. Roberts and Jay Wood, *Intellectual Virtues: An Essay in Regulative Epistemology* (Oxford: Oxford University Press, 2007), 239.
29 This is taken from correspondence with Bob Roberts.
30 Snow, "Humility," 207.
31 For a scriptural argument that accords with my perspective here, see Stephen Pardue, *The Mind of Christ: Humility and the Intellect in Early Christian Theology* (London: Bloomsbury T&T Clark, 2013).

Notes to Chapter 8 Response
(Everett L. Worthington Jr.)

1 T. S. Kuhn, *The Structure of Scientific Revolutions* (Chicago: University of Chicago Press, 1962); Peter Galison, *Einstein's Clocks and Poincaré's Maps: Empires of Time* (New York: W. W. Norton, 2003); I. Lakatos, *The Methodology of Scientific Research Programmes: Philosophical Papers*, vol. 1 (Cambridge: Cambridge University Press, 1978).
2 D. E. Davis, J. N. Hook, E. L. Worthington Jr., D. R. Van Tongeren, A. L. Gartner, D. J. Jennings II, and R. A. Emmons, "Relational Humility: Conceptualizing and Measuring Humility as a Personality Judgment," *Journal of Personality Assessment* 93 (2011): 225–34; D. E. Davis, E. L. Worthington Jr., and J. N. Hook, "Humility: Review of Measurement Strategies

and Conceptualization as Personality Judgment," *Journal of Positive Psychology* 5, no. 4 (2010): 243–52; Davis and Gazaway essay in this volume.
3 E. L. Worthington Jr., *Coming to Peace with Psychology: What Christians Can Learn from Psychological Science* (Downers Grove, Ill.: InterVarsity, 2010).
4 E. L. Worthington Jr. and S. T. Allison, *Heroic Humility: What the Science of Humility Can Say to People Raised on Self-Focus* (Washington, D.C.: American Psychological Association, 2018).
5 See *Heroic Humility*, 4; reproduced in table 8.1 for quote.
6 Worthington and Allison, *Heroic Humility*.
7 D. E. Davis, J. N. Hook, E. L. Worthington Jr., D. R. Van Tongeren, A. L. Gartner, and D. J. Jennings II, "Relational Spirituality and Forgiveness: Development of the Spiritual Humility Scale (SHS)," *Journal of Psychology and Theology* 38, no. 2 (2010): 91–100.

CHAPTER BIBLIOGRAPHY

Anscombe, Elizabeth. "Modern Moral Philosophy." *Philosophy* 33, no. 124 (1958): 1–19.
Augustine. *Letter (Ep.)* 118. Translated by J. G. Cunningham. In *Nicene and Post-Nicene Fathers*, 1st ser., vol. 1, edited by Philip Schaff. Buffalo, N.Y.: Christian Literature, 1887.
Benedict of Nursia. *Rule of Saint Benedict*. Translated by Boniface Verheyen. Atchison, Kan.: St. Benedict's Abbey, 1949.
Ben-Ze'ev, Aaron. "The Virtue of Modesty." *American Philosophical Quarterly* 30, no. 3 (1993): 235–46.
Bernard of Clairvaux. *The Twelve Degrees of Humility and Pride*. Translated by Barton Mills. New York: Macmillan, 1929.
Bommarito, Nicolas. "Modesty as a Virtue of Attention." *Philosophical Review* 122, no. 1 (2013): 93–117.
Bonhoeffer, Dietrich. *Life Together*. New York: Harper and Row, 1954.
Cassian, John. *The Institutes*. Translated by Boniface Ramsey. New York: Newman Press, 2000.
Davis, D. E., E. L. Worthington Jr., and J. N. Hook. "Humility: Review of Measurement Strategies and Conceptualization as Personality Judgment." *Journal of Positive Psychology* 5, no. 4 (2010): 243–52.
Davis, D. E., J. N. Hook, E. L. Worthington Jr., D. R. Van Tongeren, A. L. Gartner, and D. J. Jennings II. "Relational Spirituality and Forgiveness: Development of the Spiritual Humility Scale (SHS)." *Journal of Psychology and Theology* 38, no. 2 (2010): 91–100.
Davis, D. E., J. N. Hook, E. L. Worthington Jr., D. R. Van Tongeren, A. L. Gartner, D. J. Jennings II, and R. A. Emmons. "Relational Humility: Conceptualizing and Measuring Humility as a Personality Judgment." *Journal for Personality Assessment* 93 (2011): 225–34.

Driver, Julia. "The Virtues of Ignorance." *Journal of Philosophy* 86, no. 7 (1989): 373–84.

Flanagan, Owen. "Virtue and Ignorance." *Journal of Philosophy* 87, no. 8 (1990): 420–28.

Foulcher, Jane. *Reclaiming Humility: Four Studies in the Monastic Tradition*. Athens, Ohio: Cistercian, 2015.

Galison, Peter. *Einstein's Clocks and Poincaré's Maps: Empires of Time*. New York: W. W. Norton, 2003.

Garcia, J. L. A. "Being Unimpressed with Ourselves: Reconceiving Humility." *Philosophia* 34, no. 4 (2006): 417–35.

Hume, David. *Enquiries concerning Human Understanding and concerning the Principles of Morals*. 3rd ed. Oxford: Clarendon, 1975.

Kellenberger, James. "Humility." *American Philosophical Quarterly* 47, no. 4 (2010): 321–36.

Kuhn, T. S. *The Structure of Scientific Revolutions*. Chicago: University of Chicago Press, 1962.

Lakatos, I. *The Methodology of Scientific Research Programmes: Philosophical Papers*. Vol. 1. Cambridge: Cambridge University Press, 1978.

Nietzsche, Friedrich. *The Anti-Christ*. Harmondsworth: Penguin, 1968.

Nuyen, A. T. "Just Modesty." *American Philosophical Quarterly* 35, no. 1 (1998): 101–9.

Pardue, Stephen. *The Mind of Christ: Humility and the Intellect in Early Christian Theology*. London: Bloomsbury T&T Clark, 2013.

Percy, Walker. *Lancelot*. New York: Farrar, Straus and Giroux, 1977.

Pinsent, Andrew. "Humility." In *Being Good: Christian Virtues for Everyday Life*, edited by Michael Austin and R. Douglas Geivett, 242–64. Grand Rapids: Eerdmans, 2011.

Raterman, Ty. "On Modesty: Being Good and Knowing It without Flaunting It." *American Philosophical Quarterly* 43, no. 3 (2006): 221–34.

Richards, Norvin. "Is Humility a Virtue?" *American Philosophical Quarterly* 25, no. 3 (1988): 253–59.

Ridge, Michael. "Modesty as a Virtue." *American Philosophical Quarterly* 37, no. 3 (2000): 269–83.

Roberts, Robert C., and Jay Wood. "Humility and Epistemic Goods." In *Intellectual Virtue: Perspectives from Ethics and Epistemology*, edited by Michael DePaul and Linda Zagzebski, 257–79. Oxford: Oxford University Press, 2003.

———. *Intellectual Virtues: An Essay in Regulative Epistemology*. Oxford: Oxford University Press, 2007.

Schlesinger, George. "Humility." *Tradition* 27, no. 3 (1993): 4–12.

Schueler, G. F. "Why Modesty Is a Virtue." *Ethics* 107, no. 3 (1997): 467–85.

Sinha, Alex. "Modernizing the Virtue of Humility." *Australasian Journal of Philosophy* 90, no. 2 (2012): 259–74.
Snow, Nancy. "Humility." *Journal of Value Inquiry* 29, no. 2 (1995): 203–16.
Statman, Daniel. "Modesty, Pride and Realistic Self-Assessment." *Philosophical Quarterly* 42, no. 169 (1992): 420–38.
Taylor, Richard. *Ethics, Faith, and Reason*. Englewood Cliffs, N.J.: Prentice-Hall, 1985.
Thomas Aquinas. *Summa Theologiae*. Translated by the Fathers of the English Dominican Province. Allen, Tex.: Christian Classics, 1991.
Whitcomb, Dennis, Jason Baehr, Heather Battaly, and Daniel Howard-Snyder. "Intellectual Humility: Owning Our Limitations." *Philosophy and Phenomenological Research* 94, no. 3 (2017): 509–39.
Worthington, E. L., Jr. *Coming to Peace with Psychology: What Christians Can Learn from Psychological Science*. Downers Grove, Ill.: InterVarsity, 2010.
Worthington, E. L., Jr., and S. T. Allison. *Heroic Humility: What the Science of Humility Can Say to People Raised on Self-Focus*. Washington, D.C.: American Psychological Association, 2018.

Index of Subjects

African, 13–14, 25, 37n1, 37n3, 42
African-American, 19–21, 23, 37n3, 38n18, 42, 46, 110
altruism, 148, 202, 208, 212, 216
anthropology (anthropological), 14, 34, 46, 65, 68, 73n36, 108, 111, 126, 133n28, 135, 255
arrogance, 18, 28–30, 34, 113–114, 119, 142, 151, 154, 163n5, 170, 174, 181–82, 187–93, 241, 258, 260–61

benevolence, 149, 164n23, 262
Black, 10, 13–22, 24–27, 30, 32, 34–36, 38nn13–14, 38nn17–18, 39n19, 39nn21–22, 39n25, 40, 40n1, 41–42, 46, 71n9, 71n11, 77, 110
Buddhism, 217

charity, 60, 63, 76n7, 89–90, 93, 95–97, 103, 157
Christian (Christians), xi, 2, 4–5, 6n1, 7n9, 8, 10–11, 12n1, 16, 19, 21–22, 27, 31–32, 36, 37n5, 38n18, 40, 40n1, 42–44, 47, 49, 51–53, 55–56, 59–68, 70n7, 71nn11–13, 73n36, 75n1, 76nn7–9, 77–81, 83–84, 88–89, 93–98, 99n1, 100n9, 102n2, 102n8, 102n1, 103–4, 120, 122, 124–25, 127–28, 133n25, 134n9, 134n11, 135–36, 138, 143, 155–60, 162, 163n13, 166n13, 169–70, 183, 217, 219, 237–38, 241, 243–46, 249, 254–59, 263, 266n20, 266n31, 267, 267n3, 268, 269
Christianity, 2, 4, 10, 12n1, 42, 73n36, 77, 80, 95, 104, 122, 124–25, 128, 157, 219, 237–38, 244
colonialism, 14, 20, 40n7, 41
community (communities), 4, 11, 14, 16, 18–19, 22, 26, 35, 38n18, 41, 86–87, 96, 109–10, 113, 122, 124–25, 127, 130, 148, 151–52, 154, 158–62, 187, 201–3, 214, 222, 245
comparison, 21, 54–55, 80, 84, 87, 89, 95, 141, 146, 159, 163n15,

271

167, 185–86, 187, 203, 210, 223, 238, 241, 248
culture, ix, 3, 5–6, 7n4, 8, 8n13, 12, 14, 16, 20, 22, 25–30, 34–36, 37n8, 38n18, 41, 44–45, 57–59, 62–63, 70, 71n10, 78, 81, 99n1, 109–10, 113, 124, 130, 131n5, 131n6, 135, 137, 140, 142–43, 145, 148, 152, 154, 160–62, 164n18, 164n25, 165n33, 165n36, 169–70, 209, 214–15, 217–18, 230n101, 230n118, 233–34, 237–38, 247, 256

dependence, 11, 54, 65–66, 76n9, 84, 93, 97, 99, 100n11, 108, 113, 117, 121–22, 127, 130n3, 132n20, 157, 246, 249, 251–54, 256–61

effacement (effaced), 48, 60
egoism, 249
embodiment, 26, 38n13, 95, 128–29
emotions (emotional), 2, 11, 13–16, 31, 37n3, 43, 56, 69, 80, 85, 94, 99nn2–3, 101nn13–16, 101n23, 102n27, 104, 150, 163n8, 167, 213, 258–59
environment(al), 1, 7n4, 8, 45–46, 109
equality, 20, 47, 54, 58, 61–62, 64, 66, 82, 88, 258
ethics (ethical), ix, 4, 10, 12, 14–19, 21–22, 24–25, 27–28, 32, 34–36, 37n3, 40, 40n1, 40n7, 42, 59–60, 62–64, 71n10, 76n9, 78, 95, 97, 100n11, 100n12, 102n2, 102n1, 103n2, 104–5, 124, 138, 145, 155–56, 165n27, 167, 194n2, 196n1, 197, 200–201, 227n53, 229n77,

229nn82–83, 229n89, 231, 234–36, 264n2, 265n10, 265n13, 265n15, 268–69
evil, 3, 7n7, 24, 31, 50, 57, 73n26, 82, 92, 117, 128, 246, 249
exaltation, 11, 50–53, 61, 254

faith (faithful), ix, 1, 10, 27, 38n18, 39, 41–43, 50, 54–56, 59–65, 67, 71n10, 72n32, 73n36, 76n9, 78, 90, 95–97, 99n1, 100n11, 102n8, 103–4, 117, 123, 131n9, 157, 162, 166n3, 167, 254, 264n2, 265n10, 269
feminist, 16, 39n19, 39n24, 41, 60, 80, 155, 246
flourishing, ix, 4–6, 9–12, 12n3, 13–19, 23–25, 35, 40, 70, 80, 93, 95, 97–98, 99n2, 105, 113, 122, 137–40, 143–44, 146, 150–51, 153–55, 157, 166n3, 167, 190, 196n2, 225n17, 234; *see also* good life
forgiveness, 117, 140, 144–45, 164n23, 165n42, 168, 170, 228n70, 232, 236, 267, 267n7

glory, 6n1, 8, 15, 23, 49–52, 54, 57–60, 62, 66, 71n13, 78, 82, 86, 88–89, 156–57, 163n13, 166n11, 169, 218, 258
good, the, ix, 1–6, 7n7, 12, 12n3, 17, 21–22, 24, 28–29, 31, 44, 52, 54–59, 66–69, 70n7, 73n36, 80–89, 91–98, 99nn1–2, 100n4, 100n11, 101nn17–19, 101nn22–24, 104–5, 117, 119, 121, 129, 132n22, 143, 149–50, 152, 154–55, 158, 203, 241–42, 253, 256–57, 260, 265n13, 265n16, 266n20, 268

good life, ix, 4–6, 12, 12n3, 17, 21, 24, 80, 99nn1–2, 100n4, 105; *see also* flourishing
grace, 11, 25, 52, 56, 59, 62–63, 67–68, 73n34, 82, 84, 93, 95–97, 99, 110, 118, 129, 130n2, 157, 237
gratitude, 48, 54, 60, 62, 87–89, 91, 93, 101n20, 134n5, 140, 149–50, 258
Greek, 7n8, 128, 131n7, 237, 256

Hebrew, 4, 131nn4–5, 135, 156
hierarchy, 10, 36, 148, 151–53, 200, 211, 218, 223, 227n54, 229n79, 233, 235
Hindusim, 217
history (histories), 3–4, 14, 19, 20, 22, 32–34, 36, 38n18, 39n22, 42, 45–46, 70n3, 71n9, 71n13, 77, 100n11, 109–10, 112, 117, 131n5, 131n7, 131n9, 133n26, 135, 137–38, 141, 149, 153, 156–57, 174, 221, 238, 241, 244, 257, 262–63
honor (honorable), 19, 29, 46, 49–57, 60–61, 71n13, 73n34, 73n36, 74n38, 75, 81–86, 94, 108, 124, 149–50, 157–58, 251–52
hope, 1–2, 17, 22, 26, 35–36, 44, 59–60, 62, 73n36, 81, 83–84, 89, 91, 93, 95, 97, 100n11, 110, 119, 138, 157, 162, 174, 244, 250, 256, 260
humiliation (humiliating), 18, 24–25, 30, 50, 73n36, 79, 157, 246, 247, 253, 256
humility: dependence account of, 54, 65–66, 100n11, 117, 251–61; in acting, 10, 49–52, 60, 70, 72nn32–33, 73n34; intellectual, 39n1, 42, 99n1, 140, 142, 146–47, 162–63, 165n27, 165n34, 169, 173, 177, 194nn1–5, 195n6, 196n1, 259, 262, 265n17; of being, 10, 49, 70, 72nn32–33, 73n34, 73n36; limitations-owning account of, 176–77, 179, 181, 193, 194n3, 195n8, 196nn17–18, 243, 254–55, 258, 261; low-concern account of, 242, 253–54, 257–58, 260; narrow view of, 174–84; religious, 99n1, 140, 147, 259; virtue of, 4, 10–35, 37n3, 39nn22–24, 39n1, 40n2, 41–43, 47–48, 51, 56, 58–64, 70n5, 71n10, 72n28, 79–99, 100nn10–11, 101nn17–21, 102n2, 102n1, 103, 103n2, 104, 122, 124–25, 139–42, 154–59, 166n14, 167n2, 169–70, 174–85, 189–90, 193–94, 194n5, 195n6, 195nn13–14, 196n2, 197–98, 229n93, 230n116, 232–33, 237–43, 247, 254, 258, 260–64, 264nn2–5, 265nn6–7, 265nn11–15, 266n20, 266n28, 267–69; wide view of, 174–85, 194n3

immorality (immoral), 33
inequality, 152, 154
individuals (individualism), ix, 16–18, 35, 44–46, 48, 51, 64, 70, 86, 95, 101n23, 102n25, 105, 113, 117, 124, 131n10, 132n11, 132n20, 139–40, 142–45, 150–51, 153–54, 160, 164n23, 165n34, 167, 169–70, 203, 207, 217–18, 223, 225n17, 225n20, 231, 234, 247, 259

injustice, 11, 15, 58, 86, 92, 140, 149, 154, 158, 165n39, 165n42, 168, 246
integrity, 12, 14, 28, 121, 145, 148, 211, 213
intellectual (humility), ix, 5, 18, 27, 30, 39n1, 40, 40n7, 42, 99n1, 101n17, 104, 131n10, 140, 142, 146–47, 162, 163n7, 165n27, 165n34, 169–70, 173, 175, 177, 179, 182–83, 194n1, 194n3, 194n5, 195n6, 196n1, 197–98, 251, 259, 262, 265n13, 265n17, 266n28, 268–69
interdisciplinarity (interdisciplinary), 5, 139, 142, 148, 155, 159, 226n34, 231
interreligious, 59, 63, 65

Jewish, 7n9, 8, 42, 124, 133n7, 136, 166n13, 170, 183, 238, 241, 255
joy (joyful, joyless), ix, 2, 10–25, 27–33, 35–36, 37nn2–5, 37n7, 39n20, 39n23, 42–49, 54, 56–57, 59–60, 62, 64, 67, 69, 70n5, 70n7, 71n10, 99nn1–2, 100n4, 102n3, 105, 107–10, 113, 118–22, 125, 133, 150, 255–56
justice, 4, 12, 21–22, 24, 62–63, 72n32, 95, 98–99, 133, 153–54, 157, 165nn41–42, 168, 179, 191, 195n14, 212–13, 224n13, 225n19, 226n38, 228n59, 229n77, 232, 234, 236, 241, 265n12

knowledge, 24–27, 30, 33–36, 74nn34–35, 74n38, 80, 82, 86–87, 94, 108, 117–18, 128, 130, 132n12, 135, 143, 147, 157, 160, 194n1, 223, 247, 251, 265

language, 3, 7n6, 7nn8–9, 8, 26, 28, 30, 33–36, 52, 70n6, 116, 119, 140, 149, 154, 156, 158, 200, 221, 239–40, 262
leadership, 38n13, 71n11, 77, 99n1, 138, 142, 145–46, 152–53, 158, 163nn6–7, 165n26, 165n31, 167–70, 199–223, 224n6, 224nn8–9, 224nn11–13, 225n16, 225nn18–23, 225n26, 226n28, 226nn30–38, 227n39, 227n41, 227n43, 227nn46–58, 228nn59–60, 228nn64–67, 228nn74–76, 229nn77–94, 230nn95–110, 230nn117–19, 230nn1–4, 231, 231nn9–11, 231nn1–3, 233–36, 246
love, 4, 12, 15–16, 21, 23, 25–26, 30–31, 35, 37n3, 40nn7–8, 41, 43, 46, 48, 51–52, 56–57, 59–60, 62–64, 67, 69, 73n34, 73n36, 80, 82, 85, 87–90, 92–95, 101nn23–24, 102n25, 103, 105, 107–8, 112, 120–21, 124, 128–30, 156, 167, 187, 182, 229n89, 236, 245, 248, 256, 259, 262
lowliness (lowly), 4, 10, 43, 50, 53–56, 58, 60–62, 66–67, 73nn34–35, 73n38, 75, 94, 122, 124, 183, 237

magnanimity (magnanimous), iv, 11, 79–84, 86–94, 96, 98, 100nn10–11, 101n21, 102–4
marginalized, 11, 14, 18, 26, 45–46, 145
meshwork, 11, 113–16, 118, 120, 122, 124
metaphysic(s), 74n36, 77, 109, 113–14, 180, 195n14, 198

method, 5, 7n4, 8, 17, 27, 34,
    137–38, 141, 143, 146–47,
    160–62, 185, 202, 207,
    225n26, 235, 262, 264, 266n1,
    268
monk (monkish), Monastic /
    monasticism, 49, 80, 122–25,
    130, 155–59, 161–62, 166n12,
    166n1, 168, 237, 243–45,
    247–56, 264, 266n19, 268
morality (moral), ix, 3, 13–19, 22,
    24–28, 33, 35, 37n3, 39n1,
    44–45, 49, 57, 67, 70n4, 78,
    80–81, 83, 85–87, 95–97, 99n1,
    100n8, 100n12, 102n2, 103,
    105, 109, 117, 125, 137–38, 144,
    147, 155, 162, 164n22, 168, 174,
    180, 185–87, 192–93, 194n3,
    197, 213, 229n90, 237–39,
    241, 256, 260, 262–63, 264n1,
    264n3, 266n19, 267–68

narcissism (narcissist[ic]), 28, 30,
    44, 69, 94, 187–89, 192–93,
    208–9
normative (norm) / normativity,
    3–5, 7nn6–7, 9–12, 15–18,
    23–24, 27, 32, 35–36, 69, 138,
    147, 201

obedience, 25, 51, 245
ontology (ontological), 27, 50,
    73n36, 77, 113, 116, 122,
    132n11, 132, 156
oppression (oppressed), 4, 10–16,
    21–22, 24–30, 32–36, 43, 45,
    57–58, 133, 153, 246

patriarchal, 12n1, 16, 22, 24, 155,
    245
philosophy (philosophical), ix, 5,
    6n1, 7n6, 8, 11, 12, 12n1, 17,

20, 29, 32–33, 35–36, 39n1,
    40n6, 41–42, 46, 49, 64, 73n36,
    100n11, 102n1, 102–4, 110–11,
    131n7, 132n11, 133n28, 135,
    138–39, 143, 155–57, 163n11,
    166n10, 169–70, 174–76,
    178–79, 194n1, 194n3, 195n13,
    196n2, 197–98, 217, 238–39,
    242–43, 256–59, 262–63,
    264n2–5, 265n6, 265n11,
    265nn14–17, 266n1, 267–69
poor, 21–22, 47–48, 52–53, 60–62,
    73n34, 79, 123, 218, 242, 245
poverty, 20–21, 47, 50, 52, 73n34,
    252
pride, 10, 14–18, 21–22, 24,
    26–33, 35–36, 38n12, 38n16,
    39n1, 41–42, 44–48, 54–58,
    65, 69, 70n5, 71nn10–11,
    71n19, 72n28, 73n34, 74n38,
    75nn41–43, 77, 81–82, 84, 87,
    89–90, 92–93, 100n10, 119,
    159, 166n18, 167, 174–76,
    179–86, 188–93, 194nn1–3,
    194n5, 196nn2–4, 197, 197n5,
    198, 242–49, 252, 254, 258,
    264n2, 265nn8–11, 266n27,
    267, 269
proud, the, 18, 34, 45, 47, 51–52,
    55, 57–58, 66, 69, 72n33,
    73n34, 237
pusillanimity (pusillanimous), 28,
    80–81, 84, 89

race (racial), 18–22, 30, 32, 37n8,
    38n13, 41, 133n26, 188
racism, 15, 110, 165n37, 169, 187
recognition, 10–11, 31, 36, 45–46,
    50, 52–53, 61, 71n9, 71n13, 78,
    83–86, 94, 108, 121, 150, 186,
    196n20, 253

Reformation, The, 45–46, 72n32, 73n35, 78
relationships, 113–14, 122, 124–25, 134n1, 139–40, 142–45, 148, 152–54, 157–58, 185, 192, 200, 202, 209, 222
religion/religious, ix, 4, 6n1, 8, 18, 21–22, 26, 37n6, 38n11, 38n18, 39n22, 40, 40n2, 41–42, 45, 58–61, 63, 65, 73n36, 76n9, 78, 99n1, 100n5, 102n2, 103n2, 104–5, 134n9, 140, 146–47, 163n4, 163n7, 163n15, 164n16, 164nn23–24, 165nn36–39, 166nn2–4, 167–70, 196n2, 217, 230nn5–7, 231n8, 232, 234, 237, 241, 245, 259, 264n2, 265n10

science(s) (scientific), 5, 24–25, 34, 38n13, 41, 70n6, 71, 77, 91, 131n5, 132n21, 143, 145–47, 150, 153, 156, 158, 161–62, 163n4, 163n6, 163n12, 163n14, 164n23, 167n2, 169–71, 201, 203, 211, 224n6, 225n21, 226n29, 234–36, 257, 260, 266n1, 267nn3–4, 268, 269
Self, the: abasement, 44, 60, 80–84, 89, 94; abnegation, 19, 46–47, 50, 54, 155; achievement, 44–49, 64, 69, 72n28, 75n4; affirmation, 19, 46, 54; assessment, 155–56, 159, 178, 217, 241, 260, 265n8, 269; care, 26; concern, 253; confidence, 28–29, 81, 87, 94, 245; consciousness, 15, 21, 32, 73, 101n21, 174; control, 24, 31, 116–17, 251; deprecation, 178, 189, 249; determining, 114, 118, 122; emptying, 85, 120; esteem, 19, 28–29, 46, 80, 89, 218, 247; focus, 163n12, 171, 174, 208, 236, 257–58, 260, 267n4, 269; giving, 82, 84, 88, 90, 93; importance, 12, 90, 193, 200; interest, 120, 144, 153, 204, 209, 211; knowledge, 86–87, 94, 143, 251; preservation, 13–14, 18; love, 12, 25–26, 35; related, 101n24; report, 141–42, 144, 147, 153, 155, 202; respect, 18, 28, 30, 45–47, 94; righteous, 28, 186–87; sufficiency, 49, 82, 192–93, 246, 252
servant (servanthood), 47, 52–53, 56, 58, 66, 74n38, 82, 90, 123, 128, 138, 158, 199–236, 258–59
servility (servile), 28–29, 47, 124, 157, 174, 176–77, 179, 181–82, 184, 189, 193
servitude, 200, 218
Sex (sexual), 10, 15, 21–22, 26, 32–34, 95, 133n26, 188, 199
sinful, 49, 119, 248
society, 18, 20, 24–25, 32, 40, 40n1, 124–25, 158, 201–2, 215, 247
soil, 11, 107–9, 122–27, 130, 130n3, 131n5, 131n10
sovereignty, 44–45
submission, 82, 84, 98, 143, 155, 244–46

theology (theological), ix, 5, 6n1, 8, 8n12, 12, 12n1, 12n3, 15–17, 19–23, 27–28, 37nn5–7, 38n10, 39nn21–25, 40n7, 41–43, 49, 55, 59, 61–67, 70, 72n32, 75nn2–3, 76nn9–10, 76nn1–2, 77–78, 85, 89, 94–97, 99n1, 100n12, 102n2, 104–5, 130,

137–39, 143, 147–48, 155–62, 163n7, 166n3, 167, 169, 174, 178, 183, 196n2, 230n116, 233, 244, 253–54, 257, 266n31, 267, 267n7, 268
trust, 21, 40, 48–49, 52, 60, 73n36, 86, 126, 140–45, 152, 196n2, 200, 202, 205, 209, 213–14, 220, 224nn2–5, 226nn27–28, 227n41, 227n49, 227nn57–58, 228n68, 232–35, 245–46, 254–56, 263–64
truth, 3, 25, 27, 36, 50–53, 55–56, 68–69, 72n33, 73n36, 81, 108–9, 113–14, 120–21, 125, 127, 132n20, 159, 162, 256, 263

universal, 10–11, 25, 27, 32, 161

vanity, 28–29, 71n19, 75n41, 90, 160, 187, 190
vice, 2, 15–19, 21–22, 24, 27–34, 71nn10–11, 80, 82, 84, 86, 90, 92, 94, 96, 100n10, 181, 186–90, 192–93, 195n6, 196n16, 196n2, 197, 200, 251, 262
violence, 21, 34, 59, 63, 69, 75n4, 127, 133n26
virtue, 2, 4, 10–35, 37n3, 39nn22–24, 39n1, 40n2, 41–43, 47–48, 51, 56, 58–64, 70n5, 71n10, 72n28, 79–99, 100nn10–11, 101nn17–21, 102n2, 102n1, 103, 103n2, 104, 122, 124–25, 139–42, 154–59, 166n14, 167n2, 169–70, 174–85, 189–90, 193–94, 194n5, 195n6, 195nn13–14, 196n2, 197–98, 229n93, 230n116, 232–33, 237–43, 247, 254, 258, 260–64, 264nn2–5, 265nn6–7, 265nn11–15, 266n20, 266n28, 267–69; theological virtues, 22, 89, 95–97, 157; virtue ethics, 12, 15–18, 25, 32, 37n3, 60, 63, 100n11, 102n1, 155

wealth, 48, 57–59, 70, 73n34, 74n38, 188
white(s) (whiteness), 10, 14, 16–20, 24, 26–27, 29–30, 36, 38nn13–15, 39n19, 39n22, 41, 46, 71n9, 71n11, 110, 166n3, 167
womanist (womanism), 10–13, 15–17, 20–36, 37n3, 38n18, 39n19, 39n21, 39n24, 40n1, 41–42, 71n10; womanist joy, 10, 13, 15–17, 20–28, 32–33, 36, 37n3, 39n23, 71n10; womanist virtue, 10, 21, 23–26, 33, 37n3, 39n24, 41, 71n10

Index of People and Groups

Allison, S. T., 143, 156, 163, 166nn5–8, 171, 217, 230n6, 236, 258–61, 267n4, 267n6, 269
Aquinas, Thomas, 11, 14–15, 67, 71n12, 76n7, 76n9, 79, 81–85, 89, 93–97, 99, 100n7, 100nn10–12, 102n28, 102n1, 103, 103n2, 104–5, 157, 183, 194n1, 106n20, 244, 269
Aristotle (Aristotelian), 14–15, 18, 37n3, 83, 87, 99, 100n11, 101n24, 103–4, 110–11, 131n7, 132n11, 157, 189, 196n1, 197, 255, 263, 264, 264n2
Augustine of Hippo, 4, 8, 37n3, 80, 93, 95–97, 100n9, 101n24, 102nn1–7, 103, 105, 124–25, 134, 134n10, 156–57, 166n10, 166nn14–15, 167, 169, 237, 267

Benedict of Nursia, 161, 267
Bernard of Clairvaux, 122, 124, 126, 133n1, 133nn3–4, 133n6, 134, 136, 156, 159–60, 166n9, 166n18, 167n2, 244, 247, 250, 266n27, 267
Berry, Wendell, 126–28, 130, 131n5, 131n9, 134nn2–3, 135
Bonhoeffer, Dietrich, 118–19, 132n23, 133n24, 135, 248, 266nn24–25, 267

Cannon, Katie, 22–23, 32, 36, 39n24, 40, 40n1, 40nn11–12
Choe, Elise, 7n1, 8, 164n16, 168, 217, 232
Church, Ian, 173, 177, 182, 188, 194n3, 195n6, 195n8, 196nn17–18, 197
Cistercians, 122–25, 133n1, 133n6, 134, 136, 166n9, 166n12, 166n18, 166n1, 167–70, 266n19, 268

Daly, Mary, 10, 12, 12n1
Davis, Donnie, 7n1, 8, 39n1, 42, 162nn1, 2, 6, 164nn16–18, 166n2, 167n3, 168–69, 217, 224n7, 230nn113, 116, 231n7, 232–33, 235, 257, 261, 266n2

279

Driver, Julia, 239, 260, 264nn4–5, 268

Edwards, Jonathan, 16, 23–24, 27, 37n6, 39n22, 41

Floyd-Thomas, Stacey, 71n10, 133n26, 136, 186, 189

God, 4, 10, 11–12, 12n1, 15, 22–27, 31, 35, 43–44, 46–63, 65–68, 71n17, 73n36, 74nn37–38, 75nn42–44, 76n7, 76nn2–3, 77–78, 81–90, 93–99, 101n24, 103, 107–8, 112, 117–30, 132n20, 133n24, 133n26, 143, 147, 157, 162, 183, 217–19, 221, 237, 241, 244–47, 250–54, 256, 258–59, 263

Greenleaf, Robert, 201, 224n10, 224n15, 231n10, 231nn1–4, 232–33

Grenberg, Jeanine, 173, 188, 194n2, 197

Gutiérrez, Gustavo, 60, 64, 75nn2–3, 77

Herdt, Jennifer, 56, 71, 75, 103n2, 104

Holy Spirit, 31, 56, 63, 95–96, 115, 120, 126–27

Hook, Joshua N., 7n1, 8, 164n16, 168, 217, 232

hooks, bell, 17, 37n8, 41, 110, 131n6, 135

Hume, David, 17, 38n9, 41, 70n5, 77, 80, 100n8, 104, 155, 237, 256, 264, 264n1, 265n10, 268

Jesus Christ: (Jesus/Christ), 1, 4, 6n1, 8, 11, 21–22, 27, 39nn19–20, 39n1, 41–42, 47, 49–55, 58–61, 63–69, 73n36, 76n9, 77–78, 84–85, 89–90, 93, 95–97, 99, 100n12, 102n2, 103–5, 119–25, 128–30, 138, 157, 159, 201, 216–21, 224n9, 232, 238, 254, 258–59, 263–64, 266n31, 268

King Jr., Martin Luther, 19, 38n14, 38n17, 41, 46, 71n11, 77

Luther, Martin, 10, 43, 46, 48–70, 71n, 72nn30–33, 73nn34–36, 74nn37–38, 75nn42–44, 75n1, 75nn5–6, 76nn7–9, 76n3, 77–78, 119, 133

Marx, Karl, 108, 130n1, 135

Mary, 12, 43, 49, 51, 53–59, 62, 74n37

McAnnally-Linz, Ryan, 7n1, 8, 71n13, 78, 143, 163n13, 166n11, 168–69, 196n22, 217, 232

Miriam, 12, 43, 49, 57, 59

Moses, 43

Nietzsche, Friedrich, 4, 44–45, 47, 70n2, 70n4, 70n6, 71n8, 78–80, 155, 237, 256, 264n1, 265n10, 268

Paul, 4, 31, 46–47, 51, 55, 61, 65–66, 72n31, 85, 96, 120–21, 129, 217–18, 248, 258

Placeres, Vanessa, 7n1, 8, 164n16, 168, 217, 232

Plato, 2, 7nn2–3, 8, 88, 101nn23–24, 104, 105, 114

Ricciardi, Mirella, 13–14, 17, 23, 27, 37n1, 37n3, 42

Richards, Norvin, 39, 179, 185n13, 197, 240, 260, 265n6, 265n10, 268

Roberts, Robert C., xi, 11, 12n2, 28, 32–36, 39n1, 42, 79–85, 99nn1–3, 101nn13–19, 101n22, 102n27, 104, 185, 189–93, 196n22, 197n5, 242, 254, 260, 265n13, 266n28, 268

Scheler, Max, 46–49, 57, 71nn14–16, 71nn18–20, 72nn21–29, 75nn40–41, 78
Snow, Nancy, 178, 194n1, 195n12, 197, 242–43, 255, 261, 265n17, 266n18, 266n30, 269

Tangney, June, 141, 163n3, 170, 178, 195n9, 198, 228n61, 236
Taylor, Charles, 3, 6, 7n6, 7n8, 8, 8n13, 71n9, 78
Taylor, Richard, 241, 264n2, 265n10, 269
Trinity, The, 66–67

Volf, Miroslav, xi, 6, 8, 8n12, 76nn9–10, 76n1, 78, 99n2, 100n4, 105

Walker, Alice, 13–14, 24, 37nn2–3, 39n23, 42, 249, 266n26, 268
Wengst, Klaus, 7n9, 8, 42, 133n7, 134nn8–9, 136, 157, 166n13, 170
Wheatley, Phillis, 23–24, 39n22, 41–42
Worthington, Everett L., xi, 39n1, 42, 138, 143, 156, 162n1, 163n2, 163nn6–7, 163n10, 163n12, 164n17, 164n23, 165n39, 165n41, 166nn5–8, 167n3, 168–69, 171, 215, 217, 219–23, 224n7, 228n70, 230n116, 230nn6–7, 231–36, 257–63, 266n2, 267, 267nn3–7, 269

Index of Scripture

Genesis
2:17	118
4:10	109

Exodus
15	57

Deuteronomy
11:12	119

Psalms
104:27-30	119–20

Song of Songs
1:5	26

Matthew
10:22	246
11:39	4
25:21, 23	56
25	61

Luke
1:52-53	58
18:14	44

John
15:15	90

Romans
12:15	31, 55
12:3	55
12:16	55

1 Corinthians
1:9	90
4:7	68

2 Corinthians
5:16-18	121

Galatians
2:20	121
5:20-21	31
5:22-23	31

Philippians
2	49, 51, 61, 64–66, 71n17, 77
2:2-4	258
2:3	4, 85

2:3-11	217, 218		1 Timothy	
2:5	66	1:15		248
2:5-8	120	4:4-5		129
2:6	47, 66, 71n17			
2:6-7	258		James	
2:7	217, 259	4:6		237
2:7-8	157			
2:8	4, 245		1 Peter	
2:9	66	1:8		15
2:11	218, 258	5:5		4, 237
Colossians			Revelation	
1:19	128	11:18		129
2:9	128	17		57
3:12	4			